# Inequality
# CRIME &
# EDUCATION
# in Trinidad and Tobago

"Besides being a valuable contribution to the sociology of Trinidad and Tobago, this book sounds a wake-up call to politicians and policy makers. Particularly significant for public policy is Prof Deosaran's observation that the fallouts from the education system are reflected in crime, poverty and other social problems. In interpreting and explaining the painstakingly collected and meticulously analyzed data, both primary and secondary,he brings to the fore his vast experience as a teacher, researcher, policy maker and a public intellectual. While his approach is predominantly sociological, he brings in several insightful philosophical precepts and socio-psychological concepts to elucidate the educational situation in Trinidad and Tobago. Professor Deosaran's exercise demystifies many a myth and highlights some unpleasant truths. The candid fashion with which he lays bare the reality, about which there is pathetic silence, if not brazen denial, is remarkable indeed"*

Narayan Jayaram, Visiting Professor of Sociology,
National Law School of India, University of Bengaluru, India.

"ProfessorDeosaran demonstrates a deep passion and concern for the state of education in Trinidad and Tobago as the society struggles to grapple with the recurring issues of violence, indiscipline, academic under-achievement and social inequality, This book is therefore necessary reading for teachers, academics and anyone interested in the role of education in Trinidad and Tobago. It helps us to understand education and society in a manner that no other book has or will, as it incorporates most of the relevant writings on the subject in a fresh, lively and scholarly manner."

Dr Nasser Mustapha, Senior Lecturer in Sociology of Education, The University of the West Indies, St. Augustine Campus, Trinidad and Tobago

"In this book, Ramesh Deosaran, who has studied the nation's social and educational systems for many decades, demonstrates that unequal opportunity (inequality) and unequal outcomes (inequity) are both embedded in our educational system, despite a formal commitment from governments to the opposite. Deosaran describes the book as a 'wake-up call.' This book is an important intervention in a debate which is crucial to the country's future".

Bridget Brereton, Emerita Professor of History,
The University of the West Indies, St Augustine, Trinidad and Tobago

# Inequality
# CRIME &
# EDUCATION
## in Trinidad and Tobago

## *Removing the Masks*

**Ramesh Deosaran**

IAN RANDLE PUBLISHERS
*Kingston* • *Miami*

First published in Jamaica, 2016 by
Ian Randle Publishers
16 Herb McKenley Drive
Box 686
Kingston 6
www.ianrandlepublishers.com

© Ramesh Deosaran

ISBN: 978-976-637-920-9

A CIP catalogue record for this book is available from the National
Library of Jamaica.

Book Design by Ian Randle Publishers
Printed and Bound in Trinidad and Tobago

# DEDICATION

I wish for the dispossessed and socially
disadvantaged that they develop the will to survive, to
progress, to fight social injustice and inspire others.

# Contents

# List of Figures

# List of Tables

# Foreword

By Professor Emerita Bridget Brereton

The issues surrounding the academic under-performance of the government secondary schools in Trinidad & Tobago, compared with the denominational assisted schools, have been debated for many years. Very recently, they acquired fresh salience when the list of national scholarships based on CAPE results was announced and the new Minister of Education expressed his, and his government's, dissatisfaction with the small number won by graduates of the government schools. Even more controversial, however, have been the issues surrounding the process of placement in the secondary schools, and the inequities which many perceive to be inherent in that process.

In this book, Ramesh Deosaran—who has studied the nation's social and educational systems for many decades—takes up these issues (and more). He demonstrates that unequal opportunity (inequality) and unequal outcomes (inequity) are both embedded in our educational system, despite a formal commitment from governments, at least since the late 1950s, to the opposite. Deosaran describes the book as a 'wake-up call', as an intervention in a long-standing debate calling for planned, sustainable actions by the authorities. He provides a great deal of data, some new (his own recent research) but much of it already available in reports and studies going back to the 1960s, to support his intervention.

In his view, the main reason for the inequity within the education system is the 'dual' system—schools run by the government and those run by religious denominations but supported by the state—in place ever since 1870. At the secondary level, the rights of the denominational assisted schools are enshrined in the famous 'Concordat' of 1960. Deosaran argues that, in the light of recent challenges to this agreement, and ambiguities about its status in law, it is high time to revisit the Concordat and debate whether it should be revised, scrapped, or enshrined in the constitution.

For Deosaran, systemic inequality begins, or 'germinates' to use his word, in the primary schools. There are significant differences in the performance of the three types - private (fee-paying), government, and denominational assisted. Providing empirical data based on the National Tests, and on the Common Entrance Examination (1961-2000) and SEA (2001 to now) results, Deosaran shows that children from the private schools, and some denominational schools, do best overall. In the 2014 SEA, for instance, the private schools, with one per cent of all pupils, got 18 per cent of the top 200 SEA scores, while some denominational schools mainly in the educational districts of Victoria and Caroni also did remarkably well. In other words, there are' prestige' primary schools too.

At the primary level, a girl in a private or denominational school in Victoria or Caroni has a better chance, on average, of scoring high in the SEA and thus getting into a first choice, 'prestige' secondary school, when compared with other children. And entry into the high-performing primary schools is hardly a level playing-field. Entry to the private schools, fee-paying, is based on socio-economic class; entry to a 'prestige' denominational school may also be based partly on class, but probably more on ethnicity (including religion) and place of residence. All the studies done of the placement process suggest that poor, working-class, urban or semi-urban, African children, and especially boys, are the most disadvantaged group with respect to 'first choice' secondary school entry.

At the secondary level, the gap in academic performance between the 'prestige' denominational schools and most (not all) of the government schools is very wide, whether measured by the National Certificate of Secondary Education exams, by CSEC and CAPE results, or by national scholarships. The gap is a reality, so that some kind of assessment test at entry seems inevitable; parents will always want their children to get into the better performing schools. Again, the group just identified as especially disadvantaged in the SEA examination, relegated for the most part to the under-achieving government schools, performs worst at the examinations taken at the secondary level.

And of course all this affects post-secondary school trajectories. In an interesting recent study, Deosaran followed young people from twenty schools three years after they left Form 5 (CSEC level). The study shows that significantly more of those who went to denominational secondary schools were in full-time higher education than those from government schools. School type seemed to be more important here than class or ethnicity, though these did matter too, along with family structure (those from two-parent families more likely to be studying full-time) and gender (girls slightly more likely).

Does all this structural inequity in the educational system and its outcomes amount to discrimination against the most disadvantaged groups, is the process prejudiced against a particular social group? Deosaran argues that there are, incontrovertibly, 'patterns and persistence of inequalities'; if they are allowed to continue without serious efforts at reform, they could reasonably appear to reflect discrimination and a denial of the equal opportunity considered a hallmark of a modern democracy.

And so Deosaran appeals for sustained, carefully planned, and data-driven reforms in the nation's education system. He ends his book with a list of recommendations to the government, the most important being a suite of actions to improve the performance, morale and discipline of government secondary schools in the short and medium term.

This book is an important intervention in a debate which is crucial to this country's future. Let's hope it makes a greater impact than the many research studies and reports (some authored by Deosaran) calling for educational reform which have been presented to the authorities over the last fifty years.

Bridget Brereton
Emerita Professor of History
UWI, St Augustine, Trinidad & Tobago

# Preface

By Professor Emeritus Ramesh Deosaran

## THE DECOLONISATION DILEMMA

Soon after gaining political independence, governments of the formerly colonial societies in the Caribbean quickly stated objectives such as equality of opportunity, socio-economic mobility and of course, a healthy democracy. These countries, like Trinidad and Tobago, also quickened the centralisation of political power and public institutions in the belief that such centralization would speed up the social and economic transformation required for decolonisation. This ideology, driven by 'new-independence' rhetoric, became inevitable. The high expectations of the population also quickly became dependent on 'their government.' With such reciprocity, large sections of the population were almost schooled into dependency. Self-efficacy remained uncultivated. Hence, public institutions grew in number but then gradually sunk into inefficiency and ineffectiveness.

Multi-ethnic Trinidad and Tobago provides a good example. In such post-colonial pursuits the public education system, with both government and church-managed schools, quickly became of critical importance. It is from its schools that the passion for social justice and public service, the compassion for the poor and the voiceless, the thirst for knowledge and the passage for socio-economic mobility were expected to emerge. Great hopes were placed in the country's educational system. After all, if the schools should fail, the society of tomorrow would fail. And the failures would become subversive forces.

### Education: The Great Hope

In all its various forms, education and skills' training are the energizers —the creators—of economic progress and a civilized way of living, especially for developing societies with limited or diminishing physical resources. It is the passion for achievement and service that could initiate economic progress in post-colonial societies like Trinidad and Tobago. It is almost like making something out of nothing, oil and gas supply notwithstanding. This book makes an appeal for more effective utilisation of the country's educational resources, that is, having the psychological capital to maximize its natural resources and energise economic development. Any wastage through educational inequality and inequity subverts this process.

It is therefore very important that within the schools themselves, the children who are soon to become adults, must enjoy a good measure of equality of opportunity and equity to have the confidence and good spirit to develop such national purpose while also improving themselves. The education system is the cradle of democracy where, of all places, equality of opportunity, fair treatment and national ideals are expected to be nourished. I write this book with such hopes.

As an open system, education remains vulnerable to some degree of inequality and inequity, and moreso if its social environment is already infested by sharpened racial, religious and social class divisions. However, the amount of inequalities and inequities unmasked in this book is far beyond reason for a society that wishes to call itself democratic and civilized. The educational disadvantages discovered here are directly related to ethnicity, social class, parenting, place of residence and above all, the type of school a student attends.

## Education and the Underclass

Such deficits get repeated year after year, largely obscured by political and bureaucratic rhetoric and leaving schools open to racial and social class segregation. Resentment, rebellion and civil disruption by a youthful underclass are likely results. The celebrated academic success of a few attracts resentment by the many who 'do not make it.' This multi-racial society, its elite class particularly, now faces a moral dilemma in finding a justifiable way to strengthen the weak without weakening the strong. There is no doubt that the education system is elitist and inevitably capitalist-driven. Its major criterion for success, controversial as it may be, remains university education and entry into the traditional professions.

Any attempt to inquire into the educational fractures gets caught between the reluctance to stigmatise schools and the responsibility to unmask and reform the system. I choose the latter—removing the mask and looking behind the promises and gross statistics. The picture is very troubling. The statistics, from chapter to chapter, may very well attract a lighter view than mine, depending on where the reader's interest lies.

While year after year, celebrations of the deserving few take place, thousands are left stranded behind, some too far to be seen. We are yet to feel the shame of it all. Maybe I am wrong. Some will say the situation is not all that bad and it is just a case of having great expectations, too great to be realistic for a post-colonial society as ours. But after independence, we were repeatedly encouraged to have great expectations for socio-economic mobility for the freed people. Perhaps, too, my expressed concerns are motivated by my own early social disadvantages. But which writer, academic or novelist, does not put something of himself or herself into his or her work?

## Rising Above Victimhood

This book seeks to tell a story of social and ethnic disadvantage and the challenge to rise above it with a passion born of the hurt which social disadvantage inflicts. The profile of educational inequality presented here is not only an attempt to scrutinise the education system but perhaps more importantly to help inspire the socially disadvantaged to struggle above self-pity and victimhood. After all, quite a few of today's successful were once severely disadvantaged.

The expanse of data from my own research and that of others, well-acknowledged, should help attract the policy concerns required. There is evidence from the nation's prisons, its juvenile homes and, of course, its primary and especially its secondary schools. The early inequities subsequently manifest themselves in higher education too. Is one of the reasons for the ethnic and social class inequities being allowed to reach this far is out of a fear for ethnic controversy?

As several cited commentators noted, a lot of the institutional breakdown is due to the extent to which political pettiness and patronage led to misguided, defective policies. There is also the aggravating 'social contact culture' widely used for jobs and social status, thus bringing the educational system close to irrelevance. The equality challenge also comes from the increasing number of private primary schools whose students proportionally excel above those from both the denominational and government-managed schools in the SEA examination. The inevitable misfortune of the repeatedly disadvantaged in the education system is that they have to depend so much on the powerful and privileged for rescue. This situation is unfortunate for this post-colonial multi-racial society which had such high hopes after political independence for its education system. Who is responsible?

## Parenting and Community

Of course, as noted in the book, education is about structure and institutions but it is also about personal responsibility, meaning in this case, that students themselves and parents particularly must help ensure that the best use is made of the available educational opportunities.

There are, of course, social and structural challenges to families and communities that contribute to overall educational inequalities—creating a segregated educational system. But why are the disadvantages so disproportionally manifested in so many of our government secondary schools—so many of their graduates eventually seen in court and prison? Reforming the education system therefore requires wider reforms too. That is why the challenges of merit, equal educational opportunity and equity will likely arouse controversy. Merit carries logic but, unwittingly it also triggers social injustice.

## Education: Still the Great Hope

At first glance it is easy for citizens to become disillusioned and pessimistic. The media tell the story every day. And often, just when you think things will change for the better, hopes get crushed once again. But deeper reflection soon calms hurried pessimism if we recognize the causes and the possibilities that are still available. Hopefully, it is from the schools and the education system that an understanding of causes and possibilities could emerge.

Given the inherent tensions between free choice and competition in a democratic society, policy-making will always be a work in progress. A lot therefore depends on the non-partisan vision of the country's leadership, their good conscience, and their earnestness in building the consensus required for moving forward.

# Acknowledgements

Finally, in the preparation and production of this book, my deep gratitude to Mr. Ian Ramdhanie for sparing me his several week-ends for editorial checking; to publisher Mr. Ian Randle for his patience and professional courtesies and of course, my wife, Nirmala, for understanding the rigours faced. To Professor Emerita of History, Bridget Brereton, I remain indebted for her useful comments and, of course, her thoughtful Foreword. To Professor of Sociology, Narayan Jayaram, of the National Law School of India University and Dr Nasser Mustapha, Senior Lecturer in Sociology of Education at UWI, my deep appreciation for their review and comments.

Of course, any errors or related shortcomings remain mine. I also remember with deep appreciation the professionalism and civility with which former Minister of Education, Ms Hazel Manning, and Permanent Secretary, Ms Angella Jack, lent assistance in facilitating my production of the several research and policy reports cited in this book. And to all the principals, teachers and students who so willingly gave me their ideas and time, I hope this book helps provide some justification for your kind support.

**Ramesh Deosaran ORTT,**
Professor Emeritus

# Prologue

Dr. Nasser Mustapha, Senior Lecturer in Sociology of Education, UWI, St. Augustine, Trinidad and Tobago.

It is an honour for me to be given the opportunity to write a Prologue to such an outstanding and timely work by Professor Emeritus Ramesh Deosaran on education in Trinidad and Tobago. Entitled *Inequality, Crime and Education in Trinidad and Tobago: Removing the Masks,* the book is about the evolution of education in the multi-ethnic post-colonial society of Trinidad and Tobago and the implications for equality and equity. The approach is multi-disciplinary in nature as it draws from various disciplines including the politics of education, the sociology of education, the economics of education and educational psychology. The book reflects the diverse academic and public service experience of the author. In fact, I note the distinguished academic and public service experience of Professor Deosaran to help illustrate how the life experiences of an academic, inside and outside academia, can contribute to such a vividly multi-disciplinary product.

Professor Deosaran formerly served as UWI lecturer in Social Psychology, Head of the Department of Behavioural Sciences, Deputy Dean of Graduate Studies, Criminology and Social Psychology Professor, Independent Senator in the Parliament of Trinidad and Tobago, Director and Founder of both the Centre for Psychological Research and Centre for Criminology and Criminal Justice, and President (Acting) of the University of Trinidad and Tobago. He was also the founding editor of the *Caribbean Journal of Criminology and Social Psychology.* He developed several university programmes in Psychology and Criminology, all of which are now heavily subscribed. In 2013, he was awarded the nation's highest national honour, The Order of the Republic of Trinidad and Tobago. (ORTT)

As author, researcher and public intellectual, Professor Deosaran demonstrates a deep passion and concern for the state of education in Trinidad and Tobago as the society struggles to grapple with the recurring issues such as violence, indiscipline, academic under-achievement and social inequality. In this work, he is able to dissect the inter-connected and intricate issues in an objective, systematic and dispassionate style for which he is well known.

Among societies emerging from the colonial experience, often characterized by rigid stratification, elitism and restricted opportunities for the lower classes, education was perceived as the source of liberation, status attainment and success. As Professor Deosaran describes, after independence people were optimistic and had high expectations as they looked towards education as the panacea for all ills. And as the society gradually changed from one based on ascription to one based on achievement, education acted as the great equalizer by promoting social mobility on the basis of merit, instead of race or colour.

Around this time, primary education was easily accessible through both church and state schools. Though there was improved literacy, there were limited opportunities for social mobility since secondary education was still limited. This situation presented a challenge for the then government. In the struggle for decolonisation, educational policy makers restructured the system so as to increase equality of educational opportunity. Proposals to achieve these objectives included expansion of secondary school places, a common qualifying examination for selection into secondary schools (the Common Entrance Examination), a generally common curriculum, and a reduction of the powers of denominational boards.

Dr Eric Williams, the country's first Prime Minister, attempted to bring into effect a nationalist education system that would produce citizens with a new identity, new values and assimilated into the national culture rather than fragmented on the basis of race or religion. Thus, he attempted to achieve social integration and allow greater access to educational opportunity for all sectors of society. A subsequent phase of expansion started with the introduction of the Junior Secondary Schools in 1972 followed by a number of Senior Comprehensive Schools in the late 1970s.

Whereas the education system has grown considerably and appears to be more meritocratic than in previous times, the rivalry, perceptions of inequality and biases in favour of the middle class still persist. The education system is still rigidly stratified. Of course many will argue that the selection and allocation functions of education are necessary, but the lower classes will continue to feel excluded and marginalized. This of course, as Professor Deosaran graphically explains, has implications for the formation of delinquent sub-cultures.

Although universal secondary education has been achieved, and the system has grown in size, it has maintained the same stratified structure and elitist functions. The population is still concerned with their children attending the 'prestige schools'. As the author advises, unless the secondary school system is radically restructured and as long as the dichotomy between government and denominational schools persists, the Secondary Entrance Assessment (SEA), as was the Common Entrance examination, will continue to be a source of anxiety and stress for children and parents. The SEA examination continues to be very competitive. Education deteriorates into learning the tricks of the trade, how to master the examination, rather than developing one's potential to its fullest in any field. Professor Deosaran describes this as the 'tyranny of the testocracy.' The educational policy dilemmas confronting the society today are similar to those facing the country at the time of independence, except that they have grown in magnitude.

This book is therefore necessary reading for teachers, academics, or anyone interested in the role of education in Trinidad and Tobago today. It takes us on a journey back to our historical roots and at the same time looks at the contemporary issues in a broad international context. It helps us to understand education and society in a manner that no other book has or will, as it incorporates most of the relevant writings on the subject in a fresh, lively and scholarly manner.

# Introduction

## INEQUALITIES: UNPLEASANT TRUTHS

This book examines the extent to which the very optimistic, government-driven promises of the country's educational system compare with the empirical data from our research and that from several other sources. The major focus is on equality of educational opportunity and educational equity in relation to students' ethnicity, social class, gender, family background, type of school attended and place of residence.

In this sociological context, the philosophical questions of merit, equal opportunity and educational equity in a multi-ethnic society are also examined (Chapters Five and Thirteen). Use was also made of such social psychological concepts as self-esteem, racial prejudice, social perception and self-fulfilling prophesy to help explain the evolution and presence of the educational inequalities and inequities discovered.

Some unpleasant truths, usually and conveniently kept silent, are brought into the open for public attention and policy remedy. This public exposure is critical especially since, as we argue in Chapter Fifteen, and with some reference to criminological theories, much of the fall-out from the education system deviates into crime, teenage pregnancy and poverty. These youthful deficits eventually put the entire society at risk.

### Fiction and Fact

In pursuing this mission, we returned in Chapters One, Two and Three to the plantation experiences of the slaves and indentured labourers, particularly during the 19th and early 20th centuries, to help indicate how that period contributed immensely to the current ethnic diversity and evolution of the country's public educational system. Chapter Seven looks at how ethnic-driven politics helped shaped the country's dual system of education – denominational schools mixed with government schools.

Against this historical background of de-humanisation and opportunity deprivation, the post-colonial glorified obsession with education as a therapeutic and empowering instrument finds appropriate relevance and justification. More precisely, this early obsession appeared as a noble call for equality and social justice in the years soon after the country's political independence in 1962. To what extent has the education system responded to this 'noble call'?

The general purpose of the country's educational system is aptly summarized by the Ministry of Education's pledge which states:

> *Every child has an inherent right to an education which will enhance the development of maximum capability regardless of gender, ethnic, economic, social or religious background. That the educational system of Trinidad and Tobago must endeavour to develop a spiritually, morally, physically, intellectually and emotionally sound individual, that ensures that cultural, ethnic, class and gender needs are appropriately addressed.*[1]

How far have these objectives succeeded? We discovered a very surprising and troubling amount of inequality and inequity in the system. In fact, while we expected some fall-out and even delinquency out of the public educational system, as usually happens in school systems, we were quite surprised at the troubling amounts we found, especially with the vast expenditures and expansion that took place in education. We seek to remove the masks.

## THE UNPLEASANT EVIDENCE

The evidence shows that such educational inequalities and inequities have very serious, debilitating implications for the country's social and economic progress. More precisely, Chapter Fifteen, with theoretical and empirical support, seeks to make a connection between these inequities in the education system and youth deviance, especially with the young, black urban males whose under-performance receives widespread commentary. It now appears that the country's education system has a case of social injustice to answer. It is not a simple matter of 'blaming teachers.' There are serious structural deficiencies in the education system. (See e.g., Chapters Ten and Fourteen)

The fact that such inequalities and inequities are sharply related to students' race, social class, gender, family background and place of residence does contribute to the restlessness and ethnic tensions now swirling within this small, post-colonial, multi-ethnic society. Is it that the educational system has failed, or is it vulnerable and at high risk to the economic and cultural forces in the wider society?

Faced with examination-packed pressures in their early lives, primary school students especially are locked into a ruthless 'survival of the fittest' meritocracy. Cornered by very limited secondary school places of choice, these 11+ children are shunted mainly into one secondary school type or another according to their marks in the Secondary Entrance Assessment (SEA).

Those scoring 90% and over usually have the best chance of getting into a school of their choice, mainly a high-performing Denominational Secondary Schools (DSS). The rest are filtered into the Government Secondary Schools, many of which are known to be under-performing.

## The Magic of '90% and Over': Behind the Mask

This '90% and over' group usually emerges from a set of high performing primary schools for which there is a mad rush annually by parents from far and near to press for their children to get into these 'special' primary schools. Here, family ties and the socio-economic and professional background of parents provide self-serving leverage. It is from here that secondary school placement and academic output largely become shaped into ethnic and social class bias.

Between 2012 and 2015, each year the Minister of Education cited figures, publicly boasting of how many more students passed with 90% and over at the SEA examination. The unpleasant truth is that within that gross, celebrated figure existed significant but silent inequalities, persistent inequalities by students' race, social class, gender, family background and even place of residence.

These specific group deprivations were never publicly mentioned neither specifically examined by the Ministry. However, as an annual ritual, the 'first 100 students' in the SEA examinations were lavishly celebrated in top-class hotels. The masks need to be removed.

In the struggle to enter this '90% and over' group, high-priced private lessons for primary school students have now mushroomed into a very profitable industry, subverting the public school classroom and implicitly, pushing poor children into further disadvantage. As noted in Chapters Six and Ten, these feverish quests for 'prestige' school entry are largely based on the strong cultural value for grammar-type education and the traditional professions. The population sees this as good schooling, a good education. Less than five percent of secondary school students express a desire for technical/vocational programmes.[2]

## The Privatisation of Education

And so, with an increasing number of parallel private early childhood and highly 'successful' private primary schools, the public education system here is becoming more and more fractured, helplessly accommodating a disguised form of ethnic segregation and elitism, quite contrary to its original purpose. The overwhelming mission of these private primary schools is to produce children who come out in the top 100 – in the magic '90% and over' from the SEA examination. And they do succeed.

As will be illustrated later, with 12% of their students getting over 90%, these private schools are, proportionally, the most successful of the schools, even when compared to students from the 14 denominational school boards (DSB) – except one – in this respect.[3] In fact, in terms of SEA candidates, these business-driven private primary schools put up more candidates than ten of the denominational primary school boards.[4] The major objective is to eventually get these private school graduates into a 'prestige' secondary school, into university, then into one of the traditional professions. In this way, the society's social stratification order remains stagnant or suffers further inequality.

Signs of such deepening inequality were noted by educator, Lennox Bernard who, while lamenting the 'inequities in children's access to high-performing schools,' also noted that 'private schooling was becoming more effective and successful.' He called on the Ministry for a special study on this issue 'in the research-starved society.'[5] Such creeping inequalities, however, unpleasant truths as they are, continue to remain relatively obscured - so far un-noticed by public policy. The growth of private primary schools presents a serious threat to the country's inefficient and ineffective public education system – primarily to the government schools.

## Education Free, But Inequality Persists

This is the challenge facing the country's 'free' public education system now – the growing number of for-profit private primary schools. The implications are serious – politically and educationally - and will obviously make the present extent of inequalities and inequity in the public education system worse. More and more rich parents will move their children into these 'successful' high-priced private schools where individualism, testing, passing examinations and the competitive spirit are predominant.

The country's public education system will likely suffer further social and ethnic disadvantages. The Ministry of Education is now required to take well-targeted policy action against the hemorrhage. This is the phenomenon of Charter schools which is now the subject of growing controversy in the United States and England. It is essentially class warfare played out in the educational system.

There is another type of Charter school – one designed to help socially disadvantaged children. Facing City Hall objections, for example, New York parents staged street protests calling for more Charter schools. In October, 2015, thousands of parents, supported by newspaper editorials,[6] marched on New York City Hall protesting Mayor de Blasio's resistance to Charter schools. One parent said they 'were no longer going to stand for a separate and unequal education' that hurts the poor and black students.[7]

Condemning the failing public school system, another protesting parent, Jeremiah Kettridge, said that 'poor families are not prepared any longer to have their children forced into failing schools' that produce educational inequality.[8]

## Delinquency Too

The challenge in this country is not only about academic inequality. It is quite seriously also about student discipline, especially in the under-performing government schools. So those parents who are bothered about this and can afford it, feel justified in sending their children to the private primary schools. In other words, these emerging private schools illustrate the very serious consequences of allowing continued deterioration of the public school system – at least big parts of it. While the broader sociological implications are clear, the private school parents feel quite justified in exercising their democratic right.

But, as indicated above, there are different kinds of Charter schools. The corporate, business types are the ones to which former U.S. Assistant Secretary for Education, Diane Ravitch, objects. She states: 'If you want a society organized to promote the survival of the fittest and the triumph of the most advantaged, then you will prefer the current course of action' – corporate-type Charter schools.[9] She added: '*If, however, you believe that the goal of society is equality of opportunity for all children, we should seek to reduce the alarming inequalities children now have in schools.*'[10]

Yes, but what happens if these 'alarming inequalities' continue to exist in public schools – as likely seems the case? The private schools (Charter Schools) in this country are generally of the type to which Ravitch objects and the type which will likely trigger further inequalities within this country's public education system.

## Privatise to Help the Poor

The Charter schools which the protesting parents seek in New York are of the community-based type, seeking subsidies and as an alternative haven for the inefficiencies of the 'separate and unequal' government school system. There are such schools in Miami-Dade, Florida.[11] We think the day is not too far off when civic-minded organizations and Parent Teachers Associations in this country will establish Charter schools, not as an expensive business, but as a community alternative to the persistently under-performing government schools.

If they do this, it should be in the marginalised, depressed urban areas where a major challenge is from the young, black male and female. If the under-performing schools in the public education system continue their downward trend, privatisation of public education will be a welcome initiative.

It has become a betrayal of the nation's children that the authorities have not seen it fit to strategically tackle these inequitable conditions which continue to contribute to the country's segregated school system. The use of private schools for improving depressed communities is taking root across the world.

The international newspaper, *The Economist*, noted: 'This private school pattern is repeated across Africa, the Middle East and South Asia. The failure of the state to provide children with a decent education is leading to a burgeoning of private places.'[12] In its special report, the newspaper, noting 'the failure of state education,' explained how relatively economical it could be to establish such schools.[13]

The unfortunate thing for this country is that, firstly, the early signs of deterioration in public schools, especially in terms of inequality and inefficiency, were known. Secondly, no effective steps were taken or are being taken to develop and insert concrete measures to cure the existing inequities and qualitative deficiencies of the system. It is therefore no surprise that the private school system is moving in. It will be a pity, though, if this emerging, 'counter-state' movement continues to cater mainly to the already rich and privileged.

## A 'testocracy' in the Meritocracy

Given the mad rush annually for some 4,000 (limited) places in the preferred high-performing denominational (church) secondary schools, the 14,000 or so left out annually face the dismal self-fulfilling prophesy having to go, reluctantly and often with tears, to many schools not of their choice - under-performing government secondary schools. Quite often, the difference in marks for such critical diversion is very, very small. The examination-packed public education system here has turned itself into a 'testocracy' which supports the 'tyranny of the meritocracy.'

Arguing against the 'twenty-first century cult of standardized, quantifiable merit,' Law Professor Lani Guinier, in her book, *The Tyranny of the Meritocracy*, noted how the system 'values perfect scores but ignores character.' Hers is one of the several voices now calling for a realignment of the schools' objectives, from rugged individualism to 'creative thinking, collective commitment and democratic merit.'[14] The argument is not to 'destroy the concept of merit' but to redefine it in a way that creates better public virtue and promotes democratic ideals.

The current examination system is a far cry from the stated objectives (above) of the Ministry of Education. Yet it is on the scores from these tests that students are celebrated or condemned.

## School Culture: Government vs. Denominational

During our periodic visits to over sixty of the nation's secondary schools, we saw how and why one type of school differs so much from another type.[15] The numbers which measure inequality do matter. But in dealing with students' feelings and educational aspirations, hearing their voices and seeing their eyes and faces do add fuller meaning – flesh and blood – to the numbers. As we moved from one school type to another, there was joy and optimism in one type, and resentment and pessimism in the other type.

Among our interview questions, for example, we asked students how comfortable they were in their particular school. We also asked which school they had preferred to attend. The results were very clear.

The vast majority, especially the males, expressed much discomfort in the Government Secondary Schools (GSS), their major reason being they had initially expressed as their first and second choice a DSS. The collective disappointment was quite disheartening. One Form 3 boy said what was already public knowledge. He said: 'Ah doh expec' to get any passes here.' The others nodded at the self-fulfilling prophesy. The vast majority of students in these GSS's were of African descent.

Our experience at the high-performing denominational schools was quite different. During teaching time, you rarely saw a student outside. The classes worked very quietly. The students in well-fitting uniforms actually spoke and behaved differently from those in the government schools. When asked the same questions we used at the Government Schools, the students' answers were upbeat. They all proudly admitted the school was their preferred choice and how comfortable they felt there. This is the 'prestige school culture' of which Sociologist Nasser Mustapha spoke. (Chapter Seven)

These DSS were known to annually produce national and additional scholarships with media-driven celebrations, etc. There was a self-fulfilling prophesy here too, but one prophesying well-assured success and celebration. These comparisons are all part of the psychology which reinforces segregation of the country's public school system.

## 'Shame of the Nation'

All this, too, remind us of the school-based narratives of Jonathan Kozol who found gross inequities and racial segregation in America's inner-city schools. He called it 'The Shame of the Nation.'[16] The inequities and disguised segregation in our education system are rooted mainly in the black, urban communities and their schools as cited by several researchers. Our nation is yet to feel ashamed.

Educators know only too well the need to avoid stigmatizing students or schools. The psychological implications can be counter-productive. On the other hand, given the extent of inequality, structural deficits and the apparent delays in providing the required remedies, it will be to the advantage of students, teachers and parents to have these issues raised. That is, removing the masks.

The teachers themselves have passionately complained about the challenges and resources needed in their GSS. At the same time, it is to the great credit of the teachers in those affected communities who stand up and face the psychology of defeat in which such schools find themselves.

One of their loudest complaints was against parents who, as a rule in such schools, do not give them the kind of support and cooperation required for their children's academic improvement and discipline.[17] It is time to call a spade a spade in order to trigger at least a wake-up call. This is the route we choose.

Noting the 'refusal of most of the major arbiters of culture to address this subject (of educational inequity) openly,' Kozol explained that this is so because the educational disadvantages do not affect them personally.[18] It will be a further wrong, he said, to leave the subject unattended. We agree.

## Behind The Mask of Celebration

Each year, when the results of the SEA and CAPE – both national examinations – are announced by the Ministry of Education, a public drama unfolds. Take the 2015 results for example. As soon as the 443 secondary school scholarships (Open and National) were announced from the CAPE results, the celebrations over the winners started with widespread publicity. And as been happening consistently over the years, the schools which gained almost all scholarships, including the prestigious President's medals, were the denominational secondary schools.

Once again, the difference in 2015 was so staggering that the new Minister of Education, Anthony Garcia, felt compelled to report that 'the cabinet expressed its disappointment that the government secondary schools got only five per cent of the 443 scholarships.' He also noted the large extent to which the boys were lagging.[19] One denominational school, Naparima Girls' High School, for example, had 45 of its 97 candidates getting scholarships.

Such significant differences between denominational and government schools are nothing new. They were well known, except that no well-focused policy strategies were ever implemented to deal with the inequality. While the successful schools were publicly celebrating, parallel concerns were expressed by the Trinidad and Tobago Unified Teachers' Association (TTUTA) over the glaring inequality. TTUTA's President, Devanand Sinanan said: 'We must consider the social cost to the country and the fallout of such large numbers of under-achieving students being lumped into GSS, without the support systems to compensate.'[20]

To help accentuate the problem, around the same time these scholarships were publicly celebrated, several published reports emerged about student violence and delinquency in some GSS. One published report, for example, stated:

> Teachers are demanding that Minister Garcia become personally involved in taking action against the rowdy, violent and delinquent students who carried out a reign of terror at this (Government) school, attacking other students, drinking alcohol and last week, stoning a female teacher who had to lock herself into a classroom to avoid physical harm.[21]

These inequalities, flowing from the denominational vs. government school differences, have been attracting growing concerns by black academics as well (See Chapter Two). As an example, writing as a newspaper columnist, retired professor, Theodore Lewis, stated: 'The education that is dispensed in this country is of unequal quality...I believe the ascendancy of Indian children in local schools is a function of cultural reproduction. In recent decades, Indians have been more likely than Africans to graduate from university.'[22] Giving a 'warning about racial enclaves in particular elementary and secondary schools,' he added: '*While no school closes its doors to Indians, several schools at the primary and secondary level have become Indian enclaves. There is the perception that some of these schools are deliberately exclusionary. There are anecdotal reports about how impossible it is for Afro children to gain entry into a Presbyterian school in San Fernando.*'[23]

Such are the implications of inequality of educational opportunity in a society populated by ethnic diversity in a dual system of education, and with the denominational boards of school management empowered by a Concordat. The fact that denominational schools – ethnically-based as they are – out-perform the government schools will certainly attract perennial controversy until the government schools improve. It is about the politics of education in a multi-racial, post-colonial society. (See Chapters Two, Seven and Eight for further details).

Following widespread public concerns over the deficits in the education system, a newspaper felt compelled to editorialise: '*It is rather more worrisome, however, when the Minister of Education also seems at sea in respect of fundamental characteristics of the country's educational system. When asked about the vast difference in performance between the State and Denominational Schools, Mr Garcia, said that an in-depth investigation would be needed to determine this. Certainly, one explanation is the fundamental fact that the Denominational Schools always get the brightest students from the SEA.*'[24]

## SEA Inequalities: Removing the Mask

What do you say when in the SEA examination, for example, the results for a particular year (Appendix D) show that while the Hindu and Muslim primary schools had an average of 9% of their students passing the SEA with 90% and above, the Christian (Catholic, Anglican, SDA, Methodist, etc.) primary schools had an average of only 1.5% of its students passing with 90% and above. Government Primary Schools (GPS) had a 2.9% average.

Remarkably, the private primary schools had an 11.9% average passing with 90% and above. The 'in-between' Presbyterian schools had an average of 7.4%. The national average was 4.5%. This '90% and above' criterion is critical since it is the usual competitive benchmark for students to get into their first choice prestige schools, mainly the DSS.

An intriguing example of when social class ambitions crash ethnicity is the growing extent to which parents of all races and religions push to have their children enrolled in high-performing primary schools regardless of the schools' religious denomination.

These school by school inequalities should not be ignored in educational policy planning. The quick temptation is to explain these inequalities by race. This will be misleading and even unjust. To rely on religion alone is also insufficient. For example, while Hinduism, Islam and Presbyterianism are different religions, the schools under each Denomination had 9%, 9% and 7.4% respectively – similarly high proportions. Presbyterians are mainly of East Indian descent here. But as the Private schools reveal, it is not race.

## Social Psychology

Why are the average scores of the Christian primary (public) schools so much lower than even the GPS on this '90% and over' criterion – 1.5% vs. 2.9%? The plausible explanation for these primary school inequalities rests on a combination of factors – family support, commitment to education values, religious affiliation to schools, school climate, social class and the self-fulfilling prophesy. In other words, between student's race and their educational output, these appear as mediating social psychological variables along the way.

This is one example of the dynamic relationship between ethnicity and the country's dual educational system, from primary school output, secondary school achievement to students' academic and occupational status within three years after graduating from secondary school.(See Chapter Fourteen) Race and its broader coverage, ethnicity, may appear as the visible trigger - the independent variable - but with educational output as the target, there are several social psychological conditions which help put race or even sex in the shade. Such a social psychological matrix, however, does provide some optimism for educational reform. That is, while demographic factors such as race or sex are not subject to change, the mediating variables can be modified for positive outcomes. Race and sex differences appear as smoke signals, red flags. This point is important to consider when public policy is being developed.[25]

## Inequalities After Secondary School

As another indicator, while over 61% of East Indian students go on to university within three years after secondary school, only 34% of African students do so. Some 38% of 'Mixed' students also do so. (Chapter Fourteen) Here, female students of East Indian descent dominate university attendance, most of them coming from a denominational secondary school.

The inequity is also family-driven. Our study further shows that while almost 90% of students from an upper social class background go to university within three years after graduating from secondary school, less than half of the lower class students do so. (Chapter Fourteen)

All in all, however, we found that the single, most influential factor in promoting high academic and occupational status after leaving secondary school is the type of secondary school that a student attended – an institutional condition that combines race, class, gender and place of residence.

This means it is by far more likely for a student of whatever race, class or gender to reach high academic and occupational status after leaving secondary school if he or she attended a denominational secondary school rather than a government secondary school. From these and other related indicators, social and educational inequities appear quite pervasive and deep-rooted in the country's educational system. Some serious reflection and action, we repeat, are now urgently required.

## Reflection for Action

The foundation of a civilised society rests upon the proper education of its citizens. Even the government's Education Plans (e.g., 1968-83, 1993-

2003) have expressed this objective. The fact that quite often the school curriculum has been overburdened is testament to the heavy reliance which the society places upon education to shape children's minds and behaviour, and relationships between its citizens. As the inequalities began to attain visibility, it was expected that the government's Strategic Education Plan 2011-2015, would have laid out a strategic system for analysis and effective remedy. The plan failed to do so; but there is still time.

As this book argues, the quality of relationships between its citizens also determines the extent to which the society is civilized and democratic. Given the persistent inequities found between its different social groups, starting from the schools, the society is yet to be properly civilized and democratic.

For this formerly colonized society, given its relatively weak institutions and virgin economic foundations, a heavy demand is placed upon the creativity, enterprise and self-confidence of its citizens to drive the country into social and economic progress. It is an imperative also quite applicable to the other former British colonies of the Caribbean. In other words, for such newly-independent societies, psychological capital is needed to drive economic development. Such psychological capital (creativity, motivation, self-confidence, etc.) develops in at least two major ways – institutionally, through the outputs from the education system and through the quality of relationships between the different social and economic groups in the society, especially in a multi-ethnic society like ours.

It is within this broad perspective that this book is written. If, as John Dewey and a host of other educational philosophers have argued, the added-value purpose of education is to promote democracy, then certainly, the extent to which equal opportunity (process) and especially educational equity (product) exist within the education system is critical to consider. Mainly because of the hierarchical shape of the society, and the feverish, post-colonial quest for social status and socio-economic mobility, these two factors, opportunity and equity, face various barriers. These barriers are energized by the tensions between the different racial groups in the society.

A very troubling feature is that the most educationally disadvantaged group, as revealed by our data and several other sources, is the young black male and female in certain urban areas. The consequence of such persistent disadvantages is not merely group tension or envy. It is also, quite disturbing, the extent to which, such ethnic disadvantages are being played out in youthful disorder, crime and poverty. In other words, the output from secondary schooling particularly, produces some amount of celebrated successes on one hand, and some criminogenic consequences on the other hand. (Chapter Fifteen)

## Black Youth in Prison

Our visits to the nation's Remand Yard in 2013 found about 80% of the accused were between ages 18 and 35, young males of African descent. Over 90% said they attended a government secondary school with many saying they dropped out before graduating.[26] Which particular schools they attended? They were mainly from the schools in the urban communities which, from police reports, produce the highest proportion of gun-driven violence and murders. As our research further revealed, the vast majority of the population in the country's juvenile homes were black, illiterate and from single-parent homes.[27]

## The Ethnic Divide

And as the students from other ethnic groups, proportionally and consistently achieve higher academic and occupational status, this inequitable divide bears frightening consequences for the future. At the centre of this ethnic divide in education is the country's dual system of education. That is, a set of very high-performing denominational schools and many under-performing government schools. This duality is guarded by an enigmatic Concordat, a 1960 agreement between the government and the denominational bodies which allow the various denominations to manage their own schools, own the property, have a controlling role in appointing and promoting teachers and also a discretion of 20% Form One places.[28] The academic success of these Concordat-protected denominational schools is in sharp contrast to that of the government schools – a situation which produces perennial controversy and which is discussed in Chapter Six. A court has ruled that the Concordat is constitutionally protected by 'settled practice.'[29] This ruling in our view, gave overstretched emphasis on the 'rights of parents to send their children to a school of their choice' in relation to the appointment and promotion of teachers in a denominational school. In this way, the presiding judge opened a 'Pandora's Box', a situation we discuss in Chapter Eight.

As indicated earlier, disproportionate amounts of students of African descent migrate from these under-performing government schools into crime and prison. For such reasons, there have been increasing appeals for the government to 'fix' the GSS so as to make them more useful and attractive to parents and students.

## An Underclass Rebellion

Over the years, as the problem of a black, male underclass slowly reared its head as an unpleasant truth, attention to it has been quite peripheral– one plausible reason being the prevention of racial controversy. The problem, however, has now grown worse. We have therefore, with supporting data, called for urgent and serious attention to these educational challenges. If not properly and urgently attended to, the ethnic contestations over status and opportunity will likely move into more challenging scenarios. Linked to educational failure and crime, of course, are family and community dysfunctions. But by public policy and its own stated objectives, the education system has a fail-safe role to play, especially in the 'hot-spot' urban communities where youth crime and drug-abuse predominate.

Chapters Thirteen and Sixteen briefly but critically examine the concepts and educational implications of merit, equality and equity and the ideological contexts in which each concept finds itself. For example, it can be said that there is equality of opportunity and merit since every 11+ student is allowed to write the SEA. Our view, however, is to insert some compassion, some humanitarianism, into the competitive merit system so that the groups that are consistently disadvantaged by their social and economic conditions, or even by apparent discrimination, should be brought into the mainstream of competition by remedial interventions.

We also know, of course, that not all students are equally bright and further, that not all students will have the same abilities, aptitudes or academic interests. And, consequently, academic success will vary accordingly. But as Chapters Six to Sixteen show, there is much, much more to it than the relatively few individual successes at the top.

The government must now give immediate attention to the process of secondary school entrance examinations and placement, and the under-performing government schools. These are the twin disasters for many hopeful but socially disadvantaged 11+ children. Given the objectives of the publicly-funded education system, it is therefore now a matter of group human rights.

Noting the country's political independence in 1962, our early Chapters reveal the excitement and optimism over the role that education was expected to play in the decolonising process and especially in restoring the human dignity and self-confidence that the two colonized races – formerly African enslaved and East Indian indentured labourers – were denied on the plantations. In this context, it was also expected, as Chapter Two suggests, that having together suffered such humiliating plantation experiences, there would be special bonds between these two racial groups for cooperation and collective production in the post-colonial period. As the later Chapters show, however, neither the major objectives of the education system nor the collective cooperation of these two races has properly materialised.

The early promises of education have grown hollow. The ethnic tensions, spawned by the educational and political systems, are beginning to break through the limits of the national watchword – tolerance. The society – its public institutions, its civic organisations, its various elites and professionals – have much reflection and work to do.

Among our limited recommendations are an increased number of Form One places at the high-performing secondary schools, single-sex government secondary schools comparable to the denominational schools, improved legislation to help reduce the inequalities and inequities in the educational system, a review of the examination system, continued policy-directed research and resource-backed policies to improve the under-performing schools, their students and their respective communities and families.

Finally, because of the data we have discovered and their serious implications, we suspect an underclass rebellion of disorder and crime, if left unchecked, will grow into a fuller attack on mainstream society. And much of the blame will fall on the country's education system. Further details on these concerns are found in subsequent Chapters.

## NOTES

1.  National Task Force on Education (1993-2003). Ministry of Education.
2.  Several early reports indicated this very low preference for technical/ vocational programmes; e.g., Tracer Study (2001-2010) submitted to Ministry of Education, 2005. Within those who take such programmes, the failure rate as noted in later Chapters was quite high with one out of five students failing.

3.   This is the Trinidad Muslim League (TML) with 20.5 %.

4.   Ministry of Education,'Report on Secondary Entrance Assessment Examination'. 2011. (See Appendix E)

5.   L. Bernard. *Express*. September, 23, 2015. p. 14.

6.   For example, *New York Post*, September 23, 2015. p. 12.

7.   J. Ramos, *New York Post*, editorial September 29, 2015. p. 23.

8.   J. Ketrridge. Ibid. p. 2.

9.   D. Ravitch,*Reign of Error*. New York: Random House. 2013. pp. 7-9.

10.  Ibid. p. 8.

11.  Interview with Miami Dade County Charter School Board member and Director of Miami Dade College School of Justice, Dr. Ray Raimundo. October 5, 2015.

12.  The *Economist*. August 1, 2015. p. 9.

13.  Ibid. pp.19-22.

14.  L. Guinier, *The Tyranny of the Meritocracy* Boston: Beacon Press. 2015. pp. x-xi.

15.  Research Reports commissioned by and submitted to the Ministry of Education. 2006-2012.

16.  J. Kozol, *The Shame of the Nation*, New York: Random House. 2005. p. 21.

17.  These interviews are recorded in our Report, 'Voices of the Teachers', commissioned by and submitted to the Ministry of Education. 2008. Parents and guardians too, have expressed complaints against teachers, mainly about absenteeism.

18.  J. Kozol, *The Shame of the Nation*, New York: Random House. 2005. p. 21.

19.  A. Garcia, 'Govt schools get only 5 percent schools', *Guardian*, October 16, 2015. p. 3.

20.  D. Sinanan, 'Blame lack of support.' *Express*. October 17, 2015. p. 9.

21.  C. Asson, 'Stones for Miss.' *Newsday*, October 9, 2015. p. 3.

22.  T. Lewis, *Express*. October 22, 2015. p. 13. Lewis is Professor Emeritus, University of Minnesota, USA, residing in Trinidad.)

23.  Ibid.

24.  *Guardian* editorial. October 22, 2015. p. 24.

25.  See P. Wright, C. Ashvalom, T. Moffit, R. Miechand P. Silva, 'Reconciling the Relationship Between SES and Delinquency: Causation but Not Correlation'*Criminology 37*, pp. 175-184. Also, R. Deosaran 'School Violence and Delinquency: The Dynamics of Race, Gender, Class, Age and Parenting in the Caribbean' in R. Deosaran. (Ed.) *Crime, Delinquency and Justice in the Caribbean*. Jamaica: Ian Randle Publishers. 2007. pp. 89-129.

26. The author headed a cabinet-appointed inquiry into the Remand Yard of the prisons in 2013. A Report was laid in the country's Parliament.

27. R. Deosaran and D. Chadee, 'Juvenile Delinquency: Challenges for Criminology and Social Policy', *Caribbean Journal of Criminology and Social Psychology*. 1997.

28. See Concordat in Appendix A.

29. 'Kamla Jagessar v Teaching Service Commission', H.C. Action No.CV 2009-01445, 2012

# CHAPTER ONE
# Education: The Great Hope for Former Colonials

*Let us proceed to work more positively than ever towards the economic and social upliftment of the Black disadvantaged groups in our society of both African and Asian origin, as the only way to achieve the genuine national integration to which so many of us are dedicated...The history of the West Indies has been a long history of deprivations and injustices for the two numerically dominant racial groups of African and Asian origin. It is a history of deliberate and conscious discrimination against people because of the colour of their skin and notwithstanding their educational qualifications.*

Dr. Eric Williams
Former Prime Minister of Trinidad and Tobago
March 23, 1970. Address on Revolution and Dignity

*The only way to improve the quality of your life is through education and training, as it is the only passport out of poverty.*

Mrs. Kamla Persad-Bissesssar, S.C.
Former Prime Minister of Trinidad and Tobago
May 30, 2015, Address at Indian Arrival Day function

## THE PURPOSE

This Chapter looks at the glorious emphasis and hopes put on education and the implications for this post-colonial society, multi-racial society, Trinidad and Tobago. It looks back at some of the historical forces which contributed to these implications. Given how the country's educational system has evolved, some narrative about the era of African slavery and East Indian indentured labour will add fuller meaning to the contemporary relationships, especially in terms of educational opportunity, merit, occupational status, and equity.[1]

While there have been and still are post-colonial tensions arising from status competition, the quest for ethnic equilibrium uneasily continues.[2]

Such a narrative, though not exhaustive, helps provide context, 'flesh and blood' as it were, to the ongoing competition for academic and occupational status and even political power, as well as to the fluctuating tensions between these two formerly oppressed groups. There was the general feeling that these two ethnic groups – of African or East Indian descent – having suffered similar plantation conditions, should be provided with and share similar opportunities for social and economic advancement in the post-colonial era. In other words, their common suffering in the plantation should inspire both to be more cooperative than competitive rivals.

## Post Colonial Ethnic Rivalry

Justifying the need to look back at the country's colonial history in order to understand its present educational system, an Inter-American Development Bank (IDB) Report on educational equity in the Caribbean stated:

> Some of the key features and challenges for the education system in the four countries today (Trinidad and Tobago, Guyana, Jamaica, Barbados) can be traced to the historical legacy of British colonialism and to some practices adopted in earlier times.[3]

The Report added:

> It is important to understand the impact of history and tradition on the present education system here in order to arrive at more informed decisions regarding the future development of the system. One prominent example is the varying role of the state.[4]

Faced with the 1970 Black Power protests,[5] then Prime Minister, Dr Eric Williams, advocated this expectation:

> The recognition of the rights of humanity must commence with special assistance to the Black man, to make up for historical injustice and the time lost through his exclusion from the economic and social, and even political progress of the nineteenth century. I know of no better country in the world better circumscribed than Trinidad and Tobago to initiate this fundamental reconstruction.[6]

Touching on the challenge of ethnic equality, on the day before the country's Independence Dr Williams called upon the youths to teach their parents *'to live in harmony, the difference being not of race or colour of skin, but merit only, differences of wealth and family status being rejected in favour of equality of opportunity.'*[7]

These propositions for equality and equity among the formerly enslaved and indentured especially, are important to recall since they help provide a rational platform for creating an education system that generates the opportunities required.

Though the plantation conditions, with their racially divisive nature, previously fuelled mutual antagonisms between the former African enslaved and the East Indian indentured labourers, it was felt that such ethnic antagonisms would have been significantly diminished as the country moved into its political independence. As a developing, post-colonial society however, the challenge of demand and supply within an ethnically-driven multi-party system, contributed to soured relations between the different ethnic communities.

The contestations between the country's two major political parties heightened the embittered rivalry and tensions between Africans and East Indians here. No doubt, the fact that these two ethnic groups were rather similar in proportion contributed to the intensity of the competition for economic, political and educational space.[8] Tensions within the educational sector were driven by the country's religious diversity on one hand and secular pressures for equality of opportunity on the other hand.[9]

Political patronage and competition for the scarce material resources and social status produced the first major governance challenge for the post-colonial government. In fact, the People's National Movement (PNM) administration, before and just after political independence faced the challenge of how to keep its African-dominated party in power while, at the same time, maintaining ethnic harmony and equity across the other ethnic groups in the mobility-conscious society. It is a dilemma which subsequently faced East Indian-dominated parties when in power too, that is, keeping a tolerable balance between political patronage and socio-economic equity.

Further, in the early independence era, the expansion of educational opportunities without commensurate employment absorption led to inflated civil service employment and concerns with social discrimination within the private sector. The government in 1970 established a Commission of Enquiry into racial discrimination in employment.

This ethnically-driven competition for status and privilege followed political independence when there were no longer the missionaries or European planter to complain against. With such 'colonial suspects' no longer around, historian Brinsley Samaroo said *'the colonised turned inwards, seeing his fellow-colonised as the competitor and antagonist'* in educational and occupational status.[10] How much of this is today being reflected in the competition within the educational system, and how?

Following the granting of political independence during the 1960s to several Caribbean countries – from Jamaica and Trinidad and Tobago down to Guyana – the consequent upswing optimism included special emphasis on education and the preparation of Caribbean youth for the region's future social and economic challenges. The despair from colonial oppression turned into great hopes for fuller democracy and socio-economic mobility through education. In this competitive 'struggle of recovery,' however, ethnic tensions grew with mixed interpretations, especially in the linkage between education, economic expansion and politics.[11]

## Education as the Great Hope

The current parade of education as the flagship for healing the colonial wounds of neglect and oppression forms part of the great expectations so lavishly flaunted during the years soon after the country's political independence. In other words, the extent to which the marginal and underprivileged do not enjoy the promised mobility through education, to that extent would the great expectations of political independence be broken.[12]

Pledging both equality of educational opportunity and equity in 2015, the country's former Prime Minister, Kamla Persad-Bissessar, in a government-sponsored 8-page colour spread in all newspapers stated:

> The children of Trinidad and Tobago are our true national treasures. Every child in Trinidad and Tobago is equally important to me. We are working very hard to include children from all circumstances in the safety net. We are strengthening with new programmes, improving schools and learning...The Early Childhood Education Centres with their modern teaching methods will give our children the proper head start in their educational journey. This equity in education from an early age also means that all our students start off with the same advantage.[13]

Same advantage? The country is crowded by high-profile testimonies about education and training as the only way for a better life and the key out of poverty, and in consequence, by significant physical expansion and mass enrolment in education.[14] However, with such expansion, the challenges of social disadvantages by race, class and gender were yet to be dealt with. The 'advantages' are not similar.

On August 28, 2015, the former Prime Minister again said: *'Education is the most powerful asset for national development. My government is committed to education for all since each of us has the potential to do the things you wish to achieve. We provide education for all, not only for a few.'*[15] Such official commitments help set the benchmarks to assess the extent to which equality of educational opportunity and educational equity are actually achieved in this multi-ethnic society. Expanded access does not necessarily lead to equality or equity. Education for all does not necessarily mean *quality* education for all.

Further than just for economic reasons, the purpose of education, according to the former Prime Minister is also for cultural and civic purpose too.[16] Referring to the legacies of slavery and indentureship, she explained:

> In the midst of this, education remained the pillar and the unifying factor of the nation, as it was when the children of indentured labourers attended schools, overcoming language and cultural barriers and meeting other children of different origins, that commitment to a common destiny truly emerged.[17]

All this means that for over fifty years since independence, from official pledges, policies and public speeches, education was promoted as the key vehicle for self-improvement, equality of opportunity and good citizenship. How far has it succeeded?

## The Equality and Equity Challenges

At this stage, a definition of education itself will be useful. While there has been a multitude of definitions and objectives of education, we rely for relevance on the one adopted by this country's government. The government plan for educational development in Trinidad and Tobago's post-colonial society put it this way:

> What are we educating for? We are supposed to produce citizens who are intellectually, morally and emotionally fitted to respond adequately and productively to the varied challenges of life in a multi-racial developing country and to the changes which are being brought about in the economic foundations of civilisation, particularly the challenges of Science and Technology. And we are supposed to accept and cater for such inevitable situations such as the disappearance of the totally unskilled labourer.[18]

In accepting UNESCO-ECLA Education Planning Report, the government further pledged the 'responsibility of providing a balanced education for all persons.' It therefore accepted: *'General education should endeavour to develop a responsible attitude towards work, stability in relation with others, adaptability to change, the ability to think objectively and a sensitive approach to culture beyond the limits of specialization'* [19]

However, several overview studies have since expressed concern over the social and educational deficits facing youths in this country, and whether such deficits occur through personal choice, policy shortcomings or a mixture of both. For example, A World Bank Report (2003) entitled 'Caribbean Youth Development' stated: 'Factors are present in the Caribbean (Guyana, Barbados and Jamaica) that have the potential to disrupt the process of positive youth development.' Citing school drop-outs, crime and gang membership as examples of youth deviance, the Report *recommended 'reforming the education system and maximizing the protective effects of schools by improving access and retention, improving the quality of education.'* [20] To them, the issues were educational equity and equality in education.

The Caricom-appointed West Indian Commission, examining the challenges of equal educational opportunity and equity, stated in its 1993 Report:

> Nothing has come through clearer in our consultations than the vital need to improve educational infrastructure in the Region and multiply many times over educational and training opportunities for all West Indians. [21]

Referring specifically to meeting youth aspirations, the Commission added: *'If they (the youth) lose faith, the future is lost...They have not lost faith but we have found them on the edge of deep distress about conditions...about lack of opportunities in employment that leaves them idle and frustrated and tempts them down dangerous cul-de-sacs.'* [22] These popularised themes – 'our youth is our most precious resource' or that 'education is the major tool for decolonization,' etc., – have resonated across the Caribbean and this country, particularly since the country's first Prime Minister put educational development as the government's top priority for decolonization and socio-economic equality. [23]

Without aristocracies or elite legacies of their own, the descendants of slaves and indentured immigrants have been made to see education as the vital passport. Soon after the country got political independence, youth aspirations for higher education and the professional occupations soared. In fact, it was Rubin and Zavalloni's study a few years after independence on the country's secondary school students which documented the lavish academic expectations and high occupational aspirations reflecting the mood of that time. This study revealed significant proportions of students from the various social classes and ethnicities,[24] having high educational ambitions, and wishing to be 'engineers, great persons, doctors, astronauts, lawyers, neurosurgeons, etc.[25] The authors concluded: 'These students, highly aware of their conditional chances of survival in the educational hierarchy, are highly motivated to attain this most cherished goal and perceive passing the examinations as the "green light" to the future.'[26]

Noting the high academic and occupational aspirations of the young people, they added: 'There is a striking incidence of lofty, essentially unattainable or unrealized goals among lower-class students which sometimes seem to flow in a dream-like sequence.'[27] Whether through fantasy or high-self-esteem, such pervasive high aspirations emphasized the intense desire for education, at least the opportunities for education, and with the lower class particularly, the quest for equity.

In his Preface to Rubin and Zavalloni's book, prominent anthropologist Otto Klineberg sought to unmask the presumed 'fantasies' by noting: *'Unfortunately, but obviously, most of these hopes will not be realized. What happens then? What will be the consequences of disillusionment? Even if it is true that a man's reach should exceed his grasp, is it psychologically healthy to have such great discrepancy between dreams and possible achievements?'*[28]

As a tonic to enliven independence, at every turn and by every governing politician or senior bureaucrat, hope for the future was given. Proposals for personal success and mobility through education were prolific. As one of many examples, former Minister Extraordinaire and former Prime Minister, A.N.R. Robinson pledged: *'Extreme poverty is a peculiar form of slavery and indentureship. I am therefore talking about creating an enabling environment of competitive creativity among communities to demonstrate that the resources of our minds and hands are inexhaustible even if your pockets are limited.'*[29] The 'enabling environment' was expanding education and supporting facilities.

Such references are important to recall since they do provide the psychological frame of reference from which the role of education-driven status can be subsequently examined. As the years rolled on, however, some skepticism crept in. Prize-winning calypsonians, for example, produced songs severely criticising the 'deterioration' of public standards of conduct, the loss of the independence spirit and even increasing school violence and delinquency. Two notable examples are calypsonian Gypsy's *Somebody Thiefing the Soul of the Nation*, and Mighty Chalkdust's *De spirit Gone*.[30] Some calypsos go as far as to complain about the differences in ambition and success between those of African descent and those of East Indian descent.[31]

## Education as Flagship for Success

The challenges for educational infrastructure and educational opportunities, more recently, have been taken up by the government, especially by having free secondary schooling, free university education, a 65% rate of enrolment in tertiary education and an expansive school-building programme accompanied by a long list of technical and vocational training programmes.[32]

In April, 2015, the Minister of Tertiary Education and Skills Training said: 'Local tertiary education participation rates increased from 7% in 2001 to 40% in 2008...Trinidad and Tobago has surpassed its target for the tertiary education participation rate which is currently 65% in 2015.' With such an enabling environment and heavily subsidised higher education, the expectation was that substantial use would be made of them so as to improve academic and occupational mobility, especially among the poor, working class and other seemingly deprived groups in the society.

Coming to the educational inequity factor, the minister added:

> Going beyond participation, requires us as policy makers to explore human capital development from an outcomes-based perspective. For many years, education and training opportunities were restricted to a few. Those barriers have been largely overcome in Trinidad and Tobago through financial vehicles such as the Government Assistance for Tuition Expenses (GATE) programme, Higher Education Loan Programme (HELP), Financial Assistance Studies Programme (FASP), among others.[33]

Does free tuition help reduce educational inequality? Does treating unequals equally help?

Touching on the 'graduate glut,' the minister added: 'I have always maintained that the system must be equitable but at the same time all beneficiaries of the system must be held accountable.'[34] Finally glancing again at the equity factor, he said: 'Historical antecedents have led to disproportionate distribution of tertiary education and skills training.'[35]

Such celebrations of educational expansion are quite common today, and to some extent commendable. However, the fundamentals of educational inequity – disproportionality in social class, ethnicity, etc. – remain relatively unmentioned, no doubt due to their controversial nature. This remains so, even though, following the promises of political independence in 1962, this country and its respective governments appropriately cited the education system as the key agency of decolonisation, socio-economic mobility, racial equality and generally, equality of opportunity.[36]

In fact, for this multi-racial society the national anthem itself contains the pledge for social and racial equality (e.g., *Where every creed and race find an equal place*). Like the other newly independent countries in the Commonwealth Caribbean, such pledges, resting on the education system, became common.

A widely-cited calypso, encouraging youth into education, was sung by the country's most famous and celebrated calypsonian, the Mighty Sparrow (Slinger Francisco). In 1972, he sang 'Education':

> Children go to school to learn
> Otherwise later in life you go catch hell
> Your whole life will be more misery
> You're better off dead
> For there is simply no room
> In this whole wide world
> For an uneducated little boy or girl.

On several occasions, former Prime Minister Kamla Persad-Bissessar, a former Minister of Education herself, repeated her message for education as a vehicle for improved academic and occupational status. Recently, for example, she stated: 'Education is the passport out of poverty. That is why our government has emphasized education and training so as to prevent the youth from crime and instead to get opportunities for sustainable jobs and a better quality of life.'[37]

She added: 'Education is one of the cornerstones on which the unity of a nation is built. It remains my mission to continue to deliver a system where merit and ideas are fully driving forces of our politics.'[38]

No doubt, having used herself as an example, she connects this educational pledge to the labour history and the poverty-entrenched roots of the forefathers of today's generation. Indeed, there are many who have 'made it' from poverty into middle and upper class professions. But the extent to which racial and social class proportionalities, for example, arise, to that extent equality and equity in this country's education system will require consideration.

## Status Competition and Ethnic Distrust

It is quite common in this country that those Africans and East Indians who rise to high educational, occupational or political office to celebrate their individual success by referring to the poor, depressed backgrounds from which they came. Such 'rags to riches' stories are often used to help legitimise the value of the educational system without necessarily uncovering the residual challenges of equality of opportunity and social equity. In fact, in the post-colonial era the dust is not quite settled with respect to ethnic relations in the country, especially if one examines political contestations (e.g., general elections) and the repeated controversies over ethnically-driven political patronage and secondary school placement.

The related issue is not that some made it to the top; it is the contestations between the different races to reach the top, and the disproportionalities which arise, controversially, along the rough passage. This situation is orally intensified at election times, a noteworthy example of the political sociology of an ethnically-plural society. In addition to previous references to such conflicts, a dramatic example is contained in the acidic words of Imam Abu Bakr, leader of the Muslimeen insurrection of July 29, 1990:

> There is really no justice in this country. I could show you in every way that justice does not apply except for the rich and those who control the society. I think African people have suffered tremendously from dependicitis in comparison to the Indian people. You cannot talk about the population generally. You have to talk about the groups, the interests, the sectors in the society. It is groups still fighting on the plantation for their survival.[39]

The ambition-driven rivalries and stressful distrust between these two ethnic groups – Africans and East Indians – are also documented in a study, 'Employment Practices in the Public and Private Sectors in Trinidad and Tobago.' The authors concluded:

> One of the major findings was the tendency for Indians to be heavily under-represented at the higher reaches of the Public Sector. There are

no doubt historical and cultural factors which explain this imbalance. Its persistence into the present is however due to the operation of the seniority principle and to the possible influence of political will in appointments beyond a certain range.[40]

They added: 'It was also found that where merit and technical criteria must prevail, as in the Judicial and Professional Sectors, Indians were more than adequately represented.' The under-representation of Indians in the public and protective services was quite notable, but partly due to 'historical reasons.' One of the Report's recommendations to balance racial representation, was 'to ensure a measure of racial balance on all interview panels in the Public Service.'[41] The Report contained a special chapter entitled: 'Indo-Trinidadian Grievances in the National Security Services.' The mistrust went deeply on both sides.

According to the Report, Africans felt Indo-Trinidadians were 'taking over the medical profession.' Africans felt 'an Indian government will only look after Indians, etc. While Indians complained about widespread discrimination in the public sector, Africans expressed fears of Indian domination in the business and professional sectors.[42] Such fears have penetrated current debates over equality of educational opportunity and occupational status.

## Education Yes, But Different Strokes

Put briefly, however, the challenge facing this country is therefore not so much educational infrastructure or the quantity of education but as a list of researchers have found, it is more a challenge of equality of opportunity and equity among the various social and ethnic groups. In this sense, the promises and expectations for equality need to be unmasked.

After reviewing the relevant local research, sociologist Nasser Mustapha, for example, concluded:

> The impact of education cannot be ascertained on the number of school buildings, the availability of school places nor in terms of examination passes and grades. Some indication of the impact may be obtained by looking at the predicament of school leavers.[43]

That is, what happens to them after leaving school – especially the government secondary schools.

He further concluded that 'what exists in the country's educational system is a hierarchically structured system rigidly stratified along lines of social class.'[44]

As will be later indicated in greater detail, the country's dual system of education produces serious implications for equality of educational opportunity and equity among the various ethnic, social class and gender groupings both in being placed in secondary school as well as after leaving secondary school.

Some reflections on pre-independence (colonial) conditions will help provide further perspective on the role of education as a democratic instrument for socio-economic mobility among the descendants of African slaves and East Indian indentured labourers.

## NOTES

1.    While there were and still are other racial groups, e.g., Whites, Syrians, Portuguese, French, Spanish, Lebanese, Chinese, Amerindians, etc., those of African,  East Indian and Mixed descent form about 98% of today's  population.  The word, African, is used interchangeably with black, person of African descent and Afro-Trinidadian. The word, Indian, is used interchangeably with East Indian, person of East Indian descent and Indo-Trinidadian. Given the peculiar relationships between slavery and indentureship and the education system, and the current challenges in the education system, reference will be made mainly to these two racial groups. As the following references indicate, the term 'race' or 'racial' is not used in their biological sense but as socially constructed terms widely used within the population. Some of the useful writings about cultural context and competition for and distribution of status among the two racial groups are: B. Brereton, 'The Foundations of Prejudice: Indians and Africans in 19th Century Trinidad' *Caribbean Issues* 1974, (1), pp. 15-28; E. Williams *History of the People of Trinidad and Tobago* Trinidad: PNM Publishing Co., 1962; S. Ryan. 'Race and Occupational Stratification in Contemporary Trinidad and Tobago' Trinidad: University of the  West indies, ISER, 1989; D. Wood *Trinidad in Transition* London: Oxford University Press, 1968; L. Braithwaite, 'Social Stratification in Trinidad', Trinidad: University of the West Indies, ISER, 1975; Y. Malik, *East Indians in Trinidad* London: Oxford University Press, 1971.

2.    These references help reveal the tensions and struggles for ethnic and political equilibrium in the society.  B. Brereton, *A History of Modern Trinidad, 1783-1962* Kingston, Jamaica: Heinemann, 1981; 'East Indians in the Caribbean':  Second Conference, Trinidad: University of the West Indies, Faculty of Arts and Sciences, 1971; S. Ryan, 'Sharks and Sardines', Trinidad: University of the West Indies, ISER, 1992; M. G. Smith *The Plural Society in the British West Indies* Jamaica: Sangster's Book Store

Edition, 1974; D. Dabydeen and B. Samaroo (Eds.) *India in the Caribbean* Hertfordshire, England: Hansib Press, 1987; J. La Guerre (Ed.) *Calcutta to Caroni* Trinidad: University of the West Indies, Extra Mural Studies Unit, 1985; S. Ryan and J. La Guerre (Eds.) 'Employment Practices in the Public and Private Sectors of Trinidad and Tobago' Trinidad: University of the West Indies, Centre for Ethnic Studies, 1993; C. Campbell,*The Young Colonials: A Social History of Education in Trinidad and Tobago: 1834-1939*. Jamaica: The Press University of the West Indies, 1996. Among the polemicists was H. P. Singh,*The Indian Struggle for Justice and Equality Against Black Racism in Trinidad and Tobago (1956-62)*. Trinidad: Indian Review Press, 1993(Reprint of Singh's writings, etc); R. Deosaran 'The Schools and Multiculturalism: Some Psychological and Political Implications'*Caribbean Issues*, 2(3), December 1976, pp. 71-87; R. Deosaran,' Some issues in Multiculturalism: The Case of Trinidad and Tobago in the Post-Colonial Era, '*Plural Societies*, 12, (1/2), 1981, pp. 15-35; R. Deosaran.'Education, Culture and Politics' June 1976 (Unpublished graduate paper, Department of Applied Social Psychology, University of Toronto).

3.    Inter-American Development Bank,'Access, Equity and Performance'. Washington DC: IDB Bookstore. Washington. 2002. p. 37.

4.    Ibid. pp. 37-38.

5.    For a description and implications of this protest, see e.g. S. Ryan and T. Stewart (eds.) 'The Black Power Revolution of 1970'

6.    E. Williams, 'On Revolution and Dignity' in E. Williams, *Forged from the Love of Liberty: A Collection of Speeches* Trinidad: Longman Caribbean. 1981, p. 167. In using the term 'Black,' Williams used it sometimes for those of African descent only and at other times, for both Africans and East Indians.

7.    Address at Queen's Park Oval. August 30, 1962.

8.    Africans: 1946=261,485, 1960=301,946, 1970=373,538, 2013=454,182 (34.2%). East Indians: 1946=195,747, 1960=301,946, 1970=373,538, 2013= 470,118 (35.4%). As an indication of populations changes: From 1946 to 1960, Africans moved to a 37.1% increase; from 1960 to 1970 an 11.2% increase; from 1970 to 2013 a 14% increase. From 1946 to 1960, East Indians moved to a 59.4% increase; from 1960 to 1970 to a 23.71 % increase; from 1970 to 2013 to an increase of 29% (Population at 2011 census is 1,328,019, estimate, Central Statistical Office).

9.    As will be later explained, the country's dual system of education is driven by a Concordat (1960) and the state. Religious diversity: Catholic 21.6%, Hindu 18.2%, Islam 5.0%, Pentecostal (Evangelists, Gospel, etc.) 12%, Methodist 0.7%, Jehovah Witness 1.5%, Spiritual Baptist 5.7%, Baptist (Other) 1.2%, Anglican 5.7%, Seventh Days Adventist

4.1%, Not stated 11.1%, None 2.2%, Others 7.5% (Central Statistical Office, 2011).

10. B. Samaroo,' Politics and Afro-Indian Relations in Trinidad' in J. La Guerre, *Calcutta to Caroni*, p.77; J. La Guerre, J. and A. M. Bissessar,*Calcutta to Caroni and the Indian Diaspora.* (Eds.) (3rdEd.). Trinidad, St Augustine School of Continuing Studies, 2005. This collection provides some updated information regarding ethnic tensions in Trinidad and Tobago and a few other places, e.g., Guyana, Surinam, Fiji, U.S.A.

11. As an example of social and occupational stratification and the accompanying tensions and ethnic dissonance, see S. Ryan (ed.),'Social and Occupational Stratification in Trinidad and Tobago' ISER, University of the West Indies, 1989. Also, S. Ryan (with Lou Anne Barclay), *Sharks and Sardines* ISER, University of the West Indies, 1992. From his 1987 survey on the commercial successes of East Indians, Ryan stated: 'Blacks and whites have begun to express concern about this thrust; 35% of the blacks in the sample claimed that Indians had benefitted more than blacks from the 30 years of PNM rule (1956-86). Only 10 percent believed that blacks had done better. Fifty eight (58%) percent of the Indians in the sample however felt otherwise. Asked which group benefitted more when the NAR came into power in1986, only 1 percent of the blacks felt that they had done better. Twenty three (23%) percent said Indians had benefitted more'p.189. The arrival and services of the East Indian indentured labourers were consistently controversial. Some did object, others welcomed them. For example, in May 1850, two politicians in the Council, Mr. Rennie and Mr. Phillips, expressed great pleasure over the contribution of the indentured labourers. Rennie said: 'I unhesitatingly state my conviction that it, and it alone has enabled Trinidad to keep its exports and maintain even its present advanced position. The East Indians have undoubtedly exercised a powerful influence on other labourers of the colony.' Phillips added: 'Were it not for the East Indian immigration, not half a dozen sugar estates would be working now.' (Both cited in C.R.Ottley, *East and West Indian Indians Rescue*. Trinidad: Port of Spain, Crusoe Publishing, 1975, p. 44).

12. The public rhetoric just after 1962 went sky-high with calls for hard work, national commitment, honesty in public affairs and, with much gusto, the role of education in personal success and the country's socio-economic development. See e.g., R. Deosaran, *Psychonomics and Poverty: Towards Governance and Civil Society*, Jamaica, Mona: The University of the West Indies Press, 2000, pp. 2-27. For an overview of the evolution of the country's education system from colonialism to political independence, see C. *Campbell, Colony and Nation: A Short History of Education in Trinidad and Tobago 1834-1986.*

13. Published as a spread in all daily newspapers, June 14, 2015. p. 7.

14. Ibid. Former Prime Minister Mrs. Kamla Persad-Bissessar's remarks. Further and more recently, she said: 'Like me, I came from poor background but education has me where I am today. Parents and children should take your education seriously if you want to get out of poverty.' Speech at the formal opening of new building for Ministry of Tertiary Education and Skills Training, August 28, 2015.

15. Ibid.

16. Prime Minister Kamla Persad-Bissessar. *Express*, May 30, 2015. p. 7.

17. Prime Minister Kamla Persad-Bissessar. *Express*, May 30, 2015. p. 7.

18. Draft Educational Plan for Education Development in Trinidad and Tobago, 1968-83. Government Printery, Trinidad and Tobago, 1974, p. 5. For details on the multitude of definitions by John Dewey, Aristotle, Rousseau, Comenius, Plutarch, Descartes, Kant, Piaget, St. Augustine etc., see, e.g., S. Curtis, and M. Boultwood. *A Short History of Educational Ideas*. Surrey, Great Britain: University Tutorial Press, 1977; Also, R. Ulrich *A History of Educational Thought* New York: American Book Company, 1968.

19. This Report applied to all Caribbean countries. p. 5.

20. 'Caribbean Youth Development: Issues and Policy Development'. World Bank Report, Washington, D.C, 2003.

21. See e.g., *Time for Action: Report of the West Indian Commission* Jamaica: The Press, University of the West Indies. 1993. pp. 27-28. This Commission comprised 15 members with the major objective to 'formulate proposals for advancing the goals of the Treaty of Chaguaramas' which established the Caribbean Community and Common Market (Caricom) in 1973.

22. *Time for Action: Report of the West Indian Commission*, Jamaica: The Press, University of the West Indies. 1993.p 28.

23. Dr Eric Williams, *Forged from the Love of Liberty* (Selected Speeches). Longman Caribbean, 1981. See especially speeches on education (pp. 239-270 and on Independence (pp. 316-330).

24. In this book, the terms 'of African descent,' 'Africans and 'blacks' are used interchangeably, according to context, and since each has become socially acceptable. Similarly, the terms 'East Indians,' 'Indians' and of 'East Indian descent' are used interchangeably.

25. V. Rubin and M. Zavalloni. *We Wished to be Looked Upon* New York: Columbia University, Teachers' College Press. 1969.

26. Ibid. p.184

27. Ibid, p.117.

28. Ibid. p. viii.

29. Speech given at launch of National Social Development Council, Central Bank Towers, Port of Spain, October 24, 1996.

30. Gypsy's name is Winston Peters. Some verses: 'Born in a land of great

expectation, Over the years I watched its deterioration, How could some place so good turn out so bad, Where is the love we once had, Somebody thiefing the soul of the nation, Much too much political corruption, Talk about race only cause more confusion.' His other calypso, *Little Black Boy*, described the apparent lack of educational and occupational ambition and aspirations of black youths in the country. Chalkdust's name is Hollis Liverpool. By his song, he complained at the overly vulgar commercialisation of the country's culture, and in particular, how the spirit has left the country's greatest festival, carnival.

31.  In this regard, the 1988 calypso, Common Entrance by Cro Cro was very popular and racially controversial. He accused the Common Entrance system as being 'racial' in favour of children of East Indian descent and elite groups. He won the nation's highest national prize, Calypso Monarch. In this song, he accused the authorities of pro-East Indian bias in the results of the 11+ common entrance examination. His real name is Weston Rawlins.

32.  See e.g., Providing a World of Opportunity. Ministry of Science, Technology and Tertiary Education, Government of Trinidad and Tobago, 2012. Also, Administrative Report (October 2010 to September 2011). Ministry of Education, Government of Trinidad and Tobago, 2012. In the last decade, 'over US $800 million' invested in GATE, with 62,000 enrolled in 2015

33.  This provision of student financial support and related subsidies reminds me of a study I did for the Toronto Board of Education in 1975. The research report was titled 'Does Money Matter? A Study of Student Aspirations'. A review of the international literature indicated that even when money is provided for university attendance, ethnic and social class differences existed with regard to access and achievement.

34.  Fazal Karim, Minister of Tertiary Education and Skills Training. Keynote address, 2nd International Conference of Accreditation Council of Trinidad and Tobago, Hyatt Regency Hotel, April 1, 2015.

35.  Ibid.

36.  Race here is defined as a social construct, how people relate to one another, and not as a biological concept. It is used inter-changeably with 'ethnicity.' So too, 'Africans' and 'blacks' will be used inter-changeably. See R. Deosaran for a discussion on race relations. Cultural 'Dilemmas in the Caribbean' in R. Deosaran, *Social Psychology in the Caribbean* Trinidad: Longman Trinidad, 1992, pp. 265-314.

37.  Speech to formally open the new Maloney Police Station. May 27, 2015.

38.  Speech on Indian Arrival Day celebrations, *Newsday* May 30, 2015, p. 7. In fact, all public officials tend to pay high tribute to the harmonious manner in which the different races live together in the society. Both

President Anthony Carmona and then PNM Opposition Leader, Dr. Keith Rowley expressed similar sentiments as the Prime Minister on the same celebrated day regarding national unity and education. (Trinidad *Guardian* and *Express*. May 30, 2015).

39. Muslimeen Leader Abu Bakr. In R. Deosaran. A Society Under Siege. Trinidad: University of the West Indies. Psychological Research Centre. 1993. p. 254.

40. 'Employment Practices in the Public and Private Sectors in Trinidad and Tobago', S. Ryan and J.La Guerre. Centre for Ethnic Studies, University of the West Indies, St Augustine. 1993. pp. vii-x.

41. Ibid. pp. vii-x.

42. 'Employment Practices in the Public and Private Sectors', S. Ryan and J. La Guerre. Centre for Ethnic Studies, University of the West Indies, St Augustine. 1993. 'There is a deep-seated fear voiced by Afro-Trinidadians. Once an Indo-Trinidadian assumes high office in government – that individual immediately sets about bringing in more Indo-Trinidadians at the expense of Afro-Trinidadians. These perceptions are seldom backed by concrete evidence, but they are real in the minds of many Afro-Trinidadians.' p. xxix.

43. Senior Lecturer in Sociology of Education. 'Challenges to Education Reform in a Developing Country'. In R. Deosaran, R. Reddock and N. Mustapha (Eds.) 'Issues in Social Science: A Caribbean Perspective'. Trinidad: Department of Sociology, University of the West Indies, 1994. p.100; R. Deosaran 'The Schools and Multiculturalism: Some Psychological and Political Implications' In *Caribbean Issues* 2(3), December, 1976, pp. 72-87.

44. Ibid. p. 100.

# Two Races: Suffered Then, Adversaries Now

*Every child has an inherent right to an education which will enhance the development of maximum capability regardless of gender, ethnic, economic, social or religious background. That the educational system of Trinidad and Tobago must endeavour to develop a spiritually, morally, physically, intellectually and emotionally sound individual, that ensures that cultural, ethnic, class and Gender needs are appropriately addressed.*

National Task Force on Education (1993-2003)
Ministry of Education

## REFLECTIONS ON PAST OPPRESSION

The preceding chapter attempted to show how historical and political forces contributed to today's ethnic competition for status and opportunity, especially as they are related to the youths. The overall climate of public opinion after political independence expressed great expectations and high hopes that the education system would cure the wounds inflicted by colonialism, especially by the oppressive conditions of slavery and indentureship. With the current physical expansion in education, these expectations and ambitions for academic and occupational mobility remain quite strong more so as the competitive culture of materialism and conspicuous consumption gets entrenched.

To accentuate the role and value of today's educational opportunities in this multi-ethnic society, a further frame of reference is hereby provided, that is, the perverse, debilitating and inhumane conditions in which the forefathers of the present generation of Africans and East Indians lived. An appreciation of such plantation conditions and the struggles for survival, dignity and literacy will help provide a deep regard for the many opportunities which exist in education today.

In August, 2015, the son of Marcus Garvey told celebrants of the country's Emancipation Day they must learn and teach their history. He said:

> We have to learn our history because a lot of the content of today's system
> of education which is designed for us, is designed to marginalise us and
> to elevate the British to a higher level than us in terms of humanity.[1]

Though sometimes overstretched, such reflections should also
help energise the formerly oppressed people to seize and make full
use of educational opportunities. It is like a country coming from the
darkened depths of neglect to an enlightening field of opportunities.
But in this transition, the historical racial rivalries between the two
formerly despised groups, the formerly enslaved and indentured
labourers, remain fascinating, if not continuously disappointing.
That, too, has become a significant dynamic in the education system
which will be illustrated later.

## RACIAL HARMONY OR CONFLICT?

In his Foreword to David Lowenthal's 1972 book, Philip Mason
stated: *'The Caribbean was the most colonial of all societies: here the deepest
wrong was done. The mass of people had no target to aim at, no ideal vision that
was not self-defeating.'*[2] He added: *'As it eased out of colonialism, this country
remained muddled by tensions over colour, class and race and the hypocrisies that
inevitably help to smoothen relationships and decorate the tourist brochures.'*[3]

In an enlightening survey of race relations and discrimination in this
country at that time, Lowenthal concluded:

> The rosy image of multi-racial harmony, however, grossly distorts
> both the actual facts and the way they are locally seen. A sociological
> description of Trinidad depicted a society at odds with a popular culture
> of easy-going interracial mingling.[4]

Looking at race relations here, however, one can easily say that since
independence in 1962, the country has never experienced violent clashes
between Indians and Africans.[5] The electoral-driven tensions do raise
ethnic rivalries and the publicised antagonisms that go with them. The
largely plantation-derived racial stereotypes and rivalry do still swirl
around, mainly informally. Attempts are regularly made to keep such
antagonisms silent. Every year, for example, at cultural celebrations such
as Emancipation Day, Indian Arrival Day and Eid, all national leaders feel
obliged to highlight the virtues of ethnic diversity and national harmony.
Notably, the country's national watchwords are: *Discipline, Production and
Tolerance.*

At the 2015 Indian Arrival Day celebrations, the country's President, Anthony Carmona, said: *'The prominence given to our nation as a "rainbow country" has its genesis and credence in our "Calaloo culture" of which our East Indian brothers and sisters have played a principal part.'*[6] He added:

*'Every citizen of every race was a beneficiary of the sacrifice, work ethic and value system of the East Indian indentured labourers who toiled the land. East Indians have demonstrated that anything is possible and ambition can be realised from the humblest of backgrounds.'*[7]

On that same day, the then Opposition Leader, Dr. Keith Rowley, also of African descent, speaking of 'the enormous contribution East Indians have made to the country,' added that the *'influence of the East Indian indentured labourers and the generations that followed have made and continue to make an indelible impact on our society.'*[8] Speaking at his party's Emancipation Day celebrations, Dr. Rowley asked that citizens should reflect on where they came from and where they are going.

He added: *'We Afro-Trinidadians have our own strengths that others have learnt from. We can learn about the strength of the East Indian family and the industriousness of the Chinese. We can take a page from their book.'* He concluded: 'Citizens must earn respect through hard and honest work.'[9] The audience applauded. Such remarks resonated in the context of the acknowledged racial competition for equality and equity in the society.

At the country's 53rd anniversary of Independence, former Prime Minister Kamla Persad-Bissessar said: *'This country is a diverse nation of people of many origins who have been able to forge an enduring unity. We are richer for our diversity and differences and we are stronger as a nation because of the harmony which exists.'*[10] All in all, it is often whether one sees the bottle half empty or half full.

## Racial Ambivalence

At that same time, however, one week before the country's general elections on September 7, 2015, the two major political parties were locked in a very intense contest, with one party largely supported by persons of African descent, and the other party largely supported by persons of East Indian descent.[11] The respective campaign crowds and the demographics of the polling divisions reflected as much. It was described as 'the most brutal election and tribal-driven ever.'[12]

However, continuing with the racial harmony theme, an editorial in one of the three daily newspapers stated: 'The social cohesion woven from the strands of our many cultures remains a source of pride in a world where being different is not always valued or even tolerated.'[13]

Another newspaper editorialised: 'Whatever the situation is in relation to crime, this is the land of Carnival where multiple races and parties mingle, despite our differences. Over the years, many have misjudged this simple fact and sought, unsuccessfully, to agitate the masses in the hope of large-scale, open conflict. None has come, it is simply not who we are.'[14]

On that same day, however, this newspaper published an incident in which 'a Hindu shrine on the banks of the Marianne River in Blanchisseuse was vandalized on Sunday last by persons who also defaced the shrine with human filth and used a cutlass to destroy some of the clay dieties.'[15] This incident triggered extensive racial exchanges in the country's social media for several days.

This incident is noted merely to indicate that from time to time there have been episodes that do disturb one racial group or another, but, as the editorials claimed, not sufficient enough to cause riots or protracted racial hostilities. Generally, racial harmony is argued or promoted on the basis of African-East Indian relations. The fact that the country's 2011 census recorded a 'Mixed' population at 22% is seen on one hand as an expression of racial harmony, while at the same time, triggering discussions on the challenges of inter-racial marriages.

## The Black and White Controversy

What about the Whites and Syrian/Lebanese? Apart from the dilemma of definition, the white population here – less than two per cent – has generally occupied a marginal political space. An incident in August 2015 helps reveal their presence in the racial harmony and equality of opportunity discourse. A newspaper columnist and black, retired Professor, Selwyn Ryan, objecting to criticisms against then PNM Opposition Leader, Dr. Keith Rowley, implied that 'white people and near-white people, especially those in gated communities, do not generally support the PNM.[16] He wrote:

> There have been complaints over the years that our white and near-white co-citizens who live in gentrified gate communities like Victoria (Pretoria) Gardens and Goodwood Park do not as a general a rule vote for the PNM in national election and that they hear 'dog whistles' (coded messages) telling them how they should or should not vote.[17]

Being black as well, Dr. Rowley has faced comments such he 'is too arrogant, too racially conscious, and too black to be accepted by certain sections of the population, etc.'[18] Tribal politics has always posed a visible and troublesome challenge for racial harmony. In proposing explanations for anti-Rowley and anti-PNM sentiments, Ryan added: *'The white creoles, like the Hindus, Tobagonians, Muslims etc., are a tribe for and of themselves when it comes to voting and politics generally, and do their politics collectively.'*[19]

Again, social media went ablaze. Several conflicting letters were subsequently sent to newspapers. A public controversy briskly arose over race, colour, privilege and opportunity. For example, Victoria Gardens' resident, Michael Scott, tersely giving a 'white' objection to Ryan, said: *'I have come to know and befriend whites and near-whites, blacks and near-blacks, brown and near-browns, yellows and near-yellows and people of all other skin hues here. Dr. Rowley has represented the Diego Martin region for more than 20-odd years. He is a "serial underachiever" who is devoid of leadership qualities.'*[20]

Another 'white,' Frank Mouttet, wrote: *'White people are not anti-PNM or anti-Keith Rowley. They are simply anti-bad governance. They have little to cheer about under any government since Independence. Being the first to arrive after the Caribs, the whites continue to be fiercely resilient and proud of their heritage.'* He added: 'The "white people" were and continue to be saddened by what successive governments, mainly the PNM, have done to our country.'[21]

To this, Oke Zachary mockingly replied: *'I couldn't help but have a hearty laugh in Mouttet appointing himself spokesperson for T&T's white community...I suppose that chattel slavery and indentureship will always remain a charming memory for some as they offered the opportunity to become filthy rich.'*[22] Then, under the headline 'Whites should get active in politics,' black former public servant Errol Cupid complained that 'whites' opted out of politics but kept pulling the strings 'behind the scenes.'[23] Dr Rowley, however, went on to win the election.

Black trade unionist Cecil Paul angrily added: *'Mr. Mouttet, your ancestors were parasitic and got rich from free labour provided by brutally oppressed Africans. You can never become poor...Proud of your heritage, really, Mr Mouttet? You are proud of having enslaved people and brutalized them while up to today their descendants are scared by the historical, physical and mental torture as well as being economically deprived?'*[24]

But this, too, was not allowed to pass. William Als sarcastically wrote: *'The viewpoint of Cecil Paul would be amusing were it not so stupid and downright dangerous...Other Africans sold their captives to the whites or Arab traders. They sold, the Europeans bought. Mr Mouttet's ilk and yours both need to bond and work, yes, that word, work.'*[25]

Earlier though, black activist, David Mohammed, arguing that African slavery was worse than East Indian indentureship, presented ten points to prove his case. He also said: *'The truth is that there were by far more Africans in the African continent who fought against slavery than those who participated in it.'*[26]

These brief ethnographic references are noted to help indicate, as previously mentioned, the extent to which latent racial misgivings get easily triggered within this ethnically-diverse population, and also the extent to which competition for equality and equity is implicated. Such episodic racial contestations, however, usually fall as easily as they arise. The September 7, 2015 general elections exposed some of the most sinister aspects of the country's race relations.

A lot of ugly latent sentiments broke through, mainly through social media where anonymity is largely assured. Such a psychological climate is easily provoked for political advantage. That is, for example, if a party leader or supporters wish to consolidate their own racial base, they can pick some issue or complaint to publicly suggest that the other racial group is hostile against their own group or even against the racial features of their leader. When used as a psychological technique, the quickened reactions from the other side tighten racial consolidation on each side. It is consolidation by provocation. Nationhood suffers. It has happened before. And from recent experience, it seems likely to happen in future.

### After Elections, Race

Days before and soon after the country's general elections, racial exchanges on social media reached feverish and unprecedented heights. Words like 'coolie', 'nigger', 'gorillas', 'Indian whore', 'inferior people,' etc. filled the nation's airwaves. Social media and radio talk shows – like an underground information machine - engineered the racial antagonisms, crudely exposing the latent prejudices existing on several sides.

Meanwhile, the daily newspapers and television stations appealed for racial harmony. Columnist Paolo Kernahan, wrote: *'Elections 2015 opened a fissure, exposing the dark heart of racism, prejudice and negativity that pumps hatred through the veins of the nation. We bury our heads and pretend we are a melting-pot nation, a diverse mix of races and cultures, all living in harmony. This is garbage.'*[27] This is also similar to what Lowenthal said in 1972.

Newspaper columnist and Anthropologist, Dr. Dylan Kerrigan, said that *'such racist things through social media are basically a manifestation of deeper philosophical and historical problems that are embedded in our society and they come to the surface at these times.'*[28] While the post-election 'racial explosion' was taking place, the daily *Guardian* newspaper with an editorial headlined, 'Racism has no place here,' stated: *'Within hours of the announcement of the change of government, there were vile statements, threats and accusations, most of them openly racist.'*[29]

## THE POLITICS OF RELATIVE DEPRIVATION

The racial exchanges continued. columnist Tony Fraser, recapping the hostilities shared during the elections, wrote: *'The widespread practice of nepotism and the desire for total cultural, social and economic power for its tribe at all cost, was another pathology which infected the UNC.*[30] He added: *'Large groups of people now look on Indo-Trinidadian as being distrustful, money-grabbing and corrupt because of the alleged kickback deals made by the government with contractors.'*[31]

Replying to Fraser, Dirk Bosland accused Fraser of not having 'substantive fact and statistical support' for his 'allegations.' He said it was 'the PNM that emptied the treasury,' and that 'corruption continued under the PNM,' etc.[32]

As the charges and cross-charges continued, retired diplomat and senior public servant, Reginald Dumas, calling for a 'cooling down' of the exchanges, said: *'We have to confront this issue of race which we pretend is not important. Race relations is perhaps the most important factor of the society. The racial comments came from both sides. It is all around us.'*[33] Soon after the elections several calls were made for 'religious representation' in the new cabinet.

The day before the formal opening of the new Parliament, a Muslim organization, asking why there is no Muslim in the cabinet, appealed for one.[34] During the television interview, they emphasized: 'This is not a Christian country.' Before that, public appeals were also made for fuller representation of Hindus in the PNM cabinet.

Our concern, as earlier expressed, is the impact which such racial concerns and even hostilities have on the competition within the education system. Selwyn Ryan put it this way: *'The election battle we have witnessed over the past few months is the by-product of what we have done in the educational market-place.'*[35]

He added:

> The Indo-Trinis are striving to enlarge their share of the social, economic and political order, and they are doing so aggressively, employing mechanisms of education to dislodge those at the top.[36]

The data in Chapters Nine to Sixteen relate to this view.

## Slavery and Black Grievances

These periodic contestations do help, though, to illustrate the extent to which racial perceptions differ towards the same issue or event. And, almost naturally, of course, so it will be on the matters under examination in this book – equality of educational opportunity and equity. It largely depends on where your forefathers stood in the course of history or what your status is at present.[37] Hence, the data becomes helpful in taming self-serving perceptions.

That such controversies occurred at a time when there were also serious concerns by both government and the entire population over the slowed-down economy and in particular the depressed oil and gas prices, help aggravate ethnic rivalries. They put racial harmony to the test. Relative deprivation, ethnic envy and stereotyping get aroused. Now, as earlier cited, there is evidence of racial under and over-representation in certain sectors of the society, for example, in private commerce and state employment.

The extent to which such imbalances are due to the denial of opportunity, personal preference or historical circumstances has received controversial interpretations. This book will later explore the extent to which there is equality of educational opportunity, equity and under-representation by ethnicity, social class and family background in the educational sector. The anti-Rowley controversy was used as an example of the extent to which there are latent apprehensions over race, privilege and opportunity in the society. Within this, however, intriguing perceptions help drive political behavior.

Black columnist, Professor Theodore Lewis, for example, wrote: *'One of the real challenges for the descendants of emancipated slaves is that unlike other groupings of people who have come to these lands, blacks have not deliberately cooperated with each other for social and economic good.'*[38]

He continued:

> Other groupings of people who have been brought here such as the Indian indentured labourers, or who came here, such as the Syrians, Lebanese and Europeans, base their wealth accumulation on collaboration through in-group kinship. East Indians in particular have historically organized politically for the betterment of their communities.

Lewis concluded:

> We (blacks) act as individuals where other ethnic groupings act as collectives. This coming election (September 7, 2015) is a critical occasion for blacks a whole to go to the polls and make a collective statement about which party would be most responsive to our collective needs.[39]

Indeed, the PNM won the elections.

To what extent, then, can the collective needs of the country's black citizens be met by the educational system? Or the needs of citizens of all races for that matter? The issue here, of course, is feelings of relative deprivation and the extent to which such feelings are connected to the education system. Hence, Lewis, on another occasion (October 4, 2015) wrote an article headlined 'Young Afro males need more positive messages' in which he stated: *'In the current period of gang violence and murders, I think we have gotten in defensive mode and are shirking our collective responsibility to help black youths towards more wholesome alternatives. The first aspect of this would be to alter the mind-set that sees every black youth as a criminal. When did it come about that if you are a black youth in this society you shun studying, leaving that to others?'*[40]

Professor Lewis continued: *'I think the body language of schools and teachers is the culprit. A black boy of nine, ten, 11, 12 wants to be taught. You can't tell me a black boy of these ages wants to be a gunman and nothing else. The primary school has become in this country a site of divisiveness where self-fulfilling prophesy abounds. The African boy is hardhead and difficult to teach. That is the myth. This is reinforced when the SEA results come out. This progresses onto the CAPE and to the island scholarship results. There are people in this country who are perfectly happy with this state of affairs. They like it so. And the minister runs to the schools and the winner is glorified, and he is not an African boy.'*[41]

Lucidly expressing the feelings of many black citizens, he concluded: *'The education playing field is tilted. If we are serious about the socialization of the African male and what he has become in the society, we should show concern and see what we could do in our schools to fix it. I am aware this is sensitive territory...There is dire need for an examination of the status of black boys in our schools. These have become the gangsters.'*[42]

Such relative deprivation views, largely swirling underground, sometimes publicly expressed, have indeed been the subject of inquiry in several research reports as will be later illustrated. Noting the disadvantages suffered by many black youths, citizen Noble Phillip, objected to the views by 'a past president of the Chamber of Commerce' who complained that black youths were not taking up available opportunities.

Phillip wrote: *'If the scales were balanced, we may have had some persons with a different skin hue in jail for their corrupt deals over the past decade. But those persons can hire expensive lawyers to keep them from spending one night in jail. But the black young man rots, waiting his turn before the court.'*[43]

He added:

> The education system has failed the communities from which these young men come. A casual look at the SEA results will tell of the absolute failure. We have created a permanent underclass that is fodder for the devious. These persons cannot get a job, even if they stay in school and get their passes, since their home addresses and their skin colour are wrong.[44]

The headline to this article was 'Odds against many young blacks.' The connected issue to such views is that they are published, thousands of other citizens read them so the views get further distillation and social media commentary.

While the formation of racial groupings in the society is largely due to its plantation history, a lot of the current political behaviour and perceptions over inequality and opportunity is generated from the in-group vs. out-group phenomenon, that is race relations here have moved from the purely sociological to the social psychological where perceptions, reciprocity and anticipatory responses play an important part.

Under the headline, 'Scars of slavery still with us,' another black, Frederick Phillips, objected to East Indian Sahadeo Ragoonanan's letter which asked blacks to 'stop blaming slavery' for their current problems.[45] Phillips, supporting the mission for reparations, said that the social situation seen in the diaspora is a direct result of the 'trauma inherited from slavery' and that 'reparations is not cash.' He wrote: *'It has to be certain opportunities for these people to have interventions of education, health, wealth and well-being to pursue their best potential.'*[46]

Seeking to clarify the post-emancipation conditions as compared to those of indentured labourers, Patrick Bynoe wrote, *'Africans had no singular homeland to return to and had no offers to stay. Slaves and their immediate descendants helped build many of our heritage sites. They left a cultural legacy, promoted self-pride and engaged in nation-building and spread the word of freedom.'*[47] This view is apparently more optimistic than Lewis'.

The loophole in such racial controversies, however, is that in the post-colonial era, economic competition and social class penetration have significantly fractured racial homogeneity. Rarely is it accurate to say that 'all Africans think so,' or 'all Indians feel so.'[48] What is seen as a homogeneous racial group from the outside is functionally fractured inside by groupings of social class, religion, colour and, in the case of Hindus, also by caste. Each racial group has its pyramidal share of cliques, caucuses and cabals within. Economic and election financing interests conveniently cross ethnic lines. Further, the intriguing and neglected area of research is that the 'racial instinct' is not automatically aroused. It depends on the particular issue at stake. Quite often social class and economic interests trump ethnic loyalty inside and outside the racial group. The daily competition for opportunity and status is largely individually-driven – and often depending on the situation at hand.

Columnist Raymond Ramcharitar, for example, pointed out that the Africans in particular, are not a homogeneous ethnic group either. He stated: *'The indigenous black society was loosely connected in a network of Masonic and fraternal societies like The Gardeners, The Oldfellows and The*

*Mechanics. The immigrants were outsiders. Afro-Trinidad has never been and is not a monolithic group of former slaves.'*[49]

# 'ALL AH WE NOT ONE'

All this suggests that while formal claims for racial harmony gain celebrated mention, there appears to exist a 'black market underground' of racial sentiments that often shakes up the formal realm – straining the national anthem which promised a place 'where every creed and race find an equal place.' One such race-driven stimulus is the country's general elections. Ethnic sentiments are quietly expressed through the ballot box. Political contests awaken sleeping sentiments.

## Slaves to Tribalism and Race

The day before the country's last general election on September 7, 2015, the chairman of the independent Election and Boundaries Commission (EBC), Dr Robert Masson, in a public statement, said:

> A serious problem occurs when a society becomes as divisive as we are, enslaved to ethnicity and tribalism. In such an environment, excellent conditions exist for political parties, politicians and lobbyists to exploit them, to 'run amok' in order to get elected.[50]

He described the election campaign as 'the most brutish, acrimonious, rampageous, and vitriolic that I have ever witnessed.'[51] So there it is, fifty-three years after political independence, with the two major parties, each racially-driven in its own way – Africans largely on one side, East Indians largely on the other side. The racial composition of the crowds at the respective campaign meetings told the story.

Still, though, whether the society has or doesn't have a racial problem largely depends on whom you ask, and in what circumstance. In the case of the white vs. black controversy described above, the question of equality of educational opportunity and equity is also connected to social class, colour and race which is a major concern of this book. Such racial episodes are relevant.

The post-colonial cultural experience has so far been excruciatingly ambivalent. For example, on one hand there were many voices, even in the education system, for 'ethnic integration' as a mark of nationhood. At the same time, and largely for reasons of political mobilisation, other voices showed appreciation for ethnic diversity.[52]

## Racial Harmony, A Mask Over Reality?

It is within this perennial ambivalence that this issue of racial harmony and opportunity has received and still receives fluctuating, often self-serving, interpretations. There are mainly three levels at which the sentiments are expressed today – the formal level, the informal level and at the 'artistic freedom' level.

At the formal level, for example, at public religious or cultural festivals, or from ministerial speeches, the acclamation of racial harmony is prevalent. At the informal level, through social media, family conversations and same-race friendship circles, the stereotypes and related negative sentiments are privately and crassly shared in quite lively fashion.[53]

The third is the 'artistic freedom' situation where ethnic sentiments are aroused and often graphically expressed in cultural competitions or through the media.[54] Such examples often come from African-driven calypsoes commenting on educational inequality, elections or competition for employment.[55]

The pluralistic form of democracy in the country finds itself largely based on a two-party system, with each party gaining substantial support from one racial group (Africans) and the other from another (East Indians).[56] It is more than this, however. This racially-driven support is connected to the established practice of political patronage wherein whichever party gets into power, the party dispenses tremendous privileges and status positions to its supporters with all the racial implications therein.[57] The life of political parties survives on patronage. This implicitly leads to institutional racism.

Nevertheless, the post-colonial superficial pledges for 'racial and socio-economic equality' necessarily became a natural slogan for helping to create hope and faith in the country's future. Its past has been a dark, centuries-old history of imperialist-driven plantation labour, mainly through African slavery and East Indian labour indentureship.[58]

The current flush of post-colonial ambitions for equality and socio-economic success by the descendants of former slaves and indentured labourers therefore appears as a hurried enterprise to mask and compensate for the oppressive conditions which their forefathers experienced. A consideration of these oppressive colonial conditions is therefore used here to provide fuller meaning to the present interactions in the educational system between the racial groups whose forefathers once occupied the sugar plantations. [59]

It is, of course, a tribute to those who, from one generation to the next, have since borne their impoverished conditions stoically, and risen above them to succeed socially, educationally and occupationally. But many are still left behind, and with ethnic implications. It will therefore place a heavy obligation on present authorities to treat those whose educational dreams and aspirations get broken, largely through no fault of theirs, but mainly through the inequities in the system.

To help energise the way forward, to celebrate the successful while motivating those lagging behind, we now provide a summary of what those 'oppressive conditions' looked.

## NOTES

1.    Dr. Julius Garvey. *Guardian*. August 6, 2015. p. 7.
2.    In D. Lowenthal. *West Indian Societies*. London: Oxford University Press, 1972, p. ix
3.    Ibid. pp. 18-25.
4.    Ibid. Also, L. Braithwaite 'Social Stratification in Trinidad: A Preliminary Analysis'. *Social and Economic Studies*, 2(2,3), October 1953, pp. 38-61; Y. Malik. *East Indians in Trinidad*. London: Oxford University Press, 1972. For the interactions between colour, class and race, CLR James. *Beyond the Boundary*. London: Random House, 2005.
5.    The Black Power demonstrations of 1970, based as it mainly was on local control of the economy and opportunity for local blacks, did stir apprehensions among the East Indians and other racial groups. The leadership group, National Joint Action Committee (NJAC) is now a political partner with the Indian-based United National Congress (UNC) in government. As in any other small, multi-ethnic society where there is competition for status, jobs and other resources, there are quite often attendant controversies; a major trigger for ethnic antagonisms emerge at elections. The Opposition People's National Movement (PNM) is largely African-based. It is largely a case of whether the bottle is half-empty or half-full.
6.    *Newsday*. May 30, 2015. p.7.
7.    Ibid.
8.    *Express*. May 30, 2015. p.7. Such are periodic notes of racial harmony in a society which has its two major political parties racially based. That is, at this time, the United National Congress (UNC) is Indian-dominated and the Peoples' National Movement (PNM) is African-dominated. The irony in all this is that the leadership of such parties does make attempts to cultivate a multi-racial presence in their parties..

9.  Also reported in *Newsday*. July 3, 2015. p. 11.
10. *Express*. August 31, 2015. p. 5. Headline 'Let's Celebrate Our Diversity.'
11. Over ten parties were registered to contest. Almost all claim to be multiracial with a mission to unify the country.
12. By Chairman of the Elections and Boundaries Commission. *Express*. September 7, 2015.
13. *Express*. August 31, 2015. p.12.
14. *Newsday*. August 28, 2015. p. 12.
15. Ibid. p. 16.
16. *Sunday Express*. August 16, 2015. p. 13.
17. Ibid.
18. Ibid.
19. Ibid.
20. *Trinidad Express*. August 20, 2015. p. 15.
21. *Trinidad Express*. August 16, 2015. p. 13.
22. *Trinidad Express*. August 26, 2015. p. 15.
23. *Trinidad Express*. August 29, 2015. p. 15.
24. *Trinidad Express*. August 29, 2015. p. 15.
25. *Trinidad Express*. September 5, 2015. p. 15.
26. *Sunday Mirror*. June 7, 2015. p. 13.
27. *Guardian*. September 12, 2015. p.23.
28. *Newsday*. September 13, 2015. p. 9.
29. *Guardian*. September 14, 2015. p. 21.
30. *Guardian*. September 14, 2015. p. 21.
31. Ibid.
32. *Guardian*. September 17, 2015. p. 27.
33. *Guardian*. September 17, 2015. p. 15.
34. Ummah (Muslim) Organisation. Two officers on television (CNC3), September 22, 2015. This, of course, is a perennial issue of religious representation in government and in particular in cabinet. Muslims comprise 5% of the population, Hindus 25%. Quite often, some religious organizations pledge support for one or the other political party, a practice linked to the establishment or non-establishment of denominational schools.
35. *Express*. Sept. 13, 2015. p. 13.
36. Ibid.
37. For an example of 'perceptions by race,' see R. Deosaran 'The Caribbean Man: A Study in the Psychology of Perception and the Media.' Caribbean Quarterly, Vol .27 (2/3), 1981.
38. Lewis is Professor Emeritus, University of Minnesota. *Trinidad Express*. August 4, 2015. p. 13.
39. Ibid.

40. T. Lewis. Young Afro males need more positive messages. *Express.* October 4, 2015. p. 13.
41. Ibid.
42. Ibid. Lewis was appointed in 2016 by the new PNM Government as chairman of two curriculum committees under the Ministry of Education.
43. *Express.* August 5, 2015. p. 14.
44. Ibid. Some of these perceptions have their roots in reality. As a 2013 official inquiry showed, the vast majority of those in Remand Yard are black youths, with over 90% having attended or dropped out of the government secondary schools.
45. *Express.* August 10, 2015. p. 14.
46. *Express.* August 14, 2015. p. 14.
47. *Express.* August 3, 2015. p. 15.
48. It is noteworthy that when asked by researchers what race they belong to, people here identify themselves as, for example, 'Of African' or 'East Indian' descent, etc. In other words, race is used as a social construction and a mark of self-identification.
49. The often cited template is that Indians and especially Whites, Syrian-Lebanese, etc. are 'well-off' while Africans are still to catch up. Young black males are seen to be most disadvantaged. In the seventies and eighties particularly, and claimed by politician, Lloyd Best, for example, it was said that 'Indians had the economy and Africans had political power.' Such rhetoric had large holes in them. It was questionable then, if the' Africans really had political power.' The Black Power protests of 1970 questioned this assumption. As columnist, Raymond Ramcharitar, noted, the black population is far from being a homogeneous group. So too the Indians are not. See R. Ramcharitar. *Guardian.* August 26, 2015. p. A25.
50. *Newsday.* September 7, 2015. p. 3.
51. Ibid.
52. See also R. Deosaran. For discussion with examples of social tensions in the multicultural nation, see conference research and policy papers which attempt to show the continuity of ethnic tensions from the plantation culture into the post-independence era. (1) 'Cultural Conflict and Assimilation: A Psychological Agenda for Research and Public Policy'. Paper delivered at panel on 'Prejudice and Cultural Conflict' March 1,1994, Institute of International Relations, University of the West Indies, St Augustine, Trinidad. (2) 'Ethnicity and the Courts: A Clash of Cultures'. Paper delivered at conference on 'Challenge and Change: The Indian Diaspora in its Historical and Contemporary Contexts.' National Council for Indian Culture and the Institute for Social and Economic

Research, August 16, 1995. University of the West Indies, Trinidad. (3) 'Cultural Diversity and National Unity'. Paper presented on March 6, 1996, Conference on Caribbean Culture in honour of Rex Nettleford, Mona Campus, UWI, Jamaica.

53. As three examples of 'racial' statements and consequent widespread public controversy: (1) During the heated January 2013 Tobago House of Assembly elections, one People's National Movement(PNM) candidate, Hilton Sandy, told the predominantly black Tobago audience that 'a Calcutta ship is coming... and you know what you have to do.' The opposing party (People's Partnership, including the East Indian-dominated United National Congress) repeatedly attacked Sandy for being 'racist.' Tobago population is predominantly of African descent. The PNM is African- dominated. The Tobago House of Assembly, with all members of African descent, won all 12 seats. (2) In April 2014, a United National Congress supporter and member of a government state board, Jaishima Leladharsingh, through published cell phone text messages sent a series of offensive anti-black comments to a black citizen. One remark used was 'stinking niggers.' A widespread controversy arose with both the Former Prime Minister  and the Opposition Leader condemning the remarks. (3) In June, 2015, during the very heated general election campaign, one PNM candidate, Fitzgerald Hinds, was accused of making racist statements at a cottage meeting. The alleged statement, that East Indians 'are alligators from the murky lagoon,' rapidly went viral on Facebook and awakened another volatile public controversy. The Former Prime Minister, Mrs Kamla Persad-Bissessar, and other cabinet members of the People's Partnership government, publicly cited the statement and unsuccessfully called upon the PNM Opposition Leader, Dr Keith Rowley, to condemn Hinds. Such incidents may or may not be seen as just skirmishes, but more importantly is the extent to which latent ethnic antagonisms become aroused and manifested. As David Lowenthal pointed out with his own examples, such racial episodes have been and still are quite common in the society, thus contradicting the 'tourist-driven' boasts of racial harmony. Much healing work still needs to be done in this regard. During the 2015 general election campaign, attorney and former MP, Robin Montano (of White ancestry) stated: 'The racial polarisation is now worse than ever and many politicians do not even pretend to hide their racist feelings. We get racist comments (like the 'Calcutta ship' one) and nobody seems to blink an eyelash. The perpetrators of these offensive remarks are not brought to book by either the political parties or their leaders.' (*Guardian*. Wednesday June 24, 2015. p. 25)

54. This doesn't mean that there is no intra-group competition or conflict for such positions.
55. See R. Deosaran, 'Some Issues in Multiculturalism: The Case of Trinidad and Tobago in the Post-Colonial Era'. *Plural Societies*, Vol. 12, 1/2, 1981 for an analysis of the political and economic tensions between the various ethnic groups in the country. For the post-colonial era, two propositions were proposed (1) The further removed a cultural (ethnic) group is from the source of socio-economic rewards, the greater stress factors in that group's attempt to compete and gain access to such rewards (2) The further removed a cultural (ethnic) group is from the source of economic rewards, the greater the pressures for de-culturalisation and the greater the likelihood that negative stereotyping would be used to justify that group's exclusion from social and economic rewards. pp.17-18.Also see R. Deosaran, 'The Social Psychology of Cultural Pluralism: Updating the Old. *Caribbean Quarterly*, Vol. 33 (1 and 2) 1987.pp. 1-18. This paper shows some examples of cross-ethnic mobility in the decolonised stage of the country.
56. There have been political alliances but these failed to last long. The retreat into race-based political parties eventually took over once again. Notwithstanding, there are significant groups who resist and openly reject race-based parties. Yet, the core, almost guaranteed, of support for the large parties (e.g., United National Congress and its antecedents (Democratic Labour Party, and United Labour Front) and the People's National Movement), remains a diminishing but still racial base..
57. Many attempts have been made and are still being made to establish a Third Force, that is multi-racial, multi-sector party, but have not yet been able to bypass the racial pull so as to gain strong multi-racial support to capture government.
58. E. Williams (1962 *History of the People of Trinidad and Tobago*. Trinidad: PNM Publishing Co.; D. Lowenthal. (1972). *West Indian Societies*. London: Oxford University Press);J. H. Parry and P. Sherlock. *A Short History of the West Indies. (3rd Ed.)*.London: Macmillan Press. 1973. Pp. 95-111. For some details of how African slaves suffered in the slave trade, see CLR James.*The Black Jacobins*. New York: Random House (2nd Ed.). 1963. pp. 6-22.
59. There were on the plantation other racial groups, e.g., Portuguese, Spanish, French, British, etc. But given today's population: East Indian 35.4%, Africans 34.2%, Mixed 22.8%, Others 1.4%, Unknown 6.2% (Central Statistical Office Report on 2011 Census) and the two groups most affected by plantation oppression, this book focuses mainly on the East Indians and Africans.

# CHAPTER THREE

# Racial Inferiority, Cultural Resistance and Crime

*As we see our face, figure and dress in the glass, and are interested in them because they are ours, and pleased or otherwise with them according as they do or do not answer to what we should like them to be; so in imagination we perceive in another's mind some thought of our appearance, manners, aims, deeds, character, friends, and so on, and are variously affected by it. The thing that moves us to pride or shame is not the mere mechanical reflection of ourselves but the imagined effect of this reflection upon another's mind.*

Charles Cooley, The Looking Glass Self, 1922

## THE IMPOSITION OF RACIAL INFERIORITY

It was and still is heavily emphasized that the primary route for achieving socio-economic mobility from the colonised conditions is education. A knowledge of the psychological destitution and educational deprivations suffered by their forefathers should, in our view, inspire this generation of youth to take full advantage of the educational opportunities now provided.

It is for such reasons that we provide some reflections of the plantation experiences. Briefly, the situation is:

1. These two racial groups – African slaves and East Indian indentured labourers – were initially placed at the bottom of the socio-economic ladder on the sugar plantations.

2. It took over a hundred years before a basic education could be provided, and this after a lot of 'hemming and hawing' among the relevant authorities.

3. In the post-colonial era, as the education system became more formalised in the face of limited preferred places at the secondary and tertiary levels, the consequent competition triggered ethnically and class-driven controversies over equality of educational opportunity, merit and equity.

Compared to the Whites and other Europeans, the educational neglect of the former enslaved and indentured labourers continued well into the twentieth century, even after the end of slavery and indentureship.[1] In that period, the education system, in terms of both curriculum and enrolment, was riddled with social class distinctions and racial marginalization.[2] This was apart from the harsh treatment meted out by the plantation owners on the plantation fields.[3]

Noting the acute class discrimination in education, David Lowenthal wrote: '*Educational patterns throughout the Caribbean reflect, validate and reinforce these class differences. Initially, the elite were taught in Europe, the slaves not at all. The elitist secondary-school system catered for whites unable to afford education abroad and for non-whites on their way up the social ladder. Entrance was essentially limited by status. The curriculum, classical and European-oriented, was designed less to train than to confer prestige on future leaders of colonial societies.*'[4] In other words, class and racial discrimination continued to exist after colonialism.

Lowenthal further described the plantation owners' attitude to the East Indian indentured labourers this way: '*Too much literacy, as the elite saw it, would teach folk to disdain labour and would dissatisfy them with their station in life.*'[5] This was after the black enslaved, when emancipated, showed reluctance to continue work on the plantation.

## SOME NEGRO EDUCATION

Of course, while Christian groups intervened, there was no strong obligation by the colonial authorities to 'educate' the enslaved. Shirley Gordon wrote: '*One of the circumstances of slavery is that slave workers are to be kept ignorant. If they are not instructed in any arts or skills other than those required for their unpaid labour, they are less likely to resist their masters. The occasional advocates of education for slaves meant instruction in the Christian religion.*'[6]

So for both races at that time, educating them was no priority event even though in the indentured labourers' case, the British Government established conditions for education and a Protector of Immigrants.[7]

Reviewing some of the relevant statistics, Gordon added: '*On any count, popular education had not begun under slavery despite the praiseworthy striving of the missionaries.*'[8] After emancipation of the slaves, the British Government through the Act of Emancipation (1835) provided a Negro Education Grant to promote education for the ex-slaves – 30,000 pounds annually for five years at first, then have it gradually diminished until 1845.[9]

Citing the purpose of this grant, the British government in 1834 stated:

> In the appropriation of those funds, the Minister of the Crown will be guided by the principle that instruction in the doctrines and precepts of Christianity must form the basis and must be made the inseparable attendant of any such system of Education.[10]

Education for the Africans then was for Christianity. For the 'strange' East Indian indentured labourers from Calcutta and Madras, their cultural resistance to colonial, Christian-driven education posed severe challenges, to say the least.[11]

Jamaican George Beckford, linking the West Indian plantation economy to such education, said: '*Barring emigration, the only significant scope of social mobility open to them was education...slaves were only trained in skills useful to the plantation – artisan skills which could make the slave a more productive and contented servant.*'[12] Faced with a scarcity of land as well, '*there was little that black people could do to improve their lot,*' Beckford added.[13] Plantation dependency was assured.

## THE AFRICANS, CHRISTIANITY AND EDUCATION

Quite clearly, the variety of religious traditions that the enslaved brought with them from their respective African homelands was relegated by the doctrines and precepts of Christianity. It is notable that official commentaries on the need 'to educate the former Negro slaves' so often emphasized the role of Christian education in developing their 'moral character.' Little was said however of the crowded, debilitating and insanitary conditions in which such former enslaved lived and the impact such conditions might have had on their 'morality,' character and attitudes.

With slave-laden ships, the trips from Africa to the West Indies were ones of unthinkable torture and suffering. From being captured, chained on the cramped ships, starved of proper food and drink up to their plantation labour, the enslaved were treated as less than humans. In detailing 'The Atlantic Slave Trade 1440–1870,' Hugh Thomas noted the physical brutalization quite vividly.

In a case he cited, Eannes de Zurara, a courtier attached to the King of Portugal, asked silently of the slave traders and King: 'What heart could be so hard as not to be pierced with piteous feelings? For some (slaves) kept their heads low, and their faces bathed in tears. Others stood groaning, looking up to the height of heaven, crying out loudly as if asking help from the Father of Nature.'[14] De Zurara had seen 235 slaves being loaded in Guinea.[15]

In Henry Louis Gates, *The Classic Slave Narratives*, several enslaved gave personal accounts of brutal flogging, sexual exploitation and family separations which frequently occurred on the plantation and inside the Masters' homes.[16] Both body and spirit got broken.[17]

As this country, with a modern parliament, independent judiciary, free press and schools filled all across the country, looks back at its slave and indentureship history, the inspiration and drive for academic and occupational achievement, as Rubin and Zavalloni indicated, should now be of feverish proportions. Slavery experienced exceptional cruelty.

Recalling the journey from Africa, C.L.R. James noted:

> Thousands of human beings were packed in these 'dens of putrefaction.' The Africans fainted and recovered or fainted and died. Twice a day, at nine and four, they received their food. To the slave traders they were articles of trade and no more. A captain held up by calms or adverse winds was known to have poisoned his cargo. Another killed some of his slaves to feed the others with the flesh. They died not only from the regime but from grief and rage and despair...Some took the opportunity to jump overboard, uttering cries of triumph.[18]

But the torment did not end there. Prejudices, stereotypes and attitudes drove the colonisers' behaviour and public policy. Psychological brutality persisted. As hundreds of enslaved from Africa were shipped into Trinidad and the rest of the Caribbean, noted British philosopher, David Hume, wrote:

> I am apt to suspect the Negroes to be actually inferior to the Whites. There was scarcely ever a civilized nation of that complexion or ever any individual eminent either in action or speculation. No ingenious manufacturers among them, no arts, no sciences...In Jamaica, indeed, they talk of one Negro (Francis Williams) as a man of parts and learning; but it is likely he is admired for slender accomplishments, like a parrot who speaks a few words plainly.[19]

Third President of the United States, Thomas Jefferson, stated: '*I advance therefore, as a suspicion only, that the blacks, whether originally a*

*distinct race, or made distinct by time and circumstances, are inferior to the*
*whites in the endowments of both body and mind.'*[20]

## 'WASTING EDUCATION' ON AFRICANS

Such racial deprecations were quite prevalent, no doubt facilitating the importation and uses of slavery, while at the same time, releasing the plantation owners from any guilt for so doing. These deep-seated racial prejudices from such high quarters helped diminish the urgency that should have been attached to the education of the imported Africans, enslaved or freed. After all, as it seemed then, why 'waste' education on such 'inferior beings?'

Dr Williams, noting that such 'depreciation and disparagement' passed on into the period after emancipation, cited Anthony Trollope, noted British novelist, as having said of the emancipated Negro: '*But yet he has made no approach to the civilization of his white fellow creatures whom he imitates as a monkey does a man...he is idle, unambitious as to worldly position, sensual and content with little. Intellectually, he is apparently capable of but little sustained effort. He burns to be regarded as a scholar, puzzles himself with fine words, addicts himself to religion for the sake of appearance, and delights in aping the little graces of civilization.'*[21]

Discouraging any formal attempt to educate the imported Africans, Trollope added: '*I do not think that education has as yet done much for the black man in the Western world. He can always observe, and often read; but he can seldom reason.'*[22]  Such vile prejudices, shocking to contemporary society, were quite diffused among the British common folk as well in that period of colonialism and competitive imperialism.

## LOOKING TO INDIA

In the early 19th century, as the movement for slave emancipation gained momentum, the British, looking around, saw India as one of the few countries from which sugar labour could be drawn as well as possible owners of their own, small farming lands.[23] In 1814, Trinidad Governor, Sir Ralph Woodford wrote the British Secretary State with the rationale:

The cultivators of Hindoostan are known to be peaceful and industrious.
An extensive introduction of that class of people accustomed to live

on the produce of their own labour only, and totally withdrawn from African connections or feelings would probably be the best experiment for the population of this Island.[24]

In other words, from Governor Woodford's view and that of other plantation interests, the 'disciplined' nature of the East Indian labourers and the strategy of keeping them away from the allegedly less endowed Africans were among the strategies to keep the sugar plantations alive. But it was not until 1844, and after workers were brought in from France, Portugal and a few other European countries, that the British government finally agreed to ship the first batch of indentured Indian labourers - 25,000, from Calcutta and Madras, to Trinidad.

## INDIANS DESPISED TOO

As East Indian indentured labourers began to arrive, they too faced their full share of separatist prejudices, all aimed at proving how inferior the black and brown races were compared to the white colonizers, and with this, leaving plantation education as a peripheral obligation. Perhaps the most demeaning of all was James Anthony Froude, Professor of Modern History at Oxford University.

After the slaves were freed, Froude said:

> The West Indian Negro is conscious of his own defects and responds more willingly than most to a guiding hand...And with a century or two of wise administration he might prove that his inferiority is not inherent, and that with the same chances as the white he may rise to the same level. Like a spaniel too, if he denied the chance of developing under guidance the better qualities which are in him, he will drift back into a mangy cur.[25]

To fill the gap, between 1845 and 1917, a total of 143,900 indentured labourers were brought to Trinidad.[26] This policy stretched to other countries, for example, British Guiana and Mauritius. This preference for East Indian labour did not go unchallenged. With slavery ending, it was thought that such indentured importation would put pressure on the colony's housing, food supplies and wages. There was no welcome mat for the imported East Indians. They quickly found themselves at the bottom rung of the social ladder.[27]

In fact, what was essentially a mercenary-engineered clash of cultures between the colonial community and the newly arrived East Indians was given an ethnocentric interpretation by the British technocrats, the plantation owners and most intriguingly by the free, formerly enslaved Africans too. In performing their religious rites, for example, what were divine rituals back in India were now seen as 'works of the devil.' The plantocracy denigrated both races, then left each one to antagonise the other.

As Brereton noted, the indentured labourers from India came from '*an ancient and complex society, with a rigid social system, a high culture and developed religions; they came to a society where a dominant European culture co-existed with a submerged and despised African subculture.*'[28] Brereton asked: How then would they (Indian) fit into this society? The imported indentured labourers, therefore, faced their own tribulations – physical, social and psychological. From a country with a sophisticated religious and cultural system, they came here to start from scratch in a very troubled and troubling education system.

The controversy over the importation of East Indian labour was also quite intense in the British Parliament. In the House of Commons, for example, the abolitionist George Thompson savagely described the East Indians as '*indolent, mendicants, runaways, vagrants, thieves, vagabonds, filthy, diseased, immoral, disgusting, covered with sores...and a deeply demoralized class of human beings.*' He added: '*The system of emigration had been false, and to attempt to carry it out extensively would only be to create a new slave trade so as to injure materially the interests of the colonies, as to their social and moral conditions.*'[29]

The voyage from India to Trinidad was no bed of roses either. It was wretched and sickening for the contracted East Indian indentured labourers. Once taking up duties on the plantation, their lives were severely miserable. It was not what they generally expected. Ideas like equality of educational opportunity and social equity were a million miles away from the plantation realities they were about to face.

Their introverted behaviours were negatively stereotyped by the plantation owners and as well by the more extroverted Africans. Even in the early days of independence, this pattern persisted so much so that Rubin and Zavalloni remarked: '*The subordinate position of East Indians in the society reinforced tendencies to cultural conservatism, and separatist tendencies laced with pessimism with regard to equality of opportunity were strengthened.*'[30]

# PLANTATION PREJUDICES, EDUCATION AND INDIAN CULTURE

In the years after their arrival in 1845, the indentured East Indian labourers, with their strange dress, food, language and religion, were disdainfully spurned. As stated earlier, stereotypes flourished.

It is intriguing how sheer differences can get converted into stereotypes, then prejudice and discrimination. How much of these racial stereotypes exist today, not merely in the self-images of the directly stigmatized, but also antagonistically shared between the two groups – formerly enslaved and formerly indentured labourers?[31] In other words, how much of those plantation-driven stereotypes and prejudices are still held by the Africans against the East Indians, and how much still held by the East Indians against the Africans? And how does this affect the political and educational system?

While they endured the plantation denigrations, however, the indentured labourers attempted 'to save every cent' they got. It was this kind of resistance which Morton Klass wrote about in his study of an Indian village. He titled his book, *East Indians in Trinidad: A Study in Cultural Persistence.*[32] More recently, with such cultural characteristic, the East Indians here were described as the 'Unmeltable Ethnics', a dynamic mixture of cultural adaptation and persistence.[33]

It is interesting to note, however, that once working on the plantation, the indentured labourers initially attracted praise from the owners. Early on, their work was one thing, their culture another thing. The plantation owners often discriminated in their evaluations of one racial group against the other – Africans vs East Indians and vice versa - which really didn't help racial harmony around the plantation at all.

In fact, competition was aroused between the two groups for the plantation owner's affection. For example, the Union Hall Estate proprietor said he found the East Indian indentured labourers '*more intelligent, more apt, more docile, more civil, more obliging and more obedient, less easily offended, devoid of the savage disposition of the African.*'[34]

# CULTURAL RESISTANCE

Faced with a diminishing labour supply, the plantation owners, backed by very restrictive ordinances, used stronger measures to keep the East

Indian labourers in the field. Some of these ordinances were not easy for the indentured labourers to understand. In fact, these labourers, wittingly or unwittingly, showed resistance by breaking the law.

The East Indians also showed resistance with their prayers, religious practices and public festivals, unpunctuality, and often burning cane. It was also very bad for the slaves. They often opted for worship, protest festivals and rebellion in various ways. Both groups, in varying degrees, got in regular conflict with the numerous control Ordinances.

The oppressive plantation environment and the cultural resistance put up by both the former enslaved and indentured labourers continued well into the late nineteenth century.[35] Plantation conflict attracted harsh responses by the planters.

Haraksingh stated: '*Cultural resilience and adaptation might indeed be regarded as the most outstanding as well as the most persistent form of resistance among the Indian workers. Culture defined an area to which Indians, after the trials of the work place, could retreat to heal and bind the wounds.*'[36] That, too, was passive resistance.

## SOCIAL PSYCHOLOGY AND PLANTATION PREJUDICE

While harsh working and living conditions, racial prejudice and stereotyping were prevalent on the plantation, the impact of these perverse conditions upon the psyche and the mental state of the former enslaved and indentured labourers attracted psychological analysis. For example, when the plantocracy and British elite described the Africans as 'lazy', 'squanderers', 'showy', etc., and the East Indians as 'devious', 'dirty', 'immoral', 'stingy', etc., these stigmatizing epithets eventually possessed the minds of the Africans and East Indians themselves. That is, their self-perceptions mirrored the views that the slave and plantation owners, the significant others, had of them – the 'looking glass' phenomenon. In his 'Pedagogy of the Oppressed,' Paulo Freire saw the consequence as stigmatization. He said:

> Self-deprecation is another characteristic of the oppressed, which derives from their internalisation of the opinion the oppressors have of them. Often do they hear that they are good for nothing, know nothing and are incapable of learning anything – that they are sick, lazy and unproductive – that in the end they become convinced of their own unfitness.[37]

This stigmatization and self-deprecation led Africans to see the East Indians in the same way the plantation owners saw the East Indians, and the East Indians too, began to see the Africans in the same way the plantation owners saw the Africans. They did not as yet see the common enemy as colonialism and the psychology which supports it. They were common sufferers but developed a displaced antagonism against each other.

When individuals, groups or communities for that matter face a hostile, oppressive institution against which they can do nothing for alleviation, they tend to turn inwards, aggressively releasing the pent-up frustrations against vulnerable targets.[38] Recognising this psychological transference, psychiatrist Fanon stated: *'The colonised man will first manifest this aggressiveness which has been deposited in his bones against his own people.'*[39]

Of course, the mutual stereotyping, plantation prejudice and tensions between these two racial groups did not altogether originate exclusively from the planters' actions. No doubt, when first confronted, the cultural imagination of each group on the plantation got quite shook up at the other.

The differences in looks, behaviour and culture were naturally astounding and when matched with the social hierarchy of the plantation, it became almost psychologically natural for inter-personal judgements between the two groups, Africans and East Indians, to move quickly from mere cultural differences to categorization, to prejudice, then finally to hostile discrimination.[40]

Culturally different, each group developed its respective evaluations of the other. The ethnic disparities in the plantation's social and economic structure consolidated the phenomenon. How much of these qualities exist today, not merely in the self-images of the directly stigmatised but also antagonistically shared between the two groups – the descendants of slaves and indentured labourers? How much of this is the legacy of plantation psychology? How much of it is now played out in the education system? The war of words after the country's elections in 2015 and the current ethnic rivalry over educational and economic status reflect the society's plantation history.

The plantation was called 'a total institution.' Using a social psychological approach to explain how the 'total group' influences the individual, Mead stated: *'We explain the conduct of the individual in terms of the conduct of the organised social group, rather than to account for the organized conduct of the social group in terms of the conduct of the separate individuals.'*[41]

This is, according to Mead, applicable to the transformation of 'I' into 'me' as a person moves from childhood into adolescence, from being a self-driven 'subject' to a socially-created 'object', from being a human being to an 'uncivilised, inferior being.'[42] So it was for both the slaves and indentured labourers under the hands of the plantocracy.

## THE CRIMINOGENIC PLANTATION

Later on, the working and living conditions of the indentured labourers became so insanitary and harsh that many of them ran away from the plantation, often breaking the several ordinances created to confine them to the plantation. A plantation-driven criminogenic environment was born.

Trotman stated: '*Since there was little government provision for them and as they were alien newcomers in a strange land and initially without ethnic community support, they were often found wandering on the rural roadside or in the city – ill-clad, hungry and destitute. The less fortunate were picked up dead at the roadside.*'[43] Because of the destitute plantation conditions provided for them, '*malaria, hookworm, ground itch, poor sanitation and overcrowding, etc. made their lives not only miserable but infested with illnesses of various kinds.*'[44]

Several laws were made to regulate and control them, laws that they scarcely read or understood, but broke frequently. The several Ordinances (e.g., Master and Servant Ordinance of 1846, Immigration Ordinance of 1852, Ordinance of 1854), generally designed to control their labour, included many minor offences such as unpunctuality, absenteeism, drunkeness, loitering, having no pass, etc.

The prosecution and imprisonment rates for them were quite high, over 11,149 prosecutions between 1898 and 1905 (i.e., about 15% of the indentured population). As a further example, of the 8,000 indentured labourers in 1858, at least 400 were jailed for contract breaches. Later, as the indentured population grew between 1871 and 1874, there were 12,198 reported cases under the 1854 Immigration Ordinance with 3,856 jailed.[45]

After receiving complaints about the inhumane treatment meted out to the indentured labourers, an amended Ordinance was created (1899) to formalize improved living, working and safety conditions for the labourers. Just like before, and in spite of having a Protector of Immigrants, the regulations were observed more in the breach than in their application.[46]

Meanwhile, the formerly enslaved Africans began to benefit from basic Christian education while the indentured labourers remained caught up in a cultural clash over the education system. The indentured labourers' relatively uneducated status and the plantation pressures made them a marginalised community, outsiders. It was around this time that the Presbyterian Mission entered.

The relationship between these indentured conditions, the legal ordinances and the crimes consequently committed by the indentured labourers shaped the plantation into a criminogenic breeding ground for the marginalized race. That is, the barricaded East Indians, with very limited space, suppressive working conditions, destitute living and housing conditions, low wages and a hostile social environment were virtually pressured into breaking the social control laws.

There are several theories in social psychology and criminology that show how such social and psychological conditions on the plantation can instigate deviance and crime. For example, as indicated above, labeling theory, drawn from symbolic interactionism, argues that people, especially those in vulnerable positions, incorporate into themselves the views that others, especially significant others, have of them.

Cooley had proposed the 'looking glass self' as a psychological mechanism for a person to see himself as others (e.g., authority figures) evaluate him, and added to this, being shaped into the image and likeness of the superior authority.[47] This applied to both Africans and East Indians.

To the enslaved and freed Africans and indentured East Indians, the plantation owners – Whites and British – were 'superior' figures. Deviant labelling, too, in an institutional setting, stimulates the targeted person to 'live up' to the deviant label – stigmatized deviance - especially if it is one of the rare ways to get attention.

Explaining the potential for crime within authoritarian structures and superior-subordinate pressures, Quinney proposed that a person will develop action patterns that have high potential of being defined as criminal depending on the relative substance of (1) Structured opportunities (2) Learning experiences (3) Interpersonal associations and identifications, and (4) Self-conceptions.[48] Having been labeled as such, the plantation workers expected their masters to view them as 'a bunch of deviants' who needed to be controlled.

Their self-conceptions became adjusted to such anticipations. As Quinney added: *'Those who have been defined as criminal begin to conceive of themselves as criminal; as they adjust to the definitions imposed upon them.*

*That is, increased experience with criminal definitions increases the probability of developing action that may be subsequently defined as criminal.'*[49]

The related damage done to the minds of the imported East Indians and more largely so, to the Africans during the plantation setting was to increase their tendencies to commit crimes as defined in the various ordinances. Confined with limited space, harsh conditions and the severe enforcement of social control laws, their commission of crime became a form of resistance, with no moral obligation to conform to plantation rules.

## LAWS WITH NO MORAL AUTHORITY

The laws had no moral authority. They were seen to be inhumane, spiteful and for the self-serving purposes of the plantation owners. The plantation labourers had little or no property, no community stakes. The riots of the late nineteenth century (1880–1900) against the suppression of religious and cultural festivals, especially carnival (e.g., 1883, 1884) and Hosay (1884) were more active forms of resistance. Additionally, two particular factors helped stimulate the drift by Africans and East Indians into deviant activities (as defined by the several Ordinances).

The first was 'the aggressive English Chief of Police who was supported by a belligerent phalanx of Irish non-commissioned officers and by ranks filled with antagonistic Barbadians.'[50] The second was the troubling decrease in sugar prices which adversely affected the jobs and living conditions of the two besieged races. Trotman summed up the situation this way:

> The struggle for cultural hegemony in the nineteenth century therefore depended less on the socialising agencies of church and school to win consent, and more on the coercive arms of the state to enforce compliance, and in the process, large segments of the population were forced into criminal activity.[51]

These Africans and East Indians had no real roots – social or economic - in the plantation society. In varying degrees, they remained strangers to the elite and to each other. Civic commitment was denied to them. There were no core values that they found justified and by which they could have abided. And the laws, both in content and enforcement, were extremely and unjustifiably oppressive. Turning to crime became a rational adventure.[52]

These two besieged racial groups worked hard in the plantation environment, but there was no ladder for mobility, neither then nor soon after. There was scarcely any place higher up. And so, they often turned against themselves and to crime.

The criminogenic nature of the plantation system was not only that structural conditions pushed the Africans (freed or enslaved) and East Indian indentured labourers toward deviance. The apparently spiteful rulings of the colonial court also bore criminogenic traits. For example, while non-indentured labourers were forced to pay for their offences with fines – not jailed – the indentured labourers who were bound to work under law, were more often sent to jail rather than fined.

## LAWS BUT NO JUSTICE: PLANTATION STYLE

This interesting difference arose mainly in the 'off-season,' that is, when the sugar crop was not cultivated or reaped so that the planters could have afforded to have the indentured labourers in jail, and not pay them. On the other hand, the non-indentured labourer had to find work in order to pay the fines. Such discriminatory practices helped the planter save money while removing surplus labour from his charge.

Worse yet, the days the indentured labourers spent in jail were counted as 'lost days' and as such, they had to work extra time to make up for the days lost in prison.[53] Plantation jurisprudence appeared primitive, discriminatory and severely anti-labour. In the face of all this, the plantation victims remained voiceless.

Using archival data, Trotman summarized:

> In the nineteenth century, Trinidad experienced a period of fluctuating crimes against the person and the consistent criminalization of Creole culture – all derived from the direct or indirect actions of the plantocrats in their pursuit of short-term economic interests.[54]

Crime emerged out of cultural conflict. According to Trotman, it was the 'cultural orientation' of the society that was responsible for the largest category of offenses among the convicted and jailed. He said:

> A crucial element in the ideology of the plantation system was the cultural supremacy of Europe and the congenital inferiority of non-Europeans. They therefore criminalized all cultural activities that they viewed as inimical to their interests. Much of the collective violence of the period stemmed from the actions of a politically powerless class in conscious defense of their cultural interests.[55]

All this suggests that crimes by Africans and East Indians, in the late nineteenth and early twentieth centuries, were largely a frustration-driven reaction against oppressive forms of social control. This criminological explanation is different from the one that says 'social deviance leads exclusively to social control', that is to say, social control laws are justifiably developed and applied because of deviance. Stigmatization and deviance were themselves invoked by the oppressive social control laws of the plantocracy.[56]

The sharply inequitable conditions on the plantation – structural and psychological – were created much to the advantage of the plantocrats and institutional elites. The Africans and East Indians were severely disadvantaged, socially, economically and psychologically. Their deviant reactions were the only way they could have kept what little dignity they felt they had. The modern version of social reaction theory deals with situations that are largely ambiguous in the relationships between institution and offender. The plantation situation had no such ambiguity. The inequitable division of power between proprietor and worker was very clear. It was a situation beyond anomie – there were no consensual norms, no room for 'middle class aspirations' or 'natural laws of due process.' The plantation was in practice a 'prison' without bars.

In the book, *The New Criminology*, the authors stated: '*It should be clear that a criminology which is not normatively committed to the abolition of inequalities of wealth and power, and in particular, of inequalities of property and life chances, is bound to fall into correctionalism.*'[57] The plantation had no established norms for equality or against social injustice. It couldn't have. Correctionalism and social control ordinances inevitably served as 'rough justice' on the plantation.

In other words, the plantation conditions left no room for behaviour to be driven by good conscience or obedience to civil norms. Plantation workers and the attendant community had to be forcefully controlled, one result being reactive deviance – against the ordinances and one group against the other. It is from such plantation oppression and despair that the present competition for educational and occupational status is now taking place in the country.

Such reflections also help show how the template for ethnic tensions in today's society was framed. Having heard of the deprivations and educational disadvantages of their forefathers, the further question is to what extent will the present generation of youths of both races seize the opportunities now available in education for their own dignity, civility and prosperity? And how, in such quest, will the conditions for equality and equity in the education system facilitate this quest?

## NOTES

1.  The British Atlantic Slave Trade ended in 1807. Slavery was abolished in two stages, in 1834 and 1838. August 1838 marks the final end of slavery in the British West Indies. Indentured immigration ended in 1917.The last indentures were cancelled on January 1, 1920. See also C. Campbell. *The Young Colonials: A Social History of Education in Trinidad and Tobago, 1834-1939*; Also, Campbell. Endless Education: Main Currents in the Education System of Modern Trinidad and Tobago, 1939-1986.

2.  E. Williams. *Education in the British West Indies*. New York University Place Book Shop. 1968; Keenan, *State of Education in the Island of Trinidad*, 1869;

3.  See e.g.,CLR James.*The Black Jacobins*. New York: Random House (2nd Ed.). 1963; O. Patterson.*The Sociology of Slavery: An Analysis of the Origins, Development and Structure of Negro Slave Society in Jamaica*. London: Farleigh Dickenson University Press, 1975; B. Brereton.'The Experience of Indentureship', in J. La Guerre (Ed.), *Calcutta to Caroni*. Trinidad: University of the West Indies School of Continuing Studies, 1985.

4.  D. Lowenthal. *West Indian Societies*. London: Oxford University Press. 1972. pp. 117-120.

5.  Ibid, p. 118.

6.  S. Gordon. *A Century of West Indian Education*. London: Longman Group. 1963. pp. 14-16.

7.  For further details on education for East Indian indentured labourers, see C. Campbell. *The Young Colonials: A Social History of Education in Trinidad and Tobago 1834-1939, 1996*.

8.  S. Gordon, S. ibid, pp. 14-16.

9.  The Slavery Abolition Act was passed in 1833 but became effective in1834. See D. Bryden. *West Indian Slavery and British Abolition 1783-1807*, Cambridge: Cambridge University Press, 2010 for humanitarian vs. economic conflicts. For the slave's suffering through the voyage, see K. Kiple, *The Caribbean Slave Trade: A Biological History*. Cambridge: Cambridge University Press. 1984.

10. Cited in S. Gordon. 1963. p. 20.

11. See e.g. Keenan Report. 1869

12. See Beckford in *Sociology of Education*. p. 37.

13. Ibid, pp. 37-38.

14. H. Thomas, *The Slave Trade: The Story of the Atlantic Slave Trade: 1440-1870*. New York: Simon & Schuster, 1999. p. 21. Thomas also noted that 'between 1492 and 1870, approximately eleven million black slaves were brought from Africa to the Americas.'

15. Ibid. p. 21.

16. H. Louis Gates. (Ed.) *Classic Slave Narratives*. New York: Penguin Books. 2002. See e.g., *The History of Mary Prince: A West Indian Slave*. pp 231-297.

17. For a concise, interesting summary of some of the conditions encountered by African slaves coming into the Caribbean, see K. Baldeosingh. 'Better Off Free?' in *Sunday Guardian*. August 2, 2015. p.A24. After using selected data on lifestyles and quality of life, he concluded: 'It seems then, that the average Caribbean person is better off today than the average African. This, however, was at a cost of millions of people killed and brutalized through one of humanity's most shameful eras.'

18. CLR James, *The Black Jacobins*. New York: Random House (2nd Ed.) 1963. pp. 5-7.

19. Cited in E. Williams, *History of Trinidad and Tobago*. 1962. Pp. 30-34.

20. Ibid. p. 31.

21. Cited in E. Williams. 1962.pp. 31-32.

22. Ibid. p. 31.

23. Between 1845 and 1917, an estimated 149,000 indentured labourers were brought from India.

24. Cited in E. Williams, *History of Trinidad and Tobago*. 1962. p.78.

25. Cited in E. Williams, *History of Trinidad and Tobago*.pp. 110-112.

26. The first ship with indenture Indians from Calcutta, *Fatel Razack*, arrived in Trinidad from Calcutta on May 30, 1845 with 197 males and 28 females. The importation was stopped in 1917 and indenture was abolished in 1920. The last ship to arrive in Trinidad was the *SS Ganges* in April 22, 1917 with 247 males, 115 females 12 boys, 10 girls and 10 infants.

27. See B. Brereton. 1985.pp. 27-30.

28. Ibid. p. 28.

29. Cited in E. Williams. 1962. p. 100.

30. B. Strumpel. 1965. Cited in Rubin and Zavalloni. p. 200.

31. The arguments continue over which was more severe, African slavery or East Indian indentureship, especially in the context of mounting calls for 'Reparations for African Slavery.' See, e.g., article by David Mohammed, 'The-Point Contrast Between Indentureship and Slavery.' *Mirror*. June 7, 2015. p. 13.

32. M. Klass. *East Indians in Trinidad: A Study of Cultural Persistence*. Illinois: Waveland Press. 1961.
33. R. Deosaran,'The Unmeltable Ethnics'. *Newsday*. May 14, 2015.
34. Cited in D. Trotman, *Crime in Trinidad: Conflict and Control in a Plantation Society, 1838-1900*. Knoxville: University of Tennessee Press. 1986, pp. 185-186. This book provides substantial details on the relationship between crime, imprisonment and the East Indian indentured labourers.
35. D. Trotman. 1986. His book provides details especially in pp.68-140.
36. K. Haraksingh,'Aspects of the Indian Experience in the Caribbean', in J. La Guerre (Ed.) *Calcutta to Caroni*. pp. 160-62.
37. Paulo Freire. *Pedagogy of the Oppressed*. New York : Seabury Press,1974, p .49
38. This 'displacement' is one of Sigmund Freud's five subconscious defense mechanisms.
39. F. Fanon, *The Wretched of the Earth*. New York: Grove Press. 1968. p. 52.
40. See G. Allport,*The Nature of Prejudice*. New York: Doubleday. 1958. pp. 17-52. Here, Allport explains the 'natural' inclination of people to form categories of others' differences, then when lodged in a social structure, how this categorised thinking germinates into prejudice and discrimination. Allport describes social psychology as 'an attempt to understand and explain how the thoughts, feelings and behavior of individuals are influenced by the actual, imagined or implied presence of others.' This also brings to mind Charles Cooley's view that 'the imaginations that people have of one another are the solid facts of society.' It is R. Fisher (1968) who gave a more relevant definition to race relations and prejudice in the plantation: 'Social psychology is concerned with human interaction. It is the scientific study of how the behaviour of an individual is influenced by and in turn influences the action of others in the social environment. It is concerned with how an individual's thoughts, feeling and actions are intertwined with the beliefs, motives and the behavior of others are expressed in complex social structures and processes.' In *Social Psychology: An Applied Approach*. New York: St. Martin's Press. 1968. p. 6.
41. G. Mead, *Mind, Self and Society*. Chicago: University of Chicago Press. 1962. pp. 7-8.
42. Ibid, p. 8.
43. Ibid, p 186.
44. B. Brereton.'The Experience of Indentureship 1845-1917'. In La Guerre, J. *Calcutta to Caroni*. Trinidad: UWI. Extra Mural Studies. 1985. pp. 24-25. Also, E. Williams.*History of Trinidad and Tobago*. 1962.pp. 108-114.
45. D. Trotman. 1986.pp. 186-187.
46. E. Williams. 1962.pp. 103-112.

47. This shaping of the personality, even a pathological personality, has a substantial theoretical platform from symbolic interactionism and labeling to stigmatisation. E.g., see C. Cooley.*Human Nature and the Social Order*, New York: Schocken Books, 1964; E. Goffman. *Stigma*. New Jersey: Prentice Hall, 1963; E. Lemert, *Social Pathology*. New York: McGraw Hill, 1951; H. Becker. *Outsiders: Studies in the Sociology of Deviance*. New York: The Free Press, 1963.

48. R. Quinney. *The Social Reality of Crime*. Boston: Little, Brown and Co. 1970. pp. 21-22.

49. ibid., p. 22. This social reaction perspective in criminology puts the emphasis upon the social and institutional agencies and their forces upon the individual – an appropriate perspective for the plantation system.

50. D. Trotman. ibid, p. 270.

51. Ibid. p. 270.

52. The purpose here is not to provide extended theoretical explanations of crime, but to provide a crisp outline of the kind of social and physical structures which, as persuasively argued in the research literature, contribute to crime, thus making crime a 'rational' act. The plantation did provide such circumstances. References cited earlier.

53. D. Trotman. Ibid, p. 189.

54. Ibid. p. 276.

55. Ibid. p. 274.

56. See e.g., E. Lemert. *Human Deviance, Social Problems and Social Control*. New York: Prentice Hall. 1967. p. v.

57. I. Taylor, P. Walton and J. Young. *The New Criminology*. London: Routledge and Kegan Paul. 1977. p. 281.

# CHAPTER FOUR
# Plantation Pathology and Education

*Race enters as a stepchild of prejudice, above all a legacy of stereotypes developed by Europeans in the age of European expansion to world dominion. It is based above all on conspicuous physical differentiation, especially skin pigmentation and facial characteristics, which facilitate the stereotyping process which is so valuable in the maintenance of prejudice. Once established, it hardens into a systematic misperception of facts and a propensity to see all members of another racial category as looking alike.*

G. Simpson and J. Milton, Racial and Cultural Minorities, 1958

## SLAVE AND INDENTURED EDUCATION

The previous two chapters sought to show how the plantation system helped shape the social and psychological character of the forefathers of the present generation of Africans and Indians. In particular, an attempt was made to explain how much of today's racial prejudices and stereotypes originated and, at the same time, how crime became a form of cultural resistance to the oppressive laws of the plantation. This chapter now seeks to connect such experiences to the evolution of the country's educational system and the implications for both Africans and Indians.

Brought from Africa into Caribbean slavery and without much of their religious and cultural traditions, the Africans, during and after slavery, became relatively easy converts to Christianity and thereby enrolment in Christian schools (e.g., Catholic and Anglican).[1] It was different for the East Indian indentured labourers. Their transported language, dress, food, religion and stark strangeness made them difficult to convert, difficult to be assimilated in the Christian educational environment, while they themselves were reluctant to send their children to such schools.

Bringing more of their culture with them, the East Indians naturally endured stiffer cognitive dissonance to assimilate or convert. They had to divest a lot in order to accommodate the new. Such references to education for East Indian indentured labourers do not necessarily mean that the hardships of the Africans were less severe. The indentured labourers from India provide an intriguing example of cultural resistance and protective insularity which stubbornly struggled against an imperialist culture backed up by Christianity. It was a battle half-won.

As these indentured immigrants entered this 'strange land,' they found serious challenges facing the education of their children. Williams said: *'The worst victims of colonialism in this respect are the children of the indentured immigrants.'*[2] Brereton added:

> Up to around 1870 very few Indian children received any form of schooling. By the late 1860s, when the Indian population was over 20,000 there was only a handful of Indian children in the public primary schools. The Rev. John Morton, the pioneer Canadian Presbyterian Missionary in Trinidad, reported that in 1868 there was scarcely an Indian child to be found in school in the whole island.

She added:

> It was not that Indian children were excluded from the schools, but that their parents were reluctant to send them to schools run by teachers of a different race and religion, and feared that their children might be converted to Christianity.[3]

Around this time, the prejudices and stereotypes were encircling the indentured East Indians. In attempting to build a 'separate' school for East Indians in Belmont, Reverend R.H. Moor justified it in this way:

> A mixed school (i.e., for Creoles and Indians) will be a mistake. An Indian will not send his child to a Creole school. He is afraid of injustice being done his child from the Creole teacher, and of ill-usage from the Creole pupils.[4]

Reverend Moor added:

> The Creole as a rule looks down on the Indian; he is a semi-civilised being, (according to the Creole) he speaks a barbarous language, and his manners are barbarous. He comes to Trinidad to make money for there is no money in his own country, so he thinks. He takes work cheaper than the Creole will do, hence he must be ill-treated where he can be ill-treated with impunity.[5]

## CULTURAL CONFLICT IN EDUCATION

Citing several reports of the late 19th and early 20th centuries, Brereton described the humiliating stereotypes and prejudices which both the English and African inflicted on the indentured labourers. The religious practices of the 'Coolies' were seen as barbaric and violent. Their lifestyles were seen to be stingy and uncivilized. In that deprecating context, Brereton noted: *'Africans, once at the bottom of the social scale, now had an easily recognizable class to which they could feel superior.'*[6]

She summarized:

> The Indians' attitude towards money was yet another aspect of the stereotype. Thrift, with them seemed like a vice to others. The first generation of Indians especially was single-minded in its determination to save its miserable wages, even if it meant inadequate food or clothing. This contrasted with the working-class African, famous for his love of spending money lavishly on drink, food, clothes or fete...The Indians were (seen as) heathens and morally degraded.[7]

She continued:

> Morton thought Hinduism an unclean religion which fostered a low sense of sin. He judged Indians to be morally unprincipled, untruthful, revengeful and avaricious, with an obsessive respect for their sinister rites and traditions. So long as indentureship lasted, it was only too easy for Africans to despise Indians...Indians on the estates performed the low-prestige jobs, like weeding, digging and transporting cane, which Africans chose to avoid.[8]

In such demeaning circumstances, the East Indians were therefore left badly stereotyped, socially ostracized and largely illiterate. The imperialist mixture of labour migration and colonialism created a dilemma for the new migrants. How to retain a culture that is derided by others who themselves regret having lost theirs.

As a 'rescue mission,' the Presbyterian Church from Canada (Canadian Mission), between 1868 and 1900, established sixty schools for East Indians. This enterprise did not escape ethnically-driven controversy, even hostility, from the Hindu and Moslem groupings in the colony. These latter two groups were themselves struggling to open their own schools.[9]

It was cultural resistance at its peak. There was a Moslem-Hindu united front against the Presbyterian Mission, with such unity interrupted by internal differences within each religious group – Hindu and Moslem. With Canadian funding and state grants, the Presbyterians pushed ahead from 1892 to open the Naparima Teachers Training College, the Naparima Boys' College and the Naparima Girls' College. These establishments brought power and prestige to the Presbyterian educational mission while enhancing Christianity and western culture.

This further aroused both Moslems and Hindus to seek to open their own schools especially in the Chaguanas area. Their major objective was the preservation of language and culture circumscribed by the fear of having their children converted and taught by others. So intense were the conflicts that there came a call came from the Hindu-Moslem front to abolish denominational schools and for government schools to abolish the Presbyterian schools while having Hindu and Urdu as additional subjects.[10] At that time, too, religious conversion became a hot political subject.

## THE PRESBYTERIANS ARRIVE

Celebrating the success of the Presbyterian Mission, Campbell noted the records that showed how the Mission produced a creditable catalogue of firsts in trained Indians, such 'first Indians in the lower ranks of the civil service, first Indians in politics both at the Municipal and Legislative levels; first Indian professionals.'

Writing further on '*The East Indian Revolt Against Missionary Education in Trinidad 1928-1939*, Campbell stated:

> The inevitable price to be paid was the spread of Christianity at the expense of Hinduism and Islam; the advance of western civilization, including the English language to the detriment of Indian native customs and languages; and missionary favouritism towards Christian Indians.[11]

Whether it was a price to be paid, or whether the price was worth it, or whether it was a price at all, is a question for social psychological analysis from today's perspective. The answer depends, for example, on where one stands in the socio-economic continuum today.

No doubt, there was conversion, often of the proselytizing type, for example, to gain teaching appointments – with strong objections from the Hindu and Moslem groups. Today, voluntary conversion from different races occurs into Christianity, especially Pentecostal types, and less so, into Hinduism and Islam.

These are the circumstances that make the education of Indian indentured labourers and their children a very interesting sociological and psychological study, especially when their present academic and occupational status is generally considered.[12] However, in the natural course of living in what has become a multi-ethnic society, East Indians – both Hindus and Moslems – also became elasticized, that is, adopting a large measure of western culture while retaining much of their own religious and cultural traditions.[13]

Such pre-independence experiences by both Africans and East Indians bring fuller meaning to the educational and occupational aspirations of today's young people in the independence era. A plantation owner, Mr. E. A. Robinson testified before a Select Committee of the Legislative Council in 1926. When asked if having 10-year old East Indian children work 7 a.m. to 5 p.m. in his plantation would deny them an education, he replied:

> This is an agricultural country. Unless you must have children working
> in the fields when they are young, you will never get them to do so
> later...I would say educate only the bright ones, not the whole mass. If
> you educate the whole mass you will deliberately ruin the country.

Another plantation owner, Mr. C. Knox, agreeing with Mr. Robinson, said that if they were to send the 10 and 12-year old East Indian children to school, 'there would not be enough agricultural labourers in years to come.'[14]

Such plantation-driven comments provide an indication of how very far the colonial society was from educational democracy and equality of educational opportunity. How really was the situation in education for the imported labourers - slaves and indentured? It was not merely a matter of 'getting into a school' provided by the colonial administration, plantation owners or the church at that time in the nineteenth and twentieth centuries. It was also how to provide an education for the racial and religious diversity within the mass of imported labour. The challenge from the very beginning was how to get an education system, even in its barest essentials, to accommodate these 'strange' groups, particularly the East Indian indentured labourers. Such considerations, however, were severely restrained by the racial sentiments held by the colonial authorities.

## KEENAN AND LORD HARRIS

The colonial population was quite diversified. For example, in the 1808 census, the total population was 31,478 with British 1,147, French 781,

Spanish 459, Corsican 36, German 39, Chinese 22, Amerindians 1,635 and 21,895 slaves.

In 1846, Lord Harris, as the country's new Governor, found a disorganised educational system, including about forty denominational (Christian) schools, state-funded but unsupervised. The immediate challenge he found was the complex ethnic diversity of the colonised community. In 1847, the year after his arrival, he promised to submit an ordinance to the Legislative Council to establish a system of general education.

The Colonial Office appointed Patrick Keenan to inquire into the state of education in the colony. Soon after his arrival and in order to avoid having a fragmented system of education, Keenan noted that '*in contemplation of the difficulties arising from differences of race, language and religion.*' He added that Lord Harris decided to propose '*that the Government should attempt to carry out nothing more than what is generally termed secular education.*'[15] Secularism, as the presumed level playing field, was preferred to the complexities of ethnic diversity in the schools.

Between 1834 and 1851, the colony's population moved from 43,678 to 69,609, an increase of 60%. As Keenan indicated, the population then comprised 40,627 born in Trinidad, 10,812 born in different British colonies, 8,097 born in Africa, 4,915 born in other foreign countries, 4,169 were imported Coolies, 729 natives of the United Kingdom and 260 of 'miscellaneous origins.'[16] When classified according to religion, Keenan noted, 'the heterogeneous character of the population was still more striking.' There were at least ten different religious groups, including the Catholics at 43,605, Protestants grouped as 20,440, Mahometans 1,016 and Heathens at 880. (There was no classification of 'Hindus').

Given this country's existing ethnic diversity and the intermittent controversies over the ethnically-driven Concordat (dual system of education), these early attempts to accommodate diversity into a colonial-type education system are instructive. That era signaled the birth of the Concordat spirit and, as some would argue, the politics of education in the country. Noting another ethnic challenge, Keenan wrote: '*Besides those of race, language and religion, there was another difficulty – a social one, the existence of which could not be deliberately ignored. Seventeen years had passed away since the emancipation of the 20,657 slaves of the island.*'

He added:

> To such people, society was only a chaos. In it they could recognize
> neither design nor purpose, nor symmetry. For its duties, their habits

ill-suited them; for its responsibilities their intuition was defective. Nevertheless, they formed a considerable proportion of the people, and it became the duty of the State to mould them into good citizens.[17]

Educational policies at that time seemed guided by sentiments similar to those expressed by Trollope, Jefferson, and Froude. These imperial prejudices put a low value on quality education for the formerly enslaved and indentured labourers. Lord Harris wrestled with the challenge posed between ethnic diversity and a national system of education – a challenge which continued with serious political implications after the country gained independence. When Lord Harris submitted his proposal for 'a general secular system of education,' he apologetically explained:

> I decided on this plan with considerable anxiety and in no spirit of pride but rather that of deep humiliation; for I am obliged to come to the conclusion that the unfortunate differences which exist in religion could prevent any united action if that subject were introduced; and though I acknowledge to the fullest the immense importance of this subject in developing the powers of man, I thought it better, under the circumstances, that it should be left to be provided for by other means.[18]

According to the 1869 Keenan Report, in 1834, the year of Emancipation, the population was 43,678 with about one-half (20,657) Africans enslaved. Whites were 3,632; free-coloured 18,627, Aborigines went down to 762. With Emancipation, the supply of plantation labour decreased.[19] Free blacks were therefore imported from North America and other West Indian islands, and even from the 'protesting and delinquent classes' of Europe. Arriving in the midst of the already mixed community, many in these groups, much to the delight of the British, spoke English and were Protestant.

In this seminal inquiry into the education system of Trinidad, Keenan summarized:

> Here again was another new element in the constitution of the population - its peculiarity being its Protestant character. The old settlers still adhered to Catholicism, still spoke their patois of Spanish or French, still clung to their old traditions...But the supply of labour was yet unequal to the demand; and the government had to turn to a new field for fresh recruits. Accordingly, in 1845 Coolies from India were introduced for the first time.[20]

## THE PATHOLOGY OF SLAVERY AND INDENTURESHIP

Using social learning theory, it is very likely that these two affected racial groups, African enslaved and Indian indentured labourers, burdened with such dehumanizing conditions and psychological humiliations, were led into deep despair, loss of self-confidence, damaged aspirations and even neuroses. The dehumanizing European-driven denigrations (e.g., lazy, dirty, immoral, uncivilized, etc.) plastered upon these imported plantation workers would have most likely wounded their souls while they internalised and eventually believed that, in fact, they are really so. Or could at least some of them ever transcend such horrible social and psychological conditions so as to be better than what the Europeans thought of them?

## FANON, CESAIRE AND FREIRE: ON PLANTATION PATHOLOGY

This struggle over colonial oppression and its dehumanizing effects upon its imported labourers (enslaved and indentured) occupied the intellect of many scholars around the world. About seventy years ago, with damning prose and verse, two of these came from Martinique, namely, psychiatrist Frantz Fanon and poet Aime Cesaire. With psychoanalytic flair, Fanon unearthed the shaping of the inferiority complex engineered into the slave population, a condition he believed was almost irreversible.

He brashly wrote: '*For the black man, there is only one destiny. And it is white... If there is an inferiority complex, it is the outcome of a double process: primarily economic; subsequently, the internalisation – or better, the epidermalisation – of this inferiority.*'[21] In today's increasingly globalised culture, the psychological tension for the formerly enslaved and indentured people is lodged between 'black is beautiful' and 'looking to be white.' This 'colour conflict,' as one example, is now described as part of the 'mental slavery' derived from plantation psychology.

In his 'Social Stratification in Trinidad and Tobago,' sociologist Braithwaite elaborated on the extent to which the local population 'mimicked' the metropolitan and especially British lifestyles – also in the quest for 'looking like white', even in the post-independence era. For example, he, quite amusingly, wrote:

> The dark-skinned person further makes distinctions which white or fairer skinned people do not make. The phrase 'light-black' is often

used as a term of description by dark-skinned persons, while the other groups tend to be amused by this distinction. To them 'black is black' and the words 'light' and 'black' appear as contradictory terms...The root of this seems to be a psychological compensation for the lack of mobility, the individual reorganising his perceptions in order to render the wounded self-perception more acceptable.

He colourfully continued:

Occasionally, a lower class man will straighten his hair, and occasionally too, there is bleaching, of the skin and the use of a nose-straigthener in order to render the features more physically attractive...Consequently, the girls of the towns are much more influenced by the white ideals than those of the countryside.[22]

Political independence came but, according to Beckford and Braithwaite, remnants of European respectability persisted. 'Wishing to be European and white' remains a controversial aspiration within the local population. Simpson noted:

Even as cultural space opened for the emancipated Africans, respectability became a variable in that greater respect was being given to names, religious and cultural practices which duplicated or resembled Christianity or European. In this regard, the traditions brought by the slaves of free Africans from Africa struggled for their own authenticity and survival.[23]

There is a view, therefore, that even after the termination of slavery and indentured labour, the demolished self-esteem of the former plantation workers, especially the Africans, persisted and became manifest in various bizarre forms. In fact, there was a significant rise in intellectual analysis and severe condemnation of slavery and colonialism itself. Martiniquan poet, Aime Cesaire, in his *Discourse on Colonialism*, remarked: '*I am talking about millions of men who have been skillfully injected with fear, inferiority complexes, trepidations, servility, despair, abasement.*'[24]

Cesaire saw colonialism not only as racially oppressive but quite hypocritical and therefore naturally a driver of cultural imperialism. He angrily said the major hypocrisy of colonialism '*is christian pedantry which laid down the dishonest equations, christianity=civilization; paganism=savagery from which there could not but ensure abominable colonial and racist consequences whose victims were to be the Indians, the Yellow peoples and the Negroes*' (p. 33).

It was such colonised victimization that led to the massive inferiority complex that created the plantation psychology of persistent dependency later described by George Beckford in his examination of the plantation system.[25] Noting the difference between 'constitutional independence' and 'political independence,' Beckford said that though Caribbean countries gained political independence, they were *'left with a legacy of economic, social, psychological and indeed political dependency.'*[26]

Paulo Freire, dealing with psychological dependency and 'cultural invasion' in his *'Pedagogy of the Oppressed,'* passionately stated:

> Cultural conquest leads to the cultural inauthenticity of those invaded; they begin to respond to the values, the standards and the goals of the invaders...It is essential that those who are invaded come to see their reality with the outlook of the invaders rather than their own; for the more they mimic the invaders, the more stable the position of the latter becomes. The more those invaded are alienated from the spirit of their own culture and from themselves, the more the latter want to be like the invaders: to walk like them, dress like them, talk like them.[27]

Such 'invader-driven' values no doubt found their way into the education systems of the freed colonies, thus injecting, for example, a severe competition for grammar-type education as against technical vocational education. It is, therefore, more than 'dress like them,' 'whitened skin' or 'straightened hair.' Agreeing with Freire, Beckford wrote:

> Black people sought social mobility by aspiring continuously to a European way of life. Education, residence, manner of speech and dress, religious beliefs and practice, social values and attitudes and general lifestyle, all served to distinguish those black people who had made it from those who had not.[28]

The psychological challenge now facing the formerly colonised people is how to effectively escape from such 'dependency.' This would require, among other things, a selective divestment of metropolitan habits and, as far as possible, a deeper appreciation and practice of indigenous cultures – what Paulo Freire termed 'authentication.' The resistance to such transformation, however, is caught within the reciprocal relationships between psychology and economics, leaving the society's diverse 'cultures' in perpetual flux, conflict and ambiguity.

There is the psychological urge for cultural retention on one hand, and on the other hand, the instigated desire for seductive goods and services required for middle class status. There is the highly secular nature of the educational system which, as 'foreign broker,' helps keep 'local culture' fading into museums. There is as yet no 'escape strategy' from any of the four 'dependicies' earlier cited by Beckford. In fact, it looks like there will never be any escape.

The distractions in this escape strategy are the seductive cultural attractions from globalization, consumerism and capitalist-driven media. Pressed by the economics of culture, such externally-driven attractions (in dress, food, dining, songs, overseas holidays, imported luxuries, etc.) appear to be so naturally absorbed locally that rather than being elements of 'cultural invasion,' they are proudly flaunted as modern, middle-class lifestyles.

Challenges for 'cultural authentication' also emerge from conflict and competition between the various cultures within the newly-independent society itself; examples being its dual system of education and ethnic competition and patronage in its multi-party system. In other words, there is as yet no 'one national culture'. In all this, the socio-economic forces of modernization persistently shape the values and aspirations of the psychologically-vulnerable society with the education system operating as a capitalist-driven broker.

The East Indian sector of the denominational-managed schools struggles with half-hearted cultural resistance while it is an open-door for the government-managed schools. In spite of pockets of cultural retention, multi-culturalism is now subordinate to social class stratification which is itself stimulated by the capitalist-driven education system.

Like the battle for a New World Information Order in the eighties, this struggle by Caribbean societies against metropolitan lifestyles and values is a lost one, with incremental losses, surrender really, highly rated as 'globalization.' The young generation, for example, energized by mass consumerism and media-technology now functions as key drivers of metropolitanism. And they feel no loss of self-esteem or disempowerment for it. This, too, is what makes quite challenging the implementation of educational policies designed for 'indigenous' social and economic development. Many of the developmental challenges facing the country are also internally driven, such as ethnic rivalries, inequality and inequity in education and serious deficits in governance.[29] Sustainable economic development rises or falls according to how these specific challenges are dealt with.

# EDUCATION AND VALUES

What about education just after emancipation? Plantation class superiority persisted in that while education for the freed blacks was seen as the only significant scope for social mobility, such opportunities were not only quite limited but what were provided 'served further to acculturate black people to the culture of the dominant white class.'[30] The educational preference of the dominant white class was for academic, grammar-type education which led to the professions of law, medicine, engineering, etc., so even if vocational and craft courses were provided, the free blacks still felt educationally incomplete.

Beckford described some post-slavery and post-indentureship experiences which still persist in the Caribbean, even more so in Trinidad and Tobago today. For example, while there is an uneasy cultural pluralism between the different ethnic groups in the society, their social and economic aspirations are quite similar.[31] This is the difference between the arithmetic and the dynamic calculus of cultural pluralism. Further, given the limited opportunities for economic and social status, ethnic rivalries persist, often becoming quite intense at political campaigns. Cultural pluralism becomes politically fractured.

## From Past to Present

The above connections between the past and the present are used mainly to see the extent to which a population could move from such destitution into conditions not only of political independence but more precisely into higher levels of social, educational and occupational status with all its implications and complications.

The plantation 'psychology of denigration' provides the background to the anxious use of education as the current tool for gaining respect, self-confidence, social and occupational status among the different ethnic groups in the population. Therefore, the extent to which the education system fails to keep this promise would appear as an act of betrayal. On May 30, 2015, the country's former Prime Minister, Mrs. Kamla Persad-Bissessar, repeated to her audience what she has said many times before:

> Without education and training, you are doomed to remain at your same level. That is why my government provides so much money for educating the young people. My mother never went to school, she was illiterate.[32]

As will be illustrated later, such post-colonial educational ambitions are taking place in a competitive, supply and demand context which, in this multi-ethnic society, raises serious challenges of equity.

# WILLIAMS AND EDUCATION

As part of the decolonisation process, in 1965 the country's first Prime Minister, Dr Eric Williams, expressed the government's keen concerns over two related issues – equality of educational opportunity and the imbalance between grammar-type and technical/vocational training. In this regard, he celebrated the enactment of the new Education Act (1966) by proudly referring to Section 7:

> No person shall be refused admission to any public school on account of religious persuasion, race, social status or language of such person or his parents.[33]

He continued:

> We could rest satisfied with the 1965 (examination) results which show that in one respect the older (denominational) schools are paying the price for social discrimination, keeping out the better students from their classrooms, and the newer schools are going, in the not too distant future, to achieve results superior or at least equal to the results of these older schools. I present this Education Bill as a measure of integration of our society, a national system for an independent country.[34]

The challenge today, is to examine the extent to which such pledges and expectations have been realised. Twelve years after independence, Williams added:

> As colonialism drew politically to a close in 1962, Trinidad and Tobago found itself with an education system which bore all the characteristic features of cultural imperialism. There was no national outlook in education and no unified control. The curriculum of the secondary school (in 1961) was pronouncedly metropolitan in scope, orientation and character, designed to prepare the students for metropolitan examinations and metropolitan university systems.'

In rationalising his government's 1967 Education Plan, he added:

> The system showed an almost total absence of any proximation to the technical or vocational. The churches exercised extensive control of the system and were heavily subsidised by the government.[35]

With this background, and on UNESCO's advice, the government introduced the new secondary school configuration – Junior Secondary, Composite and Senior Comprehensive Schools. The consequences for equality of educational opportunity and equity were quite serious. They still are.

The descendants of imported African enslaved and East Indian indentured labourers, having endured unusual physical, social and psychological hardships under colonialism, are now feverishly consumed with aspirations for educational achievement.

Education is now widely seen in the country as 'the passport out of poverty' and a key instrument for socio-economic progress and fuller democracy. In all this, issues of equality of educational opportunity and equity reside. Can the system of education itself really fulfill such lofty aspirations and objectives?

## NOTES

1.  The cultural emasculation was quite severe, for example, they lost their original names, obliged to take on their masters' names, dress and even religion, save for some cherished traditions, e.g., Orisha, drumming.
2.  E. Williams. *History of Trinidad and Tobago*. p. 212
3.  B. Brereton.The Experience of Indentureship. In J. La Guerre (Ed.) *From Calcutta to Caroni*. Trinidad: Extra Mural Studies Unit, University of the West Indies. 1985.pp. 28-30.
4.  Cited in E. Williams. *History of Trinidad and Tobago*. 1962. p. 213.
5.  Ibid. p. 213.
6.  Ibid. p. 30.
7.  B. Brereton. Ibid. p.30.
8.  B. Brereton. Ibid. pp 28-30.
9.  B. Samaroo. The Presbyterian Church as an Agent of Integration in Trinidad and Tobago during the 19th and 20th centuries. Caribbean Studies, XIV (4), January 1975. Also C. Campbell. The East Indian Revolt Against Missionary Education 1928-1939. In La Guerre, J. (Ed.). *From Calcutta to Caroni*. pp. 117-131.
10. *East Indian Weekly*. October 19, 26, 1929. Cited in C. Campbell. p.124-125.
11. C. Campbell. Ibid, p.117.
12. Today there are 43 Hindu primary schools, five Hindu secondary schools managed by the Sanatan Dharma Maha Sabha and 25 primary and secondary schools managed by three different Moslem organisations –

ASJA, TIA, TML. From having one in 1868, the Presbyterians established 52 by 1892 and by 1900, 60 in various parts of the country. The Mixed racial category now amounts to 22% of the population.

13. R. Deosaran, 'Unmeltable Ethnics'.*Newsday*. May 14, 2015. p. 14.

14. Cited in E. Williams. *History of the People of Trinidad and Tobago*. 1962.

15. P. J. Keenan. p.9. 'Report Upon the State of Education in the Island of Trinidad', Dublin: Alexander Thom, Printed for Her Majesty's Stationery Office, 1869. Patrick Joseph Keenan was appointed by Governor Arthur Hamilton Gordon, ' to make a diligent and full inquiry into the state of education , whether secular or religious, in the island of Trinidad'. Appointed in February 1869, Keenan submitted his report in July 1869.

16. Ibid. p. 9-10.

17. Ibid. p.10.

18. P. J. Keenan. p.10. 'Report Upon the State of Education in the Island of Trinidad', Dublin: Alexander Thom, Printed for Her Majesty's Stationery Office. 1869.

19. Ibid. pp. 9-11.

20. Ibid.

21. F. Fanon, *Black Skins, White Masks*. New York: Grove Press. 1967. A later book, *The Wretched of the Earth*. New York: Grove Press. 1968, took on a much more angry tone.

22. L. Braithwaite,*Social Stratification in Trinidad and Tobago*. ISER, University of the West Indies. 1975.pp. 155-6. Such 'white-people-looking' practices, in several ways, have now become a lucrative industry through skin-whitening, hair-straightening, etc.

23. G. Simpsom, *Religious Cults of the Caribbean: Trinidad, Jamaica and Haiti*. Puerto Rico: University of Puerto Rico, Institute of Caribbean Studies. 1965.

24. Aime Cesaire, *Discourse on Colonialism*. New York: New York University Press. 2001. Cesaire was a founder of the negritude movement in Francophone literature, a devastating attack on colonialism.

25. G. Beckford, *Persistent Poverty*. New York: Oxford University Press. 1972. Here, Beckford describes how the plantation culture in the Caribbean – race, caste, subordination, etc. – creates 'static' pluralism on one hand and aspirations for 'planter' lifestyles on the other hand, thereby making the 'need to achieve' an important motive for former slaves especially. pp. 5, 64,79.

26. Ibid. p. 5.

27. P. Freire, *Pedagogy of the Oppressed*. New York: The Seabury Press. 1968. p. 52.

28. G. Beckford, *Persistent Poverty*, New York: Oxford University Press. 1972. p.38. He was dealing with the underdevelopment of plantation economies of the Third World.

29. Ethnic conflicts were cited in Chapter One. Chapters Six, Seven and Eight will describe educational 'inequality and Inequity' issues and their relationship to governance.

30. G. Beckford, *Persistent Poverty*, New York: Oxford University Press, 1972, pp. 64-65.

31. Ibid. p. 65.

32. Speech at Indian Arrival Day ceremony. Her mother, like that of many East Indian professionals in her party and government, descended from a generation of indentured labourers.

33. E. Williams. The Education Bill. Speech to the House of Representatives, December 8, 1965.

34. Ibid.

35. E. Williams, 'Education and Decolonisation in Trinidad and Tobago'. Address to Caribbean Union College. August 29, 1974.

# CHAPTER FIVE
# Promises of Education: A Critical Look

*Education has to be considered not only as a powerful tool for self-development and social integration; It has been seen as the 'great equalizer.' A review of educational history hardly supports the optimistic pronouncements of liberal educational theory. The politics of education are better understood in terms of the need for social control in an unequal and rapidly-changing economic order.*

Bowles and Gintis, 2011

## UNMASKING THE PROMISES

This chapter takes a critical look at the education system in terms of its promise and capacity to provide socio-economic mobility in an equitable manner and as well the extent to which it can operate to change the inequalities in the socio-economic order of the society itself. In other words, we consider the limitations of the education system, especially as the previous chapter indicated; great hopes are placed upon the education system in promoting the decolonisation process.

With brief reference to the international literature, we consider what lessons a relatively small post-colonial country like Trinidad and Tobago can learn in reforming its education system. A critical analysis of the education system here comes up against strong hopes and optimism over its value.

It may cause surprise, for example, to question its 'support' to a capitalist economy. Or, as some researchers pointed out, the extent to which 'meritocracy in schooling' helps legitimise inequality in the education system.

The education system here has so far been seen as a 'jobs' factory', widely accepted as such by the society, training people for a well-established hierarchy of jobs and with all the discriminatory values attached to them. Even if it is difficult to make a significant shift in this relationship, there are serious issues within the educational system that need urgent attention, the most outstanding ones being equal opportunity in education and educational equity.

As indicated above, this country's government, one after the other, pledged to use the education system to drive social and economic progress. As part of its decolonising pledges, the government aimed to reduce inequality of educational opportunity so as to increase socio-economic mobility especially among the working classes. In other words, the clarion call was to democratise the educational system in order to serve the purpose of educational equity. As the international literature indicates, however, this is a complex challenge.

The role of the education system in a democracy has always attracted much research and debate especially since it is expected to facilitate socio-economic mobility and instil the principles required for supporting a democratic society. Given the direct effects from education upon the welfare of the individual, family and society at large, such debates often pushed the issues into the political arena.[1]

Some studies focus on broad social indicators of good or bad schooling. Others, more precisely, emphasise the dysfunctional relationships between a capitalist-driven social stratification system and educational equity. The tangled pursuit of definitions for 'equality' and 'equity' also forms part of the content in later publications.

## EDUCATION: AGENCY FOR CHANGE OR VICTIM OF SOCIAL STRATIFICATION

The spirited discussion in these early debates ranged from the functional value of education for the society, its misfit for the labour market, the education system as an active agency for creating social class divisions to its being a perpetrator of an exploitative, capitalist system.

Citing a range of related studies, Bowles and Gintis (1976) and Martin Carnoy (1974) were among the early ones who viewed the educational system in America especially as almost helpless in changing society and, worse yet, in creating equality of educational opportunity. In their view, schooling is a prisoner of the capitalist society. Bowles and Gintis claimed: *'The educational system does not add to or subtract from the overall degree of inequality and repressive personal development. Rather it is best understood as an institution which serves to perpetuate the social relationships of economic life through which these patterns are set, by facilitating a smooth integration of youth into the labour force.'*[2]

Arguing that a capitalist-driven education system helps legitimise inequality, they continued: '*Beneath the façade of meritocracy lies the reality of an educational system geared toward the reproduction of economic relations only partially explicable in terms of technical requirements and efficiency standards... The yardstick of the educational meritocracy – test scores – contributes surprisingly little to individual economic success. The educational meritocracy is largely symbolic.*'[3] In their view, meritocracy in the education system masks and preserves inequality and inequity.

Bowles and Gintis' views, however, have been criticised on several grounds, such as, having little evidence, exaggerating the correspondence between work and education and ignoring the formal school curriculum. In fact, one critic, Paul Willis, produced data to show that, contrary to Bowles and Gintis' view, working class youth are not easily absorbed into the middle class, capitalist culture of the school.[4] They seek and occupy other alternatives.

The anti-capitalist commentaries not only came *before* the collapse of communism in Russia and some parts of Eastern Europe, but they failed to show the different ways in which an education system could service the economy in a democratic society and without having status differentiations in both educational attainment and occupations. Moreso, they needed to show how their version of an education system could effectively satisfy the criterion of educational equity in particular, that is, how to uplift the 'disadvantaged' groups into a place of equal advantage within a supply and demand system. In 2011, about forty years after their widely-read critique, Bowles and Gintis softened their position.

In their new Preface to a revised edition, they contritely stated: '*We are (now) more convinced that reforms of capitalism may be the most likely way to pursue the objectives that we embraced at the outset.*'[5] Of course, they still held onto their original principles such as '*a system of democratically run and employee-owned enterprise coordinated by both competitive markets and government policies.*'[6] It is in the implementation that the reservations arise.

On the other hand, what Willis, in particular, did not quite explain is how else would 'non-absorption' of working class youth into the middle class culture of the school produce socio-economic mobility which is the central argument for 'democratising' education.

Until the society becomes 'socialist,' what else do 'working class' youth do if they do not compete in such 'middle class culture' schools? Not all schools are 'middle class.' Public schools in urban areas, for example, have been criticised for a 'poverty culture,' low academic attainment and depressed socio-economic mobility. It is one of the most severe challenges of the times to get the education system unlocked from the stratification system in the wider society. The solution stops at seeking to achieve equality of opportunity and educational equity as far as practical – and to serve 'the stratified job market.'

In any case, in this country, and the Caribbean as a whole, being in school today, especially in a 'good' grammar school, is stoutly accepted as an all-embracing, legitimate passage to 'a better life.' It is the nirvana of the country and the Caribbean. This 'upward bias' ethos produces a challenge for any increase in providing technical and vocational training, a provision which unfortunately still carries lower public regard and value than the grammar-type stream, especially when such grammar stream is connected to the 'traditional professions.' The class-driven inequity is further implicated by the fact that the government-managed secondary schools also offer grammar-type subjects but with relatively low success rates.

In this context, the question is not merely whether the education system is serving capitalism or not. It is moreso, the extent to which social equity is not effectively achieved and what to do with the many who do not make it into the 'good' schools and subsequently get stuck or drift into working class jobs and incivility.

In other words, this is the extent to which the class-based stratification system and poverty are perpetuated. Getting into a 'good grammar-type school,' competitive as it is, remains a highly prized aspiration in this post-colonial culture. Political independence came, it is argued, but the colonial values in education have continued.

## MODERATE REFORMS, NOT RADICAL CHANGE

Hence, post-colonial policies in this country and the Caribbean for that matter are much more politically palatable, more publicly acceptable, to moderate, piece-meal reforms rather than radical change. Caribbean societies are fundamentally capitalist. And mainly through mass media, consumerism and the education system, the respective populations have by and large assimilated the values of capitalism. The few (Grenada, Jamaica, and Guyana) that attempted a socialist direction have either given up or have been overtaken by capitalism's first cousin – the publicly-accepted free market economy.

Critical protests against 'the education system serving capitalism' will not find much traction among the local population at present. Even inequality in education will earn mild rebuke. So too will educational inequity, even when politically-driven in our multi-racial societies. There is in this society a deeply-rooted view that merit by examination is fair, and that those who pass deserve to pass and that those who fail deserve to fail. Hopes to join the elite helps keep educational inequality alive.

Educational philosophy in this society has not as yet fully absorbed notions of distributive justice or the pernicious effects of socio-economic disadvantages upon educational opportunity. Getting into or hoping to get into a prestige school is so burning and widespread a collective desire, that it helps neutralise any possible revolt. Prestige schools, in the public mind, have earned legitimacy; they 'worked' for it.

## THE OPIUM OF CAPITALISM

It is like the opium of capitalism itself. The 'good life' is just around the corner. Work hard and be patient – quite a stabilizing principle. 'Education is the only passport out of poverty and towards a better life,' repeatedly acclaimed the country's former Prime Minister. The data presented, however, cast a shadow over such promises. Further, as an example, the 'small supply and big demand for places' in the prestige school system in the country leads to a variety of indirect and clandestine routes by parents to get their children inside. The 'prestige' school syndrome breeds corruption.

Such behaviours help create elitism by the rich and the 'well-contacted' on one hand, and filtered disadvantages for the poor and marginalised. It is therefore not surprising that debates about equality of educational opportunity got sharply linked to debates about the social class structure and the efficiency of democratic societies themselves.[7]

Notwithstanding wide public acceptance of middle class and grammar-type schools today, this country, with free tertiary education, is experiencing increasing amounts of secondary school and university graduates in the face of rather constricted labour markets. It is therefore likely that the relationship between the education system and working class mobility would suffer even more.[8]

While the education system generally provides academic and technical skills, the lingering challenge has been its role in character building. In this regard, Pitirim Sorokin in his book, *Social and Cultural Mobility*, stated:

> The education system is pretty impotent in character education...With an increase in education, suicides increase, crimes do not show any sign of decrease and mental diseases increase also. Social unrest grows. He added: Maybe education is not responsible for all this; but it is evident that the efficiency of education is limited and warns us not to trust too much of it.[9]

## LIMITS OF THE EDUCATION SYSTEM

Sorokin's view still resonates since it helps remind us of the fundamental question: What are the limits of the educational system? As an open system, taking in children from all walks of life, from varying family backgrounds, with varieties of attitudes, aptitudes and interests, with schools lodged in a variety of communities, how much could or should the school in a democratic society as ours do on its own? More precisely, how far could a government go to regulate family life? How much can an education system do, even with equality of opportunity?

The related challenge for socio-economic mobility through the education system came quite early from John Dewey when he said:

> It is the office of the school environment...to see to it that each individual gets an opportunity to escape from the limitations of the social group in which he was born, and to come into living contact with a broader environment.[10]

Such 'contact' should be more than just 'physical.' It should be an escape from the limitations of poverty and deprived opportunities as well. To what extent could the education system achieve this?

At present, this question has sharpened resonance since the rise of youth crime and delinquency is being connected to those students who leave certain types of secondary schools, especially the low-performing ones. Several studies have found that while the Denominational (government-assisted) Secondary Schools here produced significantly higher proportion of high-performing students and low rates of delinquency, the government-type schools showed the converse, that is, low proportion of high-performing students and high proportion of student violence and delinquency.[11]

In this country, whatever scepticism exists over the role of education in improving society, such scepticism is overwhelmed by the great hope and value which are formally placed on education as both mobiliser and equalizer, even for strengthening our democracy.[12]

The increases in crime, health problems and widespread institutional inefficiencies do attract public concern in this country but not yet to the extent of seriously connecting them to the value, objectives and efficiency of the increasingly expensive and expanding education system in the country. The lessons from the experiences of other countries do not attract much attention in this country.[13]

## MERIT OR ELITISM?

The debate over the education system in the United States was not as strident as that in Britain since in the case of the latter, the elitist, aristocratic nature of its school system was more deeply embedded. Hence, when attempts were made in Britain during the 1960s and 1970s to reform its educational system, the controversy between the 'traditionalists' and the 'progressives' became quite severe.

One side, backed up by the very conservative and well-publicised 'Black Papers,' the other side advocating widening educational opportunities so as to accommodate a wider spread of abilities and interests as found in the working class children.[14]

As the struggle for reforms proceeded slowly, Rubenstein and Stoneman, in their book, *Education for Democracy*, criticised the traditionalists by stating: *'More and more people are refusing to accept a system in which their children's lives are determined by selection at age of eleven...Secondary education has become increasingly comprehensive in character and entrance to higher education has become possible for more people.'*

They added: *'The traditionalists' position suggests that only by a system of elitist education can high standards be maintained. It is such attitudes which foster the continuance of gross disparities in our education system.'*[15]

## THE CULTURAL ENTRAPMENT: UNIVERSITY ABOVE ALL

As this country strives to move away from the well-grounded elitist-type of secondary education, it faces cultural resistance in the very strong public preference for 'grammar-type' and university education.[16] Such resistance, however, is not irrational given the society's value system. The resistance is related to occupational stratification, in that it is through the grammar-type education that students enter the prestigious and highly desired occupations such as medicine, law, engineering, accountancy, etc. Hence questions of equality of opportunity, merit and educational equity cannot ignore the deeply-rooted culture favouring grammar-type education heading for the established professions.

It is this frame of reference through which the society measures equality of educational opportunity and equity. Technical/vocational training and certification, as much as it is being pushed as a necessary developmental tool, is not yet any match for the grammar-school preference. There are significant differences in public respect for each, that is, apart from income benefits. The 'public respect' for grammar-type education and the upstream professions, however, cannot be seen as an arbitrary prejudice.

## WHY UNIVERSITY?

For example, the entry qualifications for the professional schools are relatively higher than those for the vocational/technical schools at the tertiary levels. Further, given the limited places usually available for applicants, many 'qualified' applicants do not get in. There is no such competition with the technical/vocational programmes. Also, it normally takes a much longer time to be trained and certified for the traditional professions. In this, however, as will be shown later shown, the equity issue arises when it is noted that a significant higher proportion of upper and middle class students gain entry into the professions from grammar schools. This tendency has become a cultural necessity, not a developmental strategy.

It is interesting to note Albert Rowe's comment regarding the resistance to the democratisation of education in England. He said:

> The present attempt at democratising education is now threatened by the traditionalists. What the traditionalists are in fact seeking to do is to continue to monopolise quality education and keep it firmly tied to their own class. They know only too well it is still true today as it ever was that the most important predictors of a child's success are not his intelligence but his parents' class, the type of school he goes to.[17]

Indeed, one of our objectives later is to see the extent to which 'parents' class' and 'type of school' contribute to students' success at secondary school.

# THE EQUITY CHALLENGE

This quest for educational democracy, underlined by the equality of opportunity ethic, is not so much to create a 'classless society,' but to open the doors more widely and equitably for lower and working class youth in particular to acquire an improved occupational status for both a better life which transcends their parents' and also to have a more direct role in determining the country's future. This is the equity challenge facing the educational system in this country.

As indicated earlier, a central part of the controversy over the utility of education is the social stratification system in a capitalist society. For example, dealing with 'functional and conflict theories of educational stratification,' Randall Collins, quite early, wrote: *'There is evidence to show that social origins affect educational attainment and also occupational attainment after completion of education.'*[18] This social origins-academic achievement connection is exactly the one which this country's educational plans sought to break and which now requires testing. This challenge sits at the heart of attempts to remove the plantation residuals.

Samuel Bowles, writing on 'unequal education,' stated: *'Unequal schooling reproduces the social division of labour. Children, whose parents occupy positions at the top of the occupational hierarchy, receive more years of schooling than working class children. Both the amount and the content of their education greatly facilitate their movement into positions similar to their parents.'*[19] Pointing to the difficulties in educational reform, Bowles further wrote: *'Unequal schooling has its roots in the very class structure which it serves to legitimise and reproduce. Inequalities in education are thus seen as part of the web of capitalist society, and likely to persist as long as capitalism survives.'*[20]

Adding to this criticism is Martin Carnoy who questioned the 'politically correct' view that *'the formal education system acts to offset social inequities and inefficiencies by being an objective selector of intelligent and rational individuals for the highest positions in the social, political and economic hierarchy.'*[21] He based his arguments *'from the analysis and interpretation of readily available books and documents.'*[22]

Carnoy further said: *'The imperial powers attempted, through schooling, to train the colonised for roles that suited the coloniser...As long as people thought that schooling did the things that the authorities claimed it did, it was hoped that they would not try to change the schools.'* As indicated earlier, it is this popular expectation that tends to neutralise any attempt towards radical reform of the education system in this country.

Carnoy felt that those who supported schooling as a means to socio-economic mobility '*wanted to perpetuate the myth to support the social structure unchanged.*'[23] Even though they advanced the cause for more technical and vocational training for decolonisation and a rejection of 'British-inspired grammar type education,' neither former Prime Minister Dr Williams nor the several government-commissioned education reports went as far as Carnoy. They could not afford to. There would have been a political price. Their proposals, therefore, remained mildly reformist with promises of socio-economic mobility.

In fact, critics like Bowles and Carnoy implicitly challenge promises like the ones put forward in this country's education reports. As earlier cited, through its more recent report, government expressed the view that through the educational system, there would be equality of opportunity regardless of gender, race, religion or social background, and this, with further opportunity for occupational mobility.

The first challenge now is  for an empirical test of this objective. The second challenge that faces this country's educational objectives is the transformation into vocational and technical training. If there is any significant ethnic, gender or social class disproportionality in allocating students to such technical/vocational training, perceptions about fairness and social justice would also arise, given the 'prevailing dominant value for academic training and university over technical and vocational training.'

## FAMILY OR SCHOOLING?

During the spirited debates in the sixties over equality and schooling, the U.S. Government established a high-powered Commission to examine the subject of equality of educational opportunity.[24] A major finding from the 1966 Coleman Report (as it was called), was that family background factors and peers showed a greater influence on student achievement than the school itself. The Report stated:

> Schools bring little influence to bear on a child's achievement that is independent of his background and general social context. Equality of educational opportunity through the schools must imply a strong effect of the schools that is independent of the child's immediate social environment.[25]

In other words, for students to enjoy equality of opportunity, the schools must make special effort to break through the social class or ethnic barriers. And the extent to which the schools may or may not be able to do this, to that extent would social class differences be perpetuated through the education system. Such intervention is in essence the pursuit of educational equity.

For such reasons, and moreso with recent evidence, the view earlier posed by Basil Bernstein in an article, 'Education Cannot Compensate for Society,'[26] becomes relevant again. Such views pessimistically argue that the school will be a 'reflection of the society' rather than having the capability to change it. That is, for example, as long as the society is social-class driven, the schools also will inevitably reflect social-class biases.

Views like those of Bowles, Carnoy and Bernstein sharply criticised the tradition of having schools for the job market as advanced by the functionalists much earlier, and even in the policies of this country. For example, in the seminal paper by Davis and Moore[27] and later by Talcott Parsons,[28] such critics further add that wherever the schools seek to provide for the job market, they merely sustain the social class discrimination existing in 'capitalist society.'

Also referring to social class perpetuation, Bourdieu and Passeron argued that the low mobility rate for working class students is more the fault of the middle class bias in the education system and not 'working class students or their culture.'[29] Taking a similar class conflict position, Raymond Boudon explained that since low social class students start from a further distance behind, upper and middle class students would naturally and logically do better in the schools.[30] Boudon presents two ways out of the stratification-locked education system. First, is for the schools to provide a common curriculum for all students and within a common period of study. The second is to have economic equality and the abolishment of social stratification. He also recognised the high improbability of either happening. We agree.

Apart from such sociologically-driven arguments though, there is a social psychological view which identifies the process of value assimilation by low social class youth, values which find discomfort or irrelevance in the middle-class school environment.[31] It is suggested that working class youth should develop psychological 'strategies,' for example, 'delay gratification and personal sacrifice' to escape their working class positions and succeed in middle-class schools.

Coleman, however, noting the middle-class culture of the school, proposed that for working class students to enjoy mobility, the schools have an obligation to over-ride entry deficits and raise the achievement levels of such students.[32] Again, this proposed intervention, he suggested, is what will help achieve educational equity – the attainment of reasonable proportionality among the social groups.

The social psychological combination of personal effort with school quality therefore is expected to facilitate school achievement. If both variables fall on the positive side, high academic achievement and upward mobility become more likely, especially for low social class students. To emphasise, personal effort can be adversely affected by destitute living conditions, parental deficits, etc., and worse yet, if the culture of the school is captured by low expectations and low academic achievement.[33] Such are the barriers which have to be overcome if the quality of educational output must achieve equitable proportions across ethnic, gender and social class groups in the society. In other words, educational equity.

The fiercely anti-establishment views of Bowles and Carnoy, though intellectually attractive, present serious problems for policy makers, especially those in post-colonial, multi-racial societies as ours. While identifying the school as 'a class-ridden agency' perpetually captured by the social class stratification from the larger society, they, like Boudon, provided no workable way to get rid of class divisions.

Neither did they consider the extent to which social differentiation of different kinds or degree would naturally arise among people in organisations. Social differentiation is a constant among people, as a vacuum that must be filled. It is the iron law of hierarchy. Hence, the need for transparent criteria and equality of opportunity in the first place.

Equity is an important part of social reconstruction, that is, for example, applying remedial interventions to lift up the disadvantaged into a proportion that is fair and reasonable to their efforts. This is more acceptable to Caribbean people and their governments though this principle has come under repeated criticisms for being insensitive to the actual needs, interests and perspectives of the historically excluded groups, that is, in determining what 'disadvantages' should be compensated for and in determining what educational opportunities are worth wanting.[34]

This country's government, of whichever party, emphatically sees the education system as a vehicle for not only economic transformation but also for democratising the system through socio-economic mobility, and primarily to working class advantage. Hence, it is therefore important to examine, as this study does, the extent to which the secondary school system provides equality of opportunity and academic attainment especially for those who need it most.[35]

To the extent that there are significant variations in educational outcomes among the different ethnic, social class or gender groupings, to that extent would the question of inequity arise. Equity is a matter of effort, proportionality and fairness. The debate over schooling, equality of educational opportunity, merit and educational equity has been lengthy, fast and furious. Interpretations shift according to the ideological framework in which the argument – pro or con – is lodged.

Bowles, Gintis and Carnoy, for example, argue that within the current capitalist systems, genuine equality of educational opportunity and equity are quite difficult, if not virtually impossible. The reforms they recommend are radical and, in our view, will not attract the popular support policy-makers require. Carnoy described the education system as 'cultural imperialism.' Jencks, like Bowles and Gintis, saw the education system and its promises as serving to 'legitimise inequality.' Passing examinations are a façade of meritocracy, they implied.

Between these attacks, there are some moderates. Halsey, for example, saw hope but with reforms. He proposed that both the structural conditions of resources as well as personal attributes of students do contribute to achievement outcomes – positively or negatively. He also pointed to the several external social forces which adversely affect working class children, thus also affecting school performance.[36] The reforms, he noted, 'will require political leadership with the will to go beyond the confines of traditional liberal assumptions.'[37]

# EDUCATION FOR SOCIAL STATUS

A critical aspect of this debate is the connection between schooling and subsequent occupational status. Noting the egalitarian concerns about the differential rewards given to different positions, and the meritocratic emphasis on the recruitment process, Parkin explained the several reasons for such seeming inequality. He referred to marketable expertise, family contacts, the manipulation of job scarcity and the neutralising roles of aspirations and the sharp differences between school types.[38] In this, 'the equalization of rewards is connected to the equalization of opportunities to compete for the most privileged positions.'[39]

Both operate in the social stratification system, he said. In this country, government's policies and the education system reside within functionalism, the kind that uses the school as a feeder for jobs, bearing different values and rewards. Its dual system of education – Denominational Assisted vs Government Schools – has produced bottlenecks for a disproportionate amount of students from poor, working class background. The point is that firstly, this country, independent since 1962, remains 'colonial' in several ways – with its education, political and legal systems still paralysed with inefficient and ineffective structures.[40]

Secondly, the economic system is fundamentally of state-capitalism with government having massive controls over employment and almost one hundred state corporations and related public bodies. As Blau and Duncan stated quite early:

> The occupational structure in modern industrial society not only constitutes an important foundation for the main dimensions of social stratification but also serves as the connecting link between different institutions and spheres of life and therein lies its great significance.'[41]

As a political institution, the state here has extensive control over the lives of its citizens and the job opportunities available.

The fact that this country is still seeking to unfold itself from colonialism, with the compelling necessity to compete for jobs in a surplus-labour market, the education system will remain a loyal, strangled servant of the rigid social stratification system with no significant change in sight, all of which bring to mind Beckford's notion of the dependence-driven plantation economy.

The Utopian proposal forwarded by Jencks is to *'equalize the value employers place on different employees.'* He added: *'This means that if we want to equalize the status of different occupations, we will have to move away from a competitive economy towards a more highly regulated system in which equality is an explicit objective of public policy.'*[42] This proposition, obviously designed for social equity, will find no kind of traction in this society. This again suggests how such 'solutions' are impossible to implement in a democracy.

The educational system here, heavily centralized, remains under elitist pressures for grammar-type education and deeply embedded aspirations for the traditional professions. As many other countries have learnt, free secondary or even tertiary education, when unscreened, does not necessarily lead to improved socio-economic mobility. That is one result of treating unequals equally.

The government 'freeness' is given to those who already have as well as those in need. Treating unequals equally maintains inequality. The country's social stratification system is doomed to remain static for a long time – and especially fuelled by the cycle of poverty and opportunity deprivation which flows from differential secondary school enrolment.

## NOTES

1.   See e.g.,'Equal Educational Opportunity', Harvard Educational Review. 1968; B.M. Sheal, 'Schooling and Its Antecedens'. 1976 (46) No. 4.pp. 463-526: E. Durkheim. 1947; 1961; A.H. Halsey, J. Floud, C.A. Anderson (Eds.).'Education, Economy and Society'.1965; J. Dewey.'Democracy and Education'. 1953; I. Illich.'Deschooling Society'. 1973; A.H. Halsey, A. Heath and J.M. Ridge,'Origins and Destinations'. 1980; S. Bowlers and H. Gintis 'Schooling in Capitalist America'. 1976; J. Douglas,'The Home and the School'.1964; P. Bourdieu and J. Passeron,'Reproduction in Education'.1977; R. Boudon, 'Education, Opportunity and Social Inequality'. 1974; Swann, Lord, 'Education for All'. 1985; G. Marshall and A. Swift, 'Social Class and Social Justice'. 1999.

Some are more 'radical' than others, for example, C. Jencks, Inequality: 'A Reassessment of the Effects of Family and Schooling in America'. 1975; J. Karabel and A. Halsey. (Eds.) 'Power and Ideology in Education'.1977;

B. Simon and W. Taylor, 'Education in the Eighties: The Central Issues'. 1981; B. Russell, 'Education and the Social Order'. 1977; J. Ford, 'Social Class and the Comprehensive School'. 1969; M. Carnoy,'Education as Cultural Imperialism'.1974; I. Morrish,'The Sociology of Education'. 1976; P. Figueroa and G. Persaud, *Sociology of Education: A Caribbean Reader*.1976; H. Ladd and E. Fiske,'Class Matters, Why Won't We Admit It?'*New York Times*. Dec 11, 2011; 'Affirmative Action: Harvard Under Fire'. *The Economist*, Nov. 25, 2014; 'Creative Destruction'.*The Economist*. June 28, 2014; 'Equity, The Glossary of Educational Reform'. May 18, 2015; Performance-based Assessment and Educational Equity. *Harvard Educational Review*. April, 1994. Vol. 64, No. 1, pp. 5-31; 'Equity and Quality in Education'. OECD. Feb 9, 2012; W. Hutmacher, D. Cochrane, and N. Bottani. (Eds.) *In Pursuit of Equity in Education*. Springer Publishing. 2001; R. Ferguson, *Toward Excellence in Education: An Emerging Vision for Closing the Achievement Gap*. Harvard Education Publishing. 2008; J. Kozol, *The Shaming of America: The Restoration of Apartheid Schooling in America*. Random House Publishing. 2005;'Educational Opportunity', Harvard Educational Review. 1968; B.M. Sheal,*Schooling and Its Antecedents*. 1976 (46) No. 4, pp. 463-526; E. Durkheim, 1947; 1961; A.H. Halsey, J. Floud, C.A. Anderson (Eds.) Education.

2. S. Bowlers and H. Gintis, *Schooling in Capitalist America*. London: Routledge and Kegan Paul. 1976.p.11.

3. Ibid. p. 103

4. P. Willis, 'Youth Unemployment: A New Social State'. In New Society. March 29, 1984.

5. *Schooling in Capitalist America*. Chicago: Haymarket Books. 2011. p.xi.

6. Ibid. p. xi.

7. See e.g.,R. Bendix and M. Lipset (Ed.),*Class, Status and Power*. (2nd ed.) New York: Macmillan. 1966. K. Eder,*The New Politics of Class*. London: Sage Publications. 1996.

8. Both government and educators have begun to express concerns about the 'graduate glut.'

9. P. Sorokin, *Social and Cultural Mobility*. New York: The Free Press. 1964. p. 502.

10. J. Dewey, *Democracy and Education*. New York: The Free Press. 1966. p.20.

11. See e.g., R. Deosaran, 'Benchmarking Violence and Delinquency in the Secondary School'. Ministry of Education. 2004, 2006

12. See e.g., Ministry of Education. *Education Plan 1968-83*; *Education for All*. 2005; Report of National Task Force in Education. 1993.

13. For example, the social class differentials in new modern secondary schools or the comprehensives.

14. A series of papers advocating the  retention of purely grammar-type and elitist schooling and attacking the intended absorption of more working class children into formal education and the upgrading of the modern-secondary schools

15. D. Rubenstein and C. Stoneman, *Education for Democracy*. Middlesex: Penguin Books. 1972. pp. 8-11.

16. This is especially seen in the first choices of both parents and students for secondary school entrance. Their first choice is for the grammar-type schools, mainly the government-assisted, denominational schools. The irony for educational equity is that such professional training is free, government subsidized for all.

17. A. Rowe, 'Human Beings, Class and Education'. In D. Rubenstein and C. Stoneman, *Education for Democracy*. Middlesex: Penguin Books. 1972. pp. 18-19.

18. American Sociological Review. 1971.

19. 'Review of Radical Political Economics'. 1971.

20. Ibid.

21. 'Education as Cultural Imperialism'. 1974.

22. Ibid. p. 3.

23. Ibid. p. 3.

24. J. Coleman, *Equality of Educational Opportunity*. Washington, D.C.: U.S. Government Printing Office. 1966. p. 325.

25. Ibid, p. 325.

26. *New Society*. 1970.pp. 344-7.

27. *Some Principles of Stratification*. 1953.

28. *Structure and Process in Modern Society*. 1960.

29. P. Bourdien and J.Passeron, *Reproduction in Education, Society and Culture*. London: Sage. 1977.

30. R. Boudon, *Education, Opportunity and Social Inequality*. New York: John Wiley and Sons. 1974.

31. See e.g., Basil Bernstein, *Social Class, Codes and Control*. 1971.

32. *The Concept of Equality of Opportunity*. 1968.

33. This line of conceptualisation is drawn from the basic social psychological formula, $B = f(\text{person and environment})$. That is, the interactionist perspective.

34. See e.g.,K. Rowe, *Understanding Equal Educational Opportunity*. New York: Columbia University. 1997. p. 4. Also, M. Carnoy who saw compensatory education as 'having low probability of success' within the existing socio-economic framework. In *Sociology of Education: A Caribbean Reader* (P. Figueroa and G. Persad. Eds.). pp.265-266.

35.  Opportunity means access, attainment means the level achieved.
36.  A. Halsey, 'Sociology and the Equality Debate'. *Oxford Review of Education*. 1975. vol. 1(1). pp. 9-23.
37.  Ibid. p. 15.
38.  F. Parkin, *Class Inequality and the Political Order*. London: MacGibbon and Kee Ltd. 1971. pp. 13-14.
39.  Ibid. p.13.
40.  A wide public discussion on the differences between functionalism and social conflict theories, between free-market capitalism and socialism will foster an understanding of the merits and demerits of the country's educational system. See e.g.,A. Giddens,*Capitalism and Modern Social Theory*. London: Cambridge University Press. 1971;J. Gurley, *Challenges to Capitalism*. San Francisco Book Company. 1976; M. Weber,*The Protestant Ethic and the Spirit of Capitalism (trans)*. New York: Charles Scribner's Sons. 1958. Also J. Lopreato and L. Hazelrigg (Eds.),*Class, Conflict and Mobility*. London: Chandler Publishing Co. 1972;J. Gray,'From Policy to Practice: Some Problems and Paradoxes in Egalitarian Reform. Education in the Eighties: Central Issues'. In B. Simon and W. Taylor (Eds.), London:  Batsford Academic and Educational Ltd. 1981. pp. 77-91;R. Brosio,*A Radical Democratic Critique of Capitalist Education*. New York: Peter Lang Publishing Co. 1994. esp. pp. 263-297, 445-620.
41.  P. Blauand O. Duncan, *The American Occupational Structure*. New York: John Wiley. 1967. p. 7.
42.  C. Jencks et al, *Inequality, a Reassessment of the Effects of Schooling in America*. New York: Basic Books. 1972. p.199. The proposals by Carnoy to change the discriminatory aspects of social stratification in order to make the education system more equitable are similarly difficult to implement in this country, or in any capitalist-embedded society for that matter. The versatility of capitalism has become well noted.

# CHAPTER SIX
# The Cultural Trap: Grammar vs Vocational

*Dare the School Build a New Social Order?*

G. Counts, 1978

*When we confine the education of those who work with their hands to a few years of schooling for the most part to acquiring the use of rudimentary symbols at the expense of training in science, literature and history, we fail to prepare the minds of workers to take advantage of this (educational) opportunity.*

John Dewey, Democracy and Education, 1916

## A POST COLONIAL CHALLENGE: PERSISTENCE OF THE COLONIAL MENTALITY

Any attempt to transform the education system will also have to change certain values about education itself and in particular, the value attached to grammar-type education and the traditional professions over technical and vocational training. The extent to which this change occurs, to that extent would the society become decolonised. Economic diversification would help reduce some of the elitism of colonialism. This chapter therefore takes us further inside the education system.

In fact, since Trinidad & Tobago and other Caribbean states became politically independent in the 1960s and onwards, pressures mounted for using the education system to build an industrial and manufacturing base rather than sticking purely to the 'colonial British grammar-type education.' It was and still is a challenge to diversify the educational system and the economy. It was also the still elusive challenge to change the value system in which grammar-school graduates attract greater public respect than graduates from technical and vocational schools. This value difference is a significant feature of our educational culture. It helps trigger inequality and inequity since it grows largely from the type of secondary school a person attends. Pointing to the deficits in the education system on July 11, 2015, the country's President, Anthony Carmona, said that the time has come for 'an overhaul of the education system,'

Soon after, on December 20, 2015, Head of the Catholic Church. Archbishop Joseph Harris, said: 'Trinidad and Tobago is going down a slippery slope. We here have not yet understood, or do not yet have the will to have a system of education which takes the learning styles and capability of students seriously.' He added: 'We have concentrated to a large extent on grammar school type of person.' He continued:

> 'As a result, teenagers were leaving school with a few passes, half educated, semi-literate and with no real employment prospects. We are then surprised when we are in trouble when in truth and in fact our education system has not helped us. It has failed.'[1]

When we asked 2,800 Form One students (of all races and social classes) what kind of education they wished after secondary school, 80% chose university education. This large proportion came from all types of secondary schools, both Denominational-Assisted and Government Schools.[2] Of course, relatively few will eventually make it to university.

Only about five percent expressed aspirations for technical/vocational training. In addition, the failure rate for those taking such training has been 'quite disturbing.' In the Caribbean Vocational Qualifications (CVQ) results for 2009 and 2010, for example, the failure rates (no full certificates) were 26% of 1,314 students and 28% of 1,718 students, respectively.[3] Later years have shown similar results.

Tackling this dilemma, the late economist and former Secretary-General of the Caribbean Community (CARICOM), William Demas, as far back as 1973 stated:

> There is need for greater emphasis on technical and vocational training. This does not mean that at the secondary level general education should be abolished and so-called practical subjects take its place completely.[4]

The challenge was more than mere curriculum structure. It was a pivotal question of values by the clients.

## DECOLONISATION BY EDUCATION

In seeking such a decolonised balance between grammar and vocational/technical education within the proposed transformation in education, the dilemma arose. For example, in July 1957, before Trinidad & Tobago gained independence in 1962, the People's National Movement (PNM) government appointed a Committee on General Education with the following terms of reference: *'To consider the operation of the educational system of the country and make recommendations on future policy related to the curriculum, the improvement of academic and other standards, and the integration of the diverse elements which comprise our population.'*

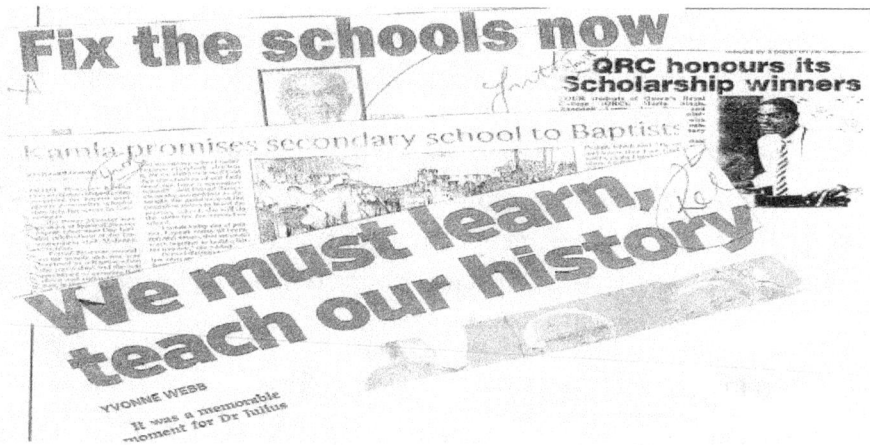

The Committee recommended 'technical and vocational skills to drive the country's post-independence industrialising and manufacturing economy.'[5] The Committee also questioned the fairness of measuring 11-plus students so early so as to allocate them into different types of secondary schools. It further expressed some concern over the prevailing dominant value for 'grammar-type education.'[6] That preference still exists today.

The Committee further agreed that:

> the normal type of secondary school should be the Comprehensive (academic and technical), provided (a) that where the existing school population warrants it, there should be separate grammar and modern schools and (b) that there should be a re-evaluation and re-organisation of the existing grammar schools.[7]

This push for technical and vocational training is important here for two reasons, both of which are relevant to the focus o educational inquality. One is that such training seemed necessary to improve the industrialisation thrust in the newly-independent country. Two, without identifying it in these early days, the authorities did not consider any possible gender, social class or ethnic differentiations that may result from mounting such technical and vocational training. However, such differentiations eventually emerged, producing implications for social and educational equity.

It might very well be that in the haste to expand and diversify the formerly colonial educational system, it was expected that the issues of social class and ethnic inequities would work themselves out. They actually did not. In fact, a purpose of the Education Committee Report in 1959 was to use the education system to achieve 'the integration of the diverse elements which comprise the population' as a means of helping to create 'one nation.' It will be useful now to test the extent to which this 1959 objective has been achieved up to 2015.

Later in 1961, the year before independence, the government appointed another committee, a Vocational and Training Committee, which recommended the establishment of the Chaguaramas Trade School. Part of the strategy was to take up the post-primary school-leavers into this Trade School.[8] A National Training Agency came soon after.

## UNIVERSITY VALUES DOMINATE

All these policies and structures for technical/vocational training, as relevant as their purpose was and still is, face a subversive value system, that is, the persistent preference by the population at large for grammar-type schools that pave the way towards the traditional professions. And that mainly starts from the brightest getting into university from a high-performing secondary school, 'brightest' meaning making high marks, for example, at the SEA in primary school, then at CSEC and CAPE at secondary school.[9]

As far back as 1973, a government National Task Force on Youth, commenting on the undesirable attitudes of youth to work, concluded that a contributory factor has been 'the open bias of many adults against 'blue-collar' or 'agricultural' jobs as opposed to 'white collar' jobs.'[10]

The choice of technical/vocational training was and is still largely seen as a default route, that is for those who are 'not interested,' do not have the 'aptitude' for grammar-type schooling or who require 'a second chance.' Such mental screening implicitly bows to the prevailing value system. The government's establishment of the Junior Secondary, Composite and Comprehensive Schools in the 1970s and 1980s was a direct attempt to help neutralize this value distinction and capture natural ability differences early.

However, the Denominational Assisted Schools still remained as traditional grammar-type schools to which parents and children remained strongly attracted. The strongly-financed offer by government to bring these Denominational Schools into the new multi-tiered system was not accepted. A 'nationalized' education system attracted strong denominational apprehensions. So while expansive school building and expensive technical equipment took place, the value-backed status quo held on.[11]

## THE EQUALITY DILEMMA

On the haunting challenge of giving equal value between academic and technical education, the government 1968-83 Education Plan stated:

> The country could not afford to perpetuate the peculiar value judgements associated with discriminating between academic and technical education.'[12]

From the 1959 Maurice Report to this 1968-83 Education Plan, the accentuation for vocational and technical education increased so as to make it attractive to all students, including those with high academic ability. But the prevailing value for grammar school education still dominated.

However, the Draft Education Plan persisted in its proposals for increased technical/vocation training and the appropriate training for teachers. Using the UNESCO-driven four-point plan for including both academic and technical courses in the senior comprehensive schools, the Education Plan viewed this *'as a socially necessary measure designed to give to technical education and the persons who pursue technical courses a more meaningful and central place in the educational system.'*[13] The Plan then concluded: *'We cannot afford to perpetuate the peculiar value judgments associated with both academic and technical education.'*[14]

Since then, several other educational reports and plans sought to pave the way for utilizing technical and vocational programmes for both curriculum and economic diversification. A subsequent National Task Force in Education, for example, proposed upscaling teacher training in technical/vocational by offering a certificate, then a B.Sc. in technical/vocational subjects.[15]

But throughout the years, the public value attached to grammar-type education and the professional routes it triggered remained quite cherished and constant. Such stubborn value persistence held serious implications for government's educational policies while putting continued stress upon the severe competition for the high-performing Denominational Assisted Schools and the Concordat system itself. The competition and consequences arising from this high value for university contribute immensely to the socio-economic inequality in the society.

Further, to help consolidate the value-preference for grammar-type courses, it became widely known that students taking technical/vocational courses had unacceptably high failure rates. The dominance of grammar school values persisted largely because of their driving force towards high occupational status and public respect.

The challenge therefore became three-fold:

1. How to create a viable workforce of technical/vocational graduates to help drive the country's industrial and diversification thrust.

2. How to improve the public respect and public value given to technical/vocational training compared to grammar-type programmes, so as to help make it an attractive training stream.

3. How to create programmes to attract those students whose aptitudes did not suit the grammar-type stream.

To these ends, a new Ministry of Science, Technology and Tertiary Education was created[16]. This ministry (name changed to Ministry of Tertiary Education and Skills Training –TEST) regularly developed lists of technical and vocational courses, a major objective being improving youth employment and serving the industrialized sectors of the country.[17] This raised another challenge – labour absorption.

## VOCATIONAL TRAINING: CINDERELLA OF THE SYSTEM

In a revised version of its technical and vocational objectives, this Ministry ambitiously stated that its programmes must be 'driven by the needs of the labour market,' and that its technical/vocational programmes 'will be strengthened as part of a seamless system to allow for alternative pathways to further and higher education.'[18]

Even this subsidized tuition and a spread of choices in technical/vocational offerings, the feverish competition, through the SEA and the high-profile celebration of secondary school scholarships, kept the public value of vocational training in its subordinate place, useful but with grammar-type education still of higher regard. In this sense, the decolonization ambitions for the education system remained a work in progress. This is understandable since, as indicated earlier, the public respect given to the traditional professions still appears unbreakable. This, of course, is an educational challenge in other parts of the world, especially in developing countries.

Pushing its technical/vocational case forward, the Ministry of Tertiary Education stated:

> The Caribbean Vocational Qualification (CVQ) is an inclusive educational initiative that will provide all secondary school students with opportunities to acquire entry-level occupational skills at Level 1.

It further stated:

> The expansion of the CVQ programme will guarantee the following: it will improve employability, that all secondary school students exit secondary schools with evidence of at least a CVQ Regionally-approved Occupational Standard.[19]

The ministry expressed plans '*to expand the technical/vocational Programs into all secondary schools.*'[20]

This expansion within secondary schools was contrary to the advice given by the government Task Force on Technical and Vocational Training. After reviewing the high failure rates in technical/vocational training programmes, the Inter-American Development Bank (IDB) also advised that such programmes be offered at post-secondary level.[21] The technical/vocational students lacked the basic educational foundation. The failure rate was quite high. For example, in 2009, 74% of those writing the examination failed to get a full certificate. In 2010, 72% failed to get a full certificate. The Task Force, too, had recommended having these programmes after secondary schooling. And so, technical/vocational training remained the Cinderella of the education system.

## YOUTH RESOURCES WASTED

The problem of equality of opportunity for technical/vocational training does not arise in the same way that equality of opportunity arises for entry into the high-performing secondary schools and university. In fact, there is at present no competition for technical/vocational education. Further, the students who enter such training are largely those who 'failed,' through the SEA 'merit' examination, to make it into high-performing grammar schools.

Their initial preference, too, was largely for grammar school and university, a dominant public value. This appears as cultural entrapment. Hence, our frame of reference for examining equality of educational opportunity and especially equity is on both grammar-type schooling and university entry. That is where the tensions arise for public policy, inequality and inequity.

Two challenges arise: (1) How to break the cultural value for grammar-type schooling, and make technical/vocational training more attractive and of greater public regard. (2) What to do with so many students who, in spite of having grammar-type abilities, do not make into high-performing grammar-type schools. The extent to which these two challenges remain without effective and ameliorative policy responses will make the government appear guilty of wasting its youthful human resources.

## NOTES

1.   Reported in *Guardian*, July 11, 2015, p A10. Archbishop's comments in *Guardian*, December 20, 2015, p. A7.
2.   R. Deosaran, 'Benchmarking School Violence and Delinquency'. 2004.
3.   Ministry of Education. Curriculum Development and Education Planning Division, 2010.
4.   Caribbean Contact. September 1973. p. 5.
5.   Education Report of 1959 of Committee on General Education. 1959. pp.180–190
6.   Ibid. pp. 180–190.
7.   Ibid. p. 67.
8.   Report of Vocational Training Committee. Government Printery. 1961.
9.   Secondary Entrance Examination (SEA), Caribbean Secondary Examination Certificate (CSEC), Caribbean Advanced Proficiency Examination (CAPE).
10.  National Task Force on Youth (Second Interim Report), Prime Minister's Office. 1973. The first interim report was laid in Parliament in January 3, 1972. Many of its recommendations focused on vocational training, apprenticeships, etc.
11.  It is argued that this value contest between grammar and technical/vocational training also rests on the fact that the traditional professions generally require more years of study. This, at least indirectly, brings us back to the public perception of intellectual competence and without giving value to the usefulness of technical/vocational training

as a means of economic diversification and even decolonizing the educational system.

12. Draft Education Plan, 1968–83. Ministry of Education. 1968. p. 33.
13. Draft Education Plan 1968–83. p. 33.
14. Ibid. p. 33.
15. National Task Force in Education. p. 48. There was also the Report of the Task Force on the Rationalisation and Coordination of Post-Secondary Technical and Vocational Training Programme. 1992. It was also here that the high failure rates were noted. pp. 152–153. See also Assessment of the Draft Education Plan 1968–83. pp. 3, 37.
16. This latter policy emerged more forcefully with the decreased emphasis on technical/vocational training in the Government Comprehensive and Composite Schools and, or more recently, the establishment of a set of specialized agencies and institutions across the country in various kinds of technical and vocational programmes, e.g., avionics, welding, metallurgy, etc., backed up by life skill courses and work force assessment centres.
17. See e.g., Policy on Tertiary Education, Technical-Vocational Education and Training, and Life-Long Learning in Trinidad and Tobago (Green Paper). Ministry of Science, Technology and Tertiary Education. Trinidad and Tobago. 2009.

    'Pathways to Living Well'. National Life Skills Programme. Ministry of Tertiary Education and Skills Training. Trinidad and Tobago. 2013.
18. Ibid. p. 5. In this revised paper (no longer a Green Paper), a policy of 'tuition-free' courses and the CVQ standard were also described.
19. Ministry of Education.Administrative Report 2010–11. p. 15.
20. Ibid. p. 3.
21. 'Access, Equity and Performance', IDB Report on Education in Four Caribbean Countries. Washington, DC: IDB Bookstores. 2002. It is also noteworthy that a large part of the country's budget goes to education – primary, secondary and tertiary. For the Ministry of Education: from $950 million in 1991 and $1.4 billion in 1996 to $4.2 billion in 2011. Overall, it was $11.2 billion in 2014–15.

# CHAPTER SEVEN
# The Politics of Education

*Democracy is a sham without a public school system   that introduces everyone to a world of ideas, values and knowledge that takes all children beyond their own narrow and private worlds.*

-William J. Reese, Public Schools and the Common Good,
Education Theory, 1988

*We ensure that every student will have the benefit of high-quality learning opportunities. Every child has an inherent right to education regardless of gender, ethnic, social, economic or religious backgrounds.*
–Ministry of Education, Strategic Plan, 2011-2015

## TOWARDS THE CONCORDAT: THE CHURCH IN POLITICS

The desire for equality of education and equity can be energized by having some understanding of the earlier 'deprivations and educational disadvantages inflicted upon the two major races' as Dr Williams indicated. As earlier discussed, during the 19[th]and early 20[th]centuries, the provision of education, of whatever kind and level, generally came quite controversially from both the church and the government. No doubt the churches, its missionaries included, saw it as their biblical duty to 'bring God' into the hearts of the slaves and then, the indentured labourers. The secular basics were peripheral.

On the other hand, the colonial government, with mixed feelings, sought to secularise the colony's educational system while expressing concern over possible proselytising of the plantation workers. In the middle were the plantation owners who were reluctant to lose their workers to the schools, even for part of the day, while also claiming that the plantation workers were 'unfit for education,' and intellectually inferior.[1]

*Newspaper clipping collage including headlines:* "Charford Court single mom celebrates as Son beats odds for SEA success", "Gopeesingh: 3,411 students suspended", "Equity in education can't work in isolation", "PM lauds political system in Arrival Day message", and a "THE EDITOR: I really do appreciate the comments about the SEA examination by TTUTA President Davanand Sinanan (Sunday Newsday). Many comments I find on target and others I believe missed the mark. I agree with his insight that the best education systems in..." with "WRITE TO: Newsday."

Naturally, tensions between church and state arose. Good intentions clashed.[2] There was also conflict between one Christian religion and another over educational control. These triangulated conflicts made the development of a coherent educational system quite difficult. There were no local powerful voices to speak for the plantation workers and to argue for their right to an education. Where some local advocacy was offered, it was merely paternalistic. That is, until the arrival of Governor Lord Harris 1846, the 1869 Keenan Report and the Missionaries.[3]

In England, the anti-slavery voices had grown while pressures for educating the East Indian indentured labourers were growing, locally and abroad. Meanwhile during the 19th and early 20th centuries, there existed for the already privileged a solidly grammar-type, elitist-driven education system in which the churches themselves participated.[4]

Notwithstanding all this, a dual system of education within the colony began to move into acceptability. Campbell stated:

> The essence of the dual system was that there were two competitive types of primary schools financed concurrently by government: government schools and denominational schools.[5]

Reviewing these early developments and the tensions over the emerging dual system, he stated:

> It was felt that the denominational schools were socially divisive and financially wasteful; that they formented religious rivalries and hardened cultural differences; promoted the spread of languages other than the English language and retarded the spread of English values and habits.[6]

These early anti-denominational views were quite similar to what Dr Williams said in 1954,[7] and to which the Catholic Archbishop, Finbar Ryan, tersely objected.

In a breakthrough example of executive power, Governor William Robinson created Ordinance 17 of 1890 which was described as the 'magna carta of the denominational system.' In this, he increased school grants, payments to teachers, improved buildings, etc. Special schools for East Indians were created. As the colony headed into the twentieth century, a few educational opportunities through competition opened for blacks.[8]

Today, the tensions still exist but for different reasons. A major source of tension is the competitive quest for equality of educational opportunity and educational equity. How did we reach here, passing over controversies and conflicts, into the compromise to establish a Concordat between the State and the Church?

## COLONIAL EDUCATION

Drawing from Campbell's work,[9] a connection between the plantation education and today's policy of 'education for all' will be briefly outlined:

1.  With the abolition of slavery in 1834, there was a move in Britain to educate the freed slaves, by philanthropists and some government officials for which an annual grant of 30,000 pounds was provided by the British government. The application of this grant was adversely affected by staff shortages, buildings and the rivalry between the Protestant and Catholic churches in the colony.

2.  Since the vast majority of the population was Catholic in Trinidad, the British government was reluctant to share the grant with the Catholic Church to build or manage schools.

3.  As the colony's new governor between 1846 and 1854, Lord Harris established several government schools out of local ward funds. In 1851, particularly, he presented his plans to form a Board of Education and an Inspector of Schools – two significant policies in the development of the island's education system.

4.  Lord Harris argued for blacks and East Indians to have improved educational opportunities from high school to the professions – but for fees.

5.  Given his apprehensions over existing religious conflicts, Lord Harris showed a preference for secular education. Naturally, the

churches raised objections. Further than this, the plantation owners were unwilling to lose their workers to schooling, expressing the view that such people were 'not fit for education.'

6.  Between 1836 and 1869, five single-sex high schools were opened in Port of Spain: St. Joseph's Convent, St. George's College, the Church of England Grammar School, the Queen's Collegiate, and St. Mary's College (1863). Three were Catholic. These schools were mainly for rich, white persons, with few non-whites. The Catholic-Protestant conflicts continued, especially between 1854–1870.

7.  The essence of the dual system of education was that there were two competitive types of primary schools financed concurrently by government: government schools and public denominational schools.

8.  It was felt that the denominational schools were socially divisive and financially wasteful; that they formented religious rivalries and hardened cultural differences; promoted the spread of languages other than the English language and retarded the spread of English values and habits.  But these opposers were not really secularists; they were Christians arguing for non-denominational schools in which they already held influence.

9.  The Education Ordinance of 1870 supported the dual system. Up to 1875, only two denominational schools qualified for state aid alongside forty-nine government schools. Under Governor Arthur Gordon, the Catholics then insisted on teaching religion in schools. They pushed for the dual system around 1860–70.

10. Governor William Robinson created Ordinance 17 of 1890 which could be regarded 'as the magna carta of denominational schools' (p.33.) As such, there were increased grants and payments to teachers, improved buildings etc.

11. By 1890, the Presbyterians created 'special schools' for Indians, but fees had to be paid with doors opened to all. At first, enrolment remained quite low.

12. Reflecting the climate of opinion at that time, several significant objections were raised regarding education for the former enslaved and plantation workers. Inspector Anderson, for example, explicitly denied any intention to promote pupils above their 'station in life.'

He defined the purpose of the ward schools as giving the common people an education in the elements of learning to make them 'industrious, contented and happy.' That is, useful for the plantation. (POSG, April 2, 1862. Report on the subject of education, 1861. Cited in Campbell, p. 69).

13. Another example: J.M. Feheney, the Port of Spain Catholic Archbishop, in his Lenten Pastoral Letter of 1883, unequivocally expounded the doctrine that the existing class structure of the colony was 'God-given' and that the aspirations of lower class children in primary schools for social mobility were unchristian (p.69).

14. College exhibition started in 1872: blacks and coloured people began penetrating the elite system of education (4 per year), mainly in law and medicine. The Civil Service exams in late 19<sup>th</sup> century opened up further opportunities for blacks at top.

15. The church still felt that education was the business of the church but the Director of Education sought to reverse this, incrementally. The dual system was regulated mainly by Ordinances 1890, 1901 and 1902 which had 'a built-in bias in favour of new denominational schools.'

16. The 1930s were turbulent times over control and funding. Ordinance 1930, for example, shifted power to make regulations from the Board of Education to the Government in Council.

17. From the late 19th century to 1960s, the tensions and power struggles over control over the dual system of education continued, with controls eventually passing from the Board of Education, then dominated by the churches in the early 20<sup>th</sup> century (1920s and 1930s) and finally to cabinet in the 1960s (p. 104).

## POLITICS AND THE CHURCH CLASH

The politics of education were significantly present as the country's dual system of education evolved, primarily between church and state with the central issues being control and funding. The eventual resolution which, somewhat restlessly, exists today is in the Concordat, essentially a sharing of rights and school control.[10]

As the multi-ethnic country headed into the 1960s, the political stage for the church-state confrontation was set. The leader of the People's National

Movement (PNM), Dr Eric Williams, had openly advocated having the country's education system centralized under government control with funding adjustments. So too did the 1959 Maurice Committee Report on General Education.[11]

As far back as 1954, Williams stated his position this way:

> I see in the denominational school a breeding ground of disunity. I see in the state school the opportunity for cultivating a spirit of nationalism among West Indian people and eradicating the racial suspicions and antagonisms growing in our midst.[12]

During his stay (1846-1854), Governor Lord Harris himself, interpreting the colony's ethnic diversity as an undesirable distraction from basic education, proposed a secular system with the church having a peripheral place. He felt that the state should also have control over the educational system with revenue drawn from local taxes. Then, like now, the church, especially the Roman Catholic, objected.

In 1960, the battle-cry for gathering the forces of the various religious groups against Williams' position came from the Roman Catholic Archbishop, the influential Count Finbar Ryan. Without mincing words and showing appreciation for the electoral power of the church, Archbishop Ryan, in a memorable sermon, said:

> While prepared to cooperate as far as possible, the Catholic Church cannot cede its ownership nor the right of direct control and management of their primary and secondary schools. The authority of the church must be safeguarded...No teacher to whom the Catholic authority objects on grounds of faith or morals shall be appointed to Catholic schools.[13]

This latter instruction eventually formed the most significant part of the 1960 Concordat. And to put political muscle into the church's position, Archbishop Ryan warned:

> Disproportionate mixing of Catholic and non-Catholic children must, as far as possible, be avoided....Catholics are roughly one third of the population. Their suffrage is no small power.

Emerging in the post-colonial era from such conditions, the government's 1968-83 Education Plan Report stated: 'A secondary school system which was born in an era of exclusivism and privilege has been changing rapidly to fit a more open system of career open to the talented' (p.37).

Indeed, the secondary school system did become more open, and still is, in terms of quantity of students entering, that is, all students had 'an equal 'opportunity' to enter a secondary school. This 'equal opportunity' arose because all students at 11+ years were allowed to write the same examination – the common entrance (CE), now the secondary entrance assessment (SEA).

Early quarrels arose about social class and ethnic bias triggered by the Concordat concessions. Staving off such allegations and noting the class-driven nature of secondary education and the role of the denominational boards, the president of a denominational board, sociologist Nasser Mustapha questioned the extent of authority which these boards really have, the Concordat notwithstanding. He said:

> It is true that they own property, make the rules and have some say in accepting 20% of their intake at the secondary school level. However, they have little control over the content of education, how it should be delivered and the values that are imparted at their institutions.[14]

However, equality and equity issues arose mainly because the proportion of students from low social class, or of African descent, for example, consistently remained under-represented in the high performing denominational secondary schools.[15]

Mustapha went further, saying:

> The system appears to be operating efficiently by providing secondary school entry to the population according to their capacity to benefit from it, but the tensions contained within the system are not equally apparent. What exists is a hierarchical structured system, rigidly stratified along the lines of social class. The conflict today is seldom between the church and state (both seemed to have achieved peaceful co-existence) but between different socio-economic groups (p. 87).

It will therefore be quite useful to find out how much has this 'exclusivism and privilege' changed and the extent to which the churches play a part. In fact, given the objective of the government Education Plan, such a measure would be an indicator of how far the decolonisation process has reached, how meaningful its promise of 'equality of opportunity' is and to what extent has educational equity been achieved in the educational system.

# EVOLUTION FROM COLONIALISM

It is relevant to note how the denominational spirit gradually found its way from colonialism into the country's education system. Regulations to the Revised Ordinances (1951-53) in Education, for example, kept the church on quite a manageable leash.

The establishment and funding of denominational schools depended on approval from the Director of Education and the Governor.[16] The Revised Ordinance stated: '*Aid will be granted only on condition that the school is open to all children without distinction of religion, race, nationality, language.*'[17] This condition, a human right really, reflected the concern that the British authorities had over the dangers of using the schools as vehicles for religious conversion. Furthermore, this conditionality eventually found its way into the current Education Act (1 of 1966), a fact about which Dr. Williams boasted a lot.

In fact, the Revised Ordinance further stated:

> The services of any teacher who attempts to exercise undue influence over the religion of any pupil shall be terminated...All teachers in Government Schools may be required to give religious instruction according to their own faith...Teachers in Assisted Schools shall give religious instruction as required by their Managers.[18]

Having no Teaching Service Commission at that time, the colony's government gave the following powers to the management of the assisted schools:

> Boards of Management of Assisted Schools shall appoint, transfer, suspend, terminate the service, or require the resignation of the teachers in their respective schools, subject to the provisions of the Education Ordinance.[19]

Such powers were implicitly subjected to those of the Director of Education. The matter of funding then became the key lever for controlling the church schools. So it was up to 1960 when 'new politics' came along, that is, heavy dependence on the votes by church members – a challenge earlier laid out by Catholic Archbishop, Finbar Ryan, against Dr Williams' anti-denominational view in 1954.

Williams said: '*I see in the denominational school a breeding ground for disunity.*'[20] The Archbishop's response was this: '*Catholics are roughly one third of the population. Their suffrage is no small power.'*[21] Muscles were flexed. The compromised route to Concordat was therefore laid.

These above reports are important to consider now mainly because they help indicate how the Concordat evolved to serve the country's ethnic diversity in spite of the surrounding 'nationalistic sentiments.' These reports also projected the country's educational objectives in a way intended to facilitate social and economic mobility and equity in the independence era. For such reasons, the subsequent assessment of the Draft Plan (1969), dealing with quality education, stated: '*The mass education system must accommodate a much wider spectrum of individual differences and needs than the highly selective elitist system had to*'[22] (p. 64).

In other words, this 1969 review suggested a refinement of what the 1968-83 Report meant by 'opening the system to the talented.' What does 'talented' mean and how is it connected to the 'elitist system?' 'Talented' was not defined. The 'elitist system' meant the grammar-school route.

At that time too, the competition to enter the high-performing secondary schools was quite severe and with repeated implications for the Concordat. The competition was generally aimed at getting into a 'prestige' school, mainly the Denominational Secondary Schools, as against a Government Secondary School. The coveted scholarships, the vast majority from the 'prestige' schools, were for academic and professional training (e.g., medicine, law, engineering, accountancy, languages, etc.).

As explained in several subsequent government reports, the four-pronged challenge for the post-colonial government became:

1.  How to diversify the secondary school curriculum so as to achieve a better spread of grammar and technical/vocational education and as well cater to the varying interests, abilities and aptitudes of students.

2.  How to improve the level of public respect given to technical/ vocational programmes and their graduates.

3.  How to accommodate freedom of students' and parents' choice in an educational system in which many secondary schools differ so much in quality of output, and

4.  What measures to use to allocate students fairly into one or the other type of secondary school, especially the high-performing ones (mainly government-assisted vs government schools).

Taking up the challenge, the Prime Minister, Dr Eric Williams, persistently argued for modifying the amount of grammar-type education so as to insert and make more attractive technical/vocational training in the secondary schools.[23] However, since the general elections and the base of contesting political parties in the 1956-62 period were largely ethnically-dominated, tensions naturally developed between the Afro-dominated PNM and the Indo-dominated Opposition, with groups of mainly Catholic Whites, Syrians, etc. in between.[24] The contestations were based more on religion than on race *per se*, the reason being the difference between government and the different churches over the control and management of the nation's schools. (Race was a factor but the collective church voice was more for religion than for race).

Most of the high-performing schools were either owned or managed by the church, with natural ethnic linkages, and any government attempt to control these schools would have been met with strong ethnically-driven political resistance.[25] Such ethnic-driven tensions spilled over into the relationships between the PNM government and managers of the denominational schools to the point where in 1960, one year before the general elections and two years before political independence, the Concordat was agreed to between the government and the denominational school boards to settle school management and ownership differences.

The Concordat was born out of politics and it survives through politics. School building programmes by denominational school boards are largely driven by the extent to which a particular Board, and by implication, its supporters, are sympathetic to the existing government.

On March 30, 2015, for example, speaking on the occasion of the Shouter Baptist Liberation Day holiday, former Prime Minister Mrs. Kamla Persad-Bissessar promised to build a secondary school for the Baptists if they supported her in the imminent general elections. She said:

> Do you want that secondary school built? God willing and with your help, we will partner to do what next you want, which is your secondary school. Just as we built your primary school, so we will do the same for your secondary school. But you have to help us.[26]

So in addition to the dominant preference for grammar-type education and challenges for curriculum diversity, the government was faced with an ethnic challenge in promoting its transformation policies.[27] Though the PNM government was largely African-based, a high proportion of its supporters were also Christian. The Catholic church played a significant part in the struggle to retain church control of its schools. In fact, the pressure against the government, as previously indicated, was largely led by the Catholic Archbishop, Count Finbar Ryan.

This leadership inspired the rest. The 1960 confrontation between the government and the church naturally had substantial ethnic implications that still exist today. The government at that time did not wish to allow the high-profile conflict to flow into the general elections. The compromise led to the formation of a Concordat signed by the Minister of Education on December 22, 1960.[28] In such circumstances, the birth of the Concordat was essentially due to pressures derived from the ethnically-driven politics of the post-colonial society. It is a good example of politics in education with implications for equality of opportunity and equity in a multi-racial society.

## NOTES

1.    C. Campbell, *The Young Colonials: A Social History of Education in Trinidad and Tobago, 1834–1939*. Jamaica, Mona: The Press University of the West Indies. 1996. p.11.

2.    See P. Keenan, *Report upon the State of Education in the Island of Trinidad and Tobago*. Dublin: Her Majesty's Stationery Office. 1869., especially pp. 8–33. Also C. Campbell, *The Young Colonials: A Social History of Education in Trinidad and Tobago, 1834-1939*. Jamaica, Mona: The Press University of the West Indies. 1996.

3.    Lord Harris established several government schools out of local ward funds. In 1851, he presented his proposals for educational reform, including a Board of Education, Inspector of Schools and increased opportunities for blacks, but for a fee. He preferred secular schools. (see C. Campbell). The Keenan Report pushed for several reforms which helped push the dual system of education further upwards.

4.    C. Campbell. pp. 5-15. For example, between 1836 and 1869, five single-sex schools opened in Port of Spain: St Joseph Convent (1836), St. George's College, the Church of England Grammar School, The Queens's Collegiate and St. Mary's College. Three were Catholic – mainly 'for the rich, white with few non-whites'. (p. 15.) Around this time, conflicts grew between the Catholic and Protestant establishments. Similar conflicts later developed in the early twentieth century within the East Indian community over educational control.

5.    Ibid, p.29.

6.   Ibid, p. 5. The Education Ordinance of 1870 supported the dual system. Up to 1875,there were only two denominational schools that qualified for state aid under the 1870 Ordinance. The following Ordinances of 1901 and 1902 also favoured the dual system with denominational schools (p. 108).

7.   E. Williams, *Education in the British West Indies*, New York: University Place Bookshop. p. 7.

8.   C. Campbell. p.72–80. The College Exhibition opened in 1872; Civil Service Examinations also gave further opportunities.

9.   C. Campbell,*The Young Colonials: A Social History of Education in Trinidad and Tobago, 1834–1939*. Jamaica, Mona: The Press, University of the West Indies. 1996.

10.  The Concordat and its implications will be discussed later.

11.  Ibid, 1959.

12.  E. Williams,*Education in the British West Indies*. New York: University Place Bookshop. 1954. p. 7.

13.  Pastoral Letter on Roman Catholic Salvation for Youth. Port of Spain, Trinidad. Catholic Printery. 1960. pp. 7-10. Around that time, of the 28 secondary schools, 18 were denominational assisted. By 1970, of the 42, 24 were denominational assisted. denominational school boards were established in 1935.

14.  He added: 'In other words, the school does not exist in a vacuum and the priorities of the wider society become the priorities of the school also. Furthermore, the stratified secondary system reflects the stratification system of the wider society. Obviously then, the culture of the 'better' schools would be the culture of the more privileged groups in the society, rather than the culture of a particular religious group.' Mustapha is President of a Denominational Board and university lecturer.

15.  See e.g.,'A Study of the Secondary School Population in Trinidad and Tobago: Placement Patterns and Practices, Centre for Ethnic Studies. 1994. University of the West Indies, Trinidad; R. Deosaran.'Benchmarking School Violence and Delinquency in the Secondary School', Ministry of Education. 2004, 2006.

16.  Revised Ordinances (1951–53), Chapter 14, No. 1. Rules and Regulations, Section 4 of Education Ordinance, Trinidad and Tobago.

17.  Ibid. Section 14, p.150.

18.  Ibid. Sections 147, 148, 151. p. 171.

19.  Ibid, Section 38. p. 155.

20.  Ibid.

21.  Ibid.

22. Assessment of Draft Education Plan 1968-83. Ministry of Education. pp. 60–70.

23. e.g., Speech to House of Representatives. December 8, 1965; Address to Caribbean Union College. August 29, 1974.

24. For details of the struggle between the different religious groups for control of schools, government grants, etc., see C. Campbell, *The Young Colonials: A Social History of Education in Trinidad 1834–1939*.

25. The general election was due the next year, in 1961. For ethnically-driven political tensions, see e.g., E. Williams, *Inward Hunger*. 1971; S. Ryan, *Race and Nationalism in Trinidad and Tobago*. 1972; J. La Guerre (Ed.),*Calcutta to Caroni* (2nd Ed.). 1985; R. Deosaran. (Ed.),*Cultural Diversity: Politics, Education and Society*. Trinidad, St Augustine: Ansa McAL Psychological Research Centre, University of the West Indies. 1995; R. Deosaran,'A Society Under Siege: A Study of Political Confusion and Legal Mysticism'. Trinidad: University of the West Indies, Ansa McAL Psychological Research Centre. 1993; R. Deosaran,'Some Issues in MultiCulturalism: The Case of Trinidad and Tobago in the Post-Colonial Era'. *Plural Societies*. Vol. 12 (1,2), Spring/Summer 1981; D. Lowenthal and L.Comitas. (Eds.).*The Aftermath of Sovereignty*. 1973; *East Indians in the Caribbean*. Trinidad: Longman Trinidad Ltd. 1992.pp. 265–367.

26. Trinidad Express. March 31, 2015. p. 3. The former Prime Minister has also appointed a member of the Baptist clergy as a Government Senator. Full support for her government also comes from the Sanatan Dharma Maha Sabha School Board, and as such, five schools have been constructed, government-funded. This follows the reluctance by the PNM government to establish more denominational schools.

27. These denominational boards included, for example, Catholic, Hindu, Muslim, Anglican, Presbyterian, Baptist, Pentecostal and Moravian faith.

28. The Government's  early intention was to have this Concordat put into law by Parliament. However, it was never taken to Parliament but put into practice over the years.

# CHAPTER EIGHT
# The Concordat in Court: Pandora's Box

*The principle of fairness holds that a person is required to do his part as defined by the rules of an institution when the institution is fair, and when one has voluntarily accepted the benefits of the arrangements or taken advantage of the opportunities it offers to further one's interests.*

John Rawls, A Theory of Justice, 1971

## THE ENIGMATIC CONCORDAT AND THE COURT

As indicated earlier, the Concordat, as enigmatic as it is, occupies a most significant place in the educational history of Trinidad and Tobago and, as well, in the contemporary status of the educational system, especially in terms of equality of opportunity. We cannot know about the education system unless we know about the Concordat.

The contents and further implications of this Concordat are therefore important to help understand the ethnic differentiations and tensions from student allocation in the secondary school system today. The Concordat, a subject of continuing controversy both in and out of court, is entitled:

'*Assurances for the Preservation and Character of Denominational Schools.*'[1] Four of the major Concordat 'Assurances' are:

1.  In relation to property, the Denominational Boards will have ownership and direct management control over their schools. (Section 1)

2.  In denominational schools, (unless the denomination concerned otherwise gives its consent), the religion of the particular denomination which owns the school will be taught exclusively and by teachers professing to belong to that Denomination. In Government Schools, all recognized religious denominations will have access through their accredited representatives during the time specified in the time-table for the teaching of Religion

to the pupils belonging to their faith. Pupils attending the schools of denomination not of their own faith will not be compelled to take part in the religious exercises or lessons of that denomination. (Section 3)

3.  Though the right of appointment, retention, promotion, transfer and dismissal of primary school teachers will rest with the Public Service Commission *(later the Teaching Service Commission)*, a teacher shall not be appointed to a school if the denominational board objects to such appointment on moral or spiritual grounds. Similarly, if a teacher be found to be unsatisfactory on these moral or spiritual grounds, the Board will have the right to request his or her removal to another school after due investigation. For these reasons, it is proposed (provided the legal and constitutional arrangements allow) that vacancies as they occur in all schools should be advertised (by the Ministry) and applications submitted in the first instance to the respective Board of Management which will examine them and forward them all with their recommendations, to the Public Service Commission (now Teaching Service Commission) for final action. (Section 4)

4.  The governing (church) bodies of the assisted secondary schools will continue to be responsible for their administration and maintenance, repair and furnishing. Those schools still continue to qualify for government aid. (Section 5)

The following are contained in Section 5 of the Concordat:

5.  The principals of assisted secondary schools will  make available a minimum of '80 per centum' of the first form entry places to those who, by passing the test, qualify on the results of the Common Entrance Examination (now Secondary Entrance Assessment) for free secondary education.

6.  The principals will be free to allocate up to '20 per centum,' the remaining places as they see fit provided normally that the pass list of the Common Entrance Examination serves to provide the pupils.

7.  Entry above the First Form will be under the control of the Minister of Education and will require the approval of the minister.

A key element of this Concordat is the phrase 'moral and religious grounds.' The interpretation and decisions on this criterion have been and still are quite controversial especially in cases of promoting or disciplining teachers of the denominational schools.[2] As will be illustrated later, the Concordat and its implications have been examined in a case involving a complaint of discrimination from a teacher in a denominational school.

The execution of the Concordat's provisions, however, are connected to the powers of the minister and Ministry of Education and, as well, to the Teaching Service Commission. As expressed in the Education Act. (No.1 of 1966),[3] the Minister of Education has over twenty-five responsibilities. Among the major ones are:

1. The promotion of the education of the people of Trinidad and Tobago and the establishment of institutions devoted to that purpose. [Section 3(a)]

2. The establishment of a system of education designed to provide adequately for the planning and development of an educational service related to the changing needs of the community. [Section 3(b)]

3. Devising a system of education calculated as far as possible to ensure that educational and vocational abilities, aptitudes and interests of the children find adequate expression and opportunity for development. (Section 4(2)(a))[4]

A particular provision, lavishly celebrated by the former Prime Minister, Dr Eric Williams over its inclusion, states:

> No person shall be refused admission to any public school on account of the religious persuasion, race, social status or language of such person or of his parent (Section 7).

This 1966 provision, however, was already included in the Revised Ordinances (51–53). This Education Act (1966) also provides for the establishment of denominational boards of management and its structure and overall jurisdiction (Sections 14-22). In particular, it is states:

> Subject to this Act, a Board shall act in accordance with any special or general directives of the Minister concerning the exercise and general performance of its powers and duties conferred or imposed on it by this Act or its Regulation (Section 16).

This latter provision is connected to the following constitutional powers of a minister:

> Where any Minister has been assigned responsibility for any department of government, he shall exercise general direction and control over that department, and subject to such direction and control, the department shall be under the supervision of a Permanent Secretary whose office shall be a public office (Section 85, Constitution).

The minister's exercise of his powers, though, has to be within the 'assurances' granted to the Concordat, especially as indicated above, where the Board's approval is required in the appointment, promotion or transfer of teachers in denominational schools. In this context, are the powers of the minister superior to those of the denominational boards as stated in the Concordat?

Since the minister's general powers are written in the constitution and the 'assurances' of the Concordat rest on 'settled practice,' not in the constitution, occasions of tension will often arise. Between the Minister of Education and the denominational boards exists a third layer of authority – the 'independent' Teaching Service Commission.[5]

Its powers, defined in the Constitution, are:

> To appoint persons to hold or act in public offices in the Teaching Service established under the Education Act, including power to make appointments on promotion and transfer and to confirm appointments, and to remove and exercise disciplinary control over persons holding or acting in such offices and to enforce standards of conduct on such officers (Section 125, Constitution).

Above these are appeals to the courts.

## CONCORDAT TAKEN TO COURT: THE JAGESSAR CASE

With such powers over the education system spread across three authorities, there will naturally be administrative and even constitutional tensions and controversies. A clash of 'rights' will ensue. One such example is the legal action taken by a teacher from a denominational (Presbyterian) primary school against the Teaching Service Commission.[6] The facts are:

1. The teacher, Kamla Jagessar, acting Vice-Principal at the Penal Presbyterian School, among others, applied for the vacant Principal's post. (According to court evidence, the Board did not receive any application from Ms. Jagessar, neither was she interviewed by the Board. She was however interviewed by the Commission).

2.  She was deemed the most senior teacher at the school and also gained the highest marks (81.5%) at the prescribed interviews.

3.  When the list of interviewed applicants and their respective marks reached the Commission, the Commission selected Ms. Jagessar for the post and informed the Presbyterian Board accordingly.

4.  The Board disagreed, and submitted its own candidate. Its Secretary, Mr. Dillon Daniel, stated: 'We regret to inform you that in accordance with paragraph 4 of the Concordat of 1960, the Presbyterian Primary Schools' Board of Education is unable to support the proposal that Ms. Kamla Jagessar be promoted to Principal.' It recommended its own candidate.

5.  Paragraph 4 of the Concordat states in part: 'A teacher shall not be appointed to a school if the denominational board objects to such an appointment on moral or religious grounds.'

6.  The Commission asked the Board to state its specific reasons for not recommending Ms. Jagessar. It was much later that the Board stated that 'she had not satisfied the requirements of the Synod of the Presbyterian Church as a communicant member of good standing.'

7.  Ms. Jagessar took legal action to obtain all names and marks awarded from the interviews conducted for the Principal's post.[7] The judge ruled that only the marks should be provided. Ms. Jagessar appealed.[8] She withdrew this appeal and then took legal action against the Teaching Service Commission.[9]

8.  A point raised by Ms. Jagessar's attorney and considered important by the defence was that the constitutional authority vested in the Commission to appoint, promote, etc. (Section 125) is superior to the Public Service Regulation (133(3)) which gave the Board the right to object to an appointment or promotion.[10] In other words, the powers and rights of the Denominational Boards were being tested in court; and with obvious implications for equality of opportunity within their schools and the educational system generally. (The Concordat is not enshrined in the Constitution)

9.  The judge ruled that the contentious Section 133(3) of the Regulations which required 'the approval of the denominational Boards' is 'neither unconstitutional nor illegal.' Even if it is found

unconstitutional, the Court indicated that it would use its related constitutional 'power of modification' to convert the 'settled practice' of the Concordat into law.

10. The judge agreed with the Board's attorney that 'at the centre of this constitutional debate is the right of a parent to select a school of his or her choice for the education of his or her child.'

11. The judge stated: 'Since 1960 the tenets of the Concordat have been the guiding principles governing the right of the church to participate in the way that Presbyterian Schools are managed and administered. It is reasonable to conclude therefore that a settled practice had developed over the years prior to the commencement of the constitution...Clearly a teacher would not be appointed to an assisted school if the Board of Management objected to that appointment on moral or religious grounds.'

12. The Court therefore ruled that in this case the Commission 'acted within the law.'

13. The Court further ruled that since the Assisted Schools are the property of the respective Denominational Boards, 'any such appointment to teach in these schools should be made subject to the approval of the owners of the property.'[II]

The court eventually ruled in favour of the Teaching Service Commission. Its counsel, Mr. Russell Martineau, SC, informed the Commission Chairman on January 25, 2015:

> The Court delivered judgement in the above matter in favour of the Teaching Service Commission. The court felt that given the important constitutional issues raised in this case, there should be an order that all parties bear their own costs.

All of the above means that with this judgement the Concordat and the rights of denominational school boards have been strengthened and the existence of ethnic diversity within the country's educational system has deepened its foothold. The judge inferred that this case has implications for a parent's right to send his child to a school of his choice, an exercise of religious rights too.

# A JUDICIAL QUAGMIRE OVER THE CONCORDAT

Several questions arise. While the ownership of property does provide certain rights to the owner, in this case, there are other rights involved, for example, the constitutional right to equal treatment and opportunity for the individual.[12] Is the Concordat, existing outside of the constitution, strong enough to defeat these other rights? Does 'settled practice' as a derivative from the Concordat, have superior status to a provision which already exists in the constitution? How far should ownership of land or a building on such land extend to other rights, for example, the rights of teachers paid by the government? To what extent and why does the Concordat clash with the Constitution (Section 4) and the Equal Opportunity Act? This case gives us an opportunity to consider, with respect, a few issues surrounding the enigmatic Concordat and the judge's ruling.

This case was about the alleged rights of a teacher in a denominational school, the Teaching Service Commission's decision and the Board's objection. The Board felt that the teacher, Ms. Jagessar, was not suitable for the maintenance of the religious character of the school. The Board, citing moral and spiritual grounds from the Concordat, said that the teacher was not a communicant in good standing for 15 years as required by the Synod.

And so the Board objected to the Commission's decision to promote her from Vice-Principal to Principal. The Teaching Service Commission asked the Board to clarify what the Synod's requirement on 'moral and spiritual' grounds actually meant. The major purpose of the Commission's inquiry was not to subvert the privileges of the Board but apparently to ensure some degree of fair treatment for the affected teacher.

Anyhow, citing several cases, the judge placed emphasis on 'the right of a parent to provide a school of his or her choice for the education of his or her child.' This 'right' seemed to have substantial influence on his final ruling against the teacher.

This implied, as the Board itself argued, that such an unsuitable teacher, as Principal, would not do justice to the religious character of the school and in this case, the parent's right to a school of his choice will be denied.

But isn't the connection between the teacher's complaint and the 'parent's right' quite a distant one? At the same time, it also appears that the distance between the 'teacher's rights' under an equality of opportunity premise,[13] and the Board's reservation is a rather grey one in constitutional terms. It is for this reason, that the Commission had cause on several occasions to ask the various School Boards to clarify their respective claims on 'moral and spiritual grounds.'

In any case, with the court's acceptance of 'settled practice,' couldn't the court rely on the Concordat as is, to make its ruling rather than stretching outside to 'the parents' right?' Note that parents prefer, among all other things, high-performing schools without regard to religious affiliation or 'religious character' of a school.

In this sense, the reliance on the parent's 'right' in order to support the Board's reservation appears overstretched. Given this ruling, however, it may be time for the government to consider putting the Concordat into the country's constitution. This will help put the required certainty into the status of the Concordat and also help put further litigation on clearer criteria.

## PARENTS' RIGHTS AND THE CONCORDAT

There is a related issue connected to equality of opportunity. The judge was influenced by the 'right of a parent to provide a school of his choice for the education of his child.' And on this, supported the Board. While a remedy for the Board's objection against the teacher was, in the judge's view, available, and was applied, what is the remedy for a parent who, in spite of his desire, is denied 'a school of his choice for the education' of his child?

More precisely, when such desired schools are available, he is denied a place for his child. In other words, his right is denied. What then? This denial gets more grievous when the school desired is one which provides the kind of 'religious character' the parent desires. This is an implication of having the secular SEA as a condition for placement at denominational secondary schools. 'Religious character' becomes subordinate to the academic (secular) reputation of the school.

The point is that since the judge put such heavy emphasis upon the constitutional 'right of a parent to provide a school for the education of his child,' what is the constitutional implication when such desired schools are available but the parent's 'right' is denied? In other words, is there any constitutional implication when a parent fails to get his child into a denominational school of his choice?

This constitutional right needs clarification as well in light of limited places at the high-performing denominational secondary schools. This right therefore does not seem to be an absolute one. And maybe, this too should be clarified.

In fact, Section 7 of the Education Act states: '*No child shall be refused admission to any public school on account of the religious persuasion, race, social status or language of such person or his parent.*'[14] Does this bring further strength to parents' rights or not? Or is academic merit allowed to trump religion, race, social status or language? What about the '20 per centum' discretion for principals? And with what implications, if any, for the Concordat and Constitution?

## CLASH OF RIGHTS: THE CASE

Important to the general theme of this book – equality of educational opportunity and equity - is the emphasis that the judge placed on Sections 4(c) and 4(h) of the constitution, as proposed by the Board's attorney, that is, the right of the individual to respect for his private and family life (4(c)), and freedom of conscience and religious belief and observance (4(h)).

In fact, the judge, seeming quite passionate on the subject, referred to several international court decisions and treaties to support the view that parents have a right to send their children to a school of their choice and 'to ensure the religious and moral education of their children in conformity with their own convictions.'

Further, given the differential manner in which SEA students are allocated to denominational and government secondary schools, the conclusion of the judge is extremely relevant:

> This Court could find no reason why the right of a parent to direct the education of his children in accordance with his moral and religious beliefs in the United States under the ECHR and in international law should not apply with equal force in Trinidad and Tobago.[15]

The Court also agreed with the Board's attorney that Section 4 of the Concordat was settled practice and further that Section 4 of the constitution itself 'converted this settled practice into a right.' This, too, is interesting. Section 4 of the constitution states: '*It is hereby recognized and declared that in Trinidad and Tobago there have existed and continue to exist, without discrimination by reason of race, origin, colour, religion or sex, the following rights and freedoms...*' Eleven 'rights and freedoms' are then listed, including 4(c) and 4(h) to which the Board used for support.

The question thus arises, what about those parents and children who apply to get into a denominational school of their religious choice but because of their SEA marks, are refused such entry? Each year, there are thousands of such cases. Which is superior – religion or marks? Then there are many who with high SEA marks choose and are taken in a school (first or second choice) which is of a religion different from theirs. Then, as reported by the Secondary School Placement Study, there are those taken into 'prestige' schools through the principal's discretion but with lower marks that many who are not.

If, as the Court felt, that the central issues are parents' and children's rights to a school of their choice, then why wasn't at least part of the judgment connected to the question of equality of educational opportunity and educational equity – issues which also have constitutional bearing? When or when not is the SEA mark not relevant in the context of the 'parent's rights?'

## THE CONCORDAT AND THE HIJAB

Energised by the politics of multi-ethnic education, the Concordat, while legitimizing the rights and privileges of the church, did and still does produce conflict with the obligations of a state-funded educational system. A particular conflict taken to court will help illustrate. This matter was known as 'the Hijab case.'[16] After six months of intense public controversy, the matter went to court in January 1995.

The issue involved an 11-year old student who passed by merit the Common Entrance Examination and was properly allocated to a place at the school of her choice, the Holy Name Convent. The child was a Sunni Muslim and the school managed by a Catholic Board of Management. The child and her parents thus insisted that she wear the hijab to this Catholic school. On the other hand, the Catholic Board and its Principal insisted that the student wear the prescribed school uniform as all other students do.[17]

After weeks of protracted negotiations between the school authorities, the parents and the Muslim leaders, the matter was eventually taken to court. Three separate but related legal instruments came into play: the country's constitution (Act No. 1 of 1976), the Education Act (Act No. 1 of 1966) and the Concordat (1960). The school principal insisted it was a 'school management issue.' The parents and the Muslim community insisted it was a 'religious rights issue.'

Ironically, the Hindu-based Sanatan Dharma Maha Sabha (SDMS) publicly agreed with the Catholic School Board on this uniform-hijab issue.[18] The presiding judge noted the 'very sensitive nature of the issues,' and 'regretted that other efforts to resolve the conflict had failed.' Finally, the judge, using the criteria of 'relevance and reasonableness,' said: '*The school does not appear to have taken into account the psychological effect of insisting that the applicant remove the hijab. The ripping away of traditions which she has so observed for half of her life...The official position of the Ministry of Education is that they do not object to the wearing of the hijab; the inference being that it is not considered to be an act of indiscipline in the several public schools in which they have been worn.*'[19]

This court ruling did not favour the powers and rights of the Board or its Principal. In the earlier cited *Jagessar vs Teaching Service Commission* case, the court showed favour.

The architecture of the Concordat is a complex one. It is subject to several compelling forces: religious rights, parents' rights, political sensitivity, grammar-type aspirations, weak government schools and strong denominational schools. The Education Act (1 of 1966) is directly connected to the scope and powers of the Concordat. And so, if any revision at all has to be done to the Concordat, the Education Act has to be amended as a priority or at least a parallel act.

An opportunity was missed by the Court, however, since the visitation of the Concordat should not be only about powers of the Board or limits of the Teaching Service Commission. To what extent is the denominational character of the church school adversely affected by taking in many children with high SEA marks but not of the school's religion?

Within the '80 per centum' placed according to results from the competitive SEA, there are thousands who wish to and get into Assisted Denominational (prestige) Schools, but not of the denomination practiced by the particular school. And parents of such children make no complaint. In fact, such parents accept the difference gladly. Have parents given up their religious rights in order to get a 'good education' in a high performing denominational school? As said earlier, educational achievement trumps religious rights. And so social class formation squeezes out cultural retention.

Annually, there are thousands of parents and children who fail to get into a school of their choice – a right which the Court itself has strongly emphasised as deserving constitutional respect. In other words, the one-track linearity which the Court undertook, wisely in some parts, seemed to have ignored the fact that, beyond the contention over Regulation 133, the case involved a clash of constitutional rights.

Since the Court ventured into the rights of parents and children to have both a good education and one endowed with moral and religious content, at least the opportunity should have been taken to suggest how equality of educational opportunity and equity could be achieved without undermining the existing powers of the Concordat and the denominational boards. It was a lost opportunity on a rare occasion.

Government should therefore be encouraged to create a much better spread of equality of educational opportunity and equity across all secondary schools, especially with the government secondary schools, and as such remove the sharp quality difference between the assisted denominational schools and the government secondary schools.[20]

# CONCORDAT REVISIONS: A PANDORA'S BOX

Regarding the Teaching Service Commission's relationship with the Boards on teacher appointments etc., the Commission in 2011 submitted several proposals to amend the Education Act. The Commission, for example, stated:

> Subsequent to the Concordat of 1960, there has been an unanticipated proliferation of denominational schools and new boards. This has left the Teaching Service Commission with the almost impossible task of adjudicating on the validity of 'moral and religious' grounds advanced by denominational boards who reject candidates that the Commission recommends on the basis of merit.[21]

The Commission added:

> It should be noted that any candidate deemed suitable by the Commission to hold an appointment, but is rejected by a Denominational Board, has access under the Freedom of Information Act to acquire the results of his/her assessment by the Commission and thereafter to challenge his/her non-appointment in Court. The Public Service Regulations (adopted by the Teaching Service Commission) bars the Commission

from appointing any candidate rejected by the Board on 'moral and religious' grounds.[22]

In its 1999 'Education for All' National Report, the Government stated that cabinet approved a committee to consider the report of the Joint Committee on the Relationship between government and the denominational boards of education and to make recommendations for a new Concordat.[23]

In fact, in 2012 the Boards themselves submitted proposals to government to make changes to the Concordat in this regard.[24]  One government after another, recognizing the high-performing schools protected by the Concordat, the implications for educational inequality  and the jealously-guarded 'assurances' guaranteed within the Concordat, have bobbed and weaved from one period to another – seemingly reluctant to touch the Concordat with  'a ten foot pole.'

This is the fearful challenge – a kind of Pandora's Box. In its 2004 meetings with the Joint Select Committee of Parliament, the Ministry of Education told the Committee that it had set up an in-house committee to review the Concordat and make recommendations. The Parliamentary Committee, in it 2005 report, urged the ministry to complete its report, submit its proposals for review, and make them known to all stakeholders.[25]

Against such background, it is urgent that both the Concordat and the Education Act (No. 1 of 1966) be reviewed and possibly integrated, or as said above, at least put the Concordat into the constitution. This story is not over.

## CONCORDAT, FUNDING PRESSURES AND TENSIONS AGAIN

Notwithstanding the Concordat arrangements, some mutual dissatisfaction still existed between government and the denominational school boards to the point where a Joint Committee was formed in 1978 to review the management control over several church schools. Subsequently, a Working Group was formed in 1981 'On the National Ownership and Joint Management of Schools.' More recently, in 2012, the Association of Denominational Boards submitted their own recommendations for the revision of the Concordat. These revisions were aimed mainly to strengthen their management control and an increase in government subventions.

After the 1960s, the Concordat experienced some restlessness over funding for school repairs, maintenance, etc. More precisely, in 1978 The

Catholic School Board initiated a proposal for the government to take over ownership of seven primary schools subject to a joint management structure.[26] The government agreed.[27] Of the eighteen Boards interviewed by the Joint Committee, only seven agreed to hand over a total of 28 primary schools to government.[28]

At this time, given the religious rights and freedoms enshrined in the constitution and the Concordat, the government sensed a possible conflict and noted: 'The Education Act, 1966 would need to be examined by the Attorney General and the Minister of Legal Affairs with a view to making any necessary amendments to meet the new concept of schools under joint management.'[29]

The government further stated: 'The constitutional provisions under Chapter 1(Section 4) of the Republican Constitution should also be borne in mind when the necessary amendments are being made.'[30] Meanwhile, all the other denominational school boards were looking on with anxiety, no doubt, recalling the former Prime Minister's publicly-stated apprehensions in 1954 against denominational schools. Their major fear was whether the PNM government was using this ground-breaking occasion as a leveraged step to nationalize all schools in the education system.

In January 1981, the year of the general elections, the Prime Minister appointed a Working Group to hold informal talks with religious bodies on the question of the revision of the Education Act (1966) with special reference to national ownership and joint management of schools.[31] This was about five months before the general election and obviously Dr Williams and his government seemed caught between their desire to nationalize the school system – if only gradually – and the suffrage powers of the eighteen denominational school boards. Of course, the Catholic Board itself seemed to have eased out of the earlier resistance of Archbishop Ryan, funding being the new pressure.[32] Would other Boards follow, and how far?

## DENOMINATIONAL TENSIONS

Now, the denominational school boards, faced with funding pressures, did not rest their 'jealous guardianship' only on grounds of religious rights, but also, and with widespread public support, on their schools being high-performing schools.[33] The country's ethnic diversity came alive as priests, pastors, pundits and imams sought to explain to their respective congregations what the school governance issues were all about – basically a clash between required funding, the Concordat and the constitution. The Working Group stated:

> It was represented that Regulations 133(2), 133(3a) and 137 (as used by Teaching Service Commission) affecting the appointment, transfer, etc. of staff in assisted schools are inconsistent with the provisions of the Constitution of Trinidad and Tobago, in particular, section 4(b) and 4(d) which guarantee equality before the law and protection from discrimination on grounds of religion by any public authority in the exercise of any functions.[34]

Modifying the recommendations of the Joint Committee, the cabinet agreed that in setting up the proposed joint state-church-community management, the constitution should have pre-eminence. The cabinet stated:

> The human rights as they relate to both teachers and pupils, who are first and foremost citizens, of the Republic of Trinidad and Tobago... The rights of teachers should not be violated on account of religious authority nor should any pupil be placed at a disadvantage as regards the physical or other conditions under which he receives his education.[35]

Here was the clash between the individual's right to equality before the law and the conditionalities set by the denominational boards. Now, the government took a powerful constitutional position at that time and with its proposal for a three-tiered management structure, sought to loosen school control by the denominational boards which were handing over their schools.

The Boards which did not agree on handing over argued that 'the right to religious education could only be effectively preserved through the exercising of their traditional right to recommend teachers for appointments, promotions, transfers,' etc. They further disagreed that 'mere access to schools for teaching religion would be sufficient to maintain the religious character of their schools.'[36]

Noting the recommendations of the 1978 Joint Committee, this 1981 Working Group saw the powers of the Concordat, Denominational Boards and even the Teaching Service Commission over teachers as 'inconsistent with the Constitution.' Now this 'inconsistency' is a critical matter, especially since, as long expected, it reached the courts some thirty years later. It is therefore important to recall exactly what the Constitution states.

The constitutional rights referred to by the Working Group are as follows: '*It is hereby recognized and declared that in Trinidad and Tobago, there have existed and shall continue to exist, without discrimination reason of race, origin, colour, religion or sex, the following fundamental rights and freedoms, (b) the right of the individual to equality before the law and the protection of the law, and (d), the right of the individual to equality of treatment "from any public authority in the exercise of any functions."'*

In spite of what the Working Group claimed, these rights are not guaranteed. They have to be tested in court, depending on the circumstances, and especially in cases where one 'right' seems to clash with another. Since today's Concordat occupies such a central place in the quest for equality of educational opportunity and equity, it is useful to recall the constitutional tensions that existed between the government and the Denominational Boards – some more than others.

In meetings with the Working Group, the Boards which did not hand over any schools, vehemently argued against any possible 'nationalization' of their schools and for the right to maintain the religious character of their schools – even while they proposed '100 percent government funding.'[37] The government eventually agreed that the education system will be three-pronged: (1) Schools managed by the government, (2) schools managed by denominational boards, and (3) schools under joint management. In order to accommodate the joint-management arrangement, the government proposed a set of amendments to the Education Act (1 of 1966).

## CONSTITUTIONAL CONFLICT

However, all of this did not effectively clarify the constitutional conflict earlier perceived by the Working Group. In fact, Working Group member and Chairman of the Law Commission, Justice E. H. Watkins, submitted an opinion on the perceived conflict.

He concluded:

Section 132(2) and 3(a) and section 137 of the Public Service Commission Regulations which have been adopted by the Teaching Service Commission purport to sanction the application of such discriminatory standards. As such they conflict with section 4(b) and 4(d) of the Constitution and are incontrovertibly unconstitutional.[38]

He further concluded:

> I am unable to discern any ground whatever on which legislation could be sustained before a Court of Law which departs in so far-reaching and radical manner against the fundamental rights and freedom of a select body of citizens of this country.[39]

This is similar to the position taken by the cabinet.

Drawing from the cabinet's acceptance of the then Prime Minister's 'Proposals on Education,' the government plan for education stated:

> That the denominational organisations be accepted as having a critical and important role in the education system particularly at the secondary level. In accepting this as a matter of policy, however, these organisations be requested to adopt the national model.[40]

And what was this national model of education? This is important to note mainly because of the denominational schools' role in providing grammar-type education from which the country's professional elites rose. The national model was *'an integrated comprehensive programme embracing the traditional academic, pre-technician, commercial, general industrial, and limited specialized craft training.'* Once this national model proposal was accepted, the government also agreed to assume full responsibility for all costs of education incurred by the denominational boards.[41] However, the denominational boards resisted.

At that time, 1969, there were 29 denominational secondary schools and 39 government secondary schools, a total of 68. In 2015, there are 39 denominational secondary schools and 86 government secondary schools, a total of 125.[42] As indicated earlier, the government wanted to have a fairly integrated curriculum in all secondary schools, with the strategic objective of building a diversified and industrialised economy. However, the heavyweight presence of the denominational boards then produced a challenge.[43]

The related, intruding fact was that the Junior Secondary School, with the shift system (though intended to be temporary), faced imminent collapse. The then prime minister's pledge 'that the three-year Junior Secondary School Programme remain an integral part of the Educational Plan' did not work out.[44]

No actual reform on the Concordat, one way or the other, has as yet taken place, suggesting, once again, the political sensitivity over matters involving educational competition within an ethnic diversity framework. It seems it has been discreetly left to the court, not the legislature, to decide.

# TTUTA AND THE COMMISSION: CALLS FOR REVISION

All in all, however, today the Boards and the Teaching Service Commission rely heavily but rather uneasily on the provisions of the Concordat subject to periodic appeals by aggrieved teachers and parents on procedural grounds and individual rights.

Linked to these individual rights and seemingly adding to potential threats to the Concordat is also the Equality Opportunity Act which extends individual rights to equal treatment from public authorities into the private sector as well. These matters are relevant as they circumscribe the 'equal opportunity' expectations which teachers, parents and students have of the secondary school system in this multi-ethnic society. And often caught in the middle is the Teaching Service Commission which publicly stated its deep concerns. In its 2010 Annual Report, for example, the Commission stated:

1. Persons who are not 'of the faith' but who have been accepted by the Boards to teach are debarred from an appointment as Vice-Principal or Principal, even if they have given long and meritorious service to the school. Such teachers are sometimes superseded by persons who are of the faith but whose competency as an academic leader falls short of the teacher who is not of the faith. This has given rise to disgruntlement, demoralization and a sense that the system is unfair.

2. It had to deal with situations where a qualified teacher who is of the faith is refused by the denomination on unspecified moral grounds while, in other cases, the objection is based on a charge that the teacher, while admittedly being of the faith, is not as regular at worship as the board of management would like (p. 12).

The Commission concluded: '*Given its constitutional responsibility to appoint teachers in all schools in a manner that is fair, consistent and transparent, the Commission sometimes finds itself challenged to accept some of the reasons being offered for denying a qualified and high performing teacher a seemingly deserved opportunity for advancement*' (p. 12).

The Teachers' Union itself has expressed repeated reservations over the Concordat and the method of secondary school placement. In a paper entitled 'Addressing Iniquity in our Education System,' its President, Devanand Sinanan, stated:

A direct result of this 20% concession to Principals has and continues to be the phenomenon of 'prestige' schools which has plagued the secondary school selection exercise since the Concordat. Superficially, this situation seemed compatible with the principle of equality of opportunity as outlined in the 15-year Education Plan. However, in reality it gave and continues to give families with close connections to the Principals of these prestigious denominational schools a distinct advantage in securing a place for their children in these schools.

Speaking on behalf the nation's 14,000 teachers, he added:

A child whose parents are in good graces with the principal has a better chance of getting his or her first choice school even though the child may have lower marks in the entrance examination. This advantageous position held by denominational schools under the Concordat is so jealously guarded that any attempt to initiate true educational reform is met with fierce resistance. It is indeed sad that all attempts at reform have skirted the issue of the Concordat.[45]

He recommended 'zoning' for secondary schools so as 'to lead to a more level playing field and reduce the level of marginalisation that many students now feel.'[46] In this context, a Report from a nation-wide study of secondary school placement noted:

At the heart of public perception of unfairness in school placement at the secondary school level is the Concordat – the agreement between the Church and State...Denominational 5 and 7-year traditional schools have been shown to be schools primarily of first and second choice. Meriting placement in any of these schools, without the hurdle of achieving the necessary C.E. score is therefore seen as unfair, and especially so when the recipients of this 'benefit' are not made public.[47]

The strength of the denominational boards does rest on the Concordat, but in addition, and in the eyes of the national community, the legitimacy of the boards rests further on the fact that they are consistently high-performing schools, thus giving the feeling that their management capabilities are of the standard required for high student academic achievement. It is partly in this context that the government has so far felt obliged the leave the Concordat alone.

In its Education Plan 1985-90, it stated its commitment this way: '*The Government acknowledges the role that the denominational bodies have played in the field of education and to re-affirm its commitment to the system of dual control that has existed in this country over the years.*'[48]

## THE DENOMINATIONAL DIFFERENCE

As will be discussed later, a significant difference between the denominational assisted secondary schools and the government schools is the extent to which one set is co-educational or not. The quality of teachers is cited as another difference. Yet another difference lies in the rate of absenteeism and lack of punctuality of teachers. Religious affiliation and loyalty to the school are also contributors. As sociologist, Mustapha indicated, such differences do contribute to the 'achievement-driven culture' of the denominational schools, apart from the additional oversight function of the Boards.[49]

From data gathered by the Ministry of Education (December 2010) absenteeism and unpunctuality are generally higher in the government secondary and primary schools.[50] For example, in one educational division, while over 10% of the government secondary school teachers were 'between 500 to 1,000 minutes late', only 2% of the denominational teachers were in that category. In another division, while 13% of the government school teachers were '1,000-2,000 minutes late,' no denominational school teacher was ever late within the one-month period. Government school teachers are also more likely to take extended sick leave than those from the denominational schools.[51]

As a means of creating a 'Concordat-like' system of school management, the Ministry advised: '*The Ministry has embarked on a process of School-Based Management with the aim of providing government schools with greater autonomy, authority and support.*' The Ministry added that these local school boards have been introduced at each government school '*to improve student performance and enrich the school environment.*'[52] The expected results have so far not been forthcoming.

Promises by the government to review the Education Act are over twenty years now. In its Annual Administrative Report (2013), the Ministry of Education stated that a policy document to guide the drafting of the Education Bill was approved in December 2009.[53] Describing staff shortages, the ministry added: '*This is a delicate piece of legislation...By the end of the reporting period; the work of the team was in abeyance pending staffing of the legal Unit.*'[54] In its later Strategic Plan 2010–2015, the ministry pledged again to review the Education Act before 2015. This review has not yet been published.

# CONCORDAT AND ETHNIC DIVERSITY

Given the linkages between religion, race, politics and education in this society, and increasing court litigation on grounds of discrimination, Government-commissioned reports on educational planning eventually began citing the ethnic and gender implications of schooling, especially at the secondary levels. Equality of opportunity slowly became a front- line issue. Individual and group rights became 'politically correct' positions. However, the distinctions between equality of educational opportunity, merit and equity still remained blurred and loosely used in the public debates.

Even the 1959 Maurice Committee's objective to use the secondary school system to 'integrate the diverse elements in the population,' remained silent. The language of 'diversity' cautiously replaced the thrust for 'integration' in the secondary schools. The first comprehensive post-independence education plan, the Draft Education Plan (1968-83), for example, had stated that '*all extensions to the school system should be geographically distributed so as to equalise educational opportunities*' (p. 3).

That was the closest the report came to considering equality of opportunity. There was nothing substantial or precise then about gender, ethnicity or social class differentiations and the objective of equality of opportunity and equity.

The former Prime Minister, Dr Williams, while celebrating the religious diversity of the society in 1965, pointed to the extent to which many children of various races and religions attended government secondary schools. He welcomed the extent to which such school-driven religious and racial mixture promoted integration.

He therefore said it would not be 'unreasonable to conclude that the principal agency for the integration of the population of Trinidad and Tobago is today the Government secondary school.'[55] Today, any thought of using the 'government secondary schools as the principal agency for integration' will be met with instant controversy.

Quite surprising too, when the Inter-American Development Bank (IDB) did a study entitled '*Access, Equity and Performance*' which included an examination of educational opportunity in Trinidad and Tobago, it stated: '*The education and training systems have to provide quality basic education to enable citizens from all backgrounds to fully participate in national development.*'[56] Under the heading, 'disparities,' it further noted that here, 'education institutions do not collect information on the ethnicity of their students.'

It correctly added: 'However, improving educational equality is implicitly related to ethnic equality.' Yet, in its suggestions for further research and analysis, it did not recommend collecting the relevant data on ethnicity and social class here in order to assess more precisely equality of educational opportunity and equity. It did speak globally about improving the quality of education and promoting equity in access to schooling.[57]

Given the country's chequered plantation history, fuelled by ethnic diversity and the accompanying contestations over status and resources, the ambivalence between ethnic diversity and ethnic integration has always haunted both public policy and political rhetoric. The Concordat is primarily based on ethnic diversity and the accommodation of religious affiliation. The Constitution, too, is primarily based on individual rights and freedoms regardless of race, colour, religion or origin.

As indicated earlier, the Education Act proudly states that no person shall be refused admission to any public school on account of the religious persuasion, race, social status or language of such person or of his parent.[58] Faced with such competing laws, therefore, this multi-ethnic society's quest for equality of educational opportunity and educational equity is still a work in progress – to say the least.

## THE PROMISES OF EQUALITY

The social and ethnic disaggregation of the national population is inextricably linked to the concept and practice of equality of educational opportunity. The concept and pursuit of equality imply that there is competition between different individuals or groups, or if not competition, there must be a distribution system that allocates equal shares. But as will be discussed later, such a distribution system cannot properly operate where the resources to share are in scarce or limited supply. One or more criteria must be established.

There will be hurdles to cross. Issues of equity get invoked when mechanisms for criteria are being undertaken or when it is found that some cannot meet the criteria because of relative disadvantages or handicaps at the starting point, and through no fault of theirs. Equality should not stop at having the same opportunity to enter the race; for example, writing the same examination. Equality of opportunity is connected to the results which is where merit clashes with equity.

In such a context, one gets the feeling that, given the ethnically-driven political tensions in the society, there was a reluctance to insert such components as race, gender or social class directly into the quest for equality and the expected outcomes of educational planning. The Draft Education Plan (1968-83) stated: 'We accept the responsibility of providing a balanced general education for all persons' (p. 5). It does not speak about inequalities which may arise between one or the other social group. However, the country's national anthem, given in 1962, contains the words: 'Where every creed and race find an equal place.'

Again, with respect to equality of opportunity, the Education Plan (1968-83) stated: *'The major thrusts towards the expansion and democratisation of secondary education were to broaden the choices available to the student and to develop a more positive attitude on the part of students and society towards all forms of employment and occupations.'*[59]

It added: 'The major thrust is to improve academic performance...and a sense of excellence with reference to intellectual standards.' The question of educational equity did not arise again, that is, the possible differences within gender, social class or ethnicity.

But it was the subsequent Government Green Paper produced by the National Task Force on Education (1993) that made the first clear, direct statement regarding equal opportunity for the various groups in the society, a policy resembling 'distributive justice.'[60]

The 1993 Task Force on Education stated:

> We are fully committed to the view that all our citizens, regardless of their gender, class, culture, ethnic origin, etc., have the ability to learn and should be provided with the opportunity to develop their potential to the fullest. We also recognise that this is the only true guarantee to sustain and improve our democratic way of life in Trinidad and Tobago.

The Report added:

> Sound and accessible education is also central to the achievement of social equity.[61]

Given the sharp relevance which equality of opportunity has for this study, we cite the Report's next statement: 'Every child has an inherent right to an education which will enhance the development of maximum capability regardless of gender, ethnic, economic, social or religious background.'[62]

This pledge sits alongside the concept of distributive justice to which John Rawls added: 'Laws and institutions no matter how efficient or well-arranged must be reformed or abolished if they are unjust.' Injustice implies that some groups are consistently left out while others are consistently and disproportionally allowed into the realm of privilege and high status.

Therefore, if the objectives of the education plans cited above are not adequately met, it means that the institutions appointed to carry out those objectives are inefficient. If the institutions do not provide equality of opportunity in access and achievement, then they are unjust.

Such conditions help put the educational plans, education system and its institutions to the test of distributive justice. That is, to what extent the Education Plan's pledge to provide equal opportunity to all 'regardless of gender, ethnic, economic, social or religious background' has been fulfilled?

The Ministry of Education '2015 Education for All' Action Plan (2006) further states: '*Critical to the effectiveness of educational policy and planning is measuring the achievement of our objectives...and accessibility to educational opportunities for all.*' Indeed, our focus is to connect the promises of educational opportunities for all with the country's ethnic diversity, class structure, gender and family background.[63] The Concordat illustrates how the politics of education plays out in a multi-racial society.

## NOTES

1.  A High Court case will be used later for illustration: High Court Action CV 2009-1445, Kamla Jagessaar vs A.G. and the Teaching Service Commission.
2.  Quite frequently, a denominational board will submit a recommendation seeking to transfer, discipline or promote a teacher on 'moral and religious' grounds without specifying the exact 'grounds.' Exchange of correspondence, meetings and even controversies result when the Teaching Service Commission asks for specific reasons. The Boards, by and large, claim that they are the ones in a position to make that judgement, not the Commission. One board, for example, at a meeting between the Commission and the Joint Select Committee of Parliament in 2012, said that the Commission and its members are not qualified to question the board's interpretation of 'moral and religious grounds.'
3.  Since 1966, this has undergone over 20 amendments.
4.  Given the minister's powers and the extent of government's control over the education system, it is felt by the boards that the system is not truly a dual system since the Boards have no authority over the curriculum or the final hiring, appointment and dismissal of teachers, etc. See N. Mustapha.

5.  This body is considered independent since its members are appointed by the country's president 'after consultation with the Prime Minister and Leader of the Opposition' Section 124 (2).

6.  High Court Action No. CV 2009-01445, Kamla Jagessar vs Teaching Service Commission. Justice Sebastein Ventour.

7.  High Court Action No. 2009-00318.

8.  CA No. 58 of 2009.

9.  High Court Action No. CV 2009-01445 on April 24, 2009.

10. The defence counsel, Russell Martineau, S.C. advised that it be taken to the Attorney General, Minister of Education and all Boards. The claimant's counsel, Anand Ramlogan became Attorney General in May 2010 and Senior Counsel in 2013.

11. This matter of ownership and jurisdiction has been subjected to several policy interventions by government. For example, see the Final Report of the Working Group on Joint Ownership and Joint Management of Schools, May 14, 1981. Also, Report of Joint Committee between Government and the Roman Catholic Authorities on the Handing Over of Seven Primary Schools, July 26, 1978.

12. Constitution, Section 4(d), (h) for example. Equal Opportunity Act, Sections 4-6.

13. Equal Opportunity Act. Chapter 22:03. Sections 4–8.

14. The implication of this Section for the Concordat was noted in a list of proposals submitted by the Ministry of Education.

15. Such judicial conclusions carry serious implications for equality of educational opportunity – a matter which will be later discussed. The judge added: 'In our jurisdiction I believe the State has a constitutional duty to protect, to preserve and to promote the diversity of choices which currently exist for the benefit of parents for the education of their children, not only on academic matters but also in matters relating to spiritual, religious and moral values.' (p.22)

16. R. Deosaran, 'Race and the Country Club, Race at the Central Bank, the Hijab and the Impotence of the Court.' Paper presented at Conference on Challenge and Change: The Indian Diaspora in its Historical and Contemporary Contexts. Institute for Social and Economic Research. August 16,1995. UWI, Trinidad.

17. Catholics comprise 30% of the population, Muslims 6%.

18. The SDMS school board manages over 43 primary and five secondary schools.

19. The judge relied on a case, Associated Provincial Picture House Ltd. v Wednesbury Corporation [1948] 1 K.B. 223.

20. Such pressure will help remove the stigma attached to the government schools while also removing the label 'prestige' from the high performing denominational schools. Several recent calls, public and official, have

been made by the author for a Task Force to examine the reasons for the relatively low performance of many government schools and make actionable recommendations for correction.

21. Proposals submitted by Commission to Ministry of Education for amendments to Education Act, especially to Clause 14)1) of the Act. November 30, 2009. The author was a member of the Teaching Service Commission (2011–13)

22. Ibid. p. 1

23. Ministry of Education. November 1999. p. 37.

24. In January 18, 2012, the Association of Denominational Boards submitted a six-page set of Recommendations to the Government for revising the Concordat. These proposals sought to confirm and some cases, strengthen the role of denominations schools to further the moral and spiritual education of students.

25. This Parliamentary Committee is empowered to inquire and report on all Service Commissions (except the Judicial and Legal Service Commission) and including the Teaching Service Commission and the Ministry of Education. The Committee Report is dated June, 2005. Trinidad and Tobago Parliament.

26. Report of Joint Committee Between Government and the Roman Catholic Authorities on the Hand-over of Seven Primary Schools by the Roman Catholic Education Board of Management and Cabinet Decisions Thereon. July 28, 1978. Government Printery.

27. The Joint Management Structure proposed by the Catholics involved the church, the state and the community.

28. These were: Anglican(3), Fundamental Baptist (1), Methodist (4), Presbyterian (4), Roman Catholic (14), Trinidad Muslim League (1), Ayra Prati-Nidhi Sabha (Vedic) (1). Those Boards not handing over: Methodist, Sanatan Dharma Maha Sabha, Tackveeatul Islamic Association, African Methodist Espiscopal, Seventh Day Adventist, Baptist Union, Moravian.

29. Ibid. p. 47.

30. Ibid. p. 47.

31. Final Report of Working Group Appointed by the former Prime Minister on National Ownership and Joint Management of Schools. May 1981.

32. The funding formula at that time: 2/3 fromGovernment, 1/3 from Denominational Boards for capital projects. Negotiations for a revised formula and school management were not successful. Denominational schools are now fully funded.

33. The reasons for such high-performance, as previously listed, include getting the students with high marks at SEA, closer teacher supervision, etc.

34. Final Report of Working Group Appointed by the former Prime Minister on National Ownership and Joint Management of Schools. May 1981.p. 8.
35. Working Group Report. p. 9.
36. Ibid. p. 12.
37. Working Group Report. p. 17.
38. Working Group Report. Appendix 1.
39. Ibid.
40. Assessment of the Plan for Educational Development in Trinidad and Tobago, 1968-83. pp.2–3.
41. Ibid. p 3.
42. As an example of the relative growth of government schools and denominational schools, from 1876 to 1887, the number of denominational schools increased from 47 to 57; for that same period government schools increased from 19 to 45. (Referenced in Campbell, p.32.)
43. Of the 39 Denominational Secondary Schools, Roman Catholic=16, ASJA=6, Presbyterian=5, SDMS=5, Anglican=4, Pentecostal=1, Baptist=1, SWAHA=1. It is no secret that in order for a School Board to establish a denominational school, the Board or broadly speaking, the racial or religious group which it represents must not be opposed to the current government. This calls for, on the part of the Boards, a special kind of pragmatic politics. In any case, the PNM's policy has been somewhat reluctant to establish more denominational schools.
44. Ibid. p. 2.
45. Paper delivered at Teachers St. Patrick District Conference. 2014.
46. Ibid. p. 3.
47. Centre for Ethnic Studies. p. 380. For example, between 1988 and 1992, 2962 students were taken in through the Concordat.
48. Ministry of Education. 1985. p. 18.
49. N. Mustapha, 'Denominational Boards and the Education Act, 1995.'
50. Ministry of Education data supplied to Parliament and Teaching Service Commission. 2011.
51. Ibid.
52. Ministry of Education Administrative Report, 2010–11. 2012. p. 47.
53. Ministry of Education, Annual Administrative Report, 2010-2011. Revised March 22, 2013. p. 39.
54. Ibid. p. 39.
55. Public Lecture on Secondary Schools. Woodford Square. October 26, 1965. In Forged from the Love of Liberty (Selected Speeches).Port of Spain, Trinidad, Longman Caribbean. 1981. pp. 242-243.
56. 'Access, Equity and Academic performance.' IDB. Washington: IDB Bookstore. 2002. pp. 24-30.

57.  Ibid. p. 47. The importance of this reference is that, once again, to note the reluctance to engage in the specifics of ethnic diversity or social class stratification in schooling as matters of equality and equity. Though, in fact, the IDB Report acknowledges the global value of educational equality, etc.

58.  Education Act No. 1 of 1966. Both government and assisted schools are defined as 'public schools' (Section 11).

59.  Draft Education Plan 1968-83. Ministry of Education. pp. 10-16.

60.  J. Rawls, *A Theory of Distributive Justice*. Cambridge, Mass: Harvard University Press. 1977.

61.  Green Paper on Education. Ministry of Education. 1993.pp. vii–ix.

62.  Ibid. p. xvii.

63.  2015 Education for All Action Plan. Ministry of Education. 2006. p. 16.

# CHAPTER NINE

# The Tragedy of Inequity

*Can citizens learn to seek their own welfare and growth, not at the expense of their fellow-men but in concert with them. The human family does not yet know the answer, but hopefully it will be affirmative.*

Gordon Allport, The Nature of Prejudice

## DOES A MERITOCRACY BREED INJUSTICE?

This chapter seeks, primarily and more precisely, to describe government's early policy framework for developing the country's education system. It also seeks to provide an overview of selection procedures for secondary school placement and the different ideologies behind educational equality. It then provides data to examine the extent to which equality of educational opportunity and educational equity have been achieved through the secondary school entrance examination and procedures, and the implications.

No doubt, since 1956 when the People's National Movement (PNM) came into government under its leader, the late historian, Dr Eric Williams, they naturally saw education as the main driver for both decolonisation and socio-economic development. According to several of its Educational Review Committees, Educational Assessment Reports and Educational and Planning and Development Reports, the policy emphasis was on physical expansion, curriculum development, teacher training and linkages with industrial development.[1]

Eventually, as the Report of the 1993 Task Force in Education noted, questions of educational inequity began creeping slowly into the educational system, especially with the government's establishment of the multi-level system of secondary schooling alongside the traditional, grammar-type government assisted denominational schools. Such observations, however, as earlier indicated, were quite global in content, and without any specific linkages to any specific variations within ethnicity, social class, religion or gender. In other words, while there was educational planning, there was little or no programmatic attention to the sociological implications of planning.

Overall, though, as earlier noted in this Report, the failure rates in the technical/vocational programmes in the new secondary schools were quite high. In the traditional examinations too, the overall failure rates of the government secondary, composite and senior comprehensive schools, especially when compared to the government assisted denominational schools, were disturbingly quite high.[2]

In addition to relatively low academic performance, the Report noted that serious problems of school violence and delinquency in these government schools escalated, a particularly troublesome issue being the shift system which the government established in order to accommodate an increased number of students writing the common entrance examination. The shift system, especially attached to the junior secondary schools, appeared as a policy failure. In terms of both delinquency and academic failure, the shift system proved to be a disaster though the intention was to widen educational opportunity for secondary school entry.[3]

Faced with widespread complaints, the government appointed a special committee 'to consider measures to alleviate the problems of the shift system.' The committee noted that the majority of children entering these junior secondary schools 'were drawn from socially deprived areas and were disadvantaged both economically and physically.'[4]

The Shift System Report concluded that 'while the designers achieved their goal of eighty percent (80%) utilization (*secondary school entry*), in so doing they destroyed any possible hope for a successful school education.'[5] The Report recommended smaller schools, zoning and the stoppage of the design of junior secondary schools.[6]

In other words, based on school-performance evidence and widespread public concerns, the junior secondary school system had failed. And connected as it was to the higher composite and comprehensive schools, these latter school types had their 14+ feeder linkage also wrecked. With this, too, equality of educational opportunity and equity suffered serious blows, especially given the generally socially deprived background from which the junior secondary school students came.

Rubbing salt in these public policy wounds was the highly visible fact that the government assisted denominational schools were consistently producing much better academic results, even capturing almost all advanced level scholarships. During these controversial years, the 1970s, school by school comparisons grew to the extent that the term 'prestige schools' became publicly attached to the denominational secondary schools – a title which remains unremovable up to today.

In its 2011 Report on the National Certificate of Secondary Education (NCSE) examination, for example, the Ministry of Education concluded that: denominational schools outperformed government and private schools in all subject areas.[7]

In the struggle to remove the stigma so generally and sometimes unfairly attached to these government secondary schools, government subsequently appointed a National Task Force on Education which concluded that concerted efforts had to be made to change the negative image and perceptions associated with these schools.[8] The Report further advised: *'In the first place, we must seek to improve the level of self-esteem of students so that they do not manifest in fact the behaviour associated with them. Positive values should be inculcated to combat the negative patterns of behaviour that students may adopt.'*[9] But how? This seems almost like blaming the victim – twice. Nothing much said then about school environment, quality teaching, parental linkages, etc., factors which impact on 'students' self-esteem.'

In the first place, the 'negative perceptions of the schools' could change by the schools' improved performance and academic output. Not firstly by students' 'self-esteem' or 'positive values.' The children's self-esteem also did not arise by magic, but apart from possible family drawbacks, the quality of schooling had something significant to do with 'students' self-esteem,' a phenomenon very likely linked to the self-fulfilling prophesy.

How is the school going to improve the self-esteem of students and change public perception if not by improved quality teaching and improved school performance, hard as it may be? That is how the denominational schools did it at first.[10]

It is from here that the positive values the Task Force called for would mainly arise. Ironically, it was a former member/secretary of the Task Force who subsequently noted the range of hardships which these students experienced and which affected their self-esteem.[11]

## EVOLUTION OF THE EQUITY PRINCIPLE

After being subjected to a series of public consultations, this Report was modified and turned into an 'Education Policy Paper (1993-2003).'[12] Here there was a better appreciation for the effects which the community, family and school environment had upon the children's social, psychological and academic condition.[13] This Report emphasized its premise this way:

> As a national community, we are fully committed to the view that all our citizens, regardless of their gender, class, culture, ethnic origin, etc., have the ability to learn and should be provided with the opportunity to develop that potential to the fullest.

The Report added: '*We also recognise this as the only true guarantee of the kind of personal and social efficacy needed to sustain and improve our democratic way of life in Trinidad and Tobago.*'[14] This was a significant step in the march towards a policy of equality of opportunity and equity *within* a multi-ethnic, class-ridden society with a colonial past. This 'liberal-egalitarian' pledge was never made so precisely before. Psychological capital was firmly recognized as a driver of education as well as economic prosperity.

Carrying its pledge further, the Plan stated that 'the educational system must provide curricular arrangements and choices to ensure that cultural, ethnic, class and gender needs are appropriately addressed.'[15] An educational equity note was further struck when the Plan advised that since '*students vary in natural ability, schools should therefore provide for all students, programmes which are adapted to varying abilities, and which provide opportunity to develop differing personal and socially useful talents.*'[16] Conceptually, this was a watershed position. Previously, education reports shunned this equality and equity challenge, drowning the issue into global statements like 'education for all,' etc.

## COMPENSATORY EDUCATION

This corollary 'compensatory education' objective commendably emphasised 'individual improvement' but did not set specific educational criteria, for example, catching up in CXC passes or SEA results. Of course, such specificity could well be operationalised within the general proposition put forward by the Plan. But this is a different proposal from one which, having noted gross academic disadvantages by race, social class, gender, school type or parental type, proposes 'group rights' to educational equity rather and compensatory education for individuals.[17]

Such an accomplishment and policy action would emerge from appropriate research and evaluation. In fact, the Plan stated:

> A basis assumption underlying these decisions on education must be informed by empirical evidence as well as philosophical orientations. To date, in Trinidad and Tobago, we have been relatively strong on philosophical orientation or judgements about education, but relatively weak on the use of empirical evidence.[18]

The Plan's position of being *'fully committed to the view that all our citizens, regardless of their gender, class, culture, ethnic origin, etc., have the ability to learn and should be provided with appropriate opportunities'* appeared as a quantum 'equal opportunity' leap from the more bureaucratically and technically-driven reports of the past.

What this 1993–2003 Plan did was to establish a policy platform on which a Caribbean sociology of education could build, that is, by seeking to measure the extent to which equality of opportunity and especially educational equity are achieved within the social and demographic factors cited in its ten-year Plan. Our connection between this Plan and its antecedent educational plans (including the Green Paper) is an attempt to indicate the evolution of policy thinking in terms of the society's multi-ethnic diversity and social class-challenges in education.

## APPRECIATION FOR DIVERSITY

In the latter case, the general purpose was 'education for all' without considering the educational inequities within the various ethnic and socio-economic groups in the formerly colonised society, and where, more precisely, remedial and compensatory interventions are necessary for equity.

Acknowledging that 'a sound and accessible education is also seen as central to the achievement of social equity,' the Plan added:

> Our learning systems, over the last two decades have not generated the expected quality of graduates in the proportions which our levels of educational expenditure per pupil have led us to hope for, and it is generally recognised that they do not cater as efficiently as they might for those who are 'educationally at risk,' as well as, more particularly, for those individuals in our community with special needs.[19]

As the 2002 IDB study on this country's educational system further noted, educational data on race or social class has been absent. The Report advised: 'Improving education equality is implicitly related to ethnic equality.'[20] However, in its recommendations, the IDB did not insert such specific data collection as a policy requirement. This apparent reluctance to connect the concept of equality of educational opportunity and equity more precisely to the challenges of ethnic diversity, social class divisions and gender restricts improved remedial targeting.

Notwithstanding the IDB Report, after assessing the data on enrolment, expenditures and quality of education, did make some relevant findings:

1. The country's 'secondary education system is diversified and fragmented. The stratification of the system both reflects and contributes to inequality and inequity in the larger society.'

2. The unsatisfactory academic performance of students in the government schools as compared to those in the denominational schools.

3. Large disparities in educational experiences characterize students from different socio-economic backgrounds and in different educational institutions.(e.g., denominational secondary vs government secondary)[21]

4. Access to schooling and knowledge favours student from higher-income households and from urban areas which causes significant inequity in education.

5. The high failure rates existed in the technical/vocational programmes and, supporting a government Report on Technical/Vocational Training, pushed for such programmes to be placed *after* the general education gained at the five-year secondary schools.[22] Subsequent research and Ministry reports support these trends.[23]

It is therefore clear at this point that from research and related authoritative assessments of the education system, the challenges of equality of opportunity and equity existed, continued to exist and, given the apparent lack of attention to the deeper side of these issues, seem likely to continue thereby contributing to a dysfunctional multi-ethnic and class-driven society.

In 1999, the Ministry of Education conducted an assessment of the education system for the years 1990 to 1998, thereby including the first five years of the 1993-2003 Plan. This assessment, entitled 'National Report on Education for All 2000,' focused mainly on administrative and physical features of the system with substantial attention paid to early childhood education and primary school system.

One of its major qualitative findings was that girls outperformed boys in the Common Entrance examination.[24] Notably, however, there were no further data or analyses on the questions of equality of opportunity or educational equity as identified in the 1993-2003 Education Plan.

In other words, at that assessment point, we did not know how far the equity objectives of the 1993-2003 Plan had been satisfied. That is, for example, that '*the educational system must provide curricular arrangements and choices that ensure that cultural, ethnic, class and gender needs are appropriately addressed.*' This is part of the equality of opportunity and equity work that needs to be done in order for the independence process and the more precise promises of decolonisation and socioeconomic mobility to be richly accomplished in this multi-ethnic society.

In this regard, the Government Education Plan stated: '*It must be realised and accepted that any Educational Plan for Trinidad and Tobago must have as one of its prime goals the preparation of our citizens leaving the secondary education sector seek either immediate employment or further education at some higher level.*'[25]

## EQUALITY OF EDUCATION: FROM POLICY TO PROOF

There are at least two major ways to assess the promise of equality of educational opportunity. One is to assess the movement of students from primary to secondary school and two, to assess the academic and occupational status of students who leave the different types of secondary schools (e.g., government secondary vs government assisted schools). We now look at the first one. The second one will be examined later.

## QUALITY BEHIND QUANTITY: THE NUMBERS STORY

Through several educational planning reports, the government from 1968 to 1983 embarked on a massive expansion of its secondary school programme, especially with its multi-tiered levels of junior secondary, composite and senior comprehensive schools. The number of government secondary schools went from 21 in 1969 to 65 in 1983, a 210% increase in fourteen years.

Within that same period, denominational secondary schools went from 29 to 28,[26] putting the total number of secondary schools from 50 in 1969 to 93 in 1983, an 86% increase. In 2015, 39 of the 125 secondary schools were denominational. This 1969–1983 period could be called the 'golden era' of educational expansion and is worth noting in order to indicate where the policy emphasis was and why the challenges for subsequent equality and equity arose in subsequent years. Today, there are 551 primary schools: private = 45, government = 138, denominational = 368. For the 125 secondary schools: government = 86, denominational = 39.

In terms of physical expansion and enrolment, there were other significant developments in the secondary school sector, particularly in the 1969-83period:

1. At all public secondary schools, enrolment moved from 30,359 in 1970 to 90,724 in 1981 – a 200% increase.[27]

2. The allocation of secondary school places also increased. Out of 29,206 students writing the Common Entrance Examination in 1968, 5,278 got placed. Out of 28,333 writing in 1983, 19,086 got placed – a placement increase of 262%.

3. In 2011, out of 17,280 students writing the SEA examination, 95% were placed into government and denominational secondary schools (2.7% into private secondary schools). Since then, in each year over 90% of students were placed in a government or assisted secondary school. Around 4% went into pre-vocational centres.

4. Government expenditure on education moved from $47 million in 1968 to $1.2 billion in 1983 – from 16% of government expenditure down to 13.2% of government expenditure.

5. In comparison, for its 2011 budget, the Government allocated $4.2 billion to the Ministry of Education, 7.43% of government expenditure. In 2015, it was over $11 billion.

# BRIDGES TO CROSS:

## CE and SEA Examinations

Given the pivotal importance of the Common Entrance Examination (CE) and its replacement, the Secondary Entrance Assessment (SEA) Examination, in terms of equality of educational opportunity and equity, it is helpful to provide some relevant evolutionary features of these two bridges to secondary schooling.

Proudly emerging from the rigid, grammar-type College Exhibition days, the government, from 1968, made significant moves to expand the educational system, physically and with enrolment. For example, the secondary school intake increased from 5,278 in 1968 to 19,800 in 1984, that is, from 18% in 1968 to 67% in 1984.[28]

The Ministry concluded that the fact that the transition rate of these 11+ students from primary to secondary school at the end of the Plan (1983) stood at 70% and that 66% of the 12-16 age group population was enrolled in public secondary schools, was sufficient proof of the progress in achieving the objectives of the Plan.[29] Today, there is universal secondary education, 95% of the 18,000 who wrote the SEA entered one type of secondary school or another.

Three deep-rooted challenges still faced the government:

1.  How to develop technical/vocational programmes to help diversify the post-colonial economy.

2.  How to invoke an effective value change in the population so that the popular emphasis on grammar-type education and university aspirations can be modified so as to make technical/vocational courses more attractive.

3.  How to develop an education system with highly visible equality of education and educational equity across all secondary schools.

Again, and quite notably, with all that quantitative proof of progress, nothing substantial was discussed about the equality or equity factor regarding ethnicity, social class, parental type, etc. No proof came forward. It seemed more a matter of numbers and physical expansion, both of which were needed at the time. But, as the history of equality of education has shown, once physical expansion gets too far ahead of equality and equity issues, it becomes very difficult to rein in the horse. The system takes on a life almost of its own.

The equality and equity issues did subsequently arise in the Ministry's Plans, but more as matters of missionary principle than of the need for evidenced-based reforms and policy action. As an example of the Ministry's early reluctance to take an evidence-based approach to the educational equity challenge, its National Test Report, as late as 2004, provided extensive details of the results by gender and by the eight Educational Districts.[30]

However, in this Report there were no published data or analysis according to school type (government vs denominational), ethnicity, social class or parental type, which are some of the critical areas to assess earlier pledges of educational opportunity and educational equity can be assessed. However, with some sense of the equity factor, the first recommendation in the Report was shyly made: '*Studies should be commissioned to provide an understanding of students' performance e.g., gender, socio-economic status, ethnicity, type of school, styles of examination and early development.*'[31]

## QUANTITY WITHOUT EQUALITY

Dealing more precisely with secondary education, the Ministry's Report contained the following:

1. Replacing the pre-1961 secondary school entry system (school examinations and few College Exhibitions), with a national common entry examination for secondary school, '*the establishment of free secondary education further increased equitable access, largely transcending geographical, ethnic, socio-economic and gender differences.*'

2. Notwithstanding marked improvements in the performance of clusters of students who perform at high levels of excellence, certain negative perceptions persist and give cause for concern.

3. Other clusters of secondary students demonstrate low levels of literacy, ambivalence to scholastic effort, lack of motivation and ambition, disruptive behaviour in and out of school.

4. Common perceptions include relative educational under-achievement of males, socio-economic and ethnic imbalances with respect to attainment and drop-out rates, increasing elitism, widening of gaps in earning potential and possible links with deviant or criminal activity.[32]

The Report then asked: 'Are these perceptions supported by primary data? Do they direct the agenda of education researchers?' Indeed, these concerns expressed so clearly in the Ministry's 2002–3 Report are the very ones which also concern this study – the promise of educational equity by 2015, the need for primary research data to examine the equality issues, etc.

While the ministry's report noted 'certain negative perceptions' regarding 'relative underachievement of males, socio-economic and ethnic imbalances,' it wisely suggested that research be done to see the extent to which such 'negative perceptions' would be supported by primary data. This is a major concern. Hence, the socio-economic, ethnic, gender and family imbalances form a major focus of our data collection and analysis.

It is notable, however, that the ministry report did not specifically identify the marked differences in quality output between the government assisted denominational schools and the government schools. These school by school differences, too, occupy a central, disturbing place in the quest for equality of educational opportunity, and more so, equality of educational output. Notably, little or no mention was made of the well-known and marked differences in both entry to and graduation from the government assisted secondary schools as compared to the government secondary schools.

Annually, crossing these two critical bridges – first, the CE examination and then the SEA – always brought joy and mostly tears by parents and children over the results. Troublesome issues of merit, equality, equity and parental dissatisfaction repeatedly arose, and still do with the SEA.

Thousands of students do not get their first, second or even third choice. Publicly grieving over her son's disappointment at the SEA results in 2013, one mother exclaimed to the television interviewer: That is 'the misery of education.' But such tears do not lead to loud protests over educational inequality. Most of the grieved are also church members. The tears also often evaporate with the great hope for another chance to get into a prestige school.

## DIVERSITY AND EXPANSION

Free secondary education came in 1961, the year of the general election and political independence. Given the predominant existence then of five-year traditional grammar-type schools, the CE examination was then designed to assess who were fit for traditional education, but as the enrollment numbers grew with varied talents, frustration seeped in. Once again, physical expansion – quantity education – faced the disconcerting challenge from quality education.

Given its early commitment to education as a major tool for decolonizing the education system, the PNM government pressed for increased secondary school enrolment, a decision which gained widespread public approval, condemning the old elitist scholarship days. But was it?

Noting the policy dilemma, the Government National Task Force on Education stated: 'Pupils and teachers were caught in a psychology of failure and experienced the frustration and rage/apathy which helplessness evokes. The social needs of the wide ability range of pupils now in secondary schools clamour for attention and response.'[33]

The Report added: 'It is not enough to place children in schools. Schools must be caring and health-giving environments which release creativity and sound human development. Investment in quality education could well prove a substantial saving to the country.' 'Such attention', the Education Report argued, 'could become a powerful preventive system saving the society from serious anti-social behavior.'[34]

From several studies – some cited earlier – the drop-out rates, violence and delinquency from the government secondary schools particularly, confirm this early warning by the Education Report.

According to a government-commissioned 'Youth at Risk' study, as the physical expansion of the secondary school system continued, so too, did the rise of failure rates, youth gangs, school violence and delinquency.[35] This report contained several recommendations regarding the marked differences between the denominational secondary schools and the government secondary schools.

Educator Lennox Bernard, for example, wrote: '*Many of the secondary schools that students in disadvantaged communities are generally assigned to were under-performing and had a low level of achievement at the CSEC level. It is clear to us that a disproportionate number of failure schools serve the poorest and most disadvantaged children.*' These children got relatively low marks at the entrance examination. These low performing schools are generally the government secondary schools (of whatever kind).[36]

## Public Rage over SEA

How long could a country, facing very strong and persistent pressures to change its secondary school placement policies, continue year after year to maintain these questionable policies? Why are the alternatives seemingly difficult to implement? Over twenty years ago, educator Gowrie put it this way:

> The Common Entrance Examination is perhaps the most controversial issue that appears to plague the nation's education system...It is now viewed in the 1990s with disdain and all sorts of negative connotations and criticisms.[37]

It has been argued that there should be no need for an entrance examination at all, given the young age of the students at hand. In any case, it is not so much that the CE examination or its successor, the SEA, is intrinsically unfair; it is that there is too much inequality between the high-performing denominational schools and many under-achieving government secondary schools. And the dispersion of students into such 'dens of inequity' puts the SEA as the chief culprit whereas the more effective solution is to develop sustainable strategies to improve the academic performance of the affected government secondary schools.

In fact, if all secondary schools, denominational and government, were high-performers and attractive to parents and students, the SEA may not be necessary at all. After all, this equity gap was well known since the 1970s after the Common Entrance began in 1961. The issue does not stop there though. What will be done with the students whose abilities and interests are not grammar-type?

## Pleas for Equity

In a persuasive appeal to remove the SEA and close the gap between the denominational and government secondary schools, educator Paula Mark wrote:

> Universal access to schooling is based on the principle of equity and social justice. Thus we are challenged to revisit policies and practices to ensure that they are equitable and just. Those policies and practices that have entrenched inequality and sustained inequity in our education system must go. The SEA is one such practice.[38]

She concluded:

> We should seek to eliminate differences among schools.[39]

Also expressing concern over educational inequity, Anthropologist Marion O'Callaghan wrote:

> Don't expect to find the daughter or son of a lawyer, doctor or well-heeled businessman being channeled to a comprehensive (school) of any sort.[40]

Noting the inequities in the education system, she added:

> Another reason concerns the greater political capacity of the middle class to intervene...Given these factors it is not surprising that Indian children do better at SEA than do 'Creoles.' These are not, however, the only factors.

On a later occasion, she wrote:

> If there is any agreement among religious authorities, it is that schools should be unequal...As long as this continues, and for as long as we remain a people steeped in religiosity that is external of religion, schools will be unequal in quality and certain strata of the society will be discriminated against.[41]

Even as low down as early childhood education, she further noted, the social class impact is felt as richer people put their three and four year-olds in prestige early childhood schools too.

It is well-known that rich parents or middle and upper class professionals gain preferential access for their children in prestige primary schools – the ones that annually generate high proportion of SEA passes for prestige secondary schools. The Study on Secondary School Placement further found that such 'privileged access' also works for children who are taken in the prestige secondary school through the twenty percent concession, or further up at Forms Two or Three. These are some of the issues, the Study argued, which help distort the merit system of the SEA.

Also tackling inequality in the country's education system was Professor Theodore Lewis, with specific aim at the role of the Concordat. He wrote:

> The state should stop using tax-payers' money to fund denominational schools. These schools should essentially be run like they are all over the world, that is, as private schools.[42]

## THE BLACK YOUNG MALE

Allegations of discrimination were also raised by black activist, David Mohammed when, after noting the ethnic-driven nature of prestige secondary schools, asked:

What about 'the poor black children'? Which government will specifically pay attention to the plight of the many brilliant students of African descent who do well in their exams but who are still not sent to the schools of their choice that they may have earned enough marks for?[43]

He added:

Most of the young black males who have found themselves on the wrong side of the law have also passed through the low-prestige school system and have hardly attended any of the top boys' colleges.[44]

Again, it must be noted, that such media-driven perceptions are read by thousands and briskly swirl through the social media. The implications for the multi-ethnic society are obvious.

In addition to the protests cited earlier, public rage over the SEA, the emergence of prestige schools and inequitable secondary school placement, have been growing over the years. A newspaper editorial stated:

The task before us all is to make all of our schools 'prestige schools' in that the quality of education, discipline and esprit de corps can become universal across the nation.[45]

No doubt this may take some time, but as the editorial advised, 'the Ministry should now plan ways to achieve it.' That was in 2013.

## SEA INEQUITY

Again, in 2014, while calling for an equalisation of secondary schools, the same newspaper editorialized:

The SEA is extremely stressful for children, parents and teachers. We'd suggest that instead of the SEA, placement could be done on a combination of zoning and course-work.[46]

Branding the SEA 'elitist and unnecessarily stressful,' Citizen Joel Quintal wrote:

Some parents who are financially and socially well-off placed are able to bypass the system by coercion, favours and the infamous Concordat. The SEA system panders to a pervasive colonial mentality. We must not continue to placate those with vested interests.[47]

Repeating previous appeals, the Trinidad and Tobago Unified Teachers' Association (TTUTA), in July 2014 said:

The SEA perpetuates inequity and marginalization among broad cross-section of the country's student population. Indeed, this system causes large numbers of people to feel they are unjustly and unfairly treated and this leads to social upheaval and unrest. This is evident in the high levels of crime and deviance currently witnessed in the society.[48]

The association advocated 'zoning' without the SEA as one solution.

As another example of public unease, Richard Thomas' letter to the editor said: *'Time to do away with the SEA due to the excessive stress on children, parents and teachers and Ministry officials.'*[49] And yet another appeal comes from T. Tam-Cruickshank who said *'Get rid of the SEA'* but do not zone children until *'all schools are of equal caliber.'*[50]

Such public frustrations over the SEA and government's lack of action are more severely expressed over social media and through television interviews, the point being that as the next SEA comes along, such public unease will increase. The central issue in the public mind is the inequalities and unfairness in the educational system. The former Education Minister, Dr Tim Gopeesingh himself, agreed that the SEA is stressful and invited suggestions for change from the public.

In a May 2014 newspaper report, after a Standard Five pupil committed suicide the day before the SEA, the former Minister said: *'Government continues to look for ways to make the exam experience easier for the thousands of pupils who sit every year.'*[51] But, as several professionals inquired, is the issue whether the examination is difficult or easy, or is it the necessity for having the examination itself?

## THE PRESTIGE SCHOOLS' DILEMMA

To the former Minister's remarks, the President of the teachers' association (TTUTA) saw this as a 'delaying tactic' and said that the Minister *'is bowing to political pressures from denominational boards which want to maintain the status quo presiding over prestige schools.'*

The association President added: *'If you take away the schools from the denominational boards, the churches will collapse. If the playing field was leveled and all secondary schools provided equity, then there would be no question of who ran the better schools.'*[52] This latter point is the most crucial of all in the quest for equality of educational opportunity and equity. The TTUTA President said: *'We have really created an artificial kind of problem by perpetuating this system of prestige and non-prestige schools. It is something we have to take serious note of.'*[53]

Both President of the National Parent Teachers Association (NPTA), Zena Ramatali, and the President of the National Primary Schools' Principal Association, Vallence Rambharat, agreed with TTUTA. *'If you are talking about quality education,'* said Ramatali, *'this exam is doing more harm than good.'*[54] Rambharat said: *'SEA is a burden to students, parents and teachers too.'*

All in all, however, and as will be discussed later, the controversy is therefore inextricably connected to six convergent structural factors:

1. That some primary schools (mainly denominational and private) generate higher proportions of students with top SEA marks compared to other primary schools - these become prestige schools.

2. That some secondary schools (mainly denominational) generate higher proportions of final examination passes compared to other secondary schools (mainly government schools).

3. That there are limited places at these high performing secondary schools.

4. (That these high performing denominational secondary schools are managed by denominational boards and have the right to accept 20% of the SEA passes from the list.

5. That such rights are empowered by the 1960 Concordat.

6. That parental and students' pressures for secondary schools of their choice, mainly denominational schools, are restricted by the fact that there are limited places at these preferred (prestige) schools – for example, in 2014, the Ministry indicated that of the 18,239 students writing the SEA, only 3,500 were able to get into the traditional five-year schools (mainly prestige schools.)

Between these structural conditions, there are a set of processes which, as some researchers have noted, do bend the secondary school placement procedures. These processes will be discussed later in reference to the Study on Secondary School Placement.

## INEQUITY BEHIND THE MASK

Within this educational matrix, there have been and still are very serious concerns over educational opportunity and equity and, in addition to other requirements, the most urgent and compelling one is to improve the under-performing government secondary schools. To mask the inequities behind seductive pledges like 'education for all' or 'education is the key passport for a better life' will eventually lead to an angry underclass of youth and discouraged parents.

After the 2015 CAPE and CSEC results were announced, for example, former Minister Tim Gopeesingh, after lavishly announcing the *'marked improvements in both examinations over the past five years,'* went onto congratulate the teachers and parents. He said, for example, that over the period 2010 to 2015, *'the pass rate of pupils achieving grades one to three has improved by 7.3%.'*

The celebration and congratulations were quite deserving, but in terms of equality of educational opportunity and equity, some key elements are still missing. How do we know that whether successes were achieved 'regardless of race, religion, social class, gender or family background' as the Ministry itself promised? These gross figures tend to mask the inequalities and inequities in the system.

## THE DENOMINATIONAL VS GOVERNMENT SCHOOLS

Educator Bernard[55] raised the challenge which has tortured one government after another, that is the well-known difference in academic performance between the denominational assisted secondary schools and the government secondary schools. That is the clash between quantity and equality with serious implications for equal educational opportunity and equity.

There are also political and ethnic implications in that should the government publicly admit to such inequities from the SEA placements, it would appear as a policy failure on their part and an attempt to bring the ethnically-driven Concordat into a protracted controversy much to the churches' displeasure and whose 'suffrage powers' have been so persuasively noted by Catholic Archbishop Finbar Ryan since 1960.

However, Bernard said:

> We have been unwilling to grapple with the failure of distinct groups of students and the class-based nature of school structures...Every year approximately 80% of students preparing to write the SEA, have their parents choose no more than 25-30 secondary schools as their first choice.[56]

He added:

Using 2011 figures, there has persisted significant difference in academic performance between the so-called 'prestige' schools and the rest of the secondary school system...This has placed considerable pressure on the majority of children being prepared for the SEA exam.

He then made the critical remark which continues to disturb parents:

Those who do not succeed in gaining admission to those 'prestige' schools generally have to cope with the psychological trauma of a deep sense of failure, some never overcome this psychological burden at the tender age of 11+...The implications related to this wide ranging low achievement of especially our male youth when linked to poverty provide a risk factor to crime.[57]

This inequity track from primary school to secondary school entry to secondary school performance has lifetime implications for the affected youth. Following the intent of the Draft 1968-83 Plan, the National Task Force on Education stated: *'On completion of five years at secondary level, the individual should be better able to lead a moral, spiritual and creative life as a responsible member of society' and should be able to continue secondary education, proceed to post-primary education either academic or technical/ vocation, join the world of work, become an entrepreneur,' etc.*[58]

Citing the former Prime Minister Dr Williams' proposals, the 1984 Assessment of the 1968–83 Education Plan stated: 'It must be realised and accepted that any Education Plan for Trinidad and Tobago must have as one of its prime goal the preparation of our citizens leaving the secondary school either immediate employment or further education at a higher level.'[59] In Chapter Fourteen, there is some evidence used to test these post-secondary expectations.

Indeed, the National Task Force on Education recognised the problem of growing inequity in the educational system. In fact, it properly expressed widespread public concerns when it said: 'The promise of free secondary education for all remains embedded in the hearts of the population and discontent will continue until all children can be placed in secondary schools that are generally acceptable to parents.'[60]

'Acceptable' means high or similar performance to denominational or other high-performing schools. It implies that zoning or random selection of student placement will not work unless government schools raise their standards.

## THE INEQUALITIES EXPOSED

In its successive Reports on the SEA examinations, the Ministry provided data consistently showing that the denominational primary schools significantly outperformed the government primary schools in this examination. The publicly-approved measure was the number from the primary school who passed for prestige schools, that is, a high performing denominational school. As one Report showed, some denominational primary schools maintained their fame over the years for producing a high proportion of prestige school passes.

Of course, some denominational primary schools did better than others in this regard. With the SEA, there was also a geographical differential, that is, out of the eight educational districts, some districts showed higher performance than others. For example, in terms of percentage of students scoring above 90% in the SEA, Caroni and Victoria districts led the other six districts.[61] The highly visible and publicly troubling differences in academic achievement (student) between the denominational schools and government schools did not attract the level of government concern they should have. The annual shedding of tears and grief by parents and children who fail to get into a denominational prestige school deserve some bold reform efforts, especially with regard to improving performance standards by the government schools, both primary and secondary. It can no longer be a matter of the educational system remaining caught between a rock and a hard place.

## NOTES

1. See e.g., Educational Development Plan for Trinidad and Tobago 1968-83 (Draft). 1968. Ministry of Education; Assessment of the Plan for Educational Development in Trinidad and Tobago. 1984; Education Plan for Trinidad and Tobago, 1985-90. Ministry of Education; Report of the National Task Force on Education (Green Paper). Ministry of Education. 1993.

2. For example, see NEC results, in Education Policy Paper (1993-2003), National Task Force on Education. Ministry of Education. 1993. p. 73.

3. See e.g., Review in Education Policy Paper (1993-2003), National Task Force on Education. Ministry of Education. 1993. esp. pp. 52-56. Also, Assessment of the Plan for Educational Development in Trinidad and Tobago 1968-83. Ministry of Education. 1984. esp. pp. 20-23 for justification, enrolment, etc. Names of these schools recently changed to just 'Secondary' with some curriculum adjustments.

4. Report of the Cabinet-Appointed Committee to Consider Measures to Alleviate Problems of the Shift System at Schools. Prime Minister's office. Port of Spain, Trinidad. 1975. pp. 18–20.

5. Ibid. p. 16.

6. Ibid. pp. 8, 20–22. Linked to the proposal for smaller schools is the 2002 Report by Dr Ralph Romain. Noting the inequitable distribution of resources across the education system and country, the Report proposed decentralisation and corrective measures including educational restructuring. Ministry of Education (Draft Final Report).

7. Ministry of Education Report on 2011 NCSE Results. p. 4.

8. Report of the National Task Force on Education. Ministry of Education. Government of Trinidad and Tobago. (Green Paper). 1993. p. 193.

9. Ibid. p. 193.

10. This troublesome distinction is due in part to the fact that students with highest marks usually get into these church schools. But a lot of other relatively 'low-marks' students get in through the 20% discretion the principals have, thus raising another issue, that of social class and religion-related contact in allocation. The tighter management controls (via School Boards) which the denominational schools have also contributed to teacher quality. In any case, the 'low self-esteem' and low academic performance in these affected government schools do not have to be so significant.

11. Referring to the problems facing such students, a former member/secretary of the Task Force, Dr Lennox Bernard, perhaps on further reflection, later said of government secondary schools: 'We sometimes forget the added challenges that some of these children experience. These include learning problems....poverty, exploitation and low educational attainment.' (*Trinidad Express*. Nov. 5, 2013. p 13.).

12. This Paper, now known as a White Paper laid in Parliament, was prepared by the National Task Force in Education which had as its basis, a Green Paper in 1993.

13. Education Policy Paper 1993-2003, National Task Force on Education. Ministry of Education, Government of Trinidad and Tobago. pp. 41–67.

14. Ibid, p vii.

15. Such 'needs' (p. xvii) require research and assessment systems – also called for by the Plan. p. 29–31.

16. Ibid. p. xvii.

17. This 1993-2003 Plan did outline a rather comprehensive list of remedial education initiatives for both primary and secondary school students. The research and evaluation required for assessing implementation have not been effectively done. The Plan did also emphasise the need for such research and evaluation (p. 29). Had this been done, the extent

of group disadvantages cited above would have been clearly noted for policy action. Also noted is the skepticism regarding the success of compensatory education mainly because of the social structure constraints, e.g., Carnoy,p. 265–266; M. Haralambos and M. Holborn, *Sociology*. London:    Collins Educational. 1995. Reviews of several compensatory education programmes, e.g., HeadStart, etc., show little success. pp. 775-759.

18. Ibid. pp. 29-31.

19. Ibid. pp. viii. The data regarding expenditure, enrolment, examination passes, etc. are in the Appendices of this 1993-2003 Educational Plan.

20. IDB Report on Education Access. p.30.

21. Ibid. pp. 168- 173.

22. Government of Trinidad and Tobago. Draft Report of the National Task Force on Technical and Vocational Training. Ministry of Education. 1995.

23. E.g., Benchmarking School Violence and Delinquency; Ministry of Education Report on 2011 NCSE Results; Ministry of Education Report to Joint Select Committee, 2013 on results for SEA, NCSE, CSEC and CAPE; Ministry Report on Cape Advanced Results. 2011.

24. National Report on Education for All 2000. Ministry of Education. Government of Trinidad and Tobago. 1999. This report included several tables on enrolment, pupil-teacher ratio, etc.

25. Assessment of Plan for Educational Development. p. 62. (Accepting then Prime Minister Dr Williams' proposals).

26. A.S.J.A. Girls' College was opened in 1976. A few denominational schools converted to government schools.

27. Ibid. p. 20.

28. Assessment of the Education Plan 1968–83. p. 70.

29. Ibid. pp. 62–63.

30. Report on National Test 2004. Ministry of Education. November, 2004.

31. Ibid. p.32. The Report reached only as far as Private vs. Public Schools. Moreover, this recommendation echoed the same objectives of a Motion filed by the author in Parliament on February 1988 and approved later that year.

32. Education for All. 2002–3.

33. Ibid. p. 52

34. Ibid. p. 52–53.

35. See e.g.,L. Bernard, 'Reforming our Education System.' pp. 346–350. In S. Ryan, I. Rampersad, L. Bernard, M. Thorpe, P. Mohammed. *No Time to Quit: Engaging at Youth at Risk*. Report submitted to Government of Trinidad and Tobago. 2013.

36. Ibid. p. 349

37. G. Gowrie, *Current Issues in Sociology and Education*. Curepe, Trinidad: DCT Publishing. 1993. p. 9.

38. Dr Mark, a former university lecturer, is a teacher development specialist. *Sunday Express*. July 26, 2015. p. 12.
39. Ibid.
40. Newsday. May 12, 2015. p. 13. Ms. O'Callaghan, former Director of Social Science programmes, UNESCO.
41. *Newsday*, August 24, 2015. p. 13.
42. *Express*, May 21, 2014. p. 14. Professor Theodore Lewis is retired Emeritus Professor, University of Minnesota. He repeated similar sentiments in another article, *Express*, May17, 2015.
43. Described as a messenger of black American activist, Farrakan. *Sunday Mirror*, July 12, 2015. p.13.
44. Ibid.
45. *Express*, September 16, 2013. p.10.
46. *Express*, March 14, 2014. p.10.
47. *Newsday*, March 23, 2015. p. 13.
48. TTUTA President, Devanand Sinanan. Newsday. July 13, 2014. p. 8.
49. Express. July 30, 2015. p. 15.
50. Express. March 14, 2015. p. 15.
51. Express. May 9, 2014. p. 7.
52. *Trinidad Guardian*, July 24, 2014. p. 14.
53. *Express*, May, 9, 2014. p. 7.
54. *Trinidad Guardian*, July 24, 2014. p. 14.
55. Former Director of the UWI School of Continuing Studies (St. Augustine).
56. Ibid. p. 349.
57. Ibid. p. 349.
58. Ibid. p. 54
59. Ibid. p. 62.
60. Ibid. p. 49. At that time in 1993, there were 101 secondary schools in the country with a total enrolment of 97,434. Government traditional schools =19, Government secondary (including JSS) = 52, Denominational Assisted = 30.
61. Ministry Report on SEA – English, Maths, Creative Writing, 2009–2011. 2014

# CHAPTER TEN
# The SEA, Public Anger and Inequality

*An interpretation of equality of educational opportunity may be evaluated properly only within the broader theory of distributive justice in which it finds its home. For it is in such a theory that determines the kinds of educational results to target and the extent to which they should be equalized.*

Kenneth Howe
Understanding Equal Educational Opportunity, 1977

## THE CONCORDAT THREATENED AND INEQUITY

Repeating the then Prime Minister's 1975 proposals to cabinet, the Assessment Report noted that 'equality of educational opportunity for all' was indeed a mission of the government.[1] But from the sociology of education perspective, 'education for all' may well unfairly disguise the hidden disadvantages affecting certain specific ethnic or social class groups with the school population – during and even after schooling. After all, the process of decolonization and the promises of political independence require improved equality of education and educational equity. The primary schools are a good place to start.

Following the introduction of free universal secondary education in 2000 and the SEA in 2001, the Ministry of Education SEA Report indicated that students are assigned to secondary schools based on four criteria – (i) order of merit (ii) students' choice of school (iii) gender and (iv) residence.

The standardised scores are combined and the composite of the standardized scores are then used to place students on the 'basis of merit and choice of schools.' In keeping with the Concordat, principals of assisted secondary schools are afforded the opportunity to choose twenty percent (20%) of the Form One intake. Low achievers (students with 30% and lower of the total composite score) are assigned to 'special' classes in schools where remedial programmes have been established to address their needs.[2]

This means students' placement is ranked on the normal curve, and not necessarily on their raw marks.[3] In that first year of the SEA, 2001, 12,197 students were placed in 5 and 7-year schools (both government assisted and government secondary schools). Almost 10,000 went to other schools (Three-year, Private, Servol, etc.). Things changed. In 2012, for example, over 93% of the 17,683 writing the SEA got into five and seven-year secondary schools; the rest into private or technical/vocational schools, etc.[4]

As earlier noted, the Concordat allowed a 20% student placement at the Principals' discretion. This agreement is intended to help preserve the religious character of the denominational schools. A clear indication of how this discretion was used came from the Study on Secondary School Placement which found a significant relationship between student race and the denominational schools in the Common Entrance.[5]

For example, *Muslim* schools selected 90.9% Indians, 5.4% Mixed and 2.4% Africans; *Hindu* schools selected 91.9% Indians, 8.9% Mixed; *Baptist* schools 61.3% Africans, 6.8% Indians, 31.8% Mixed; *Anglican* schools 43.3% Africans, 19% Indians, 36% Mixed, 0.7% Chinese, 0.2% White; *Roman Catholic* schools 20.7% Africans, 18.5% Indians, 45.5% Mixed, 3.5% Chinese, 9.4% Whites, 2.1% Syrian-Lebanese, *Presbyterian* schools 78.9% Indians, 16.5% Mixed, 1.1% Africans, 1.9% Whites.[6] Wittingly or unwittingly, the education system, to a large extent, becomes a racially segregated system. And with academic achievement also stratified by race. It is such a situation which helps contribute to the tensions between the post-independence quest for nationalism and the constitutional right to ethnic diversity.

## A RED FLAG ON EDUCATIONAL INEQUALITY

As far back as 2004, however, following its analysis of the SEA from 2001 to 2004, the Ministry's Report concluded:

1. Student selection and placement in denominational schools under the Concordat continue to disrupt placement pattern by merit.

2. The SEA placement process continues to legitimise inequities in the school system by sorting students into perceived high scoring, average scoring and low scoring groups and placing them into secondary schools likewise perceived.

3. The placement system is maintaining the notion of different types and quality of schools as well as different quality of education in the school system.

4. The steps being taken by the Ministry of Education to strengthen the Continuous Assessment Programme at the primary level should be supported by appropriate remediation programmes at the secondary level[7] (p. 53).

# Time to do away with SEA

STEADILY, the din has been increasing for the Secondary Entrance Assessment (SEA) exam to be done away with, due to the excess stress the run-up to and aftermath of this one bite at the cherry places on children, parents, teachers and Education Ministry officials.

Many also are

If T&T is to continue on its curre trajectory and accelerate towards su able economic freed... best educat...

Best ever performance in examinations, says PM

Anusha is on top

Check your Sunday Newsday.

**Son beats odds for SEA success**

Charlord Court single mom celebrates as

By MIRANDA LA ROSE

HAKEEM SAMMY, who passed for Queen's Royal College in the recent Secondary Education Assessment (SEA) examinations, defeated the odds to get the school of his choice and is now anxious to start his secondary education.

"I'm looking forward to school. I can't wait," an excited Sammy told Newsday at his family's Charlord Court, Port-of-Spain apartment yesterday.

Recalling when he was told of his results at school on July 3, he said, "I was happy and excited. The first thing

**Carmona hails contribution of East Indians to TT**

By CAROL MATROO

It has therefore been very clear from very early, and confirmed by a Report on the 2008 to 2012 SEA results, that the denominational primary schools – some much more than others – show much higher SEA performance than government schools.[8]

This 2004 Ministry Report, the first on the SEA, virtually attacked the Concordat placement system for creating educational inequity. Having said so, the Report failed to recommend any changes to the Concordat itself, or to the placement system as a whole. Perhaps, more critically, the Report failed at that crucial time and, based on the evidence, to make recommendations for improving the academic performance of the non-Concordat schools – a sin of omission which continues to haunt the educational system up to today.

After all, apart from the constitutional platform on which it is presumed to rest, the Concordat placement is based primarily on merit from the examination and parents'/students' choice. The 20% concession is an 'assurance' given by the government to the Concordat agreement. Notwithstanding this, as indicated earlier, there have been placement aberrations affecting equality of opportunity. The government will have to decide which end to tackle first or if at all – the Concordat end or the deficits at the government schools end.

## THE CONCORDAT STRIKES BACK

Faced with the persistent reluctance of government to take active steps to improve the under-performing government schools and so make them attractive to parents and students, the Concordat and the Denominational Boards, as indicated above, have been subjected to frequent attacks for having prestige schools and contributing to educational inequity. While we will consider the prestige school criticism later, it must be noted that the quarrel with the Concordat and the denominational boards also concerns the hiring and promotion of teachers.[9]

Depending on demand and supply and religious affiliation, some school boards insist on having and promoting teachers on the condition that they are of the same faith and practicing as such. This condition is allowed in the Concordat.[10] As an example, a dispute arose in March 2014 when the Anglican Education Board of Management said it does not have enough teachers to fill existing vacancies at 48 of it schools. The Anglican Board wanted Anglican teachers. At some of these schools, parents protested and a public controversy over the Concordat emerged.

A newspaper editorial headlined 'Think of the children and revisit the Concordat' wrote:

> If teachers satisfactory to the Board and the Ministry cannot be found, the Concordat is clearly failing. If only for this reason, operation of the Concordat needs to be revisited. This will be no easy task. Even the suggestion of a revised Concordat has always met with vehement opposition from all religious bodies involved. That attitude must change if the nation's children are to have their universal right to an education.[11]

The fact is, however, many Boards (e.g., Catholic Board) do not have this problem since they accept suitable teachers of a different faith.

To the accusations that they, the Boards, are 'creating prestige schools' and contributing to educational inequity, the Boards have continuously and collectively rejected these accusations. Indeed, the denominational boards have organized themselves in order to convey a collective voice where required, and to defend themselves too.

One of the Boards' leading spokesmen, Satnarayan Maharaj, Secretary-General of the Sanatan Dharma Maha Sabha (SDMS) stated: '*There are adequate historical and recent experiences to effectively defend denominational education in a culturally and religiously diverse country as ours.*'[12] He added: '*If Denominational Boards rise up, then the entire country will be rising up to support them.*'[13] Governments have recognised this.

He further defended the Concordat and the Boards in a three-part newspaper series. In one article headlined 'the Concordat revisited,' he said parents are pleased with the denominational schools since they also looked forward to their children learning the religion. He called for the Concordat to be included in the Education Act (No. 1 of 1966).[14]

His second article unleashed a severe attack on those who criticized the Concordat and denominational school boards. He wrote:

> The education system in T&T would have crumbled with alarming swiftness if it were not for the enormous presence and contribution of the several denominational boards. In recent times, it has become fashionable for a small group of idle individuals to attempt to undermine the status of the denominational schools in the education system.[15]

Criticising TTUTA, he added:

> Truancy, deviance and indiscipline are the key outcomes of the irresponsibility that will result in the positions taken by TTUTA. Some people seem inclined to demonise denominational schools as being responsible for the perceived unequal education system. This is further from the truth. All our schools have been consistently performing in various spheres – religion, cultural, intellectual, etc., with high levels of success, and so too are other denominational schools.[16]

Calling upon the government to improve performance of the government schools in his final article, he wrote:

> The enemies of denominational schools are filled with rage and envy. Those attacks are nothing but smoke screens for their own failure to achieve the standards set by denominational schools. There is a cry by people for 'a level playing field' instead of searching for solutions to improve student performance at government schools.[17]

## THE FEARSOME CHALLENGE: GOVERNMENT SCHOOLS

School type, that is many denominational primary schools vs government primary schools, generally played a very significant part in students' chances for a quality education, more precisely who gets into a high performing secondary school and who doesn't. This situation arises mainly because higher proportions of students from the denominational primary schools get relatively high marks at the SEA. And they enjoy having a higher proportion of their 'first choice' schools.

The twenty per cent Concordat discretion aside, it is argued by the school boards especially, that the placement is a merit-driven one. However, the fact that year after year, certain social groups remain disadvantaged in this merit system, suggests that something is wrong if educational opportunity and educational equity are the society's objectives. A look at the secondary school examinations indicate that the school-type educational disadvantages at entry also persist up to that level as well – as does educational output.

## THE NUMBERS OF INEQUITY

For example, in 2011, 33,138 entered for 34 subjects in the CSEC. A total of 7,183 (21.7%) passed five or more subjects. With this measure, the denominational secondary schools outperformed the government secondary schools by a ratio of 5:1. That is, for every five or more subjects passed at a government secondary, on average, five students passed at the denominational schools compared to one student in the government schools. Further, while the total number of scholarships moved from 329 in 2010 to 348 in 2011, over 90% of them were awarded to students from the denominational secondary schools.

Regarding the Caribbean Secondary Education Certificate (CSEC) examination, the Ministry's 2010-2011 Administrative Report, quite shyly, concluded: '*The Denominational Schools outperformed Government and Private Schools in all subject areas while female students outperformed their male counterparts both at the national and district levels in all subjects.*'[18]

The other Ministry Report on more detailed CSEC results clearly illustrated the very significant extent to which the denominational secondary schools outperformed the government secondary schools especially in the proportion of students who got five or more passes.[19] The results from the Caribbean Advanced Proficiency Education (CAPE) Examination 2011 were similarly disproportionate, perhaps more distressing, given the career options now open for the graduating students.

While there was some curriculum adjustments made to the traditional academic-type subjects in the secondary schools, the denominational vs government secondary school difference persisted. Part of the explanation rested on the varied natural abilities and interests of students. More precisely, students were put in a position to pursue subjects that did not reasonably suit their abilities or interests. Recognising this mismatch while proposing a diversified curriculum for the National Certificate of Secondary Education, the Ministry's Education Policy Paper[20] made this important statement:

> Over the past two decades (1970–1990), Trinidad and Tobago has developed a system of public education which at present cater for the top 75% of its 12–17 age cohort. In spite of the wide range of abilities which this secondary school population represents, the only terminal examinations available to the system are the CXC and Cambridge Certificates which are designed for the top 40% and 20% of the age group respectively, and the National Examinations Council Examinations which were designed to give certification at the craft level for a more mature clientele.

This Policy Paper concluded:

> In effect, this means that the majority of the students in the secondary school are spending five years in preparing for an examination which they do not have the remotest chance of passing. The resultant loss of motivation is at least one of the causes of indiscipline and violence with which the system is plagued.

## INEQUALITY WITH EXAMINATIONS

The difference with CAPE is usually quite astounding. For example, in the 2011 Unit 2 results, while in one educational district, 20% of students from the denominational secondary schools got Grade One, only 7% from the government secondary schools matched that performance.[21]

In another education district, the difference at Unit 1 was 31% (denominational) vs 3% (government). In fact, while five of the denominational schools got above 40% Grade One passes at Unit 1, 11 of the government secondary schools got zero passes at Grade One.

Similarly, 14 of the 41 government secondary schools got zero Grade One passes at Cape Unit 1. For all secondary schools and at both Units 1 and 2, the performance by students from the denominational schools was always much higher than those from the Government Schools. In 2010, the denominational schools were 28 percentage points higher than the government schools, with similar differences continuing in 2011 and 2012.

The examination results for 2012-2015 revealed a similar pattern: students from the denominational secondary schools showed significantly higher academic performance than students from the government secondary schools. The denominational schools also got over 90% of the national scholarships.[22]

Clearly, the type of secondary school a child attends, does make a very big difference. Generally, it seems much, much better in this regard for a child to go to a denominational secondary school than to go to a government secondary school. Such educational inequity calls out loudly for attention. All schools may not be equal; we do not really expect them to be. But such very large, recurring inequalities cannot, should not, be tolerated in a democratic, relatively well-endowed society.

Academic performance is a serious concern for government, parents and the public at large. So why then has such little attention, if any at all, been paid or is being paid to this recurring vicious assault on equality of educational opportunity and equity with the differentials of school-type? Both the political and the educational systems have failed to deliver the promise of political independence.

## THE DAMNING EVIDENCE: VARIOUS SOURCES

In the period after political independence in 1962, the country strove to utilize the Common Entrance and then the SEA not only to increase secondary school enrolment, but to establish a significant amount of educational equity. While enrolment soared into universal secondary schooling, the system faltered with regard to equity by ethnicity, social class and school-type particularly. In fact, given the 'prestige'school phenomenon, the picture of educational inequity was framed by the compounding effects of all three factors operating at once.

There are two major sources from which inequity by ethnicity, class and school type were derived or inferred. One was by the Ministry of Education Reports in which examination performance was listed by school, especially so in the last four decades. Given the denominational sector in the dual system of education, ethnicity was inferred from the list of passes. From such lists, social class required a higher level of inference, producing rough estimates.

The other source came from academic research. In this latter case, and as indicated earlier, there was and still is no doubt that the secondary school placement system is subject to gross ethnic and social class disproportions. As illustrated in the following Chapter, all studies done from the 1960s to the early years of the 21st century, found such disproportions. Some researchers termed it bias. Middle and upper class students were more successful than low or working class students. Students of East Indian or Caucasian descent were more successful that those of African descent.[23] Such differentials showed early signs of inequality and inequity.

One study, for example, found that upper social class did better than lower class students at their secondary school examination. That of course is not surprising. At that time, though, what was interesting was the significant effect 'type of school' had on academic success. That is, students from the government assisted schools performed significantly better than those from the government schools.[24] Other relevant studies cited, confirm that in this country's educational system, especially its secondary level, inequality and inequity exist in significant levels, especially with regard to ethnicity, social class, and parental type.[25]

## EQUALITY MOTION IN PARLIAMENT

In the midst of these studies and widespread public concerns over secondary school placement, two events directly related to the quest for equality of education and educational equity took place. The first was a motion moved in the country's Parliament by the author in 1988. The other was a comprehensive study of the country's secondary school placement in 1994. Let us look at the first event.

In February, 1988, a motion on 'equality of educational opportunity' was placed by the author in the Senate for debate and policy action.[26] The motion sought to capture the serious concerns of the country at that time and also to heal the gaps adversely affecting educational equality in the system. Four of the five Preambles to the motion read as follows:

1. Whereas a major goal of our educational system is equality of educational opportunity as a means towards effective political independence.

2. Whereas there is now a need to develop basic measures of equality of educational opportunity so as to assist effective educational and manpower planning.

3. Whereas the educational system has undergone extensive physical expansion since 1975 but without any systematic evaluation of the quality of education.

4. Whereas there is now a specific need to examine the degree to which the educational system has helped close the gap between the economically disadvantaged and the economically advantaged.

The motion then asked the government to undertake a nationwide study of all schools in 1988, in the first instance, of Common Entrance passes and the consequent allocation of secondary school places among the different secondary schools. The motion proposed five 'equity' variables: students' social class background, family type (e.g., single parent, guardian, etc.), gender, residence and religion.

Naturally, there was some grumbling against the motion within the denominational boards whose apprehensions were conveyed to the then Minister of Education who was himself a former principal of a prestigious denominational secondary school, Fatima College. In any case the motion was approved.[27]

# THE SECONDARY SCHOOL PLACEMENT STUDY

The second event was related to the first. In 1994, the Centre for Ethnic Studies at the University of the West Indies published what appeared as a damning report on secondary school placement in the country.[28] Its title was 'A Study of the Secondary School Population in Trinidad and Tobago: Placement Patterns and Practices.'[29] With a secondary school sample of 83,315 students from 100 secondary schools,[30] the study found:

1. While less than 25% of the students in the 5 and 7-year (prestige) schools came from low or no-income homes, as much as 50% of students in the 'new' government secondary schools came from such homes. These 'new' government schools also contained the highest proportion of Africans. (p. 24).

2. The higher the form level, the larger the proportion of students coming from upper or middle income homes, suggesting 'that students from low income homes leave school earlier than others' (p. 24).

3. Eighty-two percent (82.3%) of Indian and 80% of Chinese students lived in two-parent homes while for Whites it was 77%, Mixed 60.2%, African 52.6% and Syrian-Lebanese 50% (p. 61).

4. Whether five or 7-year schools, Indians accessed more places than any other race group. More of them also 'were placed in schools of their choice.' (p. 25).

5. The denominational schools had more students from two-parent homes than those from government schools, especially the 'new' government schools (p.44).

6. In terms of 7-year traditional girls' schools, girls of African descent comprised 20.4% while Indian girls comprised 27.2% and Mixed girls 30.1%. For the 5-year traditional schools, African girls comprised 1.9% while Indian girls comprised 9.4% and Mixed girls 5.7% (p. 51).

7. When both 5 and 7-year traditional girls' schools were combined, there was a gap of 13.5% and 14.3% respectively between the percentage of places accessed by girls of African descent, and girls of Mixed race and Indian descent respectively (p. 51).

8. Indian males accessed 26.9% of the places in 7-year schools and 37% of the places in the all boys' schools (5 and 7-year schools.). Mixed race boys had 19.1% of the 7-year schools and 28.4% in the all boys' schools. African boys held 18.1% of the places in 7-year schools and 28.1% in all boys' schools (p. 51).

9. Students from upper or middle income levels scored higher in the Common Entrance Examination (1988 to 1992) than those from lower income homes (p. 267).

10. The mean CE scores of African students were generally lower than that of all other groups, while the mean sores of White students were significantly higher than those of students identifying themselves as either Mixed or Indian. (p. 272)[31]

11. Each year (1988–1992) students of Indian descent were selected in greatest number for places in 5-year schools. Students of Mixed race outnumbered all groups for the 7-year schools.[32]

12. Among the Concordat placements, students of Indian descent each year tended to maintain their relative proportions in line with the Forms 1 to 5 school population from which all race groups were

drawn (35.7% to 35.2%)...Students of African descent were selected in much lower proportions than their ratios in the school population indicated (20% to 35%). (p. 400). The other races were selected in much higher proportions than their ratios in the population would lead one to expect (p.402).

13. Among those selected through the Concordat to 5-year assisted schools, students of Indian descent each year had higher scores than students of African descent. Indian females outperformed all others, proportionally. For entry to 7-year schools, there was no significant difference (p. 402).

14. Concordat placement in the 7-year assisted schools realised a distribution of 30.2% of students from upper income homes, 60.2% middle and 6.3% lower. (p. 406). With respect to income level homes of the general school population, the distribution was upper 6.2%, middle 49.8%, lower 38.1% (no response 6%). The inference there is that the Concordat selections are proportionally skewed towards high income homes (p. 407).

15. Overall and for each year for the Concordat intakes into both 5-year and 7-year assisted schools, there was no significant difference in the mean scores of the students by income groups and by school type (p. 407).

16. The equity question here is since the CE scores between the three income groups were not significant, why were the Concordat placements so disproportionately in favour of the upper and middle classes?

17. The Report concluded that some students from the upper income groups, with lower Common Entrance scores that those of the lower income groups do get into the 7-year schools through the Concordat, even though the mean scores are not significantly different (p.409).

18. The merit by marks vs Concordat placement was raised in terms of unplaced students. The Report stated that in each intake year, thousands of placed students had scores which were equal to, or lower than the scores made by the top scoring unplaced students; viz. 9,555 among the 1988 intakes; 6,324 in 1989; 11,128 in 1990; 8,208 in 1991; and 8,305 in 1992. Indeed, one of the main complaints by parents was and still is 'how come some students with lower

CE marks of their children getting into prestige schools while their children not getting in?'[33]

19. The study found that while a merit-driven CE mark guaranteed a preferred place that only applied within the first 5 to 9 percentage points of the top scores. It added that through the transfer system each year, students with significantly lower average CE scores than new sector placements got into 7-year government schools in two counties (p. 439).

From the analyses done, this School Placement Report concluded that through the secondary school entry examination and more particularly, the Concordat, the secondary school population was deeply stratified. The authors complained that 'the Concordat selections reinforce and ensure homogeneity in their schools.' They added: '*Homogeneity breeds polarization – a dangerous practice in a multiracial, multicultural society where people must each day work together in heterogeneous groups*' (p. 436). This view, and a few others, will be discussed later in the context of a 'clash of rights' and a related court judgement.

Regretting the public stigmatisation and low-performance of the government secondary schools, especially the 'new' ones, the Report argued that the low self-concept, damaged pride and feelings of powerlessness of the affected students in these schools would likely lead to aggression (p. 437–8).

Noting that the female of African descent was the most under-represented in the secondary school population, the authors questioned whether there was also that perceived link between education and personal social and economic mobility, could the implication be the 'feminization of poverty'? 'The Africanisation of poverty?' (p.438)

'Why also do students of African descent have consistently significantly lower Common Entrance scores than all other groups in most educational districts?' they then asked (p. 439).

# EQUALITY AND EQUITY[34]

In dealing with the challenges of equality of educational opportunity, the Report stated:

All things equal, all means to accessing the resource being the same, all groups would be expected to access secondary schooling in proportions representatives of their numbers in the relevant population. This has not been the finding in this study.

The Report further said:

> Instead, when all the pieces are put together one can say that the system (primary and secondary) is not user friendly to young people of African descent, especially females, nor to the poor, nor to those from non-nuclear families (p. 440).

The authors declared that with respect to the two majority races Africans and Indians, students of Indian descent in the secondary schools had higher average sores. More of this group than the other was in secondary school, especially in the traditional schools because among the placed students their scores were better (p. 441).

Bringing the merit principle into the 'equality-equity' challenge, they concluded:

> In this respect, Common Entrance scores were generally fairly distributed by school type but there were also too many other intervening factors impinging on the students' scores or on the placement by merit process and even on the possibility of being placed at all (p. 441).

What all this tells us is that there are hierarchies of concerns, starting first with the merit-by-marks principle, then the 80% ministry distribution of placement, then the 20% Concordat selections, then transfers, displaced students, then the results from analyses by students' race, household income, gender, residence and school type.

Regarding inequity in placement, the Report cited examples, including:

1. The unfairness in school placement because of the imbalances in available school places in different districts.

2. The transfer system which significantly allowed students with significantly *lower scores* to be placed in their school of first or second choice.

3. The Concordat selections which acted like a first hurdle to merit placement and thereafter, quite naturally broke the merit placement rhythm and perhaps too, ruptured many a student's life chances (p. 440).

Among the authors' recommendations were:

1. Abolish the Common Entrance Examination (now SEA)

2. Cease the hierarchical ranking of schools and make all schools of equal worth, with quality the main aim.

3. Give school principals and school administrators more autonomy.

4. Improve both teacher and student accountability.

5. Emphasise multi-culturalism both in instruction and curriculum.

The Common Entrance examination was abolished but its replacement, the SEA, faces the same widespread concerns. The purpose, results and comments of this Secondary School Placement Report are used to help illustrate the complexity of placement in a multi-racial, class-driven post-colonial society, and one in which competition for educational success is quite severe.

TTUTA calls for more continuous assessment

# Abolish 'stressful' SEA exam

Sue-Ann Wayow
sue-ann.wayow@trinidadexpress.com

THE Secondary Entrance Assessment (SEA) should be abolished immediately because of undue stress it causes pupils, parents and teach-

pils' competency more than the "narrow" SEA.

Sinanan made the comments after a Standard Five pupil committed suicide on Wednesday, the day before the examination.

PM: Education the passport out of poverty

Minister happy over improved CAPE, CSEC results

Anna Ramdass
anna.ramdass@trinidadexpress.com

HATS off to teachers and parents as the CAPE and CSEC results show that the pupils are excelling, says Education Minister Dr Tim Gopeesingh.

Speaking on Thursday at the post-Cabinet news conference the Office of the Prime Minister, St

The School Placement Report, preceded by a decision of Parliament, was published in 1994, over 20 years ago. Generally, the issues raised in this 1994 Report continue to exist today, for example, the ones related to the Concordat, improving the government secondary schools and the academic performance of black females. A repeat of a Secondary School Placement Study now will produce comparisons which help drive effective policy action. The extent of inequality and inequity in the education system is too glaring and worrisome to be further ignored. Roman Catholic Archbishop Joseph Harris is right. The political will has been missing in action.

## NOTES

1. Ibid. p. 48.
2. Report on the Secondary Entrance Assessment (SEA) 2001-2004. p. 53-54.
3. Ministry of Education. Trinidad and Tobago. November 2004. p. 6. Also, Ministry of Education. Report to JSPC. March 2013.pp. 35-44.
4. Ministry of Education. Report to JSPC. March 2013. pp. 35-44. Also, Ministry of Education Report. Trinidad and Tobago. November 2004. p. 6.
5. Study on Secondary School Placement. UWI: St Augustine, Centre for Ethnic Studies. 1994.p.378. The Study stated: 'Students   of Chinese, Mixed race, Syrian-Lebanese and White descent were however selected in much higher proportions than their ratios in the population would expect....Students of African descent were selected in much lower proportion than their ratio in the population...The majority of Concordat placements each year was drawn from middle and upper income home backgrounds...Students of the upper income group selected to 7-year assisted schools had lower CE scores than any of the others of the income groups in the 1989 and 1992 intakes...At the heart of public perception of unfairness in school placement is the Concordat...and especially so when the recipients of this 'benefit' are not made public and so, melt into the group who had by achievement, earned their place.' Pp. 377-380.
6. Ibid.
7. Ibid. p. 53.
8. Report on SEA Results 2008-2012, Mathematics, Language Arts Creative Writing. Ministry of Education.
9. E.g., see earlier discussion of court judgement, Jagessar vs AG, CV2009-01445.
10. Quite often, disputes of this kind come to the Teaching Service Commission for adjudication. The author was a member of the Teaching Service Commission (2011–2014).
11. *Express*, March 14, 2014. p. 12.
12. *Guardian*, September 4, 2015. Maharaj is Secretary-General of one school board, the Sanatan Dharma Maha Sabha, with 43 primary and five secondary schools.
13. Ibid. p. A 25.
14. *Guardian*, March 1, 2012. p. 29. Maharaj is a newspaper columnist and Managing Director of a television station (Jagriti), a radio station (FM 102.7) and a newspaper, *The Bomb*.
15. *Guardian*, August 21, 2014. p. 25. The SDMS has 43 primary schools and five secondary schools.

16. Ibid.

17. *Guardian* 28, 2014. p. 33.

18. Administrative Report 2010–2011. Ministry of Education, Trinidad and Tobago. p. 32

19. Report on the CSEC Examination 2011. Ministry of Education. August 2011.

20. Education Policy Paper (1993-2003). Ministry of Education National Task Force (White Paper). p. 187. Extracted from Ministry's Draft Education Plan (1992-2002). While students do have varying abilities and interests, these age-group distinctions are not as air-tight as made out to be. The lumping does not take into account the various developmental and intellectual stages of particular adolescents. These views also do not explain why in the technical/vocational courses the failure rate is relatively still high. It is well known that the quality of teaching and parent-teacher relationships, for example, do help improve student performance. This does not mean that a diversified curriculum (grammar and technical/vocational) is not useful and necessary.

21. Caroni District. This difference is even wider on some other districts.

22. This significant performance difference between denominational schools and government schools is well documented in a number of special and annual reports by the Ministry of Education, e.g., the 2011 CAPE Results.

23. The case of the East Indians is interesting since up to the early 20[th]century, they remained the least literate.

24. R. Osuju, *The Effect of Socio-Economic Status on the Educational Achievement of Form V Students in Trinidad*. Institute of Social and Economic Research, University of the West Indies, Trinidad. 1987. p. 182.

25. The concepts and implications of merit, equality and equity are discussed in Chapter Thirteen

26. At that time, 1988, the author was an Independent Senator appointed by the President (1986–91).

27. The Minister, Clive Pantin, quite an amiable person, and several other ministers and members of the Senate spoke in the debate. The National Alliance for Reconstruction (NAR) was the ruling party at the time of the motion. While they approved the motion, the nation-wide study was not then undertaken. It was not until 1992, when the People's National Movement (PNM) came into government that the study was undertaken through its establishment of the Centre for Ethnic Studies at the St. Augustine Campus of the University of the West Indies (UWI).

28. On September 1992, with government support and funding, the Centre for Ethnic Studies at UWI began preparing the study. Though

initially commissioned to examine placement through the Concordat, the Centre agreed 'that while Concordat placings were a subject of national controversy...it was felt that if there was to be any meaningful understanding of what was taking place in the school system at this level, the study had to be extended to include the entire placement process' (Foreword).

29. The Centre's joint Directors were Professors Selwyn Ryan and John La Guerre. The contracted Project leader was Dr Vena Jules.

30. At that time, the race background (self-reports) of the secondary school population was: Africans 34.4%, Indians 36.7%, Mixed 26.9%, Whites 0.9%, Chinese 0.5%, Syrian-Lebanese 0.2% and Others 4%.

31. For the period 1988 to 1992, the Concordat placements were 2,962 (3%) of the total secondary school intake. Ten percent got their first choice – 5 or 7-year school.

Students' religion in Concordat selections: Catholic 41.6%, Hindu 10.9%, E.C./Anglican 7.7%, Muslim 6.2%, Pentecostal 2.1%, Seventh Day 0.8%, Others, No Response 11.8%. Race: Indian 35.2%, Mixed 34.9%, African 20.8%, White 5.5%, Chinese 2.1%, Syrian-Lebanese 1.3%, and Other 0.2%. That time too, the government managed 294 schools (11.5%), Catholic 992 (38.7%, Presbyterian 382 (14.9%), EC/Anglican 217 (8.5%), Muslim 78 (3%), Seventh Day Adventist 22 (0.9%), Others 377 (14.7%).

32. In searching for explanatory factors regarding school placement, the regression analysis showed school choice as having highest value at 28.7%, students' CE score at 27.5%, income level 10.2%, religion 8.8%, residence 4.3%, school management authority 5.4% and race 1.5%. These relationships are compounded in varying degrees. (p.400) For example, a high proportion of White students from high-income homes will score high at CE and get their first choice.

33. The Report questioned the fact that within the five-year period, a total of 4,202 students who did not get initial first choice placement, eventually got later in as 'transfers.'

34. The authors gave their definitions of equality and equity on p. 434 of their Report.

# CHAPTER ELEVEN
# Removing the Masks: School Segregation

*Fair equality of opportunity requires that not only that legal or quasi-legal constraints in equality of opportunity be eliminated, but also that positive steps be taken to provide equality of access – and the means to achieve such equality of access to those with inferior initial competitive position resulting from family background or other biological or social accidents.*

John Arthur and William Shaw
Justice and Economic Distribution, 1991

*The education system here is not user friendly to young people of African descent, especially females, nor to the poor, nor to those from non-nuclear families.*

Study on Secondary School Placement, 1994

This country's education system moved from a colonial, plantation-driven one to a well-funded, free-tuition, dual system with an expansive education plant. It is an enlightening story to tell – from the application of brutal economics and educational deprivations in the plantation to today's policy of 'secondary education for all,' with no tuition fees even at university level.[1] Yet, still, with serious implications for equality of opportunity and equity, most of it is hidden behind the gross numbers of access and outcome.

Ministry trying to ease 'dreadful' burden

Under-performing men a big problem, says Rowley

Guyanese girl, Tobago's best in SEA

This Chapter, as a further attempt, traces the extent to which inequality and inequity is revealed by the available research.

Educational aspirations and achievement have become such cherished, even sacred objectives of individuals and public policy that the general public remains relatively undisturbed by sporadic commentaries, or even research, over systematic inequalities in the educational system, particularly of social class and ethnicity. Children and parents, especially the middle class in particular, are always 'hoping' for a 'prestige' place. Hope stifles sustained protest.

## DOES EDUCATION CHANGE OR PERPETUATE SOCIAL STRATIFICATION?

A major reason for this seeming reticence is the connection between the education system and the country's social stratification system – its elite in particular. This connection is strongly entrenched in industrialised as well as developing countries. Beteille puts it this way:

> The conceptual and empirical quest for social equality is closely linked to the society's social stratification system which in turn acts as a contributor as well as a consequence of educational inequality and inequity.[2]

As an open system, the educational system is naturally affected by a range of specific factors, for example, social class, race, gender, parenting, neighbourhood, etc. Such social and demographic factors can operate positively or negatively upon the students' academic achievement, depending on location and clientele. Because of these reciprocal relationships, the education system remains challenged by the society's stratification system, making robust education reform and quality teaching necessary, but difficult, for escaping the status quo.

In the context of equality of educational opportunity and equity, the ideological and research emphasis has been and is still placed on the extent to which any, some or all of such factors put at persistent disadvantage students from poor, working class backgrounds. What we also need to look at, for example, is the extent to which middle and upper social class students slide down from their class position in the educational system.

In his review of the equality debate, Halsey stated:

> A theory which explains educational achievement as an outcome of a set of individual attributes has lost the meaning of those structural

forces which we known as class. An adequate theory must also attend to those structural inequalities of resource allocation which are integral to a class society. Thus, any attempt to free education from its antecedents and consequences in the class system has to include structural forces as well as individual attributes. Both within and outside the formal educational system there are social forces which weigh systematically against working class children in respect of those types of learning which make for educational issues and subsequently for advantageous occupational placement.[3]

Proposing a set of conditions for structural reforms as well, he warned that 'the translation of such a theory into action would require political leadership with the will to go beyond the confines of traditional liberal assumptions.'[4]In the post-colonial societies 'where individual success in education' is so deeply cherished, such structural reforms, apart from the expenditures needed, would be fraught with sharpened political risks.[5]

Linked as it to the educational system, the occupational hierarchy is also questioned both from recruitment into it as well as from the differential status conferred on its various layers of work. 'The egalitarian critique of the class system,' Parkin said, 'raises objections to the wide disparities of reward accruing to different positions. He added:

Generally, egalitarians have espoused a view of social justice which asks that men be rewarded in accordance with their individual social needs, family responsibilities and the like, rather than in accordance with their roles in the division of labour.

## MERIT VS EQUALITY

The meritocratic critique of the class system, on the other hand, is less concerned about inequalities of reward accruing to different positions than about the process of recruitment to these positions.[6]Parkin concluded:

The prime objection raised is against present restriction on the opportunities for talented but lowly born people to improve their personal lot. Seen from this angle, social justice entails not so much the equalization of rewards as the equalization of opportunities to compete for the most privileged positions.[7]

This latter position, 'equalization of opportunities,' even with its own implementation difficulties, is more palatable at this time to the population than the socialist-driven and almost utopian ones cited earlier. Here and across the Caribbean for that matter, inequality of rewards is tolerated on the basis of the years of study and preparation as well as the cost and sacrifice undertaken to attain high-paying jobs as compared to lower paying ones. The troubling issues raised, however, concern the ways in which such occupation-reward principle is subverted and distorted, e.g., through political patronage and social contacts.[8]

Having recalled some issues of the equality debate and the several government reports promising equal opportunities for all, or having an educational system catering to varied classes and talents, etc., we now take a brief look at what the research says about inequality in education with particular reference to ethnicity, social class, gender and family background.

The Keenan 1869 Report and several research studies on the evolution of the education system in this country have looked at how one or the other ethnic, social class or sex group experienced some form of social marginalisation. Keenan considered the cultural dissonance, dislocations and inevitable discrimination experienced by the former enslaved and indentured East Indian labourers. The East Indians arrived in order to continue the sugar-cane plantation economy. At that time, they occupied the bottom rung of the socio-economic ladder. Sharp differences of religion, language, dress and customs kept them 'a society apart.'[9] Their cultural dissonance and anguish were therefore very stressful.

## UNMASKING INEQUALITY, AGAIN

In the 18th and early 19th centuries in particular, social class divisions were grossly defined with the White plantation owner, mainly Christians, at the top, the freed slaves then the indentured labourers at the bottom. The evolution of the country's education system zig-zagged under competing pressures from several sides - the British Government, the local legislature, religious groups, the plantation owners and the uneasiness from growing numbers of educated coloured people and freed slaves.[10]

Keenan noted how the cultural roots of the East Indian indentured labourers became barriers to their movement into the existing schools at the time. He advocated special schools for their children.[11]

Among the published studies that subsequently tackled academic opportunity and achievement in the Caribbean is a relatively early one in 1969 which found that a higher proportion of middle and upper social class students gained entry into the government assisted denominational schools (prestige schools) than low social class students – the prestige schools being the better performing schools.[12] Such disproportionality came largely through the Common Entrance Examination – common to all but with its fruits burdened with disproportionate representation by social class and ethnicity.[13]

These researchers also found that females, especially East Indian females, were over-represented in the prestige schools. They stated: 'Much of the egalitarianism between the sexes is in terms of opportunities for Indian girls but for Negro rather than Indian boys.' Indian boys, it was mentioned, had to lend labour support in the canefields. Another study recalled the early resistance of East Indian parents to send their children to school while attendance by Negro students increased.[14]

The authors explained that the civil service aspirations of the time must have contributed to the Negro males advancement, while the drift of Indian boys to the cane fields and labour force could account for their under-representation. Several other studies showed that indeed, from Jamaica to Guyana, students' social background did play a significant part in their academic attainment at secondary school. It was as if demography determined destiny.[15]

In their study of secondary school placement, the Centre for Ethnic Studies Report (1994) noted the ethnic imbalances in secondary school entry and more precisely, how the process was most unfriendly to the female African students.[16]

## PRESTIGE SCHOOLS UNDER ATTACK

In looking at the academic achievement (through GCE passes) of Form Five students in Trinidad and Tobago, Osuji found significant social class differences. Middle and upper social class students performed significantly better than the lower class ones.[17] Around that time, the ethnic and social class differences in the entry to secondary school and secondary school achievement became heated subjects for public debate. For example, a calypso, *Corruption in Common Entrance,* resonated with widespread controversy across the country.[18]

The calypsonian's major theme was that the Common Entrance Examination produced racially and class-biased results. With this song, he won the 1990 Calypso Monarch Crown, the nation's highest calypso award. One verse has these words:

*Because dey have to pick Baldeo, Boodoo, Krishna Maraj,*
*Hadeed, Montano, Sabga and Abraham,*
*Dey pick so much big shot children, they get jam,*
*When dey full dem big shot school right up to de neck*
*Dey send all dem poor ones to de junior sec,*
*So change your children surname*
*And don't be a fool*
*If you want your children to go to a prestige school.*

The calypso, especially with political or ethnic commentaries like this winning one, earns tremendous popular mileage and public debate. On the same inequality and deprivation theme, and with a calypso entitled 'Little Black Boy,' another calypsonian, Winston Peters (Gypsy)[19] sang:

*When you black, you just black, you can't help but be black,*
*But because you are black, don't stay in the back,*
*Look in the front, see who is doctor,*
*Look in the back, see who is lawyer,*
*Look in the back, see who is banker,*
*Look at the business, see who is the owner,*
*Look at the staff, see who is the worker,*
*Look at the drugs, see who is the gang man,*
*Look in the jail, see who you see too,*
*A little black boy jes' like you.*
*Little black boy, go to school and learn,*
*Little black boy, education is the key*
*To set you off the street and all poverty.*

These two are among many popular calypsoes alleging discrimination and also urging young black males to change their lifestyles and take their education seriously. Such poetic license helps energise the widespread controversy over secondary school placement, especially over the vast number of students who did not get into a 'prestige' school. By coincidence, the secondary school entrance examination issue eventually reached a formal political level in the country's parliament when a motion to examine equality of opportunity and educational achievement in the country was presented by the author.[20]

This motion intended to measure the output from the objectives of 'equality of educational opportunity' as promised in the several Government Plans and Reports. In 1992, and based on the motion, the government instructed that a project be undertaken on the allocation of secondary school places from the Common Entrance examination.

This motion, as approved, led to Government establishing a Centre for Ethnic Studies which, with government funding, conducted a Study of Secondary School Placement. Drawing on the substantial data collected, the Centre's 1994 report concluded:

> All things equal, all means to accessing the resources being the same, all groups would be expected to access secondary schooling in proportions representative of their numbers in the relevant population. This has not been the finding of this study. Instead when all the pieces are put together, one can say that the system (primary and secondary) is not user friendly to young people of African descent, especially females, nor to the poor, nor to those from non-nuclear families.[21]

The percentages in this report sharply raised the issue of disproportionality as a key element of educational equity, especially since the disproportionalities put African students, females and students from working class background at acute disadvantages.

The Concordat rights given to the School Boards, the Report felt, also contributed to over-representation of particular religions in students' first-choice schools (i.e., prestige schools). The Report further noted that transfers which occurred in the Government Assisted Schools *after* Form One allocations also contributed to 'unequal opportunity.' The study found that 26% of the students got their first choice school. Of this group, Chinese had the highest proportion, 53%, White 52%, Syrian-Lebanese 48%, Indians 28%, Mixed 25%, African 23%, Others 17%.

The report further noted that the 'race group which most received places they did not have as a choice were the Africans (26%) and students of Mixed parentage (25%).'[22] These results indicated an imbalance in racial and gender entry into secondary school, especially entry into the Government Assisted (prestige) Schools.

## SOCIAL CLASS AND SCHOOL VIOLENCE TOO

Such results are connected to the author's research on student violence and delinquency in secondary schools. Several focus group meetings with Form Three students were also held. At these focus group meetings in the government schools, students were asked how comfortable they felt in their particular school they attended. They were also asked which secondary school they initially chose to enter, and which one they would like to be in now. Almost unanimously, each class indicated one or the other denominational assisted school – a prestige school – within their educational division.

Three related studies between 2004 and 2010 on denominational and government secondary schools confirm the trend that: (1) there is a significantly higher proportion of middle and upper social class students in the denominational schools (2) that compared to students of East Indian descent, students of African descent generally have higher proportions in the government schools.[23] Such imbalances subsequently manifest themselves further into higher education and career choices, the significant difference emanating mainly from the type of secondary school attended (denominational vs government secondary school).[24]

With race, the 'new sector' government schools contained a higher proportion of African students than those of East Indian descent. In the denominational schools, East Indian students comprised a much higher proportion than either African or Mixed students.[25]

Regarding parental structure, 85% of the students in the denominational schools came from two-parent homes while the government schools, on the average, had 50% of their students from such homes. Is school type related to delinquency?

In particular, other analyses indicated that boys committed significantly higher proportions of delinquency than girls. The consistency of these relationships between school type on one hand and students' ethnicity, social class, family life and even gender on the other hand helps illustrate that all is certainly not well with the promises of the educational system, in particular with equality of educational opportunity and educational equity. Is it through lack of personal effort, selection process or institutional bias, or a combination of both?

The OECD's Programme for International Student Assessment (PISA) Study in 2009, as reported by the Ministry, confirmed the above results for this country. The OECD study found, for example, that 'students from the more advantaged socio-economic backgrounds are more likely to attend higher performing schools. School selection practices influence difference in performance between schools.' The study further found that 'students from single-parent families score significantly lower than students from other types of families,' and that students 'attending more socio-economically advantaged schools are more likely to have better qualified teachers.'[26]

An earlier study of juvenile homes in Trinidad and Tobago (youth sent by court, out of control, by police or parent, etc.) revealed the persistence of social class, poverty and racial imbalances in the country's educational and penal institutions. For example, students of African descent (70%) were disproportionately present in these juvenile homes compared to East Indians at 13%. Over 50% went as far as primary school.[27]

This issue of social imbalances resembled one which occurred in the nation's Remand Yard prison where accused persons await trial.[28] When over fifty of these accused (mainly ages 18 to about 30, almost all African) were asked which school they last attended, 20 percent said 'up to primary school,' with all others saying 'a government secondary school.' These two examples suggest what educational deficiencies can lead to.

## AGAIN, FIX THE GOVERNMENT SCHOOLS

From this point, and given the demographics related to secondary school entry, it is important to have as well some idea as to the more specific extent to which such imbalances exist in secondary school *output*. That is, what happens to students who graduate from the government assisted denominational schools compared to those from government schools in terms of educational and occupational status.

While colour, class and racial discrimination were clearly pronounced in the plantation era, the expectation in the independence era was that, even if racial imbalances should inevitably exist, it would be mild and manageable. However, pockets of racial and social class imbalances began to rear their respective heads sharply, especially in the passage towards enrolment in secondary schools as a major passage to success.

The Ethnic Centre Studies' Report in 1994 echoed concerns over fairness expressed by the Maurice Committee Report as far back as 1959. A study of secondary schools in 2004 also reported: '*One of the first things we noticed from our results is the relationship between students' social class (parental occupation) and the type of school they attended.*'[29] The Report added: '*More precisely, over 80% of the students sampled at the Denominational Assisted Secondary Schools came from a middle or upper class background. At the Government Secondary Schools, it is around 40%.*'

The relevant point here is that the assisted denominational schools are high-performing schools while the government secondary schools are relatively low-performers in the context of examinations. Academic performance was obviously related to social class.

These relationships, according to the Report, and as also found in other studies, help create 'the germs of socio-economic stratification for the later stages of life.'[30] '*Sooner or later*,' the Report added, '*this country will have to face the embarrassing question: Is our educational system widening equality of educational opportunity? Is it perpetuating the social stratification system? Is meritocracy (through 11+ examinations) in effect a respectable vehicle for perpetuating social stratification?*'[31]

Measures of parenting type and delinquency also produced significant differences. With the 21 acts of delinquency measured, students from the government secondary schools generally had a higher frequency of delinquent acts compared to those from the denominational assisted schools.

The difference was similar with civic attitudes. For example, when asked if they felt they had anything to lose by not attending school, over 50% of the government school students said they had nothing to lose by not attending school as against 28% from the denominational school.[32]

In a 2010 Report based on seven denominational assisted and thirteen government secondary schools, again, the delinquency rates in the government secondary schools were found to be generally higher than those in the denominational secondary schools.[33] And, once again, higher proportions of East Indian students were found in the government assisted schools compared to the government schools. More precisely, the denominational assisted schools had enrolment of 71% of East Indian descent as compared to 12% of African descent. The government secondary schools altogether had enrolment of 48% of African descent, 27% of East Indian descent and 24% Mixed; (Others = 1%).

With this and other related studies in the last forty years, there were red flags suggesting that the country's secondary school system was falling under siege by ethnic, social class and gender imbalances. As welcome as 'Education for All' policies were, the compelling issues of unequal opportunity in education and educational inequity in the context of ethnicity, social class and gender received neither clear policy nor empirical attention by government.

With the knowledge that most of the government secondary schools were relatively underperforming (for several reasons), the Ministry of Education sought as a priority to examine delinquency in these high risk ones, that is, those which, coupled with low academic performance, showed relatively high frequency of violence and delinquency. In the twenty high risk schools selected by the Ministry, the overall population was: African descent = 40%, East Indian descent = 24%, Mixed = 35%, Chinese, Syrian-Lebanese, White, etc.= 1%.[34]

In terms of the social class background of students in these high risk schools, 68% came from low, working class backgrounds, 25% from middle and four percent from upper class background (Others=3%), a social class distribution quite opposite to what was found in a related study on denominational schools.[35]

## WHAT IS RESPONSIBLE?

From this panoramic view of the social and demographic background of secondary school students and the sharp differences among school types, it gives us a picture of a significantly segregated secondary school system with all the implications for equality of educational opportunity and educational equity. What is it in the educational system that generates such inequities? Personal characteristics, selection process or institutional inefficiency and bias? As we previously said, a combination of all. Reform and remedy will therefore depend on the factors identified.

More recently, a further critique of the fairness of this country's secondary entrance examination was undertaken.[36] De Lisle said that the future of such entrance examinations *'lies not in further tinkering without evidence, but in developing a robust ongoing monitoring and evaluation system to provide information on examination processes and outcomes.'*[37]

The above differences between African and Indian students in the unequal opportunity trends should be considered in light of the earlier 1969 study which found that Africans and Indian secondary school students had similarly high academic and occupational aspirations[38] (Rubin and Zavalloni, 1969). They noted then that their results did not support 'the apparent and well-known disparity in motivations and aspirations' between the two racial groups. On the contrary, they indicated that their results revealed 'an ethos of mobility' for future mobility which cross-cuts the ethnic differences and a similar preference to delay gratification to attain future goals.

These researchers noted, however, their results were obtained a few years after the country gained political independence in 1962 when high academic and occupational aspirations were enthusiastically encouraged all around. When the 1990's came, it appeared as if the ideals and aspirations for education still existed, but the sociological fractures in achievement began to be shown more and more clearly.

Still, from the 1969 study the question arises: If both racial groups once had similarly high academic and occupational aspirations, how come more recent studies find such significant differences in actual educational opportunity and attainment in the secondary school? Furthermore, there are other studies which show that at Form One in the secondary school, students of all races (Africans, Indians, Whites, Chinese, Syrians, Mixed, etc.), have similarly high academic aspirations for going on to university. Yet, in actual attainment, a few years after, there arise significant differences with the Africans generally lagging further behind the East Indians and other racial groups.[39]

## THE SELF-FULFILLING PROPHESY COMES ALIVE

The answer may be found in the different socialisation and interaction experiences by each racial group according to the type of secondary school attended. That is, as students get placed in different school types (denominational vs government schools) and as they then move through the system, each group begins 'to see their place in the world' more sharply, that is, according to the likely consequences of social class, race and school type in the educational system. Perhaps, in the government secondary schools they begin to see themselves as others see them. The self-fulfilling prophesy comes alive. Some resist and rise, some falter and fall in aspirations and effort.

Apart from academic ability, therefore, there is a need to study the process variables, that is, the experiences which may contribute to these output differences from one point to the next in the secondary school. In tracing the imbalances in social class and ethnicity in the country's educational system since political independence, Mustapha concluded:

One can therefore say that in spite of massive educational expansion taking place, only the persons at the upper (social class) levels of the hierarchy seem to benefit. This applies to both certification and to the extent to which their formal schooling would have enhanced their life chances.[40]

In a related study, it was pointed out that the low social class (vs upper class) socialisation of students at home also significantly contributed to their non-university aspiration.[41]

Following prolonged public complaints over the SEA results in 2014, widespread concerns were expressed over the qualitative differences between primary schools and secondary schools in the country. Author and columnist Kevin Baldeosingh did an interesting analysis then, comparing primary school enrolment with the percentage of SEA passes gained in the top 200 from the 2014 examination.[42]

He found an inverse relationship between the percentage of school enrolment and percentage of SEA passes. For example, while the government schools had a 30% enrolment, they gained 7% of the top 200. The Roman Catholic schools had 26% enrolment but gained 8% of the top 200 while the Hindu schools had 10% enrolment and gained 8% in the top 200.

The Muslim and Presbyterian schools had enrolments of 4% and 15% respectively, and 13% and 18% respectively of the top 200 passes. The remarkable finding was that the private and other types of primary schools had a one percent enrolment but captured 18% of the top 200 SEA passes. Baldeosingh concluded: '*The Government primary schools did the worst, having only seven percent of the top pupils even though they account for 30 percent of total enrolment.*'[43]

Altogether then, there is a dubious claim of equality of opportunity at the secondary school entrance levels. There is the rise of prestige primary schools too, with all their social class and ethnic implications. There is a merit-driven SEA fueling a prestige-driven secondary school system with serious social stratification implications. There is, therefore, a public policy need to see what happens to those who graduate from one type, that is, the denominational schools, and their opposite type, the government schools.

## BEHIND THE MASK

The question now is this: does the education system help reinforce and paralyze the society's socio-economic stratification system or does it energize socio-economic mobility as the country's governments have pledged? The evidence cited so far generally suggests that the pledges have failed to come true. The emphasis has been on more buildings, planning reports, aggregate output and public pledges filled with hopes and promises.

Very little attempt is made by government to collect the evidence required to establish equality of educational opportunity or equity, except in the rather 'politically correct' sphere of gender. The Government-sponsored 1994 Study on Secondary School Placement was an exception, but ignored. Where the required evidence came from non-governmental sources, it also remained largely ignored.[44]

When its own aggregated data showed possibilities of inequality and inequity, no sustained attempt was made to disaggregate the data more precisely to illustrate the degree of ethnic diversity or the differences in denominational vs government school output.[45] It is from this, together with social class, family background and gender that the remedies for equality and equity will effectively arise. The mask must be removed. There is more work to be done if the promises of decolonization and equal educational opportunity are to be fulfilled.

Success and failure in education are indeed a matter of examinations, but the what possibilities students see ahead and the goals they see possible, also help shape their effort. Becker, for example, has long argued that '*if there are no available positions in the upper strata, no way of earning a living in a properly prestigeful way, schooling does not produce mobility but frustrates desire; it has no effect on the status system.*' He added: '*In such a situation disappointment may be avoided by ignoring the mobility possibility.*'[46]

This social psychological explanation, as earlier indicated, is applicable to the youthful sub-cultures now developing around the country. In particular, it is generally well known by students that getting into a government secondary school will not likely get them very far in life, compared to getting into a prestige school.

The inequality has already gripped their academic imagination hence the annual tears and joy over the SEA results. In fact, for such youths, the self-fulfilling prophesy captures their ambition and this, while they keep hearing 'the only way to improve the quality of your life is through education and training, as it is the only passport out of poverty.'[47] For them the education system is one of betrayal. There is much work to be done.

## NOTES

1.  Free secondary and university education for all (through GATE for tertiary-level education), with graduate students having to bear part of their fees.
2.  See A. Beteille (Ed.). *Social Inequality*. MIiddlesex: Penguin Books. 1974. for a wide discussion on this relationship.
3.  A. Halsey. *A Sociology and the Equality Debate*. Oxford Review of Education. 1975. Vol. 1(1).pp. 9–23. Also, p. 15.
4.  Ibid. p. 15. Also, pp. 9-23. He added: 'These include the linguistic and other stimulation in family and neighbourhood, the expectation of teachers, the efficiency of cooperation between teachers and parents, and the occupational horizons which can be seen by children at different vantage points. Above all, it is a matter of resources... The association of social class with educational achievement will not therefore be explained by a theory or eliminated by a policy which falls short of including changes in public support for learning in the family and the neighbourhood, the training of teachers, the production of relevant curricula, the fostering of parental participation, the raising of standards of housing and employment prospects and, above all, the allocation of educational resources.'
5.  For a discussion on how the education system contributes to social inequality see C. Jencks, *Inequality: A Reassessment of the Effects of Family and Schooling in America*. New York: Harper Publishers. 1972. Also, Bowles and Gintis; P. Sorokin, *Social and Cultural Mobility*. New York: Free Press. 1959. The more recent literature on local research tends to confirm a lot of what is said in the above works.
6.  F. Parkin, *Class Inequality and the Political Order*. London: MacGibbon and Kee, Ltd. 1971. p. 13.
7.  Ibid. He added: 'However both operate in the social stratification system...Rich families ensure their children are placed in the hierarchy, that is, to help institutionalise stratification. This crystallizes the class structure through time. It is this interplay between material and normative or cultural aspects of inequality which gives rise to class stratification. For stratification implies not simply inequality but a set of institutional arrangements which guarantee a fairly high degree of social continuity in rewards position of family units through generations. Without the long-term continuity provided by the kinship link it would

still be possible for inequality to persist, but not class stratification in the conventional meaning.'

8. As several critics have noted, the managed scarcity of certain top positions, the differential public respect, if not in concrete rewards, are also some of the distortions.

9. C. Jawardena noted: 'Indian culture or 'coolie' culture as it was called became a mark of low status in the eyes of the white upper status group, as well as the coloured and black groups.' '*Conflict and Solidarity on a Guyanese Plantation.*' London: Athlone Press. 1963.) Cited in M. Bacchus,*Education and Social Change and Cultural Pluralism.*Vol. 42, No. 4, Fall. 1969. pp. 368–385.

10. See for details on these struggles and the establishment of the dual system of education, C. Campbell, *The Young Colonials: A Social History of Education in Trinidad and Tobago, 1834-1939.* Jamaica, Mona: The Press University of the West Indies. 1996.

11. P. J. Keenan, *Report Upon the State of Education in the Island of Trinidad.* Dublin: Alexander Thom for Her Majesty's Stationery Office. 1869.

12. Malcolm Cross and Allan Schwartzbaum, *Social Mobility and Secondary School Selection.* 1969.

13. For a discussion on the relationship between class,culture and education, see N. Mustapha,'Class, Culture and Education', in R. Deosaran and N. Mustapha (Eds.),*Contemporary Issues in Social Science: A Caribbean Perspective.* Trinidad: University of the West Indies, Ansa McAL Psychological Research Centre. 1995. Vol. 2, pp. 78-105.

14. M. K. Bacchus, '*Education, Social Change and Cultural Pluralism.*' *Sociology of Education. Vol. 42, No. 4,* Fall. 1969.pp. 368–385.

15. See e.g. P. Figueroa and G. Persaud (Eds.),'Sociology of Education: Caribbean Reader.' 1976; N. Mustapha and R. Brunton (Eds.), *Issues in Education in Trinidad and Tobago.* 2002.

16. Study on Secondary School Placement. 1994.

17. R. Osuji. The Effect of Socio-Economic Status on the Educational Achievement of Form Five Students. Institute for Social and Economic Research,UWI, 1987.

18. Sung by Winston Rawlins, known as 'Cro-Cro.'

19. A colourful character, Peters went on to be elected as a Member of Parliament, then made Minister of Culture in 2010. He was not selected by the People's Partnership Party to contest again in the 2015 general elections. He resigned from the party about two weeks before the September 7, 2015 election date.

20. The author was then an Independent Senator in the country's Parliament; it was seconded by an attorney, Senator Allan Alexander, widely debated and finally passed. Subsequently, the study was implemented in 1994

by the PNM Government-created Centre for Ethnic Studies, University of the West Indies. The result revealed significant social class, ethnic and gender bias in secondary school placement. See Chapter Ten for details.

21. A Study of Secondary School Population in Trinidad and Tobago: Placement Patterns and Practices, Centre for Ethnic Studies, UWI.1994. pp. 44–60

22. Ibid. p. 60.

23. R. Deosaran, 'Benchmarking Violence and Delinquency in the Secondary School: Toward a Culture of Peace and Civility.' Research and Policy Report commissioned by IDB/SEMPCU, Ministry of Education, Government of the Republic of Trinidad and Tobago. March 2003. This included seven government secondary schools and three denominational secondary schools (sample = 1,800). For each of the ten schools, two classes from each Form 1, 2 and 3 were randomly chosen for the survey (anonymously done). A relevant finding was when asked if they felt they had nothing to lose by being absent from school, over 50% of students from the government secondary said yes 'nothing to lose,' while, 28% from the denominational schools said so. When asked how much more education they expect to take, 50% from the government secondary said up to university vs. 80% from the denominational schools that said up to university. Only 4% of students from each type of school expected to take technical/vocational courses. pp. 91-150. Almost 40% said 'contact is more important than ability in getting a government job.' Recommendations submitted including having substitute teachers and school safety officers.Key stakeholders were present at presentation of results and recommendations. Then Minister of Education, Ms. Hazel Manning remarked: 'This is the most comprehensive and penetrative research that has been conducted over the last decade on the subject...The benchmarks will allow us to scientifically monitor our effectiveness and strategies.' Hilton Trinidad, Port of Spain. June 16, 2014.

A subsequent study was done with 20 government secondary schools described as 'high risk' by the Ministry and the report was submitted in July 2006. There was a 2,800 student sample from Forms 1, 2 and 3. A significant proportion was 'not comfortable' in these schools. Recommendations submitted.

The third study, a 2002–2010 tracer study, included another 20 schools (a 1,293 sample obtained at Form 5 from an initial 3,500 sample at Form 1). Strong social class and ethnic differences again between Denominational and Government Schools were found. Data for students three years after leaving secondary school reveal social class and ethnic differentials continued into higher education and career choices (See Chapter 14).

R. Deosaran, 'School Violence and Delinquency: The Dynamics of Race, Gender, Class, Age and Parenting.' pp. 89–132. In R. Deosaran (Ed.),*Crime, Delinquency and Justice: A Caribbean Reader*. Kingston, Jamaica: Ian Randle Publishers. 2007.

24. Ibid. see third study, the tracer study cited above.

25. R. Deosaran,'School Violence and Delinquency,'2003, pp. 90–117. Ten secondary schools (8 government and 2 denominational) with 1,800 students; 2 classes randomly chosen from each Form. At that time, the Junior Secondary was present. The government schools contain both the traditional schools, e.g., St. George's, and the new secondary, e.g., Composite. In all of the analyses, the traditional government schools had higher proportions of two-parent homes, middle and upper class and East Indian students compared to the new secondary schools.

26. OECD Study. 2009. Cited In Ministry of Education Annual Administrative Report 2009–2010.pp. 25–29.

27. In 1997, Juvenile Homes: An Analytic Basis for Reform, Intervention and Rehabilitation. Submitted to Ministry of Social Development. October 1997. CIDA/UWI grant. 10-19 age group. Some findings: (1) 51% up to primary school, 39% up to secondary school, 2% university, 0.6% no schooling at all. (2) 70% African, 13% Indian, 18% Mixed – Africans over-represented at 38% in population and Indian at 40% in population. (3) Both parents 24%, 70% single parent or guardian, 3% living alone, 2% with friends or from orphanage. (472 Ss) Published in R. Deosaran and D. Chadee,'Juvenile Delinquency in Trinidad and Tobago: Challenges for Social Policy and Caribbean Criminology.'*Caribbean Journal of Criminology and Social Policy*. July 1997,Vol. 2 (2). pp. 36-83.

28. In 2013, the author was appointed to head a cabinet-appointed inquiry into the conditions at the Remand Yard – the place where an accused is held waiting on trial.

29. R. Deosaran,'Benchmarking Violence and Delinquency in the Secondary School: Toward a Culture of Peace and Civility' (The Summary). Research and Policy Report commissioned by IDB/SEMPCU, Ministry of Education, Government of the Republic of Trinidad and Tobago. March 2003. pp. 21-22. Seven government and three Assisted Secondary Schools were used.

30. Ibid. pp. 22–23.

31. 505 Ibid.

32. Ibid, p. 23.

33. 'Project Safeguard: Tracing Youths 2001 to 2010, Post-Secondary School Experiences. A Longitudinal Study.' Report Submitted to Ministry of

Education, Trinidad and Tobago. July 2010. Twenty separate reports submitted on disaggregated data. Above data drawn from Report No. 16 entitled 'School Type X Demographics and Civic Attitudes.pp. 22-24. Table 2.

34. R. Deosaran, 'Benchmarking Violence and Delinquency in the Secondary School' (Phase Two with Twenty High Risk Schools). Submitted to Ministry of Education, Trinidad and Tobago. May 2006. pp. 19-22.

35. Ibid.

36. J. De Lisle, 'Secondary School Entrance Examination in the Caribbean.' *Caribbean Curriculum*. 2012. 19.pp. 109-143.

37. Ibid.

38. Rubin and Zavalloni. 1969. pp. 97-98.

39. See e.g.,R. Deosaran. Tracer Study of Youths 2002–2010. Reports Submitted to Ministry of Education.

40. Education and Stratification in Trinidad and Tobago. 2002. p. 151.

41. Mustapha and Mustapha. 1997. p.81.

42. K. Baldeosingh, 'What Makes a Successful School?' *Sunday Express*. August 2014. p. 11.

43. Ibid.

44. E.g., The Study on Secondary School Placement, 1994. This Study looked at selection to Form One and how the 20% allocation was used.

45. See e.g., Ministry of Education Administrative Report 2010–2011.pp. 18–20.

46. H. Becker, 'Schools and Systems of Stratification', in A. Halsey, J. Floud and C. Anderson (Eds.). *Education, Economy and Society*. New York: Free Press,1961. p. 93.

47. Mrs Kamla-Persad-Bissessar, S.C., former Prime Minister of Trinidad and Tobago. May 30, 2015. Address at Indian Arrival Day function.

# CHAPTER TWELVE
# Behind the Masks: Inequality or Discrimination

*Special and remedial students are not ready for secondary school education. They should be limited to a few subjects only, probably Mathematics and English Language. Students required to sit the Form Three National Test are also not adequately prepared to do so. Hence plenty failures.*

Teacher from a Government Secondary School,
'Voices of the Teachers'
Report submitted to Ministry of Education, 2008

## INEQUALITY OR FAIRNESS?

In this Chapter, we seek to remove the mask more fully in order to see more precisely the extent to which inequality and inequity exist and where remedy is urgently required. Of course, it is tough for an education system to tackle the challenges of equality of educational opportunity, especially educational equity in a multi-racial, vertically privileged society as this.

As ethically and morally necessary as it is, the first reason is largely political. That is, the reforms required usually disturb the already privileged elite groups in the society, thus neutralizing the political will required. In this multi-racial society with its elections largely racially-driven, any policy changes to the racial imbalances in the educational system will invoke heated controversy. The second related reason is the lack of disaggregated data and the apparent unwillingness to gather systematically such data that would uncover the ethnic, social class, regional and family background imbalances.[1]

The Ministry of Education does collect data by denominational schools, government schools, private schools, educational districts and by the politically palatable factor, gender.[2] From these institutionally-connected data, inferences of students' ethnicity, social class and family background may be made. However, the more specific data on student ethnicity, social class and family background in relation to equality of educational opportunity and equity usually come from academic and non-governmental research.[3] The third reason is the lack of political will to undertake the substantial reforms required – even when the evidence is submitted.

The SEA proportions that go into denominational secondary schools and those into government secondary schools should be more fully and clearly published. The SEA data is usually lumped under 'Five and Seven-Year Schools' which include both government and denominational schools. This, however, is a place where the questions of inequality and merit arise.[4] As explained earlier, for a government to review the Concordat and the powers of the denominational school boards will most likely open a Pandora's Box, especially if the review is superficially argued.

Nevertheless, we now present a brief overview of the examination results from available reports which will help provide further knowledge on the extent to which inequality and inequity existin the system and possibly, the areas which require policy action for equitable remedies.

## SCHOOLS AND EXAMINATIONS

The Ministry's Strategic Plan 2010–2015[5] noted that 24% of all schools were owned by government and operated with state funding, with 76% owned by denominational boards and private organisations. There were 512 primary schools and 182 secondary schools. For Early Childhood Care and Education Centres, (ECCE), there were 170 public and 736 privately-owned.

Of the 512 primary schools in 2011, 476 were public and 36 private. Of the 182 secondary schools, 134 were public and 48 private (ECCE schools = 906). Total of all schools = 1600.[6]

The education system is based on five levels of schooling: 'Pre-Primary 3–4 years old, Primary 5–11, Secondary 12–18, Post-Secondary, (Advanced Proficiency and Technical/Vocational) and Tertiary Education.'[7]

## THE MAJOR EXAMINATIONS IN THE SYSTEM:

1. The National Tests (Primary); Secondary Entrance Examinations (SEA with a 30% Continuous Assessment Component in 2015)[8]
2. The National Certificate of Secondary Education (NCSE). The Ministry indicates this is designed for Form 3 students – a combination of continuous assessment and an examination.

3. The Caribbean Secondary Examination Certificate (CSEC). The Ministry indicates this is designed for Form 5 students 'as an exit examination.'

4. The Caribbean Advanced Proficiency Examination (CAPE–Units I and II). This is an 'advanced proficiency examination normally taken two years after Form 5.' Scholarships are based on results.

5. The Caribbean Vocational Qualification (CVQ).

6. The OECD Programme for International Student Assessment (PISA – every three years.)[9]

We now take a brief look at the results and their implications for equality of opportunity and educational equity:

# NATIONAL TEST (PRIMARY)
## (Mathematics, Language Arts, Science, Social Studies)

Public concerns sporadically point to inequalities in the SEA and CAPE results, that is, in secondary school placement and Advanced Level Open and National Scholarships. Less attention is placed on the quality of academic performance in the primary schools. However, it is from the primary school system that much of the social inequality and ethnic imbalances begin. As the Ministry's own reports indicate, such inequality in primary school performance persists from year to year and gets more tightly manifested in the SEA and CAPE examinations where the stakes are seen to be much higher.

First, inequality by Educational Administrative District. How unequal are student scores among the eight educational districts? In the Upper Level Test in 2010, Victoria and Caroni districts had consistently higher scores than the other six districts.[10] For example, while for Science at Standard 4, Victoria and Caroni had 57% and 53% passes respectively, Tobago and North Eastern had 44% and 45% respectively. Such district by district differences for the national test subjects have been rather consistent over the years, up to 2014.

In its Report on the National Tests for 2005 to 2011, two particular administrative districts – Caroni and Victoria – generally show higher performance results for all four national test subjects, and with females out-performing males from one year to the next. When the primary schools were measured with the Ministry's Academic Performance Index (API), the highest proportion of schools classified as 'mostly effective' came from Caroni and Victoria.[11]

These persistent inequalities become educational inequities especially since they appeared to be confined to certain social and ethnic groups and these disadvantaged groups lag behind in subsequent SEA passes and secondary school scholarships. Private primary schools had a significantly higher average (60%) than both denominational (50%) and government schools (47%) in all subject areas and from year to year. There were also very significant gender differences with females performing significantly better than males in all subject areas and at all the different class levels. (17,588 writing)[12] These trends express consistent inequality. The Ministry's October 2011–September 2012 Annual Administrative Report noted that there was an overall increase in student performance in Mathematics and literacy levels compared to the period 2008–2012.[13] Such gross figures, however, continue to mask the social class, ethnic and gender inequalities behind them.

We must emphasise that these persistent inequalities and inequities at the primary school level have serious implications for later educational opportunities. Table 12.1 provides another specific example of the consistent superiority of the private primary schools over the denominational and government primary schools in both mathematics and language arts. Such superiority by the private schools is demonstrated at both Standards Three and One.[14]

**Table 12.1: National Test (Mean Scores) for Mathematics and Language Arts (Standards 1 and 3) in Primary Schools (%)**

| School Type | Standard 1 | | Standard 3 | |
|---|---|---|---|---|
| | Mathematics | Language Arts | Mathematics | Language Arts |
| Private | 61 | 62 | 62 | 64 |
| Denominational | 50 | 50 | 50 | 50 |
| Government | 48 | 46 | 47 | 46 |

*Ministry of Education, National Test Report, 2005.*

At this primary school stage, the differences in academic performance between the denominational and government primary schools are not yet as significant as the differences found in the SEA, NCSE, CSEC or CAPE results. This suggests that as these primary school children grow older in the education system, the influences of differentiation – institutional, family, peers – between these three school types also grow stronger. It is almost like the work of institutional prejudice. The SEA results, for example, resemble the district by district proportions in the national test results. The educational districts of Victoria and Caroni consistently produce higher mean scores than the other six districts, thus helping to create a persistent residential bias in examination results. These performances, overall, are largely driven by the type of school attended with private schools on average much better than the denominational schools, and with government schools lagging behind.

More precisely again, in mathematics at Standard Three, while 66% of private primary school students attained Level 4 or 3, 41% of students in denominational schools and 34% in the government schools did so. These school-type differences were very similar for language arts at Standard Three.[15]The most significant implication at this primary school stage is an ethnic and social class one. That is, it is the upper and middle class parents who can more likely afford to send their children to these private schools, in addition to the other fact that it is such parents who can afford to send their children for private lessons to compete in the SEA and CAPE examinations.

The trends for the National Tests for the years 2005 to 2011 reveal similar differences between the three types of schools and from one educational district to another.[16]Given examinations as they intrinsically are, it is expected that a reasonable proportion of students will not score in the top ten or top thirty for that matter. Our concern is the troubling extent to which persistent educational inequality and inequity are systematically suffered by certain groups while other groups in the same domain consistently enjoy educational advantages over them.

At this early primary school stage, therefore, it means that if a child is female, living in either Victoria or Caroni and from a denominational or private school, compared to other students, there is a better chance on average of being a top performer in the SEA examination, getting into a denominational secondary (prestige) school and winning a national scholarship.

Given the specific objectives of these national tests and the general purpose of the education system, one would expect that these uncovered inequalities in the primary education system would be subjected to more flexible upward mobility for the social and ethnic groups so consistently marginalised and segregated. These National Tests are designed:

1.  To track the progress of students in the different schools and make comparisons

2.  To point out any teaching and learning shortcomings that may require further investigations

3.  To discriminate between essential and desirable levels of curriculum.[17]

However, when one examines the troubling trends in academic performance between these three type of schools and the ethnic, social class, gender and residential implications, the unmasked picture is one of unattended educational inequality and inequity. It is clear that educational inequality and inequity start quite early in the primary school system and get worse as students move up into the SEA and secondary school system.

The ethnic and social class inequities found at the secondary schools, and even three years after secondary schooling, germinated in the primary school system, and apparently without serious policy attention provided to close the gaps. It is also quite disturbing for a post-colonial society that relies so much on the education system for equality of opportunity and equitable socio-economic mobility to remain besieged by such repeated institutional and policy deficits.

Quietly and under the banner of a meritocracy, the education system is allowed to cultivate ethnic and social class segregation. Or is it really once again, that the education system itself is ideologically, helplessly and functionally chained to the social stratification system of the wider society?

## SECONDARY ENTRANCE ASSESSMENT (SEA)

### (Mathematics, Language Arts, Creative Writing)

Here again, there was significant gender inequality. Of the 17,268 writing in 2010, females had much higher scores. For example in 2010 again, 62.5% of females scored 90% and above while 37.5% males did so. For each year between 2005 and 2010, over 60% of females consistently scored 90% and over, compared to 40% of males consistently scoring over 90%.[18] A percentage difference of 20% is inequality. For the SEA 2011 Report, and looking at the gender inequality another way, in every year from 2007 to 2011 a much higher proportion of males than females scored below 30%. It was almost a 3:1 proportion.[19] All other SEA reports confirm this gender difference – the largest (Mean) difference being in Language Arts, a consistent 10% difference from 2008 to 2012.[20]

The trend from 2007 to 2012 indicates significant disproportionalities among the eight education districts in Trinidad and Tobago. In terms of students scoring above 90% in the SEA for the six-year period, only two districts consistently gained marks above the national average – Caroni and Victoria.[21]

More precisely, in 2012, while the national average was 4.8%, Caroni had 6.6% and Victoria 9.7% of its students scoring above 90%. In that same year, Tobago had only 0.6%, St. Patrick 2.5% and Northern Eastern 1.3%. Another example, with the national average of 7.3% in 2007, only three districts scored above this average – Caroni (8.7%), Port of Spain (7.6%) and St. George East (8.2%).

The Ministry's 2011–2012 Administrative Report published the overall SEA results but without separating the government schools from the denominational schools.[22]

## THE DANGER IN ZONING

The district distributions for the other years were similarly unequal. The implication here is that if zoning were to become a policy, equality of educational opportunity would suffer a serious blow. Generally, it is those who get above 90% in the SEA would likely get into their first choice prestige school. Two districts lead the rest consistently. For those getting 30% and less, the district distributions are also highly disproportional.[23] Getting high marks in the SEA largely depends on where you live.

## THE FLUID SEA CRITERION

Do these percentages make a difference in placement? The percentages getting 90% and above in the SEA from 2008 to 2015 are as follows: 5.6% (1,073) in 2008, 6.3% (1,111) in 2009, 5.9% (1,027) in 2010, 4.5% (786) in 2011, 4.8% (860) in 2012, 3.6% (645) in 2013, 8.9% (1,620) in 2014 and 14.1% (2,581) in 2015.[24]

In the context of limited Form One places (estimated 4,700) in the preferred denominational and traditional secondary schools, five inferences are relevant here.

1. In 2013, 66.2% and 26.3% of the 18,038 who wrote the SEA were respectively placed in government schools and denominational assisted schools. In that year, however, while only 645 (3.6%) students got 90% and above, this means in that year, 2013, many students with less than 90% marks went into these denominational schools, many of them lavishly celebrated.[25] It is therefore not true to say that only those who get 90% and above get into the preferred 5 and 7-year schools. It depends on the proportion in a particular year.

2. In 2015, in particular, the pressure for prestige school places was more intense since a higher proportion (14%) got 90% and above.

3. While the Form One places at the Denominational Schools are rather limited, the pressure by parents and children would vary according to the proportion who score 90% and above.

4. In some cases, many children getting 85% to 90%, bright as they are, quite likely, would not have gotten a place in the prestige school (7-year) of their choice. The grief and frustrations publicly displayed by these students and their parents therefore appear justified.[26] At his media conference, the former Minister of Education said that such complaints will continue until the government 'brings all secondary schools to a level of competence as we have with a lot of the Board Schools.'[27] When?

5. With such high scores in the SEA, and faced with limited prestige school places, many of them (85%–90%) would have been sent to under-performing government secondary schools. Given their SEA scores, these students are still in the high achievement, competitive realm. Why then, having such students, don't the government schools produce a higher proportion of examination passes and national scholarships?

Table 12.2 illustrates a high degree of stability in the system. Each year, about one quarter of the students writing the SEA get placed in a denominational secondary school. In fact, the total number of students writing the SEA each year, the proportions going into private schools and pre-vocational centres and the proportions getting placed in the denominational assisted sschools all show some consistency throughout the three year period.

**Table 12.2: Distribution of SEA Students Placed By School Type for the Period 2013–2015**

| Type of Institution | 2015 | 2014 | 2013 |
|---|---|---|---|
| Gov't and Gov't Assisted (Total) | 17,367 (94.9%) | 17,059 (93.5%) | 16,797 (93.2%) |
| Gov't | 12,666 (69%) | 12,167 (71.3%) | 12,062 (71.8%) |
| Gov't Assisted | 4,701 (25.7%) | 4,892 (28.6%) | 4,735 (28.1%) |
| Private | 473 (2.6%) | 598 (3.3%) | 548 (3%) |
| Pre-vocational (Servol Centres) | 445 (2.4%) | 415 (2.2%) | 262 (1.5%) |
| Total Placed | 18,285 (99.9%) | 18,072 (99.1%) | 17,607 (97.7%) |
| Number of Students to resit SEA | 25 (0.1%) | 167 (0.9%) | 417 (2.3%) |
| TOTAL | 18,310 | 18,239 | 18,024 |

*Ministry of Education Data.*

Other data show those getting 30% and less in the SEA went from 13.3% in 2008 to 11% in 2015.[28] According to teachers interviewed, this 'under 30% group' are those who can't read, can't write well and can't spell.[29] These are usually sent back to rewrite the SEA. In terms of equality of opportunity and equity, the question remains: How are the 90% and above and the 30% and less scores relate to the society's racial, social class, gender and family background diversity? Should we know? Does it matter if we know? As the earlier distributions show, however, we know for sure that there are significant inequalities in the SEA scores among the eight educational districts.

Figure 12.1 presents an interesting picture for the SEA results by school type. Using mathematics as a performance measure, the private primary schools produce much higher mean scores than either the denominational or government schools in each year – 2009 to 2011.

**Figure 12.1: SEA Results (Mean) for a Three-year Period (2009–2011): Comparisons for Math amongst Private, Denominational and Government Schools**

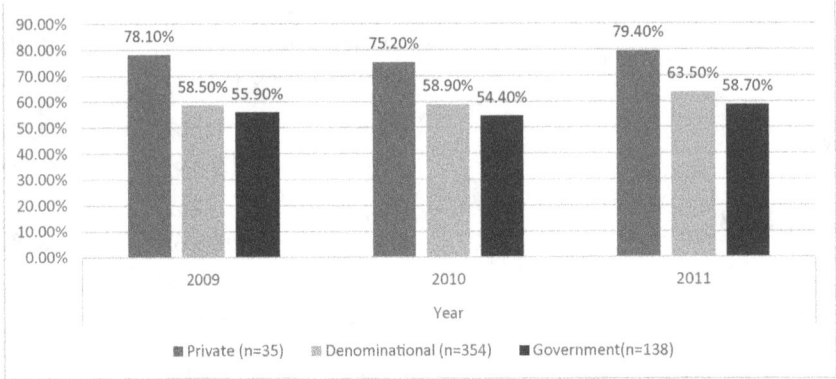

*Ministry of Education SEA Report 2011*

These private schools charge a significant fee that well-off parents are willing to pay since the schools are famously recognized for having their students placed in prestige secondary schools. This fee-paying primary school practice does raise implications for the government's free universal education policy. The second feature in Figure 12.1 is that private schools do so much better than the denominational schools.

Now the SEA improvement rates in 2014 from previous years present another interesting case. That is, the Ministry reported that in 2014 of the 18,239 writing the SEA, 8.9% scored above 90% compared with 3.6% in 2013. Further, the percentage of student scoring less than 30% went from 8.9% in 2013 down to 4.4% in 2014.[30]

But this doesn't really change things, does it? The first and second choice places available in the prestige schools remain quite constant, so what we have is a larger number of bright children fighting for the same limited places. The 'big squeeze' – educational recession. Secondly, as the Secondary School Placement Study queried with the Common Entrance, how many of those in the top 'bright' 10% were placed in a school they never chose?

Next to these 'commendable' SEA results, the Ministry wrote:

> The Ministry of Education is committed to quality education and the holistic development of the child. Our mission is to educate and develop

children who are: (1)able to achieve their full potential, (2) academically balanced,(3)well-adjusted socially and culturally, (4)emotionally mature and happy, and (5) healthy and growing normally.[31]

That year, 2014, as in previous years, the tears and dissatisfactions of both parents and children were widespread, some wondering why their children were placed in schools they did not choose while their marks were very high. They seemed not to understand the criteria for secondary school placement and the fact of limited prestige school places. A betrayal for so many.

## NCSE (NATIONAL CERTIFICATE FOR SECONDARY EDUCATION (EIGHT CORE SUBJECTS)

In 2011, of the 15,275 registered for the NCSE, 36% got five or more passes, compared to 34% in 2010 and 35% in 2009.[32] Females had a higher success rate with five passes: 43% females vs 25% males. In an unusual comparison, the Ministry reported that denominational schools outperformed government and private schools in all subject areas while female students outperformed their male counterparts both at the national and district level in all subjects.[33]

In the 2011 NCSE results, 25% failed to get any subject while 36% got five or more passes. In terms of inequality of performance, while 60% of the denominational schools got five or more passes, 26% of those in the government schools got five or more passes. Private schools got 19%.[35]

Once again, the denominational schools seemed to have earned their prestige stripes and the affection of the nation's parents and students. (Notably, while the private (fee-paying) primary schools tend to score higher than either the denominational or government schools in the SEA, the private (secondary) schools' performance at the higher examinations is generally lower than that of the other two school types.)

For the 2012 NCSE results, while the national average for five or more subjects with English A and Mathematics was 42.3%, only two districts got above this – Victoria 52.3% and Port of Spain at 51.9%. Tobago got 27.9%, North Eastern 24.1%, and South Eastern 29.7%.[36]

The differences between the denominational secondary and government schools remain astounding. For example, in 2013, while the national average for five or more passes (8 subjects listed) was 41%, almost all denominational schools went over this average. In fact, many of the 45 denominational schools got over 80% and 90% of their students with five or more passes. On the other hand, the vast majority of government schools went below this national average with almost ten (9%) getting less than five percent.

**Figure 12.2: Percentage of Students Getting Five or More Passes at NCSE 2011 x School Type**

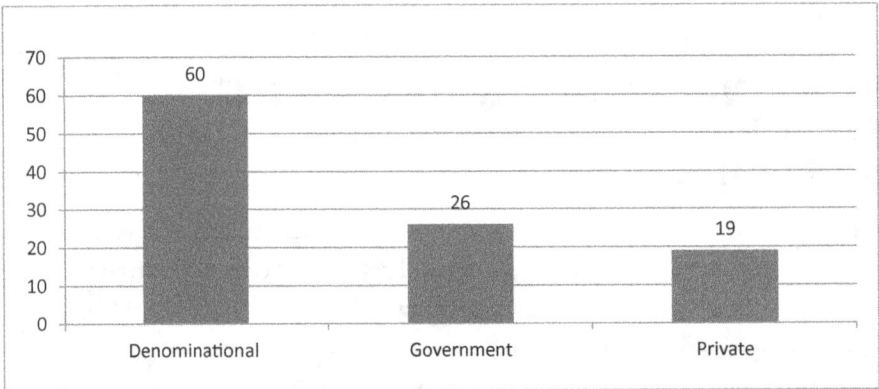

Notably, however, 12% of the government secondary schools got above 50%.[37] The published results for the CSEC examination showed similar differences between the denominational and government secondary schools.

In other words, if you want to have good chances to succeed with five or more passes, go to a school in either Caroni or Victoria or maybe, Port of Spain too. That is what zoning would imply.

## CSEC (CARIBBEAN SECONDARY EXAMINATION CERTIFICATE)

In considering equality of educational opportunity and equity, the aggregate figures are naturally inadequate. For example, in the Caribbean Secondary Education Certificate (CSEC) results for 2014, the Ministry Report showed that 56.2% of those writing the exam passed five subjects at least, compared to 52.4% in 2009. If such data were disaggregated by ethnicity, or by social class and family type, a policy-friendly picture of equality and inequity in the system would be revealed. This, of course, would depend on the educational philosophy of the government.[38]

Figure 12.3 shows the consistency of the significant difference in the CSEC results between the denominational secondary and the government secondary schools – a difference of 41% in 2008, 40% in 2009, 44% in 2010, 44% in 2011 and 45% in 2012.

The government has been quite liberal regarding scholarships. While the number went from 266 in 2009 to 348 in 2011, then to 372 in 2012, the Open Scholarships went from 65 to just 70 and the Additional from 201 in 2009 to 302 in 2012. The increase was almost all in Additional Scholarships.[39]

**Figure 12.3: CSEC Results for a five year period (2008–2012): Comparisons between Denominational and Government Schools (% with 5 or more subjects)**

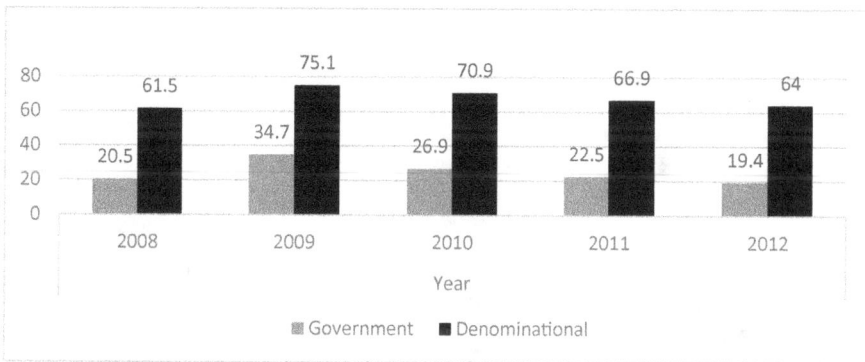

# CAPE (CARIBBEAN ADVANCED PROFICIENCY EXAMINATION)

As another illustration of inequality by district, in the 2011 CAPE–II results, Caroni, St. George East and Victoria had percentages around 70% for those who passed with Grades I–III. Tobago had 45.2%, St. Patrick 51.7%, Southern Eastern 4.2%.[40]

With CAPE I, the proportion getting Grades I–III moved from 61% in 2010 to 66% in 2014. For Unit II, 59% gained Grades I–III in 2010 compared to 68% in 2014. However, the District by District and school by school disproportionalities continued.[41]

The difference in school type attended again makes a big difference, this time in the advanced CAPE examinations. As Figure 12.4 illustrates, from 2010, 2011 to 2012, the significant difference in academic performance between the Denominational Secondary School and the Government Secondary Schools persists. With respect to students gaining Grades I–III, it was 70.6% for the Denominational Schools and 42.2% for the Government Schools. Again, the consistency of these significant differences, in this and other examinations, attract some worry.

**Figure 12.4:  Percentage of Students with CAPE Grades I–III over a Three-year Period: Comparisons between Government and Denominational Schools**

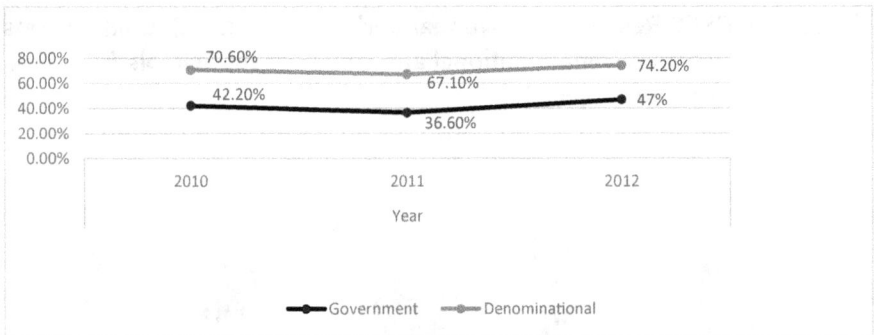

THE STRATEGIC PLAN – 2011–15: MASKING INEQUALITY
=======

In 2011, the Minister of Education, Dr Tim Gopeesingh, in the Ministry's Strategic Plan 2011–2015, listed sixteen new priority areas for attention. He emphasized that these were priority areas critical in addressing the challenges in achieving quality education.[42] Three of his pledges were:

1.  We have plans to research and understand the root causes of deviant behaviour in schools and to develop policies to prevent and eradicate negative behaviour and better manage the entire school environment.

2.  We will continually find ways to collaborate with the Local School Boards, the Denominational Boards, parents and community-based stakeholders to promote safe learning environments where human life has equal worth and where every child has an opportunity to learn and succeed.

3.  Expanding access to quality learning remains high on our agenda.[43]

In the strategic plan, the junior minister in the Ministry, Clifton De Coteau noted: *'The performance of our students in national, regional and international assessments has demonstrated the need to transform our practice of teaching to address their diverse backgrounds, aptitude and learning styles to ensure that all students are given the opportunity to succeed.'*[44]

In addition, the Strategic Plan stated: *'The plan identified three major goals aimed at enhancing and consolidating efforts in the ongoing pursuit of improved access, equity and quality of education for improved student outcomes.'*[45]

Now, the above statements made in 2011 include pledges for *'quality education, opportunity to succeed and addressing the diverse backgrounds of students.'* There was no firm commitment towards aiming for equality of educational opportunity or educational equity in the context of the society's ethnic diversity, socio-economic gaps, district disadvantages or parental background. Gender inequality did get mention mainly because there was enough published data to attract policy concern.

## INEQUALITY AND THE STRATEGIC PLAN 2011–2015

There were strong data revealing the inequalities among the eight educational districts but yet nothing firm from the strategic plan about making reforms for improving equality of opportunity. In the case of ethnic diversity and socio-economic gaps, there was neither data nor commitment in the plans or in the other ministry reports towards equality of opportunity or equity. Such data as has been found came mainly from academic researchers and other non-governmental sources.

The IDB Report on Access, Equity and Performance, for example, noting the lack of information on education and ethnic background gently stated that 'improving education equality is implicitly related to ethnic quality.'[46] It also noted that while efficiency (universal education, for example), was achieved, issues of quality and equality remain outstanding.[47]

The quest for equality of opportunity and especially equity is based not merely on 'having opportunities for all' but a serious consideration of the extent to which social and economic disadvantages persistently keep back certain groups from effectively participating in these opportunities.

After reviewing the 2010–2015 Strategic Plan, Lecturer in Education, David Subran claimed that the *'planners of post-colonial education have failed Trinidad and Tobago and it is clear that politics has sabotaged our education system in the populist decisions taken rather than decisions based on research.'*[48] He added: *'The farce of educational research becomes glaring when one sees that the Ministry's Strategic Planning Report was authored by a former campaign manager and auditor. All of the research-based papers submitted for the revision of the Education Act have been abandoned in favour of new inputs from hastily organized national consultations.'*[49]

A serious flaw in the Ministry's Strategic 2011–2015 Plan is the absence of a data-driven situational analysis to help indicate, at least, where the critical starting points are and where the benchmark destination points are so as to measure more precisely whether there are improvements or not over time. In other words, the Plan is not as 'strategic' as it should be, given the reputed role of education as the 'key passport out of poverty and for a prosperous life.'

In these respects, the plan has been too global, masking much of the inequalities, inequities and the psychological injuries lying silently below. The 'Education for All,' slogan, for example, will not capture precisely where the healing is required. Again, it is one thing for the plan to pledge improvement in students' overall academic performance,[50] but at the SEA level, for example, even when more students improve, where are the increased places in the Concordat-driven prestige schools? Or shouldn't the government schools be significantly improved to become more competitive, more attractive to parents and children?

The Ministry's strategic plan listed 'five overarching value statements:'

1. Children will achieve their potential.
2. Children will be adequately prepared educationally to fulfill their potential.
3. Children will be adequately developed socially and culturally.
4. Children who are healthy and growing normally.
5. Children who are emotionally developed, mature and happy.[51]

Now, on the face of it, these are all worthy expectations, but how can the children achieve these or be 'happy' after all the stresses, trials and tribulations from the SEA examinations? The strategic plan is quite soft here, and lacking in more realistic foundations.

## NO NATIONAL ADVISORY COMMITTEE ON EDUCATION FOR REFORMS

Maybe, part of the reason for these 'strategic' deficiencies is the failure of the Minister of Education to follow the Education Act in appointing the multi-sectoral National Advisory Committee as suggested by the Education Act (No. 1 of 1966). The Act states: *'The Minister may establish a National Advisory Committee for the purpose of advising him as to the performance of any of his responsibilities under this Act'* (Section 8).

The related value of this committee is in its intended composition – teaching profession, education experts, parents' association, school boards, community organizations, etc. On the other hand, given the fundamental issues of reform at hand, the consultations led by the Minister's consultant appear too self-serving with superficially delineated outcomes. Given its composition, this Advisory Committee would have been able to provide some ground-up proposals for educational reform and helpful understanding of hitherto unknown conditions of poverty and inequality.

In launching the strategic plan in 2011, the Ministry did announce plans to conduct a longitudinal study to determine the impact of whole-school improvement plans on students' academic achievement.[52] As of 2014, no further mention was made of any results or the stage at which this study has reached so as to inform the Ministry's planning process.

The Ministry, time and time again, in one report or another, makes promises of 'quality education,' 'equal opportunity,' etc. That is important especially since the objectives of equality of educational opportunity and educational equity, as earlier described, are superior objectives in this post-colonial era. The 2011–2015 strategic plan, for example, pledged 'to promote the rights of all citizens to quality education, from ECCE to secondary education.'[53]It didn't speak about closing the gaps of inequality and inequity.

## EQUALITY AND EQUITY: BEYOND SURVIVAL OF THE FITTEST

So far, however, the Ministry has not properly defined 'quality education' or expressed its objective of 'quality education' in quantitative, outcome terms. The 1993 Education Plan did make some attempt, but this general objective has been left too idle, too loose and too global for effective, targeted results, especially if the more refined objectives of equality of opportunity and equity are to be met for reasons of social justice and remedial action.

It needs to be emphasised, the pursuit of equality of educational opportunity and especially equity has to be examined in the realities of the multi-ethnic, class-driven, gender-conscious society as this one. It is a matter of group rights, not just 'survival of the fittest' individuals.

For example, what is the quality benchmark figure for passing secondary school examinations for those social groups consistently left behind? Restrospective comparisons alone are not enough for a strategic plan. The strategic route is to ask in advance. For example: In what year is it expected that the inequalities found in academic performance between the denominational and government schools will be significantly decreased at least, if not removed? And then work towards that target, possibly school by school.

Some related questions for a scientific approach:

1.  In what year is it expected that the inequalities found between the Educational Divisions will be decreased?
2.  By what percentage is it expected to increase the pass rate for students in the CVQ programmes?
3.  In what year is it expected that the inequality in academic performance between male and female students at secondary school be closed?
4.  In what year is it expected that a higher proportion of 'black African females' will gain entry into the Concordat-driven prestige schools?
5.  We should not be afraid ofthe Pandora's Box.

As indicated above, the Ministry pledged 'to promote the rights of all citizens to quality education.' The fact is that there is enough existing legislation to provide children with quality education.[54] So it is not really a legislative problem. It is an operational responsibility for the Ministry, so far largely unfilled. And seemingly, politics stood in the way of doing what is required, what is right.

Policy objectives like 'education for all' or 'no child left behind,' as noble as they sound, may very well mask underlying truths in an examination system. In any education system or examination, there will be results, and the persons who write the exam will individually be ranked one way or another. Such individual ranking by itself tends to obscure systematic bias or discrimination especially in societies that are multi-racial, carry historical social divisions and with various types of family structures, urban-rural differences, etc.

Of course, depending on how marked, some will pass and others will not. But if equality of educational opportunity and especially educational equity are to be served, performance measures on some, if not all of the groups cited above, must be taken for policy purposes. Further, for purposes of fairness and transparency, equality of educational opportunity and educational equity must be governed by appropriate measurement and effective policy response.

In this country, we cannot say we are pursuing equality of educational opportunity and educational equity without having quality data on the relationships at least between ethnicity, social class, region, family background and gender on one hand and educational access and achievement on the other hand. How else will we know how to help the systematically disadvantaged groups in the society? And there are. The political rhetoric must be unmasked.

## FROM BIAS TO DISCRIMINATION

Earlier, we distinguished between merit, equality and equity. So too, there are differences between proportionality, bias and discrimination. As previously presented, there is indeed strong evidence of disproportionalities within ethnicity, social class, districts, gender and family background. The evidence shows strong bias against certain of these social groups. Indeed, there are inequalities. But are these three features – disproportionalities, bias and inequalities – evidence of willful discrimination?

There have been many ad hoc protests against the 'biased and discriminatory' SEA and, in particular, the process of secondary school placement. Bias or prejudice in themselves may not necessarily lead to an act of discrimination. An act within the process may appear as discrimination, but the actor himself may not necessarily be prejudiced. While the act itself may be discriminatory, it remains a matter of proving that the actor deliberately did it.

As a special case, there is the merit-driven SEA, ministry placement (80%) by marks and the Concordat with its 20% allocation at the Principals' discretion. What is it in this process and in the three concepts mentioned above that signifies discrimination? Discrimination is described as 'unfavourable treatment based on prejudice, especially regarding race, age or sex' (*Concise Oxford Dictionary, 1995*).

From the data and analyses we have presented, does the process look prejudiced against one social group to another? Does school placement look so? After all, there were marks and a ranking. Some will naturally be left behind. At this point, how valid is the criterion to assess prejudice or discrimination? Or has the Study on Secondary School Placement made out a case of discrimination by race and social class?

In matters of prejudice and discrimination, in the sociological sense, pattern and persistence are relevant for an interpretation. We have found patterns and persistence of inequalities. If these significant patterns and persistence are allowed to continue without the required reforms, or without convincing attempts to reform, especially to the government secondary schools, such ignored persistence could take on the appearance of willful discrimination. In addition to the political obligations, the reforms required are based on the ethical and moral responsibility of the elected government and the Ministry. Behind the numbers, there is much work to be done.

## NOTES

1.    Existing aggregated data could sometimes be further disaggregated.
2.    The SEA or CAPE results, for example, are usually published under 'Government and Denominational Schools.' There is no separate column for 'Denominational Schools.' See e.g., Ministry of Education Administrative Report, October 2011–September 2012. Table 2. p. 37.
3.    See e.g., Ministry Administrative Report Oct 2010–Sept 2011, CSEC 2012 Results, p. 40; Also Ministry Report on SEA 2008–2012 Results,

p. 37. The aggregate heading '7 and 5- year Government Schools' used. Why include Denominational Assisted Schools under this heading? See, also, Ministry Report to JSC, p. 37. SEA results for Denominational Schools are sometimes published in great detail – school by school – at the back pages. It is indeed difficult for a reader or even researcher to collate these results by school type.

4.    Ibid.

5.    Strategic Plan 2011–2015. p. 10.

6.    This excludes private schools which are located in Trinidad but with Canadian, British or U.S. accreditation and governed by a private Board of Directors, including representatives from private companies and foreign missions. Students here take overseas examinations – from kindergarten to primary to secondary education. Generally, parents from energy companies, foreign missions, etc. enroll their students here.

Fees are quite expensive. For example, at Maple Leaf International School, the annual fee for kindergarten and primary is $72,450 plus $26,200 for registration, etc. This was opened in 1995. Another is the International School of Port of Spain, opened in 1994. In such international schools, issues like equality of opportunity and equity do not arise. There is also the British Academy.

7.    See Strategic Plan 2011–2015.

8.    Ministry of Education. Measuring Primary School Growth in Trinidad and Tobago. National Test 2005–2011.

9.    Annual Administrative Report, 2009–2010. p. 17.

10.   Annual Administrative Report 2009–10. pp. 18–19. 20–21.

11.   Ministry of Education. Measuring Primary School Growth. National Test, 2005–2011.

12.   Annual Administrative Report 2009–10. Inequalities in 2010, pp. 18–19, 20–21.

13.   Ministry of Education. Annual Administrative Report, October 2011–2012. p. 35.

14.   Ministry of Education. National Test Report 2005. pp. 58–76.

15.   Ibid.

16.   Ministry of Education. National Tests. Measuring Primary School Growth, 2005–2011, January 2012; National Test Trend 2009–2014, November 2014.

17.   Ibid.

18.   Ibid. p. 22.

19.   Ministry SEA 2011 Report. p. 13.

20.   Ministry Report to JSC. March 21, 2013.

21. Ministry of Education Report to Joint Select Committee of Parliament. December, 2013. p. 42.
22. Ministry of Education. Administrative Report, October 2011–2012. pp.37–38.
23. Ministry of Education Report to JSC. Also personal correspondence.
24. Educare. Ministry of Education.
25. Ministry of Education Data. The other students (7.5%) went to private schools, vocational schools, or re-sat the SEA. Also see, Educare, Ministry of Education Quarterly Publication. 2014; Ministry of Education Report to Joint Select Committee of Parliament. March, 2013.
26. Soon after the SEA results were publicly announced, for several days parents and students complained. One newspaper wrote: 'Parents have been complaining that while their children received high percentage marks, others with lower percentage marks were selected for so-called better schools.' *Guardian.* July 3, 2015. p. 4.
27. Media conference. July 2, 2015, reported in *Guardian*, July 3, 2015. p. 4.
28. Minister's media conference, *Guardian*, July 3, 2015. p. 4.
29. Voices of the Teachers. 2008.
30. Ministry of Education. *Educare.* Quarterly Publication. 2014. pp. 7–8.
31. Ibid. p.8.
32. Administrative Report, 2010–11. pp. 24–25.
33. Ibid. p. 32.
34. Administrative Report, 2011. p. 25.
35. Ministry of Education. NCSE Report, 2011. p. 14.
36. Administrative Report, 2011. p. 25.
37. Ministry of Education Report on NCSE 2010–2014.
38. Ministry of Education, Division of Educational Research and Evaluation. Preliminary Report on the CSEC, 2014. Table 1. p. 3.
39. Ministry Administrative Report, 2012. p. 28.
40. Ministry of Education Administrative Report (2010–11). 2013. p. 28.
41. Educare. Ministry Quarterly Publication. 2014. p. 7.
42. Ministry of Education. Strategic Plan 2011–2015. p. iii.
43. Ibid. pp. iii–iv.
44. Ibid. p.5.
45. Ibid. p. xiii.
46. Inter-American Development Bank, *Access, Equity and Performance.* Washington: IDB Bookstore. 2002. p.30.
47. Ibid. pp. 33–45.
48. TrinidadExpress, February 17, 2015. p. 15.
49. Ibid. The 'auditor' referred to by Mr. Subran is an election campaign advisor hired by the Education Minister. The 'politics of education'

is not confined to matters of the Concordat, but also the haste with which one government after another has opened schools without proper planning. The provision of increased secondary school places, in particular, attracts popular support, until the inequalities and other qualitative defects begin to be exposed.

50.  Ibid. p.2.
51.  Ibid. p. 5.
52.  Ibid. p. 20.
53.  Ibid. p. 25.
54.  E.g., Section 4, Education Act, No 1 of 1966.

# CHAPTER THIRTEEN
# Equality, Merit and Equity

*Throughout recorded time and probably since the Neothilic Age, there have been three kinds of people in the world, the High, the Middle and the Low. They have been subdivided in many ways, they have countless different names, and their relative numbers as well as their attitude to one another, have varied from age to age,though the essential structure of society has never altered.*

–George Orwell, Ignorance is Strength, 1984

## THE EDUCATION SYSTEM: SERVANT OR MASTER?

We now seek to clarify some of the conceptual issues involved and the extent to which a humanitarian ideology can help the educational system achieve the objectives of equality of educational opportunity and equity. The intellectual attack on the education system rests primarily on the system's reciprocal relationship with the society's social and economic structure.

That is, through its programmes and critical thinking, it is expected to close the gaps of socio-economic inequity and produce students as agents of social change. At the same time, its socialization features and training programmes essentially reinforce a stratification system that is elite-dominated, exploitative and anti-democratic.

This latter view is an attack on the functionalist nature of the education system, such as what we have, providing rewards by merit, opportunity, training students for jobs in the economic market-place, status competition, etc. These two seemingly contradictory forces struggle to mould the school agendas. It is also from this vantage point that Brosio noted that *'the school site is part of the larger struggle being fought between democracy and capitalism.'*[1] Such critics should also explain why capitalism cannot accommodate democracy. By and large, however, Caribbean societies and their education planners do not show much appreciation for the 'first force,' that is, the schools as agents of social change, neither the contradiction in the schools' purpose. State bureaucracies cannot afford to use the schools for social change. The preferred objective is 'education for jobs.' The capitalist-driven job market has little or no time for critical thinkers.

That the education system, with few fundamental adjustments, has been able to survive under 'anti-capitalist attacks' suggests at least three related things. Firstly, that the changes these intellectual attacks demand, heavily pro-socialist, do not resonate in the public mind. Secondly, the persons and institutions positioned to initiate such changes are themselves beneficiaries of the existing functionalist system.

Recognising this constraint and the role of a liberation philosophy, John Dewey said: '*The direct impact of liberty always has to do with some class or group that is suffering in a special way from some form of constraint by the distribution of powers in contemporary society.*'[2] Thirdly, critics like Carnoy, Bowles and Gintis, Brosio, even Dewey, put their alternatives in such vague, generalised manner that leaves the alternatives in suspended philosophy rather than in actionable programmes. Their one-sided attack against capitalism keeps the debate exceedingly polarized, and a long distance from reforms. We must remember that radical, revolutionary educational changes require substantial public support.

Consider, for example, the well-funded, expansive education and training programmes undertaken by the government in order to supply labour to our capitalist-driven business sector. The business sector in fact recommended the type of labour they need, and the government and workers express gratitude for the opportunity. At the same time, the government, using such labour absorption opportunities, boasts of its low unemployment rate. In such education-business scenario, how can the population be convinced that capitalism is unfriendly to the education system, or vice-versa? Is it workers' 'false consciousness' or a lack of critical thinking or just labour expediency?

This country, like the rest of the Caribbean, and as George Beckford advised, does not have the political space or economic resilience to practice the socialist-driven type of education advocated by Carnoy, Bowles, Gintis, etc. The purpose and operations of the education system here are purely of the functionalism type, serving a capitalist economy, and the governors show no interest in apologizing. To them, equality of educational opportunity remains within the mould of merit and competition, with piece-meal remedial education programmes. Radical change in the education system, even within a liberal mode, does not go down too well with an educationally-conservative, post-colonial society.

It is not easy to develop and implement education programmes effectively in a small, multi-ethnic, democratic society where competing interests press for compromise at every corner. But as has happened, from one century to another, education systems have evolved but only to the extent that the economic and political elites have allowed them to evolve.

The virtue of the critics and their philosophical propositions, however, do play a significant part in inspiring and compelling us to feel uneasy over the many deficiencies within our education system, especially with matters such as equality of educational opportunity and equity. They help push towards an ethical and moral dilemma.

It is therefore necessary for people in the Caribbean and in this country to have at least a fair and critical understanding of what the concepts equal opportunity, merit and equity mean, mainly because these are the pillars on which our education system purportedly rests. How much have we achieved? To help answer this, we now briefly consider these concepts and their implications for the education system.

Prominent critics, Bowles and Gintis put their case this way:

> An educational system can be egalitarian and liberating only when it prepares youth for fully democratic participation in social life and an equal claim to the fruits of economic activity...This is of course socialism, conceived of as an extension of democracy from the narrowly political to the economic realm.[3]

That is, the role of the school inherently carries contradictory purposes and consequences from the bruising forces of capitalism clashing with the ennobling ideals of democracy, as Dewey quite early argued in several works.[4] Pushing an activist role for the education system, Professor Brosio stated:

> The serious discussions underway in educational theory concerning class, race, ethnicity, gender and sexual preference represent significant forwarding of the democratic project and imperative. The greater inclusion of formerly marginalized persons in scholarly discourses has brought a refreshing poignancy to our studies of fairness in education.[5]

Noting the shift of emphasis from purely class analysis to ones involving *'interrelationships among class, race and gender realities in school and society,'* Broiso stated that *'these attempts were aimed at resolving tensions between structuralism and culturalism in radical educational research.'*[6] This is part of the post-modernist thrust for considering ethnic, class and gender diversity as equal opportunity and equity issues within the education system. In other words, the post-modernist validation of subjectivity and meaning became quite important in assessing the quality and status of the education system in relation to democracy itself.

## EQUALITY THREATENED

Slapping the wrists of Bowles, Gintis and Carnoy, Brosio warned that when such discourses, much undertaken within the academy, become too abstract, they lose relevance - not always *'helpful to the kind of mass-movement formation necessary to push the democratic imperative forward.'* With advice to the ivory-towered, he also added: *'The school is part of the larger society; therefore analyses that are helpful to intramural concerns are less relevant than those that address school and society in a unified manner.'*[7]

Given the slavery, indentureship and plantation history of this country, and especially after its political independence in 1962, the words 'equality' and 'equal opportunity' have dominated political rhetoric. No doubt, as Rubin and Zavalloni found, such rhetoric, connected to the role of education, inspired very high academic and occupational expectations among the youth here.[8] The limitations of the 'equality' criterion were not then, nor now, fully appreciated.

Here, the expectation of equality in the education system often carries misleading interpretations. For example, in the present system, students are ranked by their marks. Then there is the existing law of supply and demand partly regulated by the Concordat. And finally, as the curriculum planners have earlier indicated, not all students have the same academic interests or aptitudes, thus requiring different educational options.

Whether the Concordat is removed or not, the society will remain pyramidal, not rectangular, with regard to educational and occupational status and mobility unless the predominant value and reward systems are changed - a chicken and egg dilemma for a newly independent society.[9]

# OPPORTUNITY PLURALISM

It is for such reasons, that rather than pursuing equality of opportunity within the same stream of achievement, Fishkin proposed a policy of 'opportunity pluralism' to help modify the literal meaning of equality and convert it into a manageable educational policy. Will this help reduce the stresses from failure and incompatible ambitions? Fishkin, in his book, *A New Theory of Equal Opportunity*, states:

> A more pluralistic opportunity structure creates different incentives. It gives individuals the space to reflect in a more personal and ongoing way about what paths they would like to pursue and what goals in the life they value.[10]

Of course, at this point, his advice sounds like the pluralism already provided in curriculum diversity, technical/vocational training, etc. for those not getting into a prestige school. Going further, however, he proposes two options as alternatives to equality of opportunity, that is '*maximizing the minimum, or improving the opportunities of those with the least*'; and priority, that is, '*trying to improve everyone's opportunity but giving priority to those whose opportunities are the most limited.*'[11]

The critical assumption apparently made by Fishkin here, is that there are no significant value differentiations surrounding 'opportunity pluralism.' For example in our case, getting into a grammar-type prestige school, university and then into one or the other traditional professions still remains as over-powering values. Educational opportunity and success are measured mainly along these criteria.

In terms of equal opportunity and competition, that is achievement by merit, Fishkin states: '*Formal equality of opportunity at the moment of decision cannot by itself do the work that one would expect a principle of equal opportunity to do. Something more is required. At the minimum, we must also address the developmental opportunities (or a lack thereof) that precedes the contest.*'[12]

This is relevant to the SEA exam or even the CSEC exam where social class and ethnic inequalities significantly arise. But then, how much 'developmental opportunities' should be provided before the disadvantaged groups could compete on an equal footing? After all, the already advantaged are not standing still – with private lessons, more learning resources, social contacts, etc.

Now such 'proposals of hope' by Fishkin are 'within the box,' that is, contained within liberalism, and a far cry from Bowles and Gintis 'out of the box' proposition that 'the failure of liberal education reform must be linked to fundamental characteristics of the economy.'[13]

Fishkin's proposals for developmental opportunities like compensatory education itself, are designed to enable the disadvantaged to catch up, to reach the starting line so that the achievement race will have an equal opportunity start. At this point, we have to appreciate who are involved in this contest. The society does have an established elite, particularly in the business and professional class. But a large part comprises the *noveau riche*, a newly-arrived middle class.

After all, as a post-colonial society with very large sections of its population emerging from poverty and depressed opportunities, the middle or upper class status is quite new to these persons, having struggled up mainly through grammar-type schooling. This group, both of African and East Indian descent, have already made the extra effort, sacrifice and, coupled with their natural ability, to reach the top where the places are limited.[14] It requires a special amount of compassion and nobility to give way now. They feel they deserve the status. In the end then, and in many ways, the educational reforms sought for equal opportunity and equity depend on 'compassion and moral obligation', at least until the competition for status diminishes or disappears.[15]

In addition, while Fishkin's 'maximin' and 'priority' principles are drawn from a 'libertarian- egalitarian' perspective, there are practical limits, falling as they do partly within the realm of compensatory education – a controversial alternative in itself. Further, we need to be clear about who exactly will trigger and sustain the application of these 'developmental opportunities, especially if it means reducing their class position.' This is the dialectical question. There are already rising concerns here, for example, over the extent to which a government should or could reach into the lives of families.

## AFFIRMATIVE ACTION

Another alternative, especially where 'developmental opportunities' are absent for disadvantaged black youth, is a policy of affirmative action, controversial but with strong backing from blacks and other minorities, especially in the United States, England and increasingly so, in the Caribbean. After examining several landmark cases dealing with discrimination, Professor Randall Kennedy lists four of the major arguments for affirmative action: (1) Seeking reparatory justice, (2) Creating diversity, (3) Facilitating integration, and (4) Countering racial prejudice.[16]

Professor Boxill put these arguments into two routes. He said '*backward-looking arguments justify preferential treatment considered as compensation for past and present wrongs while forward-looking arguments justify preferential treatment considered as a means to future and present goods.*'[17]

Furthermore, he explained, and as indicated earlier for this society, the allegation will have to be well-grounded in order to prevent counter-allegations of discrimination by other groups who may get left out through affirmative action for others.

Faced with such protracted, socially-divisive issues, resort has often been taken to the courts hoping for sober, penetrating, just and sustainable conciliation. This is what happened in the case over the legality of the Concordat.[18] This court route has been usefully exemplified by Donald Horowitz in his book, *The Courts and Social Policy*, as well as by Michael Rebell, in his *Courts and the Kids*.[19]

In both books, the matters involved inequitable funding, and stopping or preventing overt or covert discrimination of poor, minority groups and children. Of course, litigation will not always solve all socially-rooted problems, but at least it will help inspire and drive legislation and citizen's movements.[20]

Nevertheless, as Professor Chemerinsky said: '*Without judicial action, equal educational opportunity will never exist.*'[21] To this, Rebell added: 'Only with court involvement has our nation made significant in-roads into our intractable educational inequities. This is not to say that the courts alone have in the past or can in the future ensure educational equity.'[22]

The issues of equality of educational opportunity and educational equity contain questions of philosophy and education itself. In our ethnically-driven electoral system, these issues are also seriously political. It is therefore quite important that the policy objectives are non-discriminatory and transparent, with results faithfully compared to objectives.

We need to know the conditions, qualitative and quantitative, required to implement such objectives. We also need to know how far and with what empirical evidence, these policies of equal opportunity, as expressed in government report, are being achieved and with what implications for ethnic, social class and gender diversity.

Next, what are the 'developmental opportunities' required to achieve 'equal opportunity' for the disadvantaged? After all, as the famous Coleman study warned, equal opportunity does not necessarily guarantee equal results. It cannot.

## IMPROVE GOVERNMENT SCHOOLS OR 'SEGREGATION IN DISGUISE'

As evidenced earlier, the educational imbalances here include social class which is compounded by race. Dealing with the Concordat and the denominational assisted schools, Mustapha noted that the process of secondary school enrolment serves moreso to tighten the society's social class hierarchy. The well-known inequities of race and class in secondary school enrolment and success arise mainly because of the glaring and recurring achievement deficiencies in many government secondary schools – a phenomenon which one regime after another has failed to tackle head-on.[23] As evidenced by the several studies cited earlier, the notable differences in school type, if not unchecked now, would likely aggravate 'racial segregation in disguise.'[24]

Therefore, before we seek to apply any one or more of the 'affirmative action' reasons forwarded by Kennedy in our situation, we will have to establish, at least prima facie, that the social class and ethnic disproportionalities found in the process of secondary school enrolment are deliberate or victims of very inefficient or unlawful procedures.

The glaring fact is that the inequalities perpetrated by the sharp differences in school-type outputs here cannot continue if the equal opportunity and educational equity pledges of the government policies are to be fulfilled among the various races and social classes here.

Much more is needed than what the *'Jagessar v Teaching Service Commission'* case cited earlier on the Concordat offered. It is true that that case involved a charge of discrimination brought by a teacher against the Denominational Board and the Teaching Service Commission, and in which the judge, using the Concordat, rest his ruling on the rights of a parent to send his child to a school of his choice and also the Board's rights to property and the preservation of its religion. But nothing about the rights of a parent to get his child enrolled in a school of their choice where *preferred places* are limited, or whether the Concordat process itself is discriminatory in the secondary school placement process. It appears as a clash of constitutional rights. In that regard, judicial clarity may be needed.

# RESISTANCE TO REFORMS

Howe, in his book, *Understanding Equal Educational Opportunity*, further noted that since the

> celebrated Brown v Board of Education decision in 1954, the quest for equality of educational opportunity has been extended from its original focus on race to encompass other sources of discrimination such as disability, language and gender.

The functionalist, merit-driven basis on which the country's educational system operates seems to have failed in terms of equality of opportunity and equity. The obstacle to fundamental changes, however, is that there are strong, deeply embedded aspirations, maintained by the general population for a place at the top, and believing further that education is the key passport to prosperity and a better life. And that they have a chance. This neutralizing dynamic keeps protest and mass movement for change dormant, except for the mild, ad hoc 'grief and tears' annually flowing over the SEA results.

It is interesting that there are no such 'grief and tears' over the secondary school results which reveal very pronounced differences in ethnicity and social class. One commentator, Professor Theodore Lewis, calling for an examination of the status of black boys in our schools, said:

> 'The educational playing field is tilted. If we are serious about the socialisation of the African male, and what he has become in the society, which is someone who does not pass for a prestige school and never wins the scholarships at A-Level, then we should show concern about this and see what we could do in our schools to fix it.'[25]

# INEQUALITY IN SCHOLARSHIPS TOO

In the 2013 CAPE results for example, no government secondary school got an Open Scholarship. Neither did any receive a President's Medal. All these national awards went to students from denominational secondary schools. Forty of the nation's 134 secondary schools received scholarships – Open and Additional. Eleven (or 13%) of the 86 government schools got only 'Additional Scholarships' while over 75% of the denominational secondary schools got both Open and 'Additional Scholarships.' This means that for every six denominational schools that got scholarships, only one government secondary school got – and only 'Additional Scholarships' at that.[26]

That's where the public focus is set – on passing examinations and scholarships. The fundamental educational reforms proposed by Carnoy, Gintis, etc., are quite far from the political and public mind here. The major purpose of the educational system, as we said, is functionalism and closely linked to the requirements of the capitalist business class. Surplus labour is put into stagnant job positions.

## THE EQUITY CHALLENGE CONTINUES

From evidence presented so far, we are faced with significant gaps within race, religion, social class and gender in academic opportunity and achievement, more precisely in the context of secondary school entry. The disproportionalities are extremely troubling since secondary schooling has very serious implications and consequences for life chances in further studies, occupational careers and the virtues of good citizenship.

Furthermore, since government spokespersons, especially one Prime Minister after another, have publicly and repeatedly advanced education as 'the key to prosperity and a better life,' then surely it becomes necessary for government to ensure that the mechanisms - qualitatively and quantitatively – are put in place for all groups to have equal opportunity and reasonable academic achievement. Promising 'education for all' merely protects the hidden injuries and disparities of social class and ethnicity.

The concepts of equality of educational opportunity and equity have naturally been used to treat the disparities within a social and distributive justice model, but also within an operational framework, that is, to question the extent to which the very objectives of the government's several education plans have been achieved or not. The data suggests significant reforms are needed.

## EQUALITY AND EQUITY: DEFINITIONS

What makes an examination of equal educational opportunity and equity so vital to this county? A starting point is with the sociological concept of equality itself. The concept necessarily admits firstly, that there are different social groups present in the society. Secondly, these groups need to be examined and compared with regard to the relationships (e.g., rights and duties) between them to see the extent to which equality or inequality exists.[27] The country's ethnic diversity exists under a national anthem which pledges a place 'where every creed and find an equal place.'

Among the important relationships between the groups are three inter-related systems – economic, political and educational.[28] The education system has reciprocal relationships with the other two. In the competition within each system – given the supply and demand challenges – racial, social class and gender tensions arise, often intensified by allegations of unfairness and discrimination. It therefore becomes necessary for tax-supported public policies to be transparently developed and equitably applied among the different ethnic groups. It will be of concern if the education system, directly or indirectly, throws up significant degrees of ethnic or social class discrimination, and leaving such discrimination unattended.[29]

Hence, given the subject of this book – equality of educational opportunity and equity – at least two minimal conditions are required. One, each group is identifiable enough to be measured.[30] Two, there is a defined criterion on which the groups are measured – that is, educational opportunity for limited places. In other words, the education system now in the independence era is strongly obligated to help correct the wrongs of inequity from the colonial past.

The presence of prestige primary and secondary schools, the use of a common examination at 11+ and the uneven selection process for secondary schooling – all combine to leave the educational system open to allegations of bias, inequality and discrimination. The troubling fact is that, given that 'equality of educational opportunity' has been so frequently cited as an official educational objective, there has been no concerted attempt to define, discuss and operationalise the objective in the relevant reports and plans.[31]

Even in the several research studies which have dealt with ethnic and socio-economic gaps and disproportionalities in secondary school enrollment, the concept of equal opportunity and equity have been used without substantial definition.

An attempt, though quite cryptic, was made to define both equality and equity in the local Study of Secondary School Placement. Here 'equality' was defined in terms of 'group proportionality.' 'Equity' was defined mainly in terms of the 'unfair' criteria in allocating students, especially with reference to the Concordat.[32]

Interestingly, an Assessment Report of its Education Plan (1968-83), cautiously stated: '*The term "quality education" has proven to be a somewhat elusive concept and would appear to mean different things to different persons. The qualitative aspects of educational planning deal with changes and adaptations. Quality education is concerned with bridging the gap between what goes on in the classroom and the world in which we live.*'[33] Nothing yet about inequality within ethnic diversity or social class.

The Report added: '*Quality education seeks to redress imbalances and maladjustments between schooling and the labour market, between schooling and family life, between schooling and citizenship and finally between schooling and living.*'[34] The fearsome challenge was not undertaken. That is, no promise to examine or at least make some reference to equality of educational opportunity among the various ethnic and social class groups as a criterion for connecting 'schooling and the world,' or between 'schooling and family life or citizenship.' It would appear as if such differentiations were to be left to the market-place and survival of the fittest.

Given the opportunity deprivations suffered by forefathers of both Africans and East Indians on the plantation, as cited by Dr Williams, and the promises of remedy made in the years soon after independence, the justifiable expectation is that careful attention would be paid to creating at least a level playing field for the descendants.

The evidence cited so far illustrates that having equality of opportunity for secondary school entry is not sufficient. And the policy remedy is seriously mitigated by the politics of ethnicity and constitutional rights. Equal opportunity in education and academic achievement are connected to other forces and opportunities in the wider society.

Throughout his book, *Understanding Equal Educational Opportunity*, Kenneth Howe argued that a clear understanding of the 'equal opportunity' concept is necessary if reforms are to be relevant and effective. In locating this view into a social justice model, Howe cited three liberal-democratic traditions to help energise an understanding of this 'pivotal' concept.[35]

'Equal opportunity' is defined in *Black's Law Dictionary* (5th ed.) and referenced by selected court judgments as *'The condition of possessing substantially the same rights, privileges, and immunities and being liable substantially to the same duties.'* In education, it essentially means providing similar opportunities for every social or economic group involved. It does not necessarily mean equality in academic performance. Opportunity means access, not necessarily achievement. Equity involves comparative outcomes between identified groups. And the remedies for curing disadvantages.

Given the obvious need for this country to undertake urgent reforms in its education system, especially with regard to opportunity and related qualitative issues, an improved consideration of the concepts of equality of educational opportunity, merit and equity will assist in not only developing the required reforms but also in implementing them. After all, educational reforms have their limits, particularly in this society with a dual system of education and an embracing, protective and protected Concordat.

## THE ISSUE: QUANTITY AND EQUALITY.

In moving forward in this regard, the following three platform issues are noted:

1.  There is no doubt that the government, one after the other, has significantly increased the number of school buildings, school places and facilities, especially at the secondary and technical and vocational levels (1961–2013).The building of early childhood centres by the 2010–2015 government has also been significant. However, the human rights' issue of quality education and the implications for social imbalances in the expanded system have not been properly articulated by government, quite possibly, because of their politically sensitive nature.

While such expansions were taking place, the challenges of quality of education became a policy and research concern, especially from the 1970s when, for example, complaints of ethnic and social class discrimination in public and private institutions became politically-driven.[36] The number of school places inevitably opened the doors to concerns over quality of education and equity.

2.   Several education planning reports (1968–2004) pledged in varying degrees to secure equality of educational opportunity with regard to socio-economic, ethnic and gender differences. It became evident that quality of education resulted in 'quality for some.' The updated focus must now be on quality as fairly and proportionally spread across all ethnic, social class and gender groups – without implicit or explicit discrimination.

3.   Alongside these reports, questions need to be asked regarding educational democracy, social justice and the challenges of providing equality of educational opportunity and equity, especially in the context of a newly independent, multi-ethnic society forged from a labour history of African slavery and East Indian indentureship.[37]

## THE POLICY DILEMMA OF EQUALITY

This great hope for education as a flagship vehicle for individual and national development was colourfully expressed in several official reports on the country's educational policies. An official Report which assessed the Government 1968-83 Education Plan stated that *'education was the main medium through which the country's social, cultural and economic transformation could be achieved.'* Referring to the system of the sixties, the Report added: *'The existing education system was one that was geared to the needs of a colonial society,'* hence the 1968-83 Plan was devised *'to strive continuously towards the creation of an egalitarian society.'*[38]

Now, the concept of an egalitarian society inevitably implies equality of opportunity within the various social groups in the society. It requires comparisons. 'Education for all' does not explicitly meet this criterion.[39] Again, the notion of equality and even egalitarianism was mentioned but nothing further in the Education Plan. It is like a heavy courtship without a marriage.

For example again, the government's 1985–90 Education Plan stated: *'Trinidad and Tobago recognizes that its greatest resource is its people and that its greatest hope for the future lies in the full development of the potential of its children. The programmes of education provided must therefore cater for the spiritual, moral, intellectual, aesthetic, physical and vocational development of the student'* (p. 15).

The Education Plan then listed twenty-one strategies and methods to accomplish this overall objective. None of the twenty-one included the specific routes towards equality of educational opportunity, or the challenges of educational equity in a multiracial society.  Such policy challenges in a dual system of education should not remain blurred or swallowed in generalised objectives.

In its earlier section, the Plan listed nine major strategies of the new education plan and twenty-six measures to achieve these strategies at the earliest opportunity. Again, none of these strategies contained any strategy, policy or measure to ensureequality of opportunity or educational equity, especially within the secondary school, in terms of either input or output.[40]

As stated earlier, this is part of the challenge to which the former Prime Minister, Dr Eric Williams, referred to when he spoke about the 'historical deprivations which these two numerically dominant groups, Africans and Indians, suffered.' The dynamics of inequality cannot be hidden within the aggregates, especially when the society faced throughout the sixties and seventies widespread allegations over discrimination in public institutions andrelated social and economic sectors.

Expressing its underlying convictions, the Plan added: '*There is now an urgent need to focus attention on the improvement of the quality of education in all our institutions.*' It then added: '*It is almost unnecessary to state that all students cannot arrive at the same level of academic attainment at the same time and that the programme of education must be adjusted to suit the needs of the individual student.*'[41]

True, while *all* students cannot achieve academically at the same time, the challenge for educational planners in a multi-ethnic society, is to identify which ethnic group or socio-economic group is moving ahead or being left behind compared to others and for what reasons. In a sociological sense, it is a matter of group rights.

On the other hand, given the ethnically-based politics then and now, matters about racial equality or even social class discrimination tend to create such protracted public controversies that it is likely felt such sensitive issues should be left to work themselves out within the institutions themselves.

That is, in the case of education, to the market place of individual academic achievement and merit. The implications for educational equity were yet to be precisely considered.

## EVOLUTION OF THE EQUITY PRINCIPLE

However, the principle of educational equity did come into gentle prominence in the mission statement of the National Task Force in Education appointed by government in1993. The mission statement: *'To promote equity and excellence, providing a viable humane and comprehensive educational policy framework.'*

Stating its philosophy of education, the Task Force Report said its *'members believe that every child has an inherent right to an education which will enhance the development of maximum capability regardless of gender, ethnic economic, social or religious background.'* And *'that there is a need to create and sustain a humanized and democratized system of education.'*[42]

But like previous reports, this one had no data to show the extent to which equity has been achieved among the various social groupings regardless of gender, ethnic, economic, social or religious background. However, the Report showed significant progress by precisely linking, at least conceptually, the challenge of equality of educational opportunity and equity to ethnicity, social class and gender. It acknowledged the need for empirical evidence to support its philosophical positions. In fact, the Report commendably added: *'In Trinidad and Tobago, we have been relatively strong on philosophical orientations or judgements but relatively weak on the use of empirical evidence.'*[43]

## MAKING EQUALITY WORK

Researchers and commentators rhetorically use the term equality of educational opportunity, especially with regard to ethnicity (e.g., race and religion) and social class, but do not insert it within a workable policy framework. From a policy and fairness doctrine point of view, the following nine issues are therefore useful to consider:

I.  First of all, we must recognise that once we use the words 'equality of educational opportunity' we admit that one, there are limited opportunities; two, that these opportunities are of great value in society; three, that there are different social and ethnic groups legitimately competing for these limited opportunities.

2. We must also recognise the difference between equality of educational *opportunity* and equality of educational *attainment*. Opportunity is access. Attainment is academic achievement. Academic opportunity does not necessarily lead to academic achievement.

3. Given that there is a limited number of high-performing denominational secondary schools[44] annually offering an estimated 4,700 preferred Form One places with some 18,000 students writing the entrance examination, allocation is generally based on the results from the SEA examination. Students are placed by merit in the competitive system. As indicated earlier, through the Concordat, principals also have a discretion to select 20% from the 'pass' list.

4. This 'merit-driven' system results in around 75% who wrote the common examination not getting into a school of their choice. And from evidence cited, the group getting into the prestige school is proportionally dominated by those of middle and upper class, of East Indian descent and from two-parent homes.

5. Assuming that there is no corruption, the case for educational equity must take into consideration: (i) All students have an *equal opportunity* to write a *common* examination, and (ii) Allocation to secondary schools is primarily based on a marks-driven *merit* list.

6. But do these conditions truly satisfy equality of opportunity? Yes, but up to a point. That is, the opportunity to write the common examination is subverted by the troublesome fact that not all primary schools are equal in output. There are prestige primary schools too, denominational mostly, many of which produce a high proportion of highly-placed students from the competitive examination results, and who eventually get into their first choice, prestige secondary schools - again, denominational schools mostly.

7. These church schools therefore produce quality output from bottom to top - from primary to secondary - quite legitimately. Within this legitimate purpose, however, ethnic and socio-economic inequality arises as an unintended consequence of the conflict between freedom of choice and merit in the free-market place of educational opportunity.[45]

8.  Within this conflict, two critically related issues arise: (i) The country's constitution and the Education Act allow parents the freedom to send their children to a school of their choice regardless of race, religion, origin or colour. The constitution also allows the church freedom of religion, thought and expression, assembly and association. The 1960 Concordat strengthens these rights and freedoms. (ii) There is an urgent, compelling need to improve the quality output of the government-managed schools, both primary and secondary, making them more academically attractive to both parents and students.

9.  Equity is a more demanding criterion than equality of opportunity or even merit. Equity essentially means *'fairness, the application of principles of justice to correct or supplement the law or a regular procedure.'*[46] It is part of an adjustment exercise. In the case of the education system, equity therefore means to provide remedy to the socially disadvantaged on the assumption that with such remedy, they would have better chances of success. In this sense, equity is an attempt to supplement the regular system, to enable the disadvantaged to catch up. It is equity by remedy.[47] In this sense, inequities occur when biased or unfair policies, practices or schools contribute to a lack of equality in educational performance, results and outcomes.[48] The quest for educational equity presumes that not all students start the race from the same line. Some start from far behind others – although they are judged and expected to reach at the same finishing line.

A lot of the arguments for fairness emerged from John Rawls 'Theory of Justice' in which he explained that the application of fairness carries two related parts: the first is institutional, that is, its rules and 'practices must be just;' the second are mutual obligations, that is, 'the requisite voluntary acts.'[49] This matter of 'mutual obligations' is important in the discussion of equality and equity since it encourages the disadvantaged to feel obliged to make some effort to escape his or her misfortune.

The pressures for self-serving advantage are also recognised by Rawls when he says: *'Official rhetoric cannot create a world without selfishness or a world where no one uses competitive advantage for*

*personal gain. It can, however, often help create a world where people feel
ashamed about such behaviour.'[50]*

Given the severe competition for prestige school places, and the struggle
to enter traditional professions amidst a surplus labour situation in the
country, it is highly unlikely that even shame would inspire the fulfilment
of mutual obligations by the already privileged.[51]

Given the history of class conflict and social inequity, it seems very
unlikely that objectives of equality of educational opportunity or moreso,
educational equity, would be achieved through the contrite hearts or civic
duty of one person to another. Referring to failures in the social contract, it
was said: *'Men's rationality is in practice always pitted against the passions of
an unthinking self-interest.'[52]*

A Policy paper by the Organisation for Economic Co-operation and
Development (OECD) states:

> Equity in education has two dimensions. The first is fairness which
> basically means making sure that personal and social circumstances,
> for example, gender, socio-economic status or ethnic origin – should
> not be an obstacle to achieving educational potential.[53] The OECD
> further indicated that the second dimension is inclusion, that is, having
> a basic minimum standard of education for all.[54]

Within the rights and freedoms cited above for both parents and the
church, how can educational equity be attained given the present forces
of merit and allocation? In the present circumstances, it cannot, since it
means, most of all, that the different social groups writing the examination
should be reasonably, if not equally, represented in entering the prestige
secondary schools. That is, at least similar in proportion to their numbers,
an argument put forward earlier by the Report on Secondary School
Placement.

Such proportional representation will mean a quota system - affirmative
action - in order to achieve educational equity. But equity is both process
and product. It also requires fairness, fairness according to student effort
and in a merit-driven way. In other words, you cannot just pick up students
from a particular social group and allocate them into secondary schools,
especially the prestige schools, merely in accordance with their respective
proportions in the population. There are gateways to education based on
effort, ability, aptitude and available places.

With these conditionalities, therefore, in order to achieve the effort required to succeed academically, and for educational equity to be achieved, effective measures (e.g., resources and programmes) must be taken to improve the academic abilities of the currently disadvantaged students so that, as a group, their proportion will be improved and become similar to those of the currently successful.[55]

But even with this 'equity by remedy,' there will still be a merit list because of the limited places now available in the high-achieving secondary schools. All schools are also not equal. With all the rapid building expansion taking place, there is a serious, gaping inequality gap among the government schools particularly – both primary and secondary – compared to the denominational schools. All 11+ children will write the same examination but not all enjoy the same quality of school environment.

Let us look at a possible but improbable situation. Assuming that with the already bright students and those uplifted by remedial interventions, everyone of the 18,000 writing the Secondary Entrance Assessment examination falls within the 95–100% range, how will the allocation for the estimated 4,700 available Form One places be equitably done? Or, even if 10,000 students make 98%? Who from this list would be chosen to fill the 4,700 places? How would this be done? The magic of statistical standardization will leave chaos behind. The point is as long as there are such a relatively small number of prestige school places compared to the number of children writing the SEA, the problem of educational inequity will exist.

## EQUITY BY REMEDY

So far, therefore, the attainment of educational equity remains one of proportionality (equal proportions) through remedial measures. We repeat, improved equity relief can surely come with improved government attention and policies for the government schools. It would also be educational folly and politically explosive now to place students by zoning or by random allocations - as proposed by some academics and commentators. Given the consistently-high performance of many denominational (prestige) schools and the 'untouchability' of the Concordat, the most equitable policy option is therefore to have the low-performing government-managed primary and especially secondary schools become attractive to both students and parents.[56]

Part of the government schools' low performance is due to the fact they continually get students who rank relatively low in the SEA examination. A chicken and egg situation develops. However, there is evidence that many of these prestige schools started with average and less than average students – and from working class homes too. The policy option here, in addition to more resources and after careful study, is to provide these government schools with more efficient and appropriately-trained teachers, performance benchmarks and more effective management and accounting systems.

## THE EQUITY DILEMMA, AGAIN

The equity debate is stimulated by public statements and research findings that low social class, students of African descent and from single–parent homes are disadvantaged in terms of getting into high-performing schools, mainly the prestige schools.[57] This pushes the equity challenge further. For example, if educational equity eventually means getting equal proportions of various social groups in high-performing schools, how will this proportion be determined, from which particular social group?

Will it be driven by selection by race, religion, social class, parental type or driven by gender? It will be impossible to select a student from all categories at the same time, isn't it? Or does the push for educational equity mean that all students who seem to be lagging behind be given remedial treatment and support without regard to race, social class, parental type or gender?

A student from an upper social class background, for example, may have low marks – a low performer. We already have some of these but in relatively small proportion. Will they be given remedial treatment to catch up and so contaminate the proportional representation criterion for equity? Also, a student of African descent may already be a high performer, with high marks. We already have some of these. We also have East Indian students from two-parent homes who get relatively low marks. Such possibilities create difficulties for secondary school placement by proportional representation, as the School Placement Study proposed, by representativeness.

Even if educational equity is the objective, that is, through proportional representation, what is the criterion for selection for remedial education in order to catch up? Or are we going to select all those who are falling behind regardless of race, social class, gender or parental type? This is not what the researchers have been calling for. Their expressed concerns are, for example, having working class students and female African students become higher academic achievers and getting into the prestige schools in greater proportions.[58] How exactly then are we going to achieve this? By affirmative action, by remedial education or by changing and sanitizing the Concordat process? Or by all three?

Compared to lower class students, students from the middle/upper class, as a group, are already highly represented in entering high-performing schools. But with a remedial education policy for proportionally disadvantaged, there may be allegations of social discrimination if you leave out an upper/middle class student with low marks. To avoid this allegation, if the policy is to apply remedial treatment to all with low marks - even to the middle/upper class students with low marks – these would be so few in number that the proportional representation policy may not be overly disturbed. But the basic principle will be shaken up a bit.

## THE SOLUTION AGAIN: IMPROVE GOVERNMENT SCHOOLS

Remedial interventions for the disadvantaged students and improvements to the government-managed schools seem more practical policy options for now. Of course, this discussion is based on the fact that entrance into a high performing (prestige) school with limited places, is a highly sought-after choice. That means, entrance into a grammar-type secondary school from where further education into one of the established and respected professions (law, engineering, medicine, accountancy, languages, etc.) is facilitated.

At present, the entire equality of educational opportunity and educational equity issues rest on the value which the population puts on a grammar-type education. The government, however, has developed a significant range of technical/vocational programmes across the country – from welding, avionics, oil drilling, farming, etc.[59] As indicated earlier, however, very few secondary school students look forward to entering such programmes.[60]

## CULTURAL RESISTANCE

If the population develops a higher regard for technical/vocational courses, and the entrepeneurship that emerges from such training, the pressures for equality in education and equity would be dampened. The frame of reference would change. Further, it is not merely a matter of income. It is more a matter of the relationship between the dominant cultural value for grammar-type education and the public respect given to one type of education as compared to another type. As in the old colonial days, the struggle is still on for grammar-type education. A massive psychological change of values is required.

The need to diversify the education system while catering to varying student abilities and aptitudes under one roof was attempted in the 1970's with the Junior Secondary-Composite-Senior Comprehensive School configuration. Such varied nomenclatures have been condensed today into just high school or secondary school. But the prestige school – grammar-type of education – remains of pristine choice.

Citing significant racial, gender and class imbalances in secondary school entry, the 1994 Secondary School Placement Study stated: 'All things equal, all means to accessing the resources being the same, all groups would be expected to access secondary schooling in proportions representative of their numbers in the relevant population.'[61] Here, equity is implied through proportional representation, if certain utopian conditions are present. But that exactly is the problem.

As we said before, all things are not equal but could be made reasonably equal if the under-performing government schools improve. Through remedial interventions and equal 'access to resources', the disadvantaged could gain fuller representation in their desired secondary schools. But the equity challenge does not end there. Places at university are less than the demand. Will these 'remedied' students be prepared to compete up there too? Further ahead, too, the high quality, high-paying occupations are much less than the demand and are quite competitive. Remedial interventions and quota system can only reach so far in a society that is inherently competitive, or as Bowles and Gintis complained, severely capitalist.

## THE EDUCATION SYSTEM: A PRISONER OF SOCIETY?

All in all therefore, while critical theorists see educational reform for educational equity as almost a hopeless case, there is a liberal group who see limited reforms possible, fuelled by supportive parents and student ambitions on one hand, and remedial programming on the other hand. The explanation of working class under-achievement through a culture deficit paradigm, unfortunately, not only blames the victim but acknowledges the superiority of the middle and upper classes.

This debate over equality of educational opportunity and equity has been caught between different ideologies. For example, here is Carnoy:

> The new education should instead be designed to create or reinforce a non-hierarchal society in which property will not have rights over people, and in which daily, no person will have the right of domination over another. This would be an 'egalitarian' society in which everyone is the same; people will have different work but that work will not give them authority over the lives of others. Work will be done *for each other*, out of common agreement and understanding.[62]

More moderately, and arguing for 'a fair society,' Corning proposed a proper balance between three fairness precepts: 'equality in relation to our inescapable needs, full and fair recognition for merit, and a proportionate reciprocity.'[63] He admitted, though, that the difficulties exist not in these ideas but in their implementation without interest group tensions. At the end of his book, he confessed: "There are no easy answers to this problem' of creating a fair society.'[64]

The reforms required for this country's education system will not come through radical ideologies, as intellectual seductive as they may be. Neither will they come through Utopian proposals, attractive as these too may be. The first step, with public support and political will and courage, is to implement strategies to improve the performance of the government secondary schools so as to make them attractive to both students and parents.

Unless we want the government to wage a protracted war with the country's churches, the policy option quite possible but so far lazily treated, is to form an effective partnership between teachers, parents, community and state to improve both the academic performance and student discipline in the many government secondary schools now needing serious attention. This attention should be linked to the primary schools for it is from there that the reform challenges begin. That is why the minister should have appointed the National Advisory Committee, to help energize this process.

Given the social and occupational structure of the wider society, the education system will naturally find itself with a middle class culture, and in conflict with working class habits. In this post-colonial society, it is officially and commonly admitted, that the education system must serve society and the economy.

Through consumerism, conspicuous consumption, mass media, job-market demands, high occupational and academic aspirations, the society is now irreversibly capitalist, and comfortable with middle class values. The extent to which the schools achieve and practice middle class values and aspirations, to that extent would the schools appear successful, even to working class parents. Therefore, the objectives of this country's educational plans can only be moderately reformist and captured by capitalists values.

For example, while the elitist preference for grammar-type education flourished during the colonial era,[65] it still persists as a driving force behind the inequities experienced in the educational system. In this regard, Carnoy argued that while some of the poor succeed, '*instead of trying to understand why so few of their low-income class moved up in relative status, the successful congratulate the inequitable school system.*'[66]

In his study of equal educational opportunity in this country, Baksh found significant social class differences in secondary school students' educational and occupational aspirations and recommended that longitudinal studies be done to clarify these social class and related sociological differences.[67] Given the social class, ethnic, gender and students' family type imbalances in relation to their secondary schooling, it will be also quite useful to find out what happens to students three years after graduating from the government assisted denominational schools and government schools respectively.

Of course, not everything that one wishes for in life will get fulfilled. But after hearing so much about 'education is the passport out of poverty and for a better life,' then to have students' aspirations so repeatedly broken will bound to have psychological repercussions.

It will therefore be useful for public policy to verify the extent to which such disproportions persist after students leave Form Five in secondary school. In other words, to what extent does the social stratification system in the society perpetuate itself through or in spite of the educational system? What difference does secondary schooling make, if any?[68]

A meritocracy in a competitive context is essentially a 'weeding out' process. However, any system of acclaimed meritocracy in a multi-racial society which persistently holds down students from low, working class homes or from a particular ethnic background, to a depressing extent, to that extent the meritocracy becomes unmasked, socially unjust and in need of review. For educational equity, a meritocracy has to mean much more than everyone writing the same examination.

The first prime minister did not cater for this when he addressed youths at an Independence Day rally. He wished then for educational equity in the academic results from both denominational schools and the government secondary schools.[69]

## SOME FURTHER POLICY ISSUES

The practice of giving private, extra lessons for those preparing for the SEA is now an industry, thus putting an extra cost to poor parents. The social and political contacts that some parents have also do help in getting their children into a 'good' primary school – even though such parents live a far distance from the school, thus pushing less endowed parents and their children who live nearby the school lower down or entirely out of the acceptance list. This is an informal but crucial area where educational inequity is created.

At this point, there are three related policy issues.

1. Clearly, more primary and secondary government schools need to be improved regarding the quality of their educational output.

2. The research evidence strongly suggests that, while the Ministry and teachers do have an important role to play, if the required social and psychological support do not adequately come from parents, especially working class parents and the community, the social imbalances and inequality in secondary schooling will not be significantly improved. Shared responsibility should be clearly articulated and invoked. If not, the privileged will continue to remain so. High-achieving schools are found to have strong, very supportive Parent-Teachers' Associations.

3. What might be useful to consider is to create some benchmark goals to help quantify the extent to which, proportionally, the currently disadvantaged social groups show improvement year to year. Such as is done with trends in crime and health for example.

In all this, policy-makers and even researchers must be careful not to ignore the downward slide and mental collapse of some middle and upper social class students in secondary schools. That is, as academically bright as they were in entering a prestige secondary school, as they move from Form One into Form Two or Form Three, their academic interests and performance deteriorate. This is a neglected area of policy attention. A downslide slide by the middle class could be as worrisome, even more painful than the frustrated ambitions of the lower class.

## SINGLE-SEX FOR EQUALITY?

It is quite notable that the very successful denominational assisted secondary schools are either all-male or all-female whereas the government secondary schools generally include both sexes (Queen's Royal College, for example, an exception). Is such a difference related to academic success? Does it affect equality of opportunity to learn? Many teachers, citing instances of illicit sexual acts between boys and girls in the mixed schools as an example, expressed preference for single-sex schools.[70]

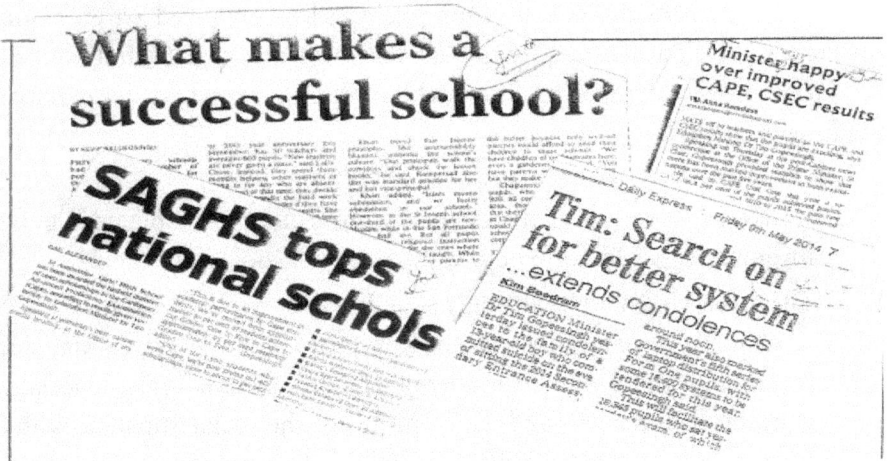

Another common reason by teachers were 'distractions' by one or the other sex. Several educators have also expressed views in one direction or another so much so that in 2010, the Ministry of Education said it 'piloted a new strategy – the Single Sex School Conversion Project.'[71]

The Ministry explained its rationale this way: '*The Ministry acknowledges that students learn in different ways, and that there are discernable differences in the manner in which boys and girls assimilate information. The project therefore takes account of these differences and is intended to enhance students participation and performance.*'[72] This is an important intervention.

What was this single-sex project like? A group of students from the 2010 SEA placement process were assigned to Form One in 20 selected government secondary schools throughout Trinidad. The conversion will take place on a phased basis into single sex schools.

The Ministry stated that by 2015, 10 schools would have been converted to male only and 10 schools to female only. Listing the twenty schools selected, the Ministry pledged that the outcome of this measure should result in an improvement in the performance of male students and an enhancement in the performance of female students.[73] No report yet. The results are anxiously awaited.

## NOTES

1.   R. Brosio, *A Radical Democratic Critique of Capitalist Education*. New York: Peter Lang Publishing. 1994. p. 31. See also M. Carnoy and H. Levin, v*Schooling and Work in the Democratic State*. Stanford: Stanford University Press, 1985 for an extensive discussion on these relationships and in particular the contradictions.

2.   J. Dewey, v*Liberalism and Social Action*. New York: G.P. Putman's Sons. 1935. p. 62.

3.   Bowles and Gintis, *Schooling in Capitalist America*. p. 14. Further, pp. 10-105 lay out their foundation principles.

4.   *Freedom and Culture*, New York: G.P. Putman and Sons. 1939; *Democracy and Education*. New York: The Free Press. 1916. p. 99.

5.   A. Brosio, *Radical Democratic Critique*. p. 612.

6.   Ibid. pp. 614-615.

7.   A. Brosio. pp. 612-622.

8.   Ibid. Such expectations were tied with notions of equal treatment, equal opportunity, etc.

9.   G. Beckford and others have argued that many colonial and plantation values are still dominant in this and other Caribbean societies, especially in the competition for educational and occupational status.

10.  J. Fishkin, *Bottlenecks*. New York, Oxford University Press. 2014. pp. 10-15.

11.  ibid.

12.  Ibid. pp. 12–13.

13.  Bowles and Gintis, p.101.

14.  This is a general comment in that merit-driven socio-economic mobility in the country is distorted by political patronage, social contacts, white collar crime, money laundering and illegal drug trafficking.

15.  Dewey himself struggled with this dilemma. The competitive structure and stratification of the society do shape a lot of what we call 'human nature.' A Darwinian view, however, suggests that such qualities like competition and envy are instincts for self-preservation and survival.

16. R. Kennedy, *For Discrimination: Race, Affirmative Action and the Law*. New York: Vintage Books. 2013. especially pp. 78-140. Kennedy provides a concise but well-documented case for affirmative action, mainly for blacks, in the U.S. A central focus is university admissions.

17. Cited in Kennedy. p. 80.

18. Jagessar v Teaching Service Commission

19. D. Horowitz, *The Courts and Social Policy*. Washington: Brookings Institute. 1977. M. Rebell, *Courts and Kids: Pursuing Educational Equity Through the State Courts*. Chicago: University of Chicago Press. 2009.

20. For example, Civil rights legislation like the Civil Rights Act of 1964, *Brown vs. Board of Education*, 1954 and No Child Left Behind Act, 2001 have all been encouraged by protest movements.

21. Cited in Rebell, p. 5.

22. M. Rebell, *Courts and Kids: Pursuing Educational Equity Through the State Courts*. Chicago: University of Chicago Press. 2009.

23. There have been some successes with a few government secondary schools, in particular, Couva East and San Fernando Central, for example, with scholarships. In 2013, Couva East got five 'additional', the highest ever achieved by a government secondary school. Whenever such events occur, they appear as 'big' surprises, making big media headlines. The number of CSEC passes and scholarships, as earlier pointed out, far exceed those by the government secondary schools. These comparisons are made to embarrass but to encourage the government in particular to inquire and provide all resources – human and physical – to improve performance in its government schools.

24. As already explained, these deficiencies are multi-facetted: students with higher marks chose and enter the denominational schools. The denominational schools have an added oversight management layer – the Board. The religious matching between teacher and school, as Keenan noted, create added obligations; the large size of the government schools, have been noted as being counter-productive, etc. Several public calls to government for a multi-sectoral inquiry has so far not been successful.

25. *Express*. October 4, 2013. p. 13.

26. Press Conference by Minister Dr Tim Gopeesingh. September 20, 2013. Also published in *Trinidad Express*. September20, 2013. p. 5.

27. See *Black's Law Dictionary* for definition of 'equality.'

28. The legal system is also a system, but will require a more distant analysis.

29. Ethnicity and race are used interchangeably. Race used a social construct. Ethnicity includes race, religion, customs, etc. The distinction will be made where necessary.

30. As indicated previously with percentages – Africans, East Indians, Chinese, Whites, Syrian-Lebanese, Mixed. Given the plantation, slavery, and indentureship background in this book, the opportunity and equity issues are being related mainly to Africans and East Indians as identifiable groups.

31. The general stated objective has been on gross enrolment. The opportunity and achievement differentials among the different races, religions, social classes, etc. were left for non-governmental researchers to identify. As indicated previously, disproportionalities in race, religion, social class, etc., in public services given the political climate, governments and their respective agencies keep far away from publicly raising these issues. Others, community activists for example, do. The establishment of an Equal Opportunity Commission is intended to deal with allegations of job discrimination in both the private and public sector

32. Ibid. p. 440–441.

33. Assessment of the Plan for Educational Development in Trinidad and Tobago, 1968 to 1983. Ministry of Education, Government of Trinidad and Tobago. October 1984. p. 63.

34. Ibid. p. 63.

35. K. Howe, *Understanding Equal Educational Opportunity*. New York: Columbia University, Teachers College. 1997. pp. 15-16. His three traditions: libertarianism, utilitarianism and liberal-egalitarianism.

36. Such public complaints were largely triggered by the Black Power protests and marches in April 1970, leading to a public inquiry and several policy adjustments by the then PNM Government.

37. See e.g., P. J. Keenan, 'Report Upon the State of Education in the Island of Trinidad', Her Majesty's Stationery Office. 1869. Also, C. Campbell, *The Young Colonials: A Social History of Trinidad and Tobago 1834-1939*.

38. 'Assessment of the Plan for Educational Development in Trinidad and Tobago 1968-83. Ministry of Education. Government of Trinidad and Tobago.' October 1984. p. 1. There was the proposal to have any extensions to the school system 'geographically distributed so as to equalize educational opportunities' to 'centralise the more expensive higher educational facilities.'p.2.

39. This Assessment Report also included some proposals from the 'Prime Minister's Further Proposals to Cabinet in Education' October, 1975.

40. Education Plan 1985-90. Ministry of Education. pp. 10–14.

41. Ibid, p. 8–9. In its two related 'Evaluations' of both goals and system, the concepts equality of education or equity did not specifically arise. pp 52, 70. Perhaps, the collected data would subsequently point in these directions.

42. Report of the National Task Force on Education (Green Paper). Ministry of Education. Government of Trinidad and Tobago. 1993. pp. 5-6.

43. Ibid. p. 73.

44. These high-performing secondary schools are commonly called and widely recognised in the society as 'prestige schools.' For ease of communication, therefore, we use the term 'prestige' where applicable.

45. Similar to the social injustices perpetrated by the free-market economy of capitalism. This clash between freedom of choice, parents' preference and ranking by merit helps uncover the subtle connection between the education system and social class driven society — a point made by several authors earlier mentioned.

46. *Concise Oxford Dictionary*. (9th Edition).

47. For further details on the concept of 'equity' see *Black's Law Dictionary (5th Edition)* – 'Equity is justice administered according to fairness as contrasted with the strictly formulated rules of common law. It is based on a system of rules and principles which originated in England as an alternative to the harsh rules of common law and which was based on what was fair in a particular situation. One sought relief under this system in courts of equity than in courts of law. The term 'equity' denotes the spirit and habit of fairness, justness and right dealing which would regulate the intercourse of men dealing with men.' The objective is 'to render the administration of justice more complete, by affording relief where the courts of law are incompetent to give it, or to give it with effect.' The provision of 'compensatory education' as a remedy and for the creation of educational equity has been described as 'deficient' since it apparently ignores 'the more fundamental structural problems of schooling itself'. (see Chapter 7 for discussion.) For increased relevance to our work is the definition provided in Cochran's *The Law Dictionary*: 'Equity is a type of justice that developed separate from the common law. Equity courts allowed themselves latitude of construction and assumed, in certain matters such as trusts, a power of enforcing moral obligations which the courts of law did not admit or recognise.' In our work on educational equality and equity, and given the economically-determined constraints, we attach great importance to the requirement of 'moral obligations.'

48. *The Glossary of Educational Reform*, May 18, 2015. For further details on educational equity, see 'Reference-based Assessment and Educational Equity', Harvard Education Review. April, 1994. Vol. 64, 1. pp. 5–31; 'Equity and Quality in Education', OECD. February 9, 2012; W. Hutmacher, D. Cochran and N. Bottani (Eds.), *In Pursuit of Equity in Education*, Springer Publications. 2001.

49. J. Rawls, *A Theory of Justice*. Cambridge, Mass: Harvard University Press. 1971. pp. 11–14.

50. Ibid. p. 264.
51. This view is related to the failure of Adam Smith's hope for a harmonised economy based on mutual dependence of skills and services.
52. I. Taylor, P. Walton and J. Young, *The New Criminology*, London: Routledge and KeganPaul. 1977. p. 4.
53. OECD Policy Brief, 'Ten Steps to Equity in Education'. 2008.
54. Ibid.
55. The Government Task Force on Education did note the serious equity gaps and recommended several measures for restoration and equity. For example: 'Greater effort must be put into providing educational enrichment courses...The opportunity exists for an appropriate agency to provide daily enrichment and/or remediation programmes that will prove beneficial to these disadvantaged students.' p. 51.
56. There are some provisions for remedial learning for those students who fall below an overall mark acceptable at the time. It is known, however, that the majority of these students under remedy are Africans, of working class background and single-parent homes. The challenge, therefore, is not to wait until such students write the SEA but through pre Standard Five assessment to provide strong remedial education so as to enable them to compete fairly and equitably at Standard Five. There are no available data on the extent to which these students subsequently gain entry to prestige secondary schools. Normally, students have two chances to write the SEA.
57. Centre for Ethnic Studies Report on Secondary School Placement. 1994.
58. 'A Study of Secondary School Placement', Center for Ethnic Studies.1994.
59. There is growing concern that the economy and private sector at present cannot accommodate the large number of graduates from these expanding technical//vocational sectors. Then-PNM Opposition Leader, Dr Keith Rowley has called the expanding tertiary education sector 'paper mills.' (Television, CNC3, interview with hostess Hema Ramkissoon. Tuesday June 6, 2015. 6.30 a.m.) He said that the large sums of money spend are not giving the taxpayers value for money, that there is too much government-directed education, thus restricting choice, enterprise and creativity. The government's claim is a '60% enrolment in tertiary education.'
60. Less than 4% express such interest from our three surveys in secondary schools. R. Deosaran, 'Benchmarking Violence and Delinquency in Secondary Schools'. 2006; R. Deosaran, 'Project Gateway: A Tracer Study', 2008. Reports submitted to Ministry of Education.
61. Summary Report of Centre for Ethnic Studies. UWI, St Augustine. 1994. pp. 28-29.
62. M. Carnoy p. 366. Carnoy's Utopianism recalls Adam Smith advocacy of inter-dependent expertise and traders which, moral sentiments

notwithstanding, became a shrewdly-run hierarchical system of profit-making, quite self-serving at the top.

63. P. Corning, *The Fair Society*. Chicago: University of Chicago Press. 2012. p. 170.
64. Ibid. pp.170–190.
65. See C. Campbell, *The Young Colonials: A Social History of Education in Trinidad and Tobago, 1834–1939*.
66. M. Carnoy. p. 29.
67. I. Baksh, *Caribbean Sociology: Introductory Readings*. Jamaica: Ian Randle. 1984. p. 722.
68. The government's policy is to increase the secondary school to tertiary education enrolment from the present 40% to 65% in 2015. (Free education through GATE) While in the nineties, more secondary schools were built to accommodate all 11+ students rather than catering only for those who 'passed the Common Entrance Examination,' the social inequities in academic achievement among secondary schools persisted. The sharp differences between quantity and quality education still exist.
69. Ibid.
70. Voices of the Teachers. Research Report on 20 Schools submitted to Ministry of Education. 2008.
71. Ministry of Education. Annual Administrative Report 2009–2010. p.14.
72. Ibid. p. 14.
73. Ibid. pp. 14–15.

# CHAPTER FOURTEEN

# After Secondary School What? The Inequities Continue

*Yet for all its success, modernity is an ambivalent condition. There is far beneath the surface, a sense that something is missing: economic growth and political freedom do not seem enough. Capitalist economics and liberal democratic politics have prepared the basis for a good life, but its actual attainment seems just beyond the possible.*

Alan Wolfe, Modernity and Its Discontents, 1989

## WHAT HAPPENS TO THEM AFTER SECONDARY SCHOOL?

Now that we have seen the significant imbalances in ethnicity, social class, gender and even in family life with regard to placement and academic performance in secondary schools, it will be helpful to take a look, even a preliminary one, at what happens to these students to see, more precisely, to what extent any further inequities arise three years after leaving these different types of secondary schools.

These queries of post-secondary schooling are directly connected to the initial placement of students into the different types of secondary schools – the denominational secondary and the government secondary. In other words, initial secondary school placement could eventually have serious consequences – good or bad – for students' lives after graduating from school.[1] Such possible consequences make SEA and secondary school placement critical educational policy matters. The above queries therefore bring into sharp focus, in terms of both public policy and the promises of decolonisation, the tensions between equality of educational opportunity, merit and equity.

## IS SOCIAL STRATIFICATION PERPETUATED?

Our trigger question is this: Does the merit-driven system for secondary school entry have implications for subsequent social inequality and educational inequity? Further, does the education system perpetuate the social stratification system rather than closing the gaps and energising socio-economic mobility as promised?

What are the options available to the government in achieving social equity through the educational system? How can educational inequity be quantified? And what are the quantified thresholds that will permit claims of equity for social class, racial, gender or family type groups of students?

Several of the ministry's reports promised equitable access, the elimination of social and gender disparities by 2015, improvement in every aspect of quality in education, and a secondary education system with increased equitable access, largely transcending geographical, ethnic, socio-economic and gender differences.[2]

Our study therefore sought to find out more precisely, the extent to which students took up higher education or entered the job market three years after Form Five and whether, as a test of social equity, such choices were related to their social, racial, gender, family life background and the type of secondary school attended.

In addition to these questions of post-secondary equity (educational and occupational status), we also considered the implications for delinquency and youth crime. It is therefore a study in the sociology of education with implications for the role which education plays in civility and maintaining or changing the country's social stratification system.

## HAVE THE PROMISES FAILED?

Before moving into the data though, it will be helpful to recall more precisely the equality and equity promises made by the government. The Ministry of Education's Report on 'Education for All' stated:[3]

1. 'Education for All' is about equipping our people on an equitable basis for life.

2. 'Education for All' is about assuring our children adequate earning potential.

3. It is about being able to appreciate oneself and the basics of respectful interaction with others, and ensuring for all a good quality of life.

4. Ensuring that by 2015 the learning needs of all young people are met through equitable access to appropriate learning and life skills programmes.

5. Improving every aspect of the quality of education, and ensuring their excellence so that recognised and measureable outcomes are achieved by all.

6. The time is therefore opportune to mobilise all sectors of the national community in the interest of the education of our youth.

7. It is time for our NGO's to be brought more fully into the righting of social imbalances at the family level.

## MAJOR OBJECTIVE

In such circumstances, we therefore found compelling reasons to do an exploratory study of what students do three years after they leave Form Five in secondary school. A more precise understanding of what they do will help contribute to improved policy-making to help fulfill the promise for equality of opportunity and educational equity.

The major assumptions here are:

1. Going on to higher education (e.g., university) just after or within three years after leaving Form Five in secondary school is a better opportunity for social prestige, high occupational and professional status (socio-economic mobility).

2. Getting into a job rather than in higher education just after or within three years of leaving Form Five in secondary school would likely diminish the opportunity for upward socio-economic mobility.

There is of course the matter of income, that is, for example, a welder or plumber may make more money than a lawyer. But such individual workers like plumbers, clerks, drivers, etc. will not occupy high positions in social stratification – in terms of respect and policy influence particularly. This, apart from the fact, that some jobs, the professions mainly, take a much longer time to qualify, etc. In other words, just as we have prestige schools, so too do we have prestige occupations.

Here, we do not question the usefulness or necessity of the different jobs. Or even their relative scarcity. As discussed earlier, it is a matter of the burning aspirations of both parents and students and the well-established public respect given to the traditional professions. Further, we make the claim that this post-colonial society is steeped in the values of functionalism[4] – with substantial tolerance for educational drop-outs and marginalization. The competitive education system is looked upon as the major vehicle for fulfilling the requirements of an elitist-driven stratification system.[5]

# SIX SPECIFIC OBJECTIVES:

1. Whether continuing into higher education (e.g., university) or getting a job three years after Form Five would vary according to the social class background (parental occupation) of students.

2. Whether continuing into higher education or getting a job three years after Form Five would vary according to the type of secondary school (government assisted vs government secondary) students attended.

3. Whether continuing into higher education or getting a job three years after Form Five would vary according to the gender of students.

4. Whether continuing into higher education or getting a job three years after Form Five would vary according to the racial background of students.

5. Whether continuing into higher education or getting a job three years after Form Five would vary according to the parental structure of students' homes (e.g., two-parent homes vs single-parent or guardian homes).

6. Would the strain felt between the academic and occupational aspirations of these secondary school students and their academic attainment have any criminological implications?

To help answer these questions, we used a sample of 1,293 students from 20 secondary schools spread across the country – seven denominational assisted schools and thirteen government secondary schools.[6] We measured their educational and occupational status three years after they left Form Five.[7] *(See Appendix M for details on sample, measures, etc.).*

# RESULTS

## Social Class and Students' Post-Secondary Destination

The results in Figure 14.1 show that while 60% and 85% of the middle and upper class students respectively got into 'studying only,' that is into higher education (post-secondary studies or university) three years after Form Five, only 31% of the low social class students did so.

With respect to students who ended up 'working only' three years after leaving secondary school, the proportion was 32% for low social class students, 19.5% and 7% for middle and upper class students respectively.

**Figure 14.1: Social Class x Student Status Three Years After Form Five**

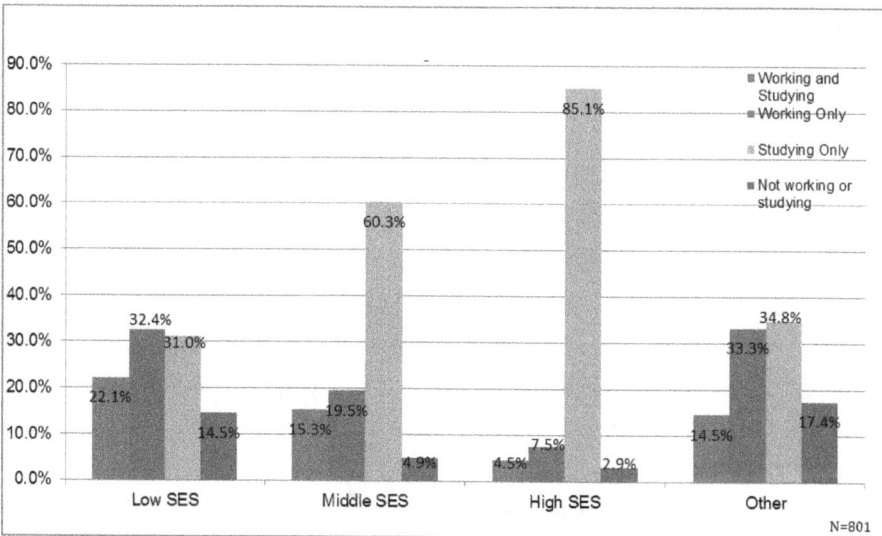

The related aspect to these results is that the jobs that students got were 'low-paying, working class' jobs. (Over 90% of the jobs gotten were low, working class jobs) Since a much higher proportion of low social class students ended up 'working only' in such jobs three years after leaving Form Five, the implications for socio-economic mobility become obvious.

The proportions for 'neither working nor studying,' that is the 'idle' group, three years after leaving Form Five, were 15% for low social class students, 5% for middle and 3% for upper social class students. For the fourth category, 'both working and studying,' the proportions were 22%, 15% and 4% for low, middle and upper class respectively. ('Other' includes pensioners, retirees, unemployed, etc.) That 22% of the low social class students chose to both study and work is a good sign of mixing economic necessity with personal enterprise.

In fact, given the wider opportunities for part-time studies and time-off allowances for employees to study, a combination of 'studying only' and 'studying and working' help strengthen the promise of socio-economic mobility. Fifty-three per cent (53%) of the low social class group fall into this combination while 75% of the middle and 90% of the upper social class group did so – a significant difference, but still providing positive signs for the low social class

The Pearson correlation test on these relationships showed a correlation (r) of .34, significant at the p < .01 level. That is, the higher the social class background of the student, the more likely he or she will go on to study only rather than enter the job market three years after leaving Form Five in secondary school.

## Social Class and Kind of Institution Attended Three Years After Form Five

To further strengthen the assumption that studying three years after leaving secondary school would increase the student's chances of getting a well-regarded job or preparing for a profession, we now look at what kind of studying was involved by those who chose to go on studying. That is, what kind of institution was involved in terms of potential social mobility and professional status.

As Figure 14.2 shows, the higher the social class status of the student, the more likely that student will enter UWI or a foreign university three years after leaving Form Five. The data shows 61% and 83% for middle and upper class respectively as against 35% for lower class. Low social class students are more likely to enter the College of Science, Technology and Applied Arts of Trinidad and Tobago (COSTAATT), private business schools or other institutions (e.g., technical/vocational institutions).

**Figure 14.2: Social Class x Academic Institution Persons Enrolled in Three Years after Form Five %**

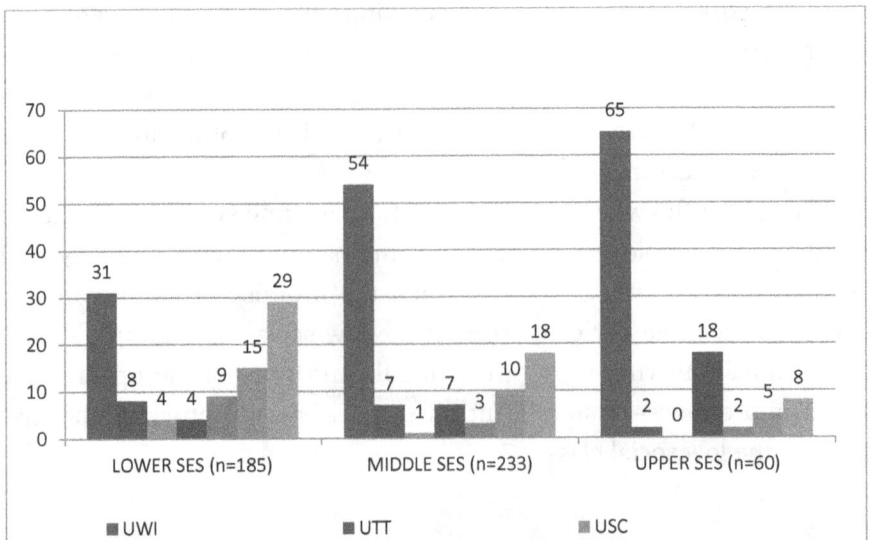

Almost 53% of the low social class former Form Five students entered such programmes as against 31% and 15% for middle and upper class respectively.

The correlation (Pearson correlation) between the social class background of students and the likelihood of entering a university rather than other types of education is r = .25, p < .01) More precisely, the higher the social class background of students, the more likely they would go on to higher education at university three years after leaving Form Five.

## Would the Type of School Attended Make a Difference Three Years After?

Figure 14.3 shows that while as many as 71% of students from the government assisted schools (prestige) chose to 'study only' three years after leaving Form Five, 34% and 28% of those from government secondary colleges and other government schools (e.g., Composite) respectively chose to 'study only.'

The inverse occurred for 'working only.' While 38% of those from government schools chose to 'work only' three years after leaving Form Five, the proportion for students from the prestige schools was much less, 12%. For those 'neither studying nor working,' that is being idle, the proportions were 18% for the government secondary schools and only 4% for those from the government assisted schools (prestige schools.)

**Figure 14.3: School Type x Student Status Three Years After Form Five %**

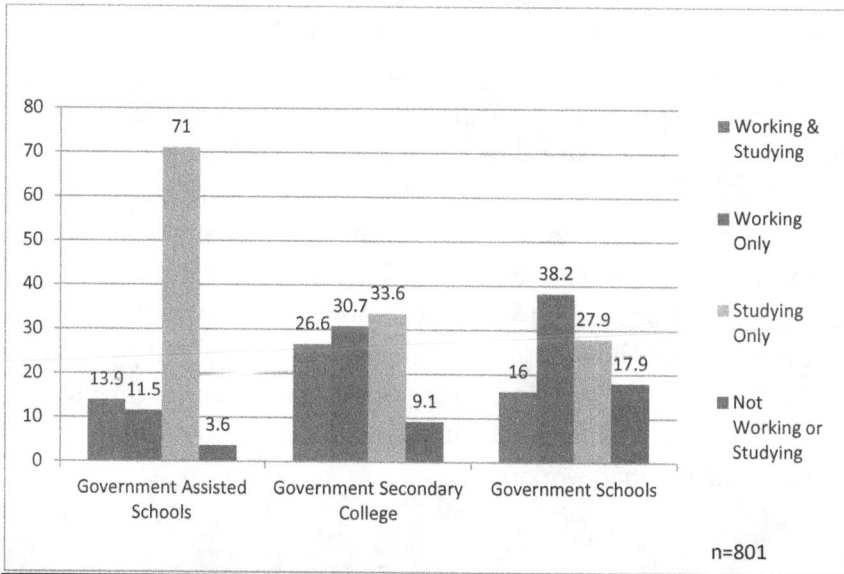

Those from government secondary colleges (27%) and other government schools (16%) had the highest proportion 'working and studying,' commendably suggesting, once again, economic necessity as well as individual enterprise, apart from issues of academic prowess. While not having the benefit of attending a prestige school, these may well be the ones still struggling to make ends meet while still looking at the future. They have not given up.

The Pearson test shows a significant relationship between the type of secondary school attended and what students do after leaving Form Five. That is, those who attended a government assisted school were more likely to go on to study only, while those who attended the government schools were more likely to enter the job market. ($r = .42$, $p < .01$) That is, the more academically prestigious the school attended, the more likely students will continue into studying rather than entering the work force.

Clearly, the extent to which further studies, that is, post- secondary studies, lead to higher social and occupational status, to that extent would attendance at a government assistedschool more likely acquire such status.

## Would Students' Parental Type Make a Difference?

Would a single-parent/guardian or two-parent home make a significant difference in whether the secondary school graduate choose to study or work three years after Form Five? The data from Figure 14.4 says likely yes. The data shows that while 50% of those from a two-parent home got into 'studying only' three years after secondary school, the comparable proportion was 29% for mother-only homes and 23% for 'other' homes (e.g., father-only, step-father, guardian, aunt, etc.)

While studying only may be the premier position, especially for the former Form Five graduates, those who study and work show special mettle, especially if they come from 'Mother Only' or 'Guardian' types of homes. Figure 14.4 also shows that while 17% of the 'Both Parents' group studied while working, the proportion was 19% and 21% for 'Mother Only' and 'Other' types of homes. The two-parent advantage still appears operational.

The Pearson test showed a significant correlation between parental type and the likelihood of studying three years after leaving Form Five. ($r = -18$, $p < .01$) That is, students with two-parent homes are more likely to continue studying than working.

**Figure 14.4: Parental Background x Student Status Three Years After Form Five %**

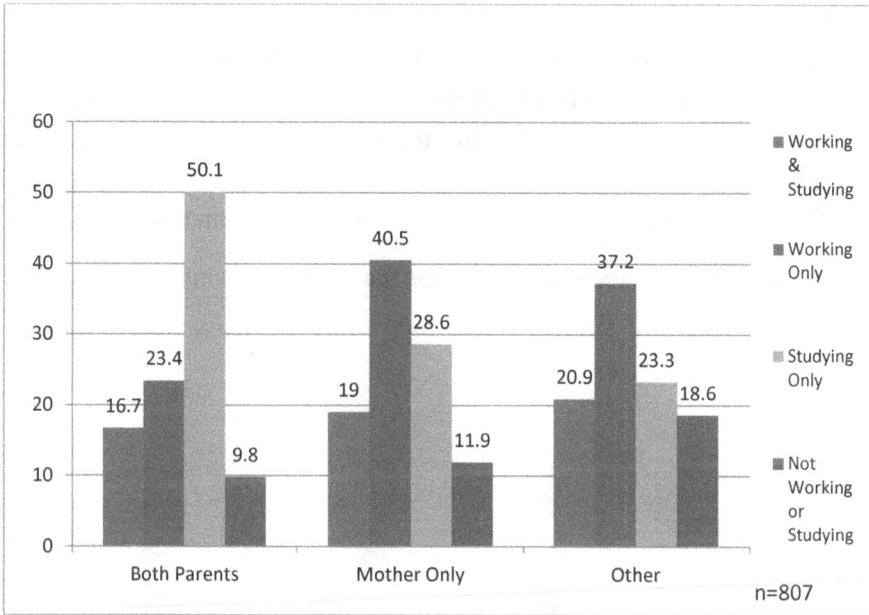

It is also useful to note from an earlier study that a higher proportion of students from two-parent homes (80%) got entry into government assisted denominational schools compared to 11% from 'Mother Only' and 9% from 'Other' homes.[8] Other studies revealed similar trends from Form One up to Form Five.[9] From the data seen and related studies, it seems that the combination of two-parent homes with attendance at a prestige school helps paralyse the country's socio-economic stratification structure.

## Is Race Related to What Students Do Three Years After Form Five?

The data shows (Figure 14.5) that while 61% of students of East Indian descent got involved in 'studying only,' only 31% of those of African descent did so three years after Form Five. The comparable proportion for racially Mixed students was 37%. With regard to 'working only,' that is getting into the work force exclusively three years after Form Five, 19% of East Indian students did so, compared to 36% and 25% for African and Mixed students respectively. For the group 'working and studying,' the proportion was 20% of African descent, 13% East Indian and 24% Mixed.

A Chi-square test revealed a significant relationship between race and what these students did three years after leaving Form Five. ($\chi^2 = 68.45$, df 6, p< .01)

All in all, therefore, these results suggest that the social and economic structure in which the 11-plus student is located largely and eventually determines what he or she will end up doing further up, three years after leaving Form Five at secondary school. In terms of probability, it is almost as if demography determines destiny - socio-economic status.

**Figure 14.5: Race x Student Status Three Years After Leaving Form Five %**

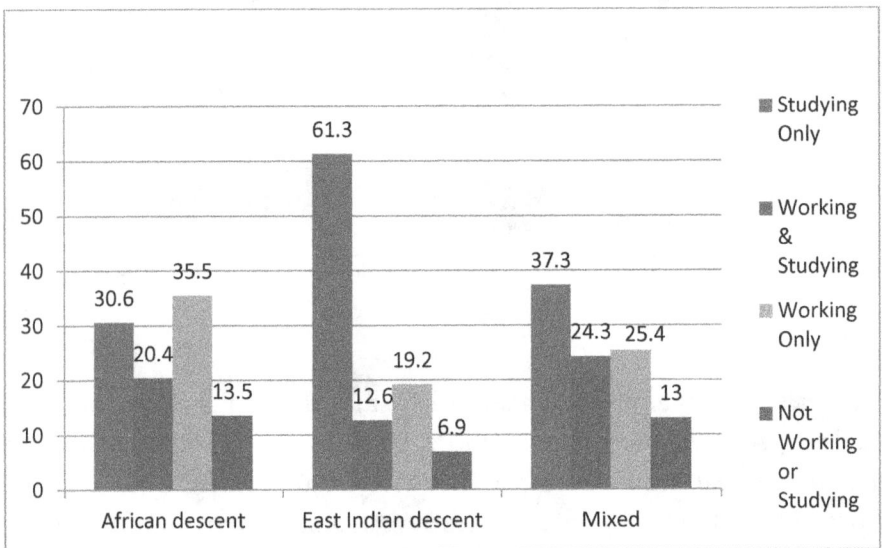

Figure 14.6 shows that while 61% of students of East Indian descent were in university three years after Form Five, 34% of those of African descent and 38% of the Mixed group did so. The trend was opposite for technical/vocational institutions. While 57% and 52% of those of African and Mixed descent respectively went into Technical/vocational institutions, 37% of East Indians did so. Clearly, entering university seems to be the strongly preferred route for the Form Five graduates of East Indian descent. The Chi-square test showed a significant relationship between race and the kind of academic/training institution students went to three years after Form Five. ($\chi^2 = 24.68$, df = 4, p < .05)

**Figure 14.6: Race x Academic Institution Attendance Three Years After Form Five %**

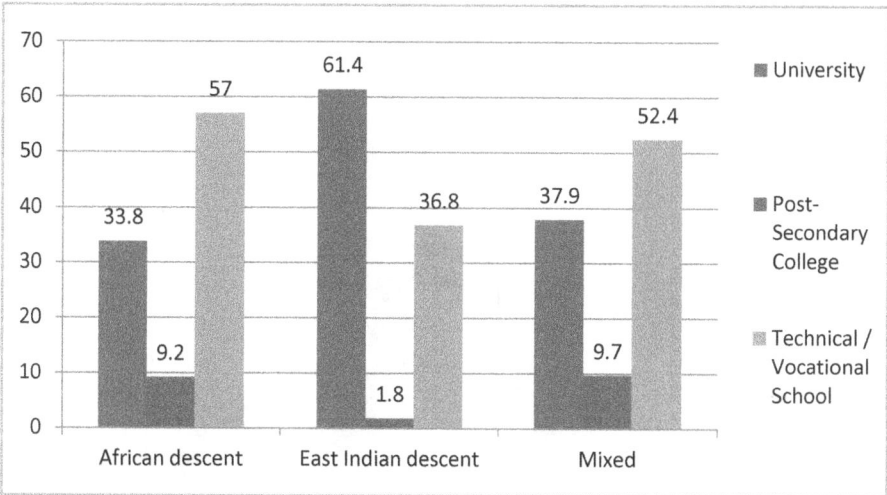

**N.B. 'University'** *includes University of the West Indies (UWI), University of the Southern Caribbean (USC), University of Trinidad and Tobago (UTT), foreign universities not included in this analysis. 'Post-Secondary College' includes College of Science, Technology and Applied Arts of Trinidad and Tobago (COSTAATT) and Cipriani College for Labour and Cooperative Studies while 'Technical/Vocational' includes the John Donaldson Technical Institute, San Fernando Technical Institute, etc.*

## Would Gender Make a Difference Three Years After Form Five?

As Figure 14.7 shows, while 51% of females 'studied only' three years after leaving Form Five, the proportion for males was 42%. The relationship was opposite for 'working only', that is, 35% for males vs 18% for females who 'worked only.' For 'working and studying,' the proportions between the sexes were the same, 17%. In terms of 'neither studying nor working,' quite surprisingly, the proportion of females was higher than that for males (14% vs 7%).

Figure 14.8 shows that a slightly higher proportion of females than males went into university (51% vs 49%). On the other hand, while 48% males went into technical/vocational institutions, the proportion was 43% for females. A higher proportion of females (7%) than males (4%) went into other institutions like Cipriani College for Labour and Cooperative Studies and COSTAATT.

**Figure 14.7: Gender x Student Status Three Years After Form Five %**

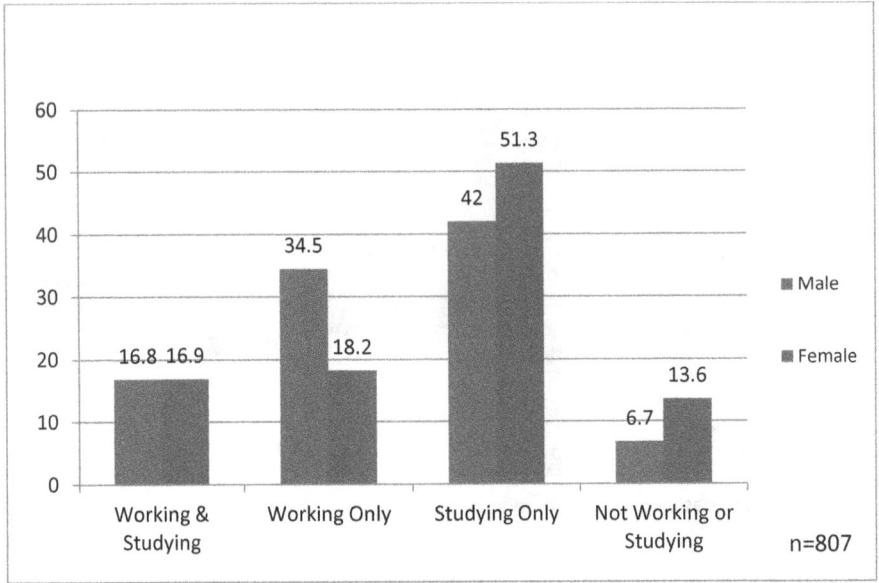

**Figure 14.8: Gender x Tertiary Educational Institute Attendance Three Years After Form Five %**

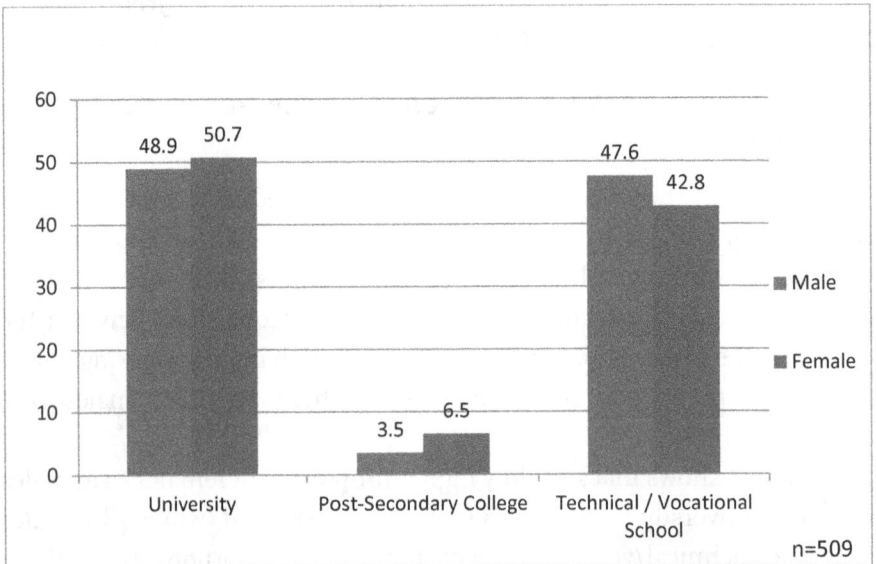

## THE MULTIPLE REGRESSION

So far, with regard to (a) students' social class, (b) school type attended and (c) parental structure, significant relationships have been found with each of the following: (d) studying or working (e) institution entered and (f) type of programme undertaken. It is useful to find out what are the relative influence of each independent variable (a to c) on the three dependent variables (d to f).

The multiple regressions for each equation are:

1. Studying or working = 0.267 + 0.357 (school type) + 0.115 (parental type) + 0.349 (social class) + 621.7

   F= 64.55, d.f. = 3, 709, p < .01

2. Academic programme entered = 0.160 + 0.683 (school type) + 0.037 (parental type) + 0.194 (social class) + 718.5

   F = 40.90, df = 3, 451, p < .01

3. Academic institution entered = 0.727 + 0.119 (school type) + 0.035 (parental type) = 0.075 ( social class) + 32.8

   F = 12.51, df = 3, 267, p < .01

From the above analysis, school type seems to have the greater weight than the other variables upon what a student does three years after his or her secondary school. This implies that the better academic and occupational advantages emerge from attendance at denominational secondary schools rather than at the government secondary schools. And, as the data indicates, the foundation for this result is largely laid in the primary school system.

## THE 'AFRICAN YOUTHS IN DANGER' STUDY: THE POLITICAL FACTOR

In August 2015, during a political town hall meeting, then PNM Opposition Leader, Dr Keith Rowley (now Prime Minister) gave an interesting example of the challenges facing policies to prevent young black males from drifting into deviance. He indicated that while his party (PNM) was in government before 2010, they had 'serious concerns over these youths, especially in identifiable 'hot spot' areas.'

He stated: '*We had several programmes for these black, under-performing urban youths because we found them under-performing and getting into crime.*'[10] Dr Rowley continued: '*But when the UNC government (United National Congress) came into power in 2010, they rejected these programmes, saying it was "a race thing." But now that they are in power, they are trying to put them back.'*[11]

These concerns over black youths were and still are quite prevalent, and in constant search for solutions. Before Dr Rowley's remarks, the Public Services Association (PSA), one of the country's leading trade unions, in 2006, had also expressed similar concerns and contacted the author to see what kind of research project may help throw some light on the issue.

Given all the data already known, the suggestion was to see how the 'mind' of these black youths worked, especially in terms of their academic and occupational aspirations. More precisely, since these 'high risk' youths generally went to government secondary schools, it was felt that a sample of black youths from such schools would help fill some of the blanks. From this preliminary study, it was felt a larger study could emerge later.

## THE ASPIRATIONS OF BLACK YOUTHS

As indicated above, in 2006 the Public Services Association (PSA) requested that a study be done on the subject. The PSA's rationale was its observance of the *'relatively high rate of crime and violence committed by young black males, especially along the East West corridor.'*[12] It was a justifiable concern. After reviewing the relevant research, for example, a 2013 Report concluded: *'There is obvious justification for the focus on young black males as a group particularly at risk.'*[13]

## CONCERNS

It was already noted that young black youths dominated gang membership, showed relatively higher crime rates and came from higher rate of single-parent homes. Such structural factors were already known. We wanted to find out, more precisely, the extent to which a sample of black youths were clear on their future academic and occupational goals and the extent to which there were any differences between those from the government secondary school and the denominational secondary school.[14]

We felt that the clearer and more committed the youths are to their future academic and occupational goals, the less likely they would drift into criminal habits. This was our general hypothesis. We therefore sought to uncover the motivation and attitudes which help to drive such youths towards incivility. It was therefore a preliminary study for prevention and early counselling.

## SAMPLE AND FOCUS GROUPS

A brief summary of the method and relevant findings are hereby presented.

We selected five government secondary schools (3 in north Trinidad and 2 in south Trinidad) and one denominational assisted secondary school for comparison. The five government schools were identified as 'high risk' schools by the Ministry of Education. Ten black Form Five students were selected from each of the six schools for focus group sessions. (Total 60 students)

The main focus group questions were:

1.  What are your main career or job interests after leaving school?
2.  What kind of academic/training preparation do you intend to take, if any?
3.  What kind of obstacles you foresee in fulfilling your ambition?
4.  How comfortable are you in this school?
5.  How much do you like coming to school?

From their answers, follow-up questions were used for clarity, etc.

Apart from the interviewer, three trained observers scored the students' answers within a range of 1(low) to 5 (high). Seven specific categories were used in scoring their answers. For example, if these Form Five students defined their 'expected career'*very specifically* as against *vaguely*, they would get a mark of 5 or close to 5. If they showed *great confidence* in explaining their further education or career choice, they too would get 5 or close to 5, etc. If, however, they wavered, appeared confused or showed little or no knowledge of a future career, the mark would be low, i.e., 1 or close to 1.

## RESULTS

Table 14.1 shows the results for each of the six schools. Clearly, on all seven (7) criteria, the government schools boys showed a vagueness about occupation, a lack of career commitment, a poor understanding of how to reach their goals and discomfort with both school and teacher relationships.

This table also shows how different the government school boys were from the denominational school boys. Two government school groups had mean scores as low as 1.6 and 1.7 respectively out of a possible Mean score of 5. These boys seemed in very great need of career guidance, confidence boosting and mentoring. They are at risk.

Table 14.1: Government Schools vs Denominational Schools: Career Uncertainty (1=low, 5=high)

| School | Career Specificity | Career Confidence | Career Preparation | Academic Interest | School Comfort | Teacher-Student Relationship | Access to Opportunities/ Obstacles | TOTAL SCORE& MEAN |
|---|---|---|---|---|---|---|---|---|
| EW Corridor -1 Gov't School | 2 | 2 | 1 | 2 | 1 | 2 | 1 | 11 $\overline{x}$ =1.6 |
| EW Corridor -2- Gov't School | 3 | 2 | 2 | 2 | 3 | 2 | 2 | 16 $\overline{x}$ =2.3 |
| EW Corridor -3 Gov't School | 2 | 2 | 1 | 2 | 2 | 2 | 1 | 12 $\overline{x}$ =1.7 |
| South -1 Gov't School | 4 | 3 | 2 | 2 | 2 | 2 | 2 | 17 $\overline{x}$ =2.4 |
| South -2 Gov't School | 3 | 3 | 3 | 2 | 2 | 2 | 3 | 18 $\overline{x}$ =2.6 |
| Prestige -1 Denominational | 5 | 5 | 5 | 5 | 4 | 3 | 5 | 32 $\overline{x}$ =4.6 |

(Project Headway: African Youths in Danger. R. Deosaran. 2006)

The two (2) South government school boys were not far behind with overall Means ($\overline{x}$) of 2.4 and 2.6 respectively. And the denominational school? Table 14.1 further shows that boys from this school had a higher overall Mean ($\overline{x}$) score of 4.6. That is, they showed greater confidence, specificity, knowledge and interest in the careers they chose.

The government school boys were rather vague, quite rambling, when it came to stating an occupational aspiration, a career goal. Their career preparation was also quite poor and disconnected. It was generally a case of 'not sure.' Those who identified something specific said 'welding,''mechanic,''coast guard,''police,''army,''chef,'etc. One particular boy from a government school said he wanted to be 'a doctor.' The rest of the boys in the group burst out laughing loudly, as if such career aspiration was impossible in that environment. It isn't only the social class implications of chosen careers; it is also the lack of commitment to what is chosen.

The boys in all government schools also anticipated difficulties in their future – much more than those from the denominational school. They had scores of 1, 2 and 1 respectively on this factor, anticipating failure and obstacles. The Denominational School boys had a score of 5 on this same factor. To them, their future seemed quite certain.

The 'middle class'disconnect of these government school boys became quite apparent when we looked at the results from the denominational school. The boys in this prestige school responded with such specificity and confidence that their chosen career looked a done deal.[15] Unlike the other boys, these prestige school boys were able to identify a relative who had a job like the one they now aspire to. And it was 'surgeon,"accountant,' "engineer,"architect,"lawyer' and even 'psychiatrist.' It was more than just dreaming. They explained quite precisely the kind of subjects to be taken, and even the places where such professions are taught. These spoke about 'professions,' not just 'jobs.'

## CONCLUSION

Given the widespread concerns cited earlier overyoung black males, these preliminary results suggest that though students entering these government schools did have relatively low Common Entrance marks, it is evident that such secondary schooling made little or no difference in helping to move them out of poverty or out of their original social class positions. For them, the former Prime Minister Kamla Persad-Bissessar's repeated advice that education is the only passport out of poverty does not resonate.

One of the recommendations made was for the government to establish a strategically-configured set of Career Empowerment Centres around each government secondary school – with government-labour-private sector-school partnership. This should be connected to the guidance and counselling diagnostic services of the school. The structural conditions (e.g., poverty, community infrastructure, etc.) are noted but these call for a different study and integrated solutions.

## NOTES

1.   The word 'graduating' is important here. That is, we counted only those who graduated. There are many students who left secondary schools, moreso, the government secondary schools before Form Five or before

graduating. Our results will therefore be quite conservative, that is, if the status of those 'drop-outs' were counted, the inequities could have been worse.

2. See e.g.,'Education for All.' Statistical Digest. Ministry of Education, 2002–3.pp. 22–58.

3. Ibid. pp. 22–58.

4. Largely inspired by the 'functionalism' papers of K. Davis and W. Moore in the 1940s, social stratification became a very controversial topic of intellectual debate, especially by counter-views from the social conflict theorists. Functionalism, for example, argues for the justifiable prestige given to certain jobs over others, for the extra training, etc. required, and high/respect, incentives, etc. Critics, for example, M. Tumin and W. Wesolowski, cited the many distortions which undermine functionalism, the main ones being inequality of opportunity and the perpetuation of elitism.

See e.g., K. Davis, K. and W. Moore, *The American Sociological Review.* Vol. 10. 1945. pp. 242–249. Reply by M. Tumin, 'Some Principles of Stratification', *The American Sociological Review.* Vol. 1 (2). 1953; R. Aron, 'Social Class, Political Class, Ruling Class', *European Journal of Sociology.* 1960. Vol. 1. pp. 260–281. Later critics include C. Anderson, *The Political Economy of Social Class.* New York: Prentice Hall. 1974. esp. pp. 76-115 on inequality, social class, and education. More recent writings on educational inequality and social class have been cited in earlier chapters.

Though early writings, these papers outlined the major contours of functionalism and the criticisms. In this country, it is well known, but implicitly supported, that political patronage and soil contacts play very significant roles in subverting the intended values of educational certification and socio-mobility. government and other official pledges of education as 'the key passport out of poverty and for a more prosperity' merely disguise these underlying forces of inequity and iniquity.

5. Between the ideal and the practical in this country, however, the values of functionalism are widely practised and governed by the middle and upper social classes especially (many noveau riche, conspicuous consumption, etc). The neutralizing factors are the feverish aspirations and hopes by the low, working class to join them. George Beckford's book, *Persistent Poverty*, provides some insight into the plantation-derived class obstacles to equality, especially pp. 84–120, 215–250.

6. Denominational Schools = 41% of sample, Government Secondary/College = 18%, Government Composite, Comprehensive, etc. = 38%. The three private schools used for the original Tracer Study were omitted.

This 'post-secondary study' is part of a larger longitudinal study (2001-2009) which traced students from Form One through Form Three to Form Five and three years after. The Tracer Study Report submitted to Ministry of Education. R. Deosaran, 'Project Safeguard: Tracing Youths 2001-2010, Post-Secondary School Experiences.' Ministry of Education, Trinidad and Tobago. July 2010.

7. As is usual with such tracer studies, it took great effort to reach students three years after they have left their Form Five. School records, addresses, etc, were used to reach them.

8. R. Deosaran, 'Benchmarking Student Violence: Towards a Culture of Peace.' 2005

9. E.g., R. Deosaran. Project Safeguard: Tracing Youths 2001 to 2010. 2010.

10. Town meeting, together with PNM election candidates, Mr. Stuart Young and Fitzgerald Hinds – both lawyers. Also reported in television station, CCN, channel 5, Wednesday, August 19, 2015, 9 p.m. On September 7, 2015, the 'UNC' (People's Partnership) Government lost the election to Dr Rowley's PNM.

11. The Ryan Report referred to is the Government-commissioned report entitled: 'No Time to Quit: Engaging Youth At Risk.' 2013. The Governing party, the People's Partnership, has complained and replied that the 'urban hot spots of crime' were under the PNM and still are for a long time.

12. In the letter by the PSA President Ms Jennifer Baptiste to undertake the study.

13. See e.g., 'No Time To Quit: Engaging Youth At Risk.' Committee on Young Males and Crime in Trinidad and Tobago. Report to former Prime Minister, Government of Trinidad and Tobago, 2013. This is apart from numerous other sources – the police, media reports, research reports previously cited. Black youths outnumbered Indian youths in the prisons, juvenile homes, etc.

14. 'African Youths in Danger on the East-West Corridor', R. Deosaran. October, 2006. Preliminary Research Project partially funded by Public Services Association of Trinidad and Tobago. We agree this focus group exercise involved a relatively small sample (60), especially with one Denominational School, but as a preliminary study, the results could provide a plausible basis for a more systematic and larger study.

15. This DenominationalSchool was also located along the East-West corridor but comprised students who did very well in the then Common Entrance Examination.

# CHAPTER FIFTEEN

# Strain, Failed Ambitions and Crime

*Students from the community are now immune to crime that takes place around them. Recently, past members of the school were 'gunned down' near the school and students saw this as normal. Student delinquency has increased by answering back teachers, fighting, etc. It is now too much to handle. There is now a trend whereby female students are outnumbering boys in giving trouble at school.*

Teacher, Government Secondary School.
Voices of the Teachers, Report submitted to Ministry, 2008

What then, are some of the deleterious consequences of 'bad' schooling or consistently having certain social groups excluded or dropping out of mainstream education? In this chapter, we seek to connect what happens in the education system, the deficits particularly, to youth deviance. Our earlier analyses have uncovered sufficient data and widespread concerns to indicate that flowing from the education system and secondary schooling particularly, there is the growth of a poor, youthful and marginalised underclass.[1]

## FROM SCHOOLING TO UNDERCLASS

Many of these have had frustrated ambitions, unable to cope with grammar schooling, from fractured family backgrounds and communities, or went to low-performing secondary schools where failure was the early self-fulfilling prophesy. Indeed, the 'underclass' has been described as 'hostile street and career criminals, skilled entrepreneurs of the underground economy, passive victims of government support and the severely traumatized.'[2] Another related description is: 'The underclass has been transformed from surplus and discarded labour into an exclusive group of black urban terrorists.'[3] Our view is that, once poor and single-parented in a low-performing secondary school, for example, many black males particularly have drifted out of school and into an underclass culture.[4] Increasing concerns have therefore been expressed over ineffective secondary schooling and youth crime.

For example, the former head of the country's Public Service, in making the link, said: '*When you are not educated and you can't get work, the only thing you do is to shoot a gun or live and have children with women out of wedlock.*'[5]

Making this same education-crime link, former Prime Minister Kamla Persad-Bissessar stated:

> Education is the passport out of poverty. That is why our Government has emphasized education and training so as to prevent the youth from crime and instead to get opportunities for sustainable jobs and a better quality of life.[6]

Writing on '*The Effect of Dropping out of High School on Criminal Behavior,*' Terence Thornberry *et al* noted that when the school serves as 'a source of failure and frustration for students, this increases delinquency' both in and after their dropping out. This implies that the school has failed as an agent of social control.[7] And, quite plausibly in this middle-class driven society, out of the strain from failed and frustrated aspirations, the drift to deviance by such students becomes a less stressful option.[8] The country indeed became decolonized by having political independence, its own legislature, fair and free elections, independent judiciary, wavering industrialisation and other related structures.

But while decolonisation by structural changes took place, the society became captured, inevitably perhaps, by western values of status competition, debt-ridden consumerism, conspicuous consumption and rugged individualism. Then there is the Frantz Fanon 'wish to be white' syndrome which drives a cosmetic and body-change industry of its own. Largely, the value penetration, energised by mass communication, appears happily as 'westernisation by invitation.' The 'spiritual' and 'anti-foreign' resistance from the church or a few intellectuals quickly become yesterday's news.

Sociologists, Haralambos and Holborn noted:

> Individual achievement and materialism are major values in Western industrial society. Individual achievement is often symbolized and measured by the quality and quantity of material possessions that a person can accumulate.[9]

This 'deculturalisation' process and status struggle have serious implications for the poor, especially for the poor youth whose academic under-achievement is no match for the middle class culture of 'status by material possessions.'

By government policy and personal desire, education was actively promoted as the key passport out of poverty and towards a better life. The education itself, in spite of attempts to decolonise, became an instrument for academic competition and widely-preferred grammar-type schooling towards the traditional professions. The consequences of the failures and strains from the educational system therefore become important matters in terms of equality of opportunity, equity and deviance as a substitute for academic failure.

## GROWTH OF FRUSTRATION

As the government National Task Force on Education and the IDB Education Report on Access and Performance confirmed, by giving secondary school places to all, serious academic and psychological problems emerged with students. Firstly, they were not all sufficiently prepared as yet, even in the basics, for secondary schooling. Secondly, very many did not have the aptitude nor the interest in grammar-type subjects.

The chairman of the National Energy Skills Centre (NESC), Feroz Khan, recently noted: '*Part of the challenge that we face in crime and other social issues is because students are falling out of the secondary school system with nowhere to go.*' He advised technical and vocational courses. The related fact is, however, even with such courses, the failure rate is relatively high, mainly because of students lack of knowledge in basic education. The young black males, it is argued, are the major casualties of a broken education system.[10]

As such, the absence of effective public policy responses aggravates a problem that needs healing. The marginalised products of such inequality have attracted serious concerns about youth crime in several studies and reports previously cited - for example, the Secondary School Placement Study, the National Task Force on Education and the more recent 'No Time To Quit Study of Youths at Risk.'[11]

## FROM PSYCHOLOGICAL STRAIN TO CRIME

From the social class and racial inequities discovered in our data so far, it seems quite plausible that many of the affected youth would have experienced disappointments and frustrations, even becoming enraged, at the treatment meted out to them by a stubborn secondary school placement system and their self-prophesied failures, particularly at the under-performing government secondary schools.[12]

In reviewing the 'weaknesses' in the delivery system of education in the country, the National Task Force on Education said: 'All of the foregoing factors serve to increase the proportion of students who we eventually label as 'educationally at risk.'[13]

With regard to secondary school placement, the Report added:

> The majority of students find that though they have secured a place at a secondary school, their needs are often not met and at the end they are faced with failure. Pupils and teachers are caught in a psychology of failure and experience the frustration and rage/apathy which helplessness evokes.[14]

From the various theories in criminology, we chose social reaction theories to help explain the deviance committed by the plantation workers in their oppressive conditions of labour. We now need a different kind of explanation for the increase in lawlessness, crime and gang formation by high-risk young people here.[15] A recent study on young males and crime in this country provided a panoramic view of youth crime and lawlessness.[16]

That study concluded:

> The young male population that is more at risk of directly being caught in the criminal world of drugs, guns and deadly violent crime are of African descent...This study takes the view that young males, particularly young Afro males are seriously 'at risk' and are seriously 'in trouble.'[17]

One of its authors, Ryan, added: 'We argue that the elites and the politicians are largely responsible for the outcomes that are by-products of a flawed, class-driven model of development.'[18] Another study in 2012 on race and crime in Trinidad, noted that 'increasing amounts of crime and violence were found mainly in Afro-Trinidadian communities.' The study further found that '83% of the gangs in Trinidad were African while 13% were East Indian.[19]

From the research, commentaries and even the calypsoes earlier cited, a sharpened focus has been placed on the black male youth and the disadvantages endured. Professor Theodore, wrote a newspaper column on the subject entitled 'Young Afro males need more positive messages.[20] More sharply, black activist, David Mohammed, in his column, noting the advantages of other ethnic groups, asked: 'What about the poor black children?'

From the research provided, the educational system, while it confers celebrated success upon a relatively few, it seemingly leaves behind large numbers of frustrated working class, black youths lodged in criminogenic circumstances. As pointed out earlier, from Form One to Form Five in the government secondary school, a large proportion of students, lower class and all, expressed aspirations for university and thereby a middle class life. Few of the lower class make it, thus leaving behind a significant proportion experiencing the strain of aiming for society's success goals but without having the means to achieve them. These fall into the high-risk group that Ryan cited.

Many of these, of course, would have previously been disappointed in not getting into a preferred prestige school. Such repeated disappointments would likely shift such youths, socially strained as they are, into more comforting sub-cultures that are in opposition to the mainstream values they wished for but could not achieve. Citing results from the 2011 CSEC examination, educator Bernard found that 16.6% of those who sat the exam from 'hot spot' areas never passed an exam as compared to 9.5% in 'non-hot spot areas.' These hot spot areas are African-dominated.

Further, the percentage that 'never passed an exam' was 75% in Beetham Gardens, quite high in comparison with other areas.[21] Both areas are known to contain significant amounts of high risk African youths. In connecting schooling with high risk youth, Bernard said: *'Many of the secondary schools that students in disadvantaged communities are generally assigned to were under-performing.'*[22] These are mainly the government secondary schools.

Bernard added that those students from such areas particularly who fail to get into a prestige school 'generally have to cope with the psychological trauma of a deep sense of failure.' He concluded:

> All students now proceed to the secondary school but it does not address the more salient features of inequity.'[23] He further noted the extent to which such disadvantages of the male youth 'provide a risk factor to crime.[24]

## FROM INEQUALITY TO CRIME

What is the connection between such 'strained' high-risk youths and delinquency and crime? What are some of the additional social and psychological conditions which may trigger their deviance?

In seeking to explain working class youth and crime, sociologist Robert Merton, borrowing from Emile Durkheim's theory of anomie, pointed to the prevailing ethos of America, the dominant value, which was 'the acquisition of wealth and status.[25]

Given the feverish competition for educational and occupational status in this country now, we, like Merton, begin by briefly referring to the early work of Emile Durkheim who examined the implications between aspirations and frustration particularly.[26] More precisely, from this Merton later promoted a structural strain theory to help explain deviance, that is, the extent to which the disparity between cultural emphasis on 'success goals' and expectations for their achievement produces strain-driven deviance.

Durkheim had earlier argued that anomie is a social condition in which the social norms are no longer effective in regulating behaviour, when these norms become loosened, fragmented and are substituted by other values in the society.[27] In other words, a condition as anomie may breed lawlessness.

Durkheim famously stated: *'With increased prosperity, desires increase. Overweening ambition always exceeds the results obtained, great as they may be, since there is no warning to pause here.'*[28] Such psychological connections are relevant to the rapid rise in status expectations, and have profusely captured the minds of young people in Trinidad and Tobago, even those whose resources and means to achieve the success goals are quite limited.

In explaining suicide of the upper social classes in France, Durkheim indicated that the discrepancy between high aspirations and the inability to achieve them produces psychological strain. Social disorganisation creeps in. Such high aspirations, he noted, emerged from the egalitarian promises inspired by the French Revolution.

## THE STRAIN FACTOR

Our concern here is not about suicide but we are still concerned with the link between the dominant value for middle class success and failed aspirations because it does have some relevance to the youths of this country. Our high aspirations and expectations were triggered not by any revolution but largely by the rousing rhetoric of equality and socio-economic mobility after gaining political independence in 1962.

Our further premise here is that this former British colony, Trinidad and Tobago, is now immersed in American values, and the frenzied quest for material success, social status and prestige – all of which are not within the reach of many.[29] And much of the relative shortfall in such reach is directly attributable to secondary school placement and lack of academic success. Or put another way, since this society is so soaked with aspirations for middle class success goals, if legitimate means to achieve them are not available, then quite likely, the disadvantaged youths will feel pressured to utilise illegitimate means.[30]

It needs to be emphasised that Trinidad and Tobago experienced lavish promises of an egalitarian society and a flush of high aspirations and expectations soon after it gained political independence in 1962. Such heightened aspirations apparently remain undiminished up to the present and with serious social and psychological implications, especially with the relative oil and gas prosperity which the country traditionally enjoys.[31] The concept of psychological strain therefore does have relevance to this country.

The population's feverish quest and keen competition for luxury goods and conspicuous consumption have been regularly criticised by the clergy and several highly-placed public officials. In August, 2015, for example, the country's President, in his Independence Day message said: 'Post-colonialism has led to gross materialism. Money must not rule this town of ours, but rather character, integrity and decency.'[32]

Merton, noting the dominant value of and the competitive quest for wealth and status, explained that the pressures for such goals are spread equally across all social classes but the legitimate means to achieve such goals are differentially distributed across the social classes. This brings to mind the words of the country's first prime minister when he said in 1975, many in the society 'have champagne tastes but mauby pockets.'

Upper class persons have greater access to education, role models and social contacts which empower them to compete successfully for wealth and status, especially through the education system. The lower class has no such advantage although all classes are repeatedly encouraged to aspire to higher education.

## CHAMPAGNE TASTES BUT MAUBY POCKETS

Adding a social psychological interpretation to Durkheim's views, Merton famously and quite early stated:

It is only when a system of cultural values extols, virtually above all else, certain *common* symbols of success *for the population at large* while the social structure rigorously restricts or completely eliminates access to approved modes of acquiring these symbols *for a considerable part of the same population*, that antisocial behaviour ensues on a considerable scale.[33]

Soon after independence, our secondary school students have held and still hold high academic aspirations.[34] As indicated earlier, about 80% of them from all social classes in Form One held high aspirations for university education and professional occupational status. And the extent to which barriers appear to deny them access, to that extent will some psychological strain result and illegitimate routes adopted. In the end, they would likely also devalue such middle class values or, in addition, seek alternative interests and means of satisfaction.[35]As our data in Chapter Fourteen indicates, even among those low social class students who made it through Form One up to Form Five - only 30% of them as against over 70% middle and upper class – eventually continued into 'full-time study only' three years after leaving Form Five. It seems that, in spite of their apparent academic ability and free university tuition, the interest and value which many low social class students initially put into education become diminished through experiences in the Government Schools. It is worse for those who left the Government Secondary school before reaching Form Five!

## STRAIN ADAPTATIONS

Merton proposed 'five modes of adaptation to strain,' two of which are of criminological interest here - the 'innovators' and the 'rebels.' (The other three are the conformists, ritualists, and the retreatists.)[36] The *innovators* are the ones who still value the dominant middle class goals of society but recognise their own social class or resource limitations, or are denied the opportunities to achieve these valued goals.

They therefore seek alternative routes to achieve them, that is often 'illegal means to succeed in society.' Such alternative and illegal routes are facilitated in an environment where the law enforcement rate is ineffective and low, where academic competition and success are prolifically acclaimed and where the means to success goals are inequitably spread across the various social class and ethnic groups.[37]

The *rebels* are the ones who become cynics, who reject the values and goals of mainstream society and even the legitimate means to achieve them. These rebels create their sub-cultures, their own value systems.

Indeed, a large proportion of the frustrated, stressed and strained were in our government secondary schools, or dropped out prematurely. Merton's high aspirations-strain-differential opportunities model is therefore likely to occur here with the adaptive response being to reject that which they found exceedingly strained to get, and consequently set up or join an alternative value system – mainly for respect.

The drift into a gang culture would therefore likely to occur. As indicated earlier, Merton's low class-success goals-strain-deviance model does not necessarily run up a straight line. If that were all it takes, it would be a rather permissive theory. There must also be some facilitating environmental conditions such as community fragmentation, weak law enforcement, low detection rates, weak parental norms and controls, etc.[38] And of course, the opportunity.

In dealing with the 'ecology' of crime, Stark made several propositions. Three of these are: (1) Living in stigmatised neighbourhood causes a reduction in an individual's stake in conformity, (2) More lenient law enforcement increases the incidence of crime and deviance, and (3) Stigmatised neighbourhoods  tend to be overpopulated by  the most demoralised kinds of people.

While there is an issue of 'cause and effect', the propositions regarding neighbourhood status remain plausible. Many of our high risk youths live in such neighbourhoods. It is such structural elements which help attract strain-driven deviance and the notion of an underclass. In other words, much of delinquency or gang formation is social psychological, that is the interaction between personality characteristics and the facilitating environment.[39] Such an interaction perspective helps prevent overuse and abuse of personalised labelling and stigmatisation. The explanatory burden also rests on environmental conditions.

## LAW AND THE LOSS OF MORAL AUTHORITY

A key environmental psychological element is the extent to which the community possesses or loses its moral authority to control deviance.[40] In the case of the crimes by plantation workers, we argued that such crimes were committed, and guiltlessly so, because the social order had lost its moral authority, notwithstanding its authoritarian structure. Norms of civility and fairness were fundamentally absent. So it is in the eyesof many black youths cited by local studies.[41]

The over-riding issue is the absence of psychological attachment to the mainstream. There is no moral obligation to obey. Durkheim puts it this way:

> The more weakened the groups to which the individual belongs, the more he consequently depends on himself and recognises no other rules of conduct than what are founded on his private interests.

Self-serving reasoning enters and, according to criminologists Taylor *et al.*, falls into the passions of an unthinking self-interest.[42]

The data does show that there is strain upon many young people here, especially those who face challenges in secondary schooling. But, as indicated earlier, such strain does not automatically cause deviance. We here have attached such strain, where it exists, to local environmental conditions which help convert psychological strain into crime or deviance.[43] This is where the existing theory can be modified for local application. This, apart from Merton's matrix where not everyone 'strained' enters crime.

## THE ENVIRONMENT TOO

The strain between the opportunity structure of society and the social and psychological conditions of the lower class youth helps make them rebellious against mainstream society with deviant consequences such as burglary, larceny, robbery, drug-trafficking - absorbed within a gang culture.

The theory of deviance therefore moved from Durkheim's anomie to Merton's opportunity structure, then to the 'illegitimate opportunity structure' proposed by Richard Cloward and Lloyd Ohlin.[44] Given this country's post-independence development, the erratic rise of status expectations, the public dominance of success goals and social class fragmentation, these theories do have relevance here. The theoretical connections, when narrowed and slightly modified, hold a logic that is applicable. While outlining their 'general theory of crime,' criminologists Gottfredson and Hirschi explained that while 'there are multitudes of theories of criminality, in fact, the number of truly distinct explanations is small.'[45] We agree.

# CARIBBEAN CRIMINOLOGY

During the 1990s, concerted attempts were made to create a 'Caribbean Criminology' in which many of the existing theories were revised for Caribbean application, especially in the area of delinquency.[46] It was generally felt then that: (1) There was a need to integrate some of the relevant theories since they appeared so dispersed.[47] (2) While the local data and context may be different there was enough for modifying existing theories to provide explanations.[48] This is what we do.

Along the East-West corridor (i.e., from Carenage, Diego Martin, Arima to Sangre Grande), there is much delinquency and youth violence, perpetrated by numerous gangs and school drop-outs.[49] With such combination, it is plausible to apply Cloward and Ohlin's theory of illegitimate opportunity structure to gang formation and youth crime in such districts. The theory could be modified, as earlier noted, to accommodate local peculiarities such as politically-patronised hooliganism and make-work programmes which help contribute to a restless underclass.

# OPEN-DOOR DELINQUENCY

Society's opportunity structure, a functional model of society really, is therefore a variable, ranging from legitimate to illegitimate points of entry. The 'illegitimate opportunity structure' in the East- West corridor does help attract the 'strained' secondary school student who searches for a sub-culture for comfort, status, a networked belonging and achievable status or respect.

In extending Merton's opportunity structure theory into a sub-culture domain, Cloward and Ohlin explained that just as legitimate opportunities are available across all social groups, so too illegitimate opportunities are available and, more precisely, they attract and are mostly exploited by the frustrated low class youth. They argue that spread of illegitimate opportunities is organised and integrated.[50]

Inserting the psychological implications of such a phenomenon, they stated:

> When pressures from unfulfilled aspirations and blocked opportunities become sufficiently intense, many lower-class youth turn away from legitimate channels, adopting other means, beyond conventional mores, which might offer them a possible route to success-goals.[51]

When the marginalised, strained status of the government school graduate, for example, are combined with their deviant civic attitudes,[52] the combination makes it relatively easy for them to enter the structured gang culture of illegitimate opportunities.[53]

In this way then, it is not the poverty into which the student is born that necessarily causes crime. It is more so his poverty linked to the strain he feels from having aspirations and enticements to celebrated socio-economic goals, but for which he has limited opportunity to access. And if education, secondary schooling in particular, makes their aspirations so unattainable, then the criminogenic implications may be quite serious. After all, our data shows that as much as 18% of them from the government schools (vs only 3% from the denominational assisted schools) were 'neither studying nor working.'[54]

In seeking possible links between educational attainment and youth crime, and noting students' need for strong peer relationships in the secondary school, Ricardo Sabates stated: 'One may expect that peers are a protective factor against criminal behaviour but they can also promote anti-social and criminal behaviours as peer effects are very strong in criminal decisions.'[55]

Sabates' view falls with the domain of differential association, as an explanation for delinquency. His view is also relevant to the 'illegitimate opportunity structure' perspective especially where there are connections between a student's deviant peers and a criminogenic environment. The student could be drawn into the illegitimate opportunity structure, as already experienced by his deviant peers. The student gets immersed into a culture of 'deviance without guilt.'[56]

Sabates concluded:

> Increasing educational attainment as a narrowly-defined policy is unlikely to reduce crime, unless accompanied by reductions in social inequalities, increasing opportunities for young people at risk of social exclusion and adult outcomes of deprivation, and a more active role of families of fostering learning and preventing anti-social behaviour in early years.[57]

We agree that while equality of educational opportunity and attainment are being pursued, a sustaining set of conditions must also be pursued for their success. However, we believe that increasing educational attainment can also help lead to reductions in social inequalities.

While we agree on 'preventing anti-social behaviour in early years,' the research so far cited indicates that the youths without adequate educational attainment are the ones most likely to be delinquent and move into gang membership – educational achievement does help reduce crime.

It is noteworthy that at a mass gathering of Catholics, the country's Catholic Archbishop, Joseph Harris, said: '*Until exclusion and inequality in this society and between people are reversed, it will be impossible to eliminate violence and crime.*'[58]

## PATHWAYS TO REFORM

What in essence Sabates is saying, however, almost like Bowles, Carnoy and Gintis, is that while educational attainment is being pursued, significant reforms in the social and economic order must also take place. But the dilemma that faced these critics is the same one facing Sabates. That is, how do you get the policy-making elites and the already privileged to make the proposed fundamental changes, especially with political risks facing them?

The above discussion includes reference to several theories in order to help make sense of the previous relationships cited. Given the manner and depth to which 'success values' and 'greed for status' have spread across this formerly colonised society, we believe that 'strain through frustrated opportunities' also applies to the middle class in our society, except that possibly, this group may have better access to both legitimate and illegitimate outlets. Social comparison and energised feelings of relative deprivation play an important part in the struggle for the society's success values.[59]

Further, compared to middle class students, the low class, African students who get in or prematurely drop out of the government secondary schools are more likely to ease out of the queue towards middle class success goals, in anticipation of failure, and move into 'less stressful' criminogenic endeavours. Such a possibility may be qualified by the fact that this newly-independent country does not as yet have a solidified middle class, given the relatively new routes suddenly available for upward mobility. The society is still in the *nouveau riche* stage.

Here, social class by income or occupation largely lacks the values that discretely separate the middle from the lower class. This is one reason that helps make strain theory somewhat elastic in its application to this society.

The form by income or even occupation may be there but not the substance that creates discrete social class distinctions.

While such theories are quite plausible they are not laws, in that, for example, it is not that all low class students go on to commit crimes because they were vexed and felt strained that they did not get the secondary schooling they desired, or felt very unfairly treated. Some do, but not all. Apart from significant statistical probabilities, for certain problems even small numbers can do great damage. In terms of crime and systematic socio-economic marginalisation, for example, we do not need inordinately large numbers to attract public policy attention. Such dysfunctional conditions help create social injustice and an uncivil society. Leaving such conditions unattended is a slap in the face of a modern democracy.

From the evidence seen from several sources, in particular the potential for crime and deviance, we believe there is enough inequality and inequity in the educational system to attract public concern and educational reform. Since the fundamental reforms required depend upon the government, the political will must be activated one way or another.

## THE UNDER-CLASS

The value of the above discussion on marginalised or high-risk youth is to help energise the quest to reduce the amount of inequality in educational opportunity and inequity because, we believe, like Sabates, Merton and Cloward and Ohlin, that it is the strain from such inequalities and inequities that contributes significantly to delinquency, crime and underclass formation.

The low-performing government secondary schools education must not continue to be a major springboard for much of the deviance the society now experiences. As educator Lennox Bernard advised: 'Fix the schools'. We earlier proposed that the application of strain or opportunity structure theories should consider the kind of society in which such theories are applied.

Briefly, this society, as a newly independent one and relatively fresh out of colonialism, faced pressures for quick development and institutional decolonization with the new government striving to 'earn its stripes.' Apart from the tensions discussed earlier, such pressures led to the maintenance of very centralised administrative systems and a strongly functionalist mode of education and socio-economic order. Any small, newly independent country who departed from this route would eventually become compelled to return to it, even after experimenting with alternatives. This has been the Caribbean experience, and with all the strains generated. Still, however, there are reforms possible which could be functional, fair, more efficient and with a reduction in social injustice.

## NOTES

1.  White collar crime or crimes by middle class or the wealth are not dealt with here.
2.  Cited in John Hagan, 'The Poverty of a Classless Criminology.' *Criminology*, Vol. 31 (1). pp. 2.
3.  Ibid. p.2.
4.  For further readings on the causes and prevention of juvenile delinquency, see e.g., J. R. Weiss, R. Crutchfield and G. Bridges, *Juvenile Delinquency* (2nd ed.). London: Sage Publications. 2001.
5.  Dumas, R. *Newsday*. September 13, 2015. p. 19.
6.  Speech at formal opening of new Maloney Police Station. May 2, 2015.
7.  T. Thornberry, M. Moore, and R. Christenson, 'The Effect of Dropping Out of High School on Subsequent Criminal Behaviour', *Criminology*, Vol. 23. 1985. p. 3.
8.  See for a discussion on strain theory, R. Agnew, 'A Revised Strain Theory of Delinquency', *Social Forces*. Vol. 64. pp. 151–167.
9.  M. Haralambos and M. Holborn. *Sociology*. London: Collins International. 1995. p.5. This is in addition to the visible expansion of highly-priced houses, gated communities. This modernisation (vs tradition) process is a large subject fit for sustained social science analysis. For a useful discussion on social class formation, deculturalisation, materialism and the dilemmas of socialism and capitalism, see, e.g., A. Vidich (ed), '*The New Middle Classes*. New York: New York University Press, 1995; Earlier but very informative works - M. Weiner (ed), *Modernisation, The Dynamics of Growth*. New York: Basic Books, 1966; P. Sorokin. *Social and Cultural Mobility*. New York: The Free Press, 1959; S. Chodak, *Societal Development*. New York: Oxford University Press, 1973; L. Harrison, *Underdevelopment is a State of Mind: The Latin American Case*. Boston: Center for International Affairs and Harvard University Press, 1985
10. See e.g., Professor Emeritus Theodore Lewis. 'Young Afro Males need more positive messages.' *Express*. October 4, 2013. p. 13. Also, Professor Selwyn Ryan, 'Schools in Turmoil.' *Express*. November 9, 2014. p.13. Educator Dr Lennox Bernard, 'Fix the schools now.' *Express*. November 5, 2013. p. 13. Dr Keith Rowley, 'Under-performing men a big problem,' *Express*. August 8, 2015. p. 19.

11.  See particularly papers by Ryan and Bernard.

12.  While all government schools are now called secondary or high schools (no longer composite or comprehensive), the distinctions between the traditional five-year government secondary schools and the former 'new' composite and comprehensive schools largely remain.

13.  National Task Force on Education. p.2.

14.  Ibid. p. 52.

15.  There is a variety of theories used to explain crime, e.g., Deterrence, Psychogenic, Social Structure, Strain, Social Process, Social Reaction, even Marxist types – Radical Criminology. For detail see e.g.,S. Brown, et al. *Criminology: Explaining Crime and Its Context*, Ohio: Anderson Publishing. 1998;F. Hagan, *Introduction to Criminology*, California: Nelson Hall Publishing. 1994.

16.  See e.g., Committee on Young Males and Crime in Trinidad and Tobago. Executive Summary. (S. Ryan, et al), 'No Time to Quit: Engaging Youth at Risk', St Augustine: School of Education. University of the West Indies. 2013. p. 11. A previous study by the World Bank in 1998 entitled 'Trinidad and Tobago Youth Development' contains a wide discussion – with data – on youth at risk, including young black males.

17.  Ibid. p. 16.

18.  S. Ryan, 'Another Look Inside the Book Bag', Committee on Young Males in Trinidad and Tobago. p. 16. Selwyn Ryan is a Professor Emeritus of Political Science, University of the West Indies.

19.  A. Kalunta-Crumpton,'Race, Ethnicity, Crime and Criminal Justice in the Americas', 2012. Cited in *No Time to Quit: Engaging Youth At Risk*. 2013. p. 26.

20.  *Express*. October 4, 2013. p. 13.

21.  L. Bernard, 'Reforming our Education System', in *No Time To Quit*. p.347.

22.  Ibid. p. 347.

23.  Ibid. p. 349.

24.  Ibid. p. 349-50.

25.  R.Merton,'Social Structure and Anomie',*American Sociological Review*. 3. pp. 672-682; R. Merton,*Social Theory and Social Structure*. New York: The Free Press. 1968.

26.  E. Durkheim,*Suicide: A Study in Sociology (trans)*. J. Spaulding and G. Simpson. New York: NY: The Free Press. 1951. p. 246.

27.  E. Durkheim,*Suicide: A Study in Sociology*, New York. The Free Press. 1951.

28.  Ibid.p. 253

29.  Such value immerges mainly from mass advertising and consumerism, cable television, international travels, numerous shopping malls

political rhetoric and high-mobility pledges, etc. The nouveau riche culture includes intense competition for social status and class competition.

30. See R. Cloward and L. Ohlin,*Delinquency and Opportunity: A Theory of Delinquent Gangs*, Glencoe, Il: Free Press. 1960.

31. R. Deosaran, *Psychonomics and Poverty: Towards Governance and Civil Society*, Kingston: University of the West Indies Press. 2000, pp. 5-40. In fact, a very high positive correlation (r = .80) was found between the rise of this country's GDP from 1962 to 2010 and the serious crime rate.

32. Carmona, A. reported in *Express*. August 31, 2015. p. 17.

33. R. Merton,'Social Structure and Anomie', *American Sociological Review*. Vol. 3.pp. 680.

34. E.g., see Rubin and Zavalloni. 1968; R. Deosaran, 2005, 2008.

35. This strain reduction mechanism is explained in cognitive dissonance theory.

36. R. Merton, *Social Theory and Social Structure*, New York, NY: The Free Press. 1968.

37. This of course does not explain all crime. It however emphasizes the relationships between lower class groups, middle class aspirations, success goals, strain and differential opportunities. For a critical review of strain theory, see R. Agnew, 'A Revised Strain Theory of Delinquency', *Social Forces*. 1985. Vol. 64. pp. 151-167.

38. R. Stark gives a good account of the relationship between neighbourhood quality and deviance. See 'Deviant Places: A Theory of the Ecology of Crime', *Criminology*. 1987. Vol. 25. pp. 893-909.

39. Such a perspective also includes George Herbert Mead's 'symbolic interactionism.' See E. Schur, *Labeling Deviant Behaviour: Its Sociological Implications*, New York: Harper and Row. 1971. pp. 15-25

40. Such as public perception of excessive corruption, inefficient and effective state institutions including the Police Service, etc.

41. See e.g.,'No Time To Quit: Engaging Youth At Risk.' 2013.

42. Taylor et al. *New Criminology*. p. 4.

43. R. Stark gives a good account of the relationship between neighbourhood quality and deviance. See 'Deviant Places: A Theory of the Ecology of Crime',*Criminology*. 1987. Vol. 25. pp. 893-909.

44. R. Cloward and L. Ohlin, *Delinquency and Opportunity*, New York: The Free Press. 1966.

45. M. Gottredson and T. Hirschi, *A General Theory of Crime*, Stanford, California: Stanford University Press. 1990. p. 111.

46. See e.g.,R. Bennett and J. Lynch, 'Towards a Caribbean Criminology: Problems and Prospects', *Caribbean Journal of Criminology and Social Psychology*, January 1996. Vol. 1(1), pp.8-36.

47. See Taylor et al, *The New Criminology*, for a critique of the numerous theories in criminology and their application to youth crime and delinquency. For several further attempts to integrate criminological theories, see S. Brown, E. Esbensen and G. Geis, *Criminology: Explaining Crime and Its Context*, Cincinnati, Ohio: Anderson Publishing. 1998. pp. 385-410.

48. G. Jarjoura and D. May, 'Integrated Criminological Theories to Explain Violent Forms of Delinquency',*Caribbean Journal of Criminology and Social Psychology*, January and July, 2000. Vol. 5 (1&2). pp. 81-100. Also,B. Forst and R. Bennett. 'Unemployment and Crime: Implications for the Caribbean',*Caribbean Journal of Criminology and Social Psychology*, January/July 1998. Vol. 3 (1&2). pp.1-28; R. Deosaran and D. Chadee, 'Juvenile Delinquency in Trinidad and Tobago: Challenges for Social Policy and Caribbean Criminology',*Caribbean Journal of Criminology and Social Psychology*, July 1999. Vol. 2 (2), pp. 36-82.

49. E.g., see Education Ministry's Statistical Digest. 2002-3; R. Deosaran, 'African Youths in Danger', 2006; 'No Time to Quit, Engaging Youth At Risk', 2013.

50. For an integration of anomie, illegitimate means and cultural transmission, see R. Cloward. Illegitimate Means, Anomie and Deviant Behaviour. American Sociological Review. 1959. Vol. 24, p. 164; Quite an early but still useful paper in the mode of theory integration.

51. Ibid. p. 105.

52. R. Deosaran. 2005.

53. The drift into deviance is even more likely with those who drop out of the government secondary school before they reach Form Five or graduate

54. The others were studying full-time, working full-time, etc. See Chapter 13.

55. R. Sabates, 'Educational Attainment and Juvenile Crime', *British Journal of Criminology*. 2008.48.pp. 395–409.

56. E.g.,A. Calvo-Armengol and Y. Zenou,'Social Networks and Crime Decisions: The Role of Social Structure in Facilitating Delinquent Behaviour',*International Economic Review*. 2004.45. pp. 439–458. See D. Matza, *Delinquency and Drift*, New York: Wiley. p. 1064.

57. Sabates. p. 407.

58. Mass at Corpus Christi, Queen's Park Savannah. *Guardian*. June 20, 2015.

59. See e.g.,R. Deosaran *Psychonomics and Poverty*, for the active role of relative deprivation in social class formation in this society.

# CHAPTER SIXTEEN

# Discussion: School Type, the Cradle of Inequality

*Psychological capital is the motivation to build physical capital. It includes trust, civic attitudes, the achievement motive, relative deprivation and feelings of personal well-being. It has a vital role in academic achievement.*
Ramesh Deosaran, Psychonomics and Poverty, 2000

*Tensions have increased between efficiency and ethics, between consumption and distributive justice, and between monetary gain and morality. Equality of opportunity may well call for institutional action designed to redress previously existing and inherited disadvantages.*
Douglas Vickers, Economics and Ethics, 1997

## THE EQUALITY CHALLENGE FOR THE GOVERNMENT SCHOOLS

In this final Chapter, we review some of the major findings and their implications, highlight some relevant subjects for further discussion (e.g. conservatism, humanitarianism), discuss the dilemmas (conundrums) which equality and equity policies face in a democratic society, and finally propose a list of actionable programmes and policies. Given the data presented so far, the challenge for equality of educational opportunity and educational equity remains in urgent need of attention.[1] In particular, it may appear as irresponsibility on the part of the relevant authorities if no urgent and serious attention is given to the repeated deficits of so many under-performing government secondary schools and their fragmented communities.

Further, it now remains a challenge for the government to define its concepts of educational equality, measure the derived outcomes, reform where remedies are needed and with a sharp eye for continuous improvements.

# EDUCATIONAL INEQUALITIES: DISCRIMINATION UNMASKED

The data earlier presented from the SEA, NCSE, CSEC and CAPE examinations and the role of the Concordat uncovered disturbing instances of inequality and inequity in the education system. We saw surprising amounts of bias regarding race, social class, gender, parental background and even place of residence in the system.

Where it is exclusively used, the 'examination by merit' system seems to be producing persistent social disadvantages. Merit does not always serve social justice. Much of the healing must start from the primary school and the relationship between schooling and the family too. Proportionally, students of African descent are consistently behind those of East Indian descent. Low social class students remain relatively stagnant in their position while the middle and upper classes show increased gains, females continue to outperform males, students from two-parent homes consistently perform better than those from single-parent homes, and examination passes largely depend on where in the country students live.

Extremely worrisome, too, is that the government secondary schools consistently show significantly lower academic performance than the denominational secondary schools with serious implications, especially for the young, black male. These disproportionalities appear consistent year after year.

A very notable difference uncovered is in the extent to which the private primary schools consistently outstrip both the denominational and government primary schools in the SEA examination. And in the midst of all this uneasily sit the Concordat and the process of secondary school placement. The educational system is tragically fractured and heated by an environment filled with ethnic antagonisms and status competition.

# MONEY IS NOT ALL

All this also mean that vast expenditures on the education system and expanded enrolment do not necessarily create equality of opportunity or equity in the system. In fact, the gaps of inequality get worse. And this is the system that was supposed to help 'heal the wounds of colonialism,' of providing fair opportunity and mobility for the socially disadvantaged.

The annual celebrations over SEA passes and scholarships merely mask the equitable realities. The mask has been removed. But what about after these students *leave* secondary school at Form Five?

# AFTER SECONDARY SCHOOL, WHAT?

We now provide a brief summary of some inequalities students experience *after* leaving secondary school, and the sociological implications. A measure of socio-economic mobility, we repeat, is the extent to which a student occupies or heads towards an occupational status higher than that of his or her parents or guardian.[2] As earlier explained, we defined 'university' as high academic status mainly because of its potential to lead to a high-paying, relatively respected and influential job – including one of the traditional professions.

Therefore, if a student enters university, especially UWI as the leading institution, or takes up full-time study within three years after Form Five, and his or her father is a vendor, chauffeur, or office clerk, it is very likely that that student would eventually occupy a higher occupational status than his father.[3]

# SOCIAL CLASS

Table 16.1 provides an overview of the educational and occupational status of the students three years after they left Form Five.

As the table shows, 47% of the low social class group went to university (UWI, UTT, USC = 43%; foreign university = 4%) three years after Form Five.[4] These broke ranks and 'crashed' the class barrier. These are the 'gate-crashers' or 'escapists' depending on how one looks at it. Further, 31% of them went into 'full-time studies only' and 22% into 'studying and working.'[5]

If UWI alone is used as the yardstick, it will be 31% low social class going to UWI. In this respect, it looks like free secondary and university education has some way to go for low social class students. *(The extent of group under or over-representation will be illustrated later)*.

What is the position with the middle and upper classes? Some 85% of the upper class went to university (local 67%, foreign 18%) - a percentage difference of 38% between the upper and low social class students.

Some 85% of the upper class students also went into 'full-time studies;' only 5% 'working and studying.' Again, when UWI is used as the yardstick here, we found 65% of the upper class going to UWI, a difference of 34% between upper and low social class for UWI attendance.

**Table 16.1: Proportions of Social Class, Race and School Type: Original Form Five Sample X Proportions who Entered University Three Years After Leaving Form Five (%)**

| | | In Original Sample (Form5) | In University | Full-Time Studies Only | Studying and Working | Working Only | Neither Studying nor Working |
|---|---|---|---|---|---|---|---|
| Social Class | Lower | 52 | 47 | 31 | 22 | 33 | 14 |
| | Middle | 40 | 69 | 60 | 15 | 20 | 5 |
| | Upper | 8 | 85 | 85 | 5 | 7 | 3 |
| Race | African | 30 | 47 | 30 | 20 | 36 | 14 |
| | East Indian | 45 | 72 | 61 | 13 | 19 | 7 |
| | Mixed | 25 | 49 | 37 | 24 | 25 | 13 |
| School Type | Denominational | 40 | 77 | 71 | 14 | 11 | 4 |
| | Government | 60 | 40 | 31 | 18 | 35 | 14 |

Note: Some percentages have been rounded off. Also foreign universities included here.

For the middle class, 69% went to university (local 62%, foreign 7%): 60% 'full-time studies,' 15% 'working and studying.' Again, if UWI is used as the yardstick, it will be 54% middle class going to UWI. However measured, comparatively speaking, the middle and upper social classes substantially held on their class positions. These are the 'retainers.'

If, as an estimate, we use 'not studying or working' and 'working only,' then we may say 10% of the upper class skidded down from their original class position in the sample, and 25% of the middle class did, especially since, as we gathered, over 90% of these early jobs were 'working class jobs.'[6] This proportion who 'didn't make it,' who descended from their high status, are the 'sliders.' The low social class students could only move up or stay put.

## DRIFTERS, STAGNANTS, CLIMBERS AND RETAINERS

Five percent of the middle class and 3% of the upper class were 'neither studying nor working.' Altogether, this 'neither studying nor working' are the 'drifters' (Table 16.1).

The low social class group who are 'working only,' well, while they may have future plans, for now, they can be classified as the 'stagnants.'

In terms of education and socio-economic mobility therefore, this implies that about five out of ten low social class students, three years after leaving Form Five, were heading for an occupational status higher than their parents. *(Many of these came from the denominational secondary schools.)*

Seven out of ten middle and upper class students went to university. In fact, this is the post-independence experience: while the low social class is moving up, the middle and upper classes are moving up too, but in greater proportions. Notably, when UWI alone was used as the criterion, these differences were wider among the social classes. The mobility trajectory, however, is, in fact, more forcefully propelled by race and moreso by the type of school attended.[7]

# STRATIFICATION PERSISTS: TYPE OF SCHOOL

In this post-colonial, multi-racial, dual educational environment, social stratification in the educational system includes race and the type of secondary school attended as contributory factors to upward mobility.

Table 16.1 also shows that the type of secondary school attended, whether denominational or government, made a bigger difference than social class or race. Some 71% of those who attended a denominational school went into 'full-time studies only compared to 31%, on average, for those from government secondary schools – a difference of 40%. Some 77% of students who came from denominational secondary schools went into university three years after compared to 40% of those who came from the government secondary schools – a difference of 37%. See Table 16.1 also. More concisely, while a student from a denominational school, on average, has 8 out of 10 chances to enter university, a student from a government school has 4 out of 10 chances (see Table 16.2).

**Table 16.2: School Type x Persons Attending University Three Years After Form Five (%)**

| School Type | UWI | UTT | USC | Foreign | Total |
|---|---|---|---|---|---|
| Government-Assisted | 61 | 4 | 1 | 11 | 77 |
| Government | 23 | 9 | 5 | 3 | 40 |

As the multiple regression test showed, the type of school attended provided the greatest weight to upward mobility. In terms of 'not studying or working' – the idle group of 'drifters' – while the denominational schools produced only 4%, the government schools, on average, produced 14%, a very significant difference again.

## RACE

Does race make a difference? In fact, as Table 16.1 shows, while 47% of students of African descent went into university three years after secondary school, as much as 72% of East Indian descent did so, 49% of the Mixed group also did.

The table shows that while 30% of students of African descent ended up 'studying only' three years after leaving Form Five, 61% of those of East Indian descent did. The comparative proportion for the Mixed group was 37%. As indicated before, the majority of 'studying only' group were also in university.[8]

Overall, this implies that as far as the traditional professions are concerned, it is very likely that a higher proportion of East Indians will proceed into such professions than Africans. Table 16.1 suggests the extent to which race, social class and especially school type contribute to the perpetuation of the stratification system of this post-colonial society – a phenomenon of inequality quite distant from what was promised soon after political independence.

## TWO-PARENT VS SINGLE-PARENT

Whether a student came from a two-parent or single-parent/guardian background, it makes a significant difference too. Figure 14.4 shows that while 50% of those from a two-parent home went into 'full-time studies' within three years after leaving Form Five, 29% of those from single-parent/guardian homes did so. Further, the vast majority of those from two-parent homes also went to denominational secondary schools.

Table 16.3 highlights that there are differences between the living arrangements of students and those that went on to university education three years after form five. For instance, it shows that of those students who lived with both parents, 65% of them went on to university. This compares to 52% of those students who lived with single parents or other arrangements.

**Table 16.3:** Living Arrangements x University Attendance Three Years After Form Five (%)

| Living Arrangements | UWI | UTT | USC | Foreign | Total |
|---|---|---|---|---|---|
| Both Parents | 48 | 7 | 2 | 8 | 65 |
| Single Parents / Other | 32 | 9 | 4 | 7 | 52 |

## Gender

The data on gender show that while the differences are generally not as dramatic as those for social class, race, school type or parental type, the trend is that females are ahead of the males in 'studying only' and 'going to university' – the upward mobility instruments (Figure 14.7). While 51% of the females were 'studying only,' 42% of males did so three years after leaving Form Five. For 'working only,' the proportions were 35% males and 18% females.

It remains a bit puzzling though, that while 14% of the females remained idle, 'neither studying nor working,' only 7% of the males did so. This 14% group of female 'drifters' may possibly be connected to the rise in female crimes, teenage pregnancy and the cycle of female poverty.

The 1994 Study on School Placement concluded that the education system *was not user-friendly to people of African descent, especially females, nor to the poor, nor to those from non-nuclear families.*[9] That situation has not changed. Like the young, black male, some special policy-action attention should be placed on the young, black female in secondary schools.

## BLACK YOUTH UNDERCLASS

A high proportion of low social class students - 47% - ended up 'not studying or working' or 'working only' (Table 16.1). In fact, as much as 14% were 'neither studying nor working' – a significant revelation of class-driven inequality and, as 'an idle' group, the most vulnerable and high risk of all. Almost all came from the government secondary schools. Notably, these reached up to Form Five. Therefore, we believe, all things put together, the 'idle, drop out' rate will be higher for those low social class students who failed to reach Form Five. This group of drifters very likely form the black, urban youth underclass.

## THE GATE-CRASHERS

The education system cannot appear to remain biased or discriminatory, especially, as the evidence shows, against poor, black males. This apparent neglect will likely turn back and bite the society. Given the organic nature of society, this will be a price to pay. This is the message also emphasized by the cabinet-appointed study entitled 'No Time To Quit: Engaging Youth At Risk.'[10]

That is why the low class 'gate-crashers' and 'escapists' we found from this study, those who forced themselves through, should be doubly celebrated – effort pays off in a  democracy; except that such a struggle will be experienced again by the others coming behind them. The already privileged and powerful are culturally and economically embedded.

The evidence of inequality and inequity, flowing mainly from the government secondary schools, must not be allowed to remain idle. Ameliorative policies need to be put within a social justice, humanitarian philosophy.

Therefore, the duty of educators, policy-makers and the people's representatives is now to make this burden of the affected as light as possible. And if there is competition in the education system, it must be on equal and equitable grounds as far as possible. Social justice and humanitarianism deserve no less.

## WORSE FOR SCHOOL DROP-OUTS

It is important to note that the groups examined in Tables 16.1 and 16.3 have all graduated from Form Five. For those low class persons who left *before* reaching Form Five, we believe that, as a group, their subsequent academic and occupational status would be significantly lower than that of the low social class group that remained up to Form Five. These drop-outs from the government secondary schools, we believe, will likely form part of the criminogenic underclass.

## SCHOOL TYPE, AGAIN

The type of secondary school students attended played a significant part. Over 70% of those who entered 'full-time study' came from denominational secondary schools compared to 31% from the government secondary schools (Table 16.1). The opportunities for secondary school are available, but the quality is conditional on merit from the SEA. So too are university opportunities – by merit.

As secondary school placement data shows, equality of educational opportunity, on the face of it, does not necessarily lead to equality of educational achievement – or occupational status. Even if this is acceptable – everybody cannot end up equal – the humanitarian worry, as our evidence shows, is why do certain social groups consistently have such lower proportions of educational success - from SEA, through secondary school, after leaving secondary school and up to university level?

## EDUCATION AS PASSPORT TO BETTER LIFE. FOR WHOM?

It is almost misleading to youths to advocate education as the 'key passport' out of crime and for better life when the road is so twisted, prejudiced and apparently discriminatory for those who are starting far behind. That is why there is such a serious concern particularly for the young black males in this society. The education system is not used as it should. And this, of course, is related in cyclical fashion, to family life and community deficits.

Moreso, under the heading, 'Equality,' it was the conclusion of the Study on Secondary School Placement:

> When all the pieces are put together, one can say that the system (primary and secondary) is not user friendly to young people of African descent, especially females, nor to the poor, nor to those from non-nuclear families.[11]

We believe from reports on teenage pregnancy, media reports and our interviews with teachers, that that situation has not changed. It is likely to worsen.

## REPRESENTATIVENESS BY RACE, CLASS, SCHOOL TYPE

### Social Class

The percentages in Table 16.1 allow a comparison to be made on the extent – all things being equal – to which race, social class and type of secondary school attended are each under or over-represented in their academic and occupational status three years after Form Five.

**Figure 16.1: Proportion of Persons Who were at University Three Years
After Form Five Compared to their Original Social Class
Proportion in the Sample**

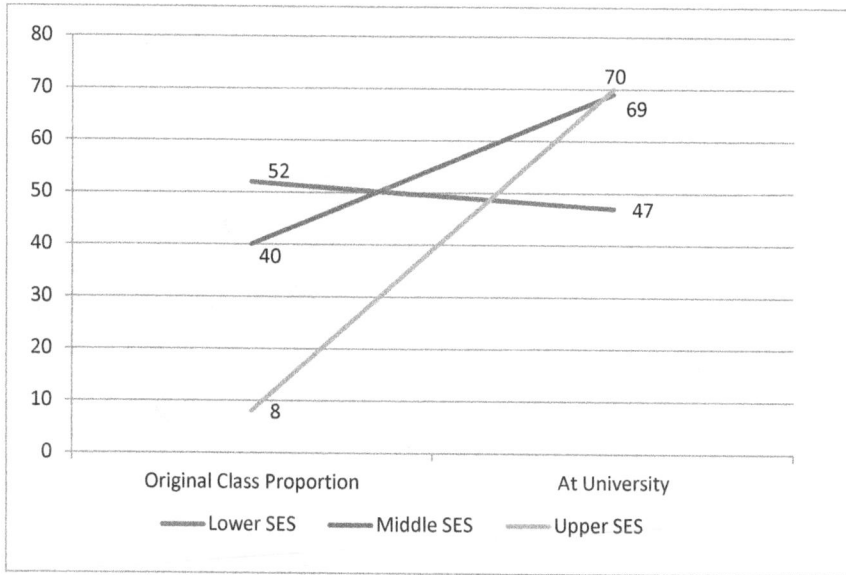

For example, while there may be some satisfaction in seeing 47% of the low social class in university, their proportion in the sample is 52% (a negative difference of 5%). The proportions of middle and upper class in the sample are 40% and 8% respectively, but their proportions in university are 69% and 85% respectively – large positive difference. Figure 16.1 illustrates the proportional inequalities of social class.

Class inequality seems not only to persist, but to be widened in the post-secondary period. It also appears that with free tuition for all – poor and rich together - this inequality gap looks likely to remain so for a very long time.

**Race**

Compared to their original proportion in the sample, Africans are reasonably represented in university attendance. But the equality test is of one of relative mobility. So, as Figure 16.2 illustrates, while the Mixed group is slightly better represented than the Africans, the Indians are by far over-represented compared to both. While the proportion of Indians in the sample was 45%, 72% of them went to university. For Africans, the proportion was 30% in sample and 47% in university, and for the Mixed group, 25% to 49%.[12]

**Figure 16.2:** Proportion of Persons of Different Races Who went to University Compared to their Original Racial Proportion in the Sample (%)

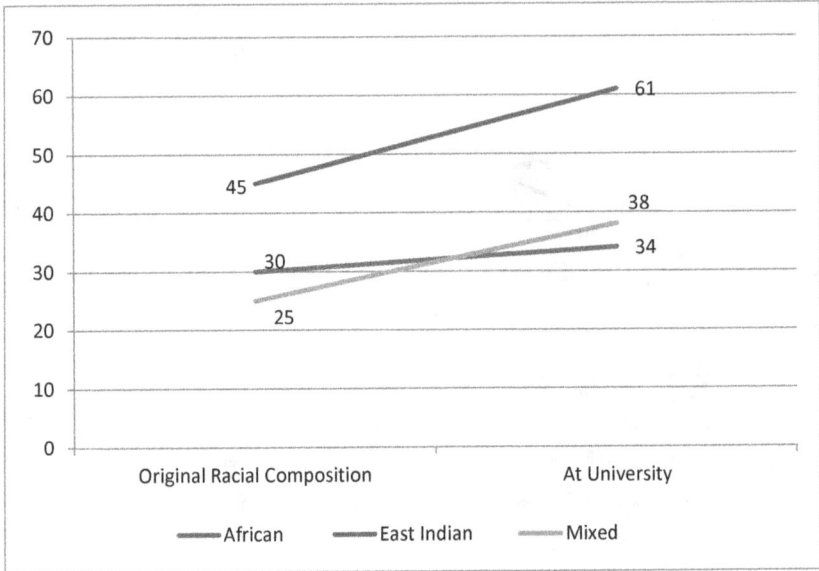

**Figure 16.3:** Proportion of Persons Who went to University Compared to the Type of Secondary School They Originally Attended

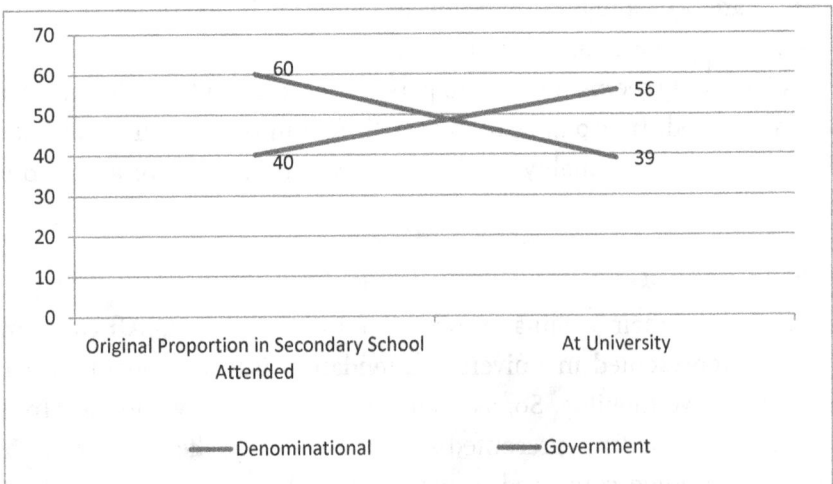

## Type of School

As evidenced in almost all the data presented previously, the type of secondary school attended makes a very big difference. Figure 16.3 shows, for example, that while those in the denominational schools comprised 40% of the sample, the proportion of them who went to university three years after Form Five was as much as 77% – vastly over-represented. For the 60% of those in the government schools, the proportion who went to university was 40% – a measure of under-representation.

# THE MIXED GROUP: A RACIAL ENIGMA

References to freedom, equality and dignity soon after the country gained independence in 1962, pertained almost exclusively to the 'formerly oppressed African slaves and East Indian indentured labourers.' No mention was then made of the products of inter-racial sexual relationships and marriages. These products were known as marginal 'douglas,' almost as a racial aberration, not as a specific group deserving policy attention.

As the late Dr Williams said in 1970:

> Let us proceed to work more positively than ever towards the economic and social upliftment of the Black disadvantaged groups in our society of both African and Asian origin, as the only way to achieve the genuine national integration to which so many of us are dedicated.[13]

### Nothing about 'douglas.'

The Mixed group now stands at 23% of the population with 7.7% of African-Indian mixture and 15.3% described as 'Mixed Others.' While mainly for historical reasons, we have focused on Africans and East Indians (each around 35%) in our equality and equity discourse, 23% is too large to ignore in both research and public policy now. It is high folly to ignore the sentiments and status of this Mixed group in politics now. Quite a few of them contest elections and are in high office too. It is not quite clear on which side, if any, the racial affection or self-identity of the 7.7% douglas generally falls – on Africans or East Indians. If, for example, they identify with either Africans or Indians, then the respective advantages and disadvantages would be accordingly felt.

In terms of equality of opportunity and equity in education, their proportions are sociologically quite important. For example, a higher proportion of them than Africans went into 'full-time studies only' three years after Form Five (37% vs 31%. It was 61% for the Indians.) A similar proportion of Mixed and Africans remained idle, 'not studying or working', as drifters (13% to 14%). See Table 16.1.

While 49% of the Mixed group went into university, 47% of the Africans and 72% Indians did so. Over half of both Mixed and African groups (52% and 57% respectively) went into technical/vocational training. Generally then, compared to the Indians, both Africans and the Mixed group appear disadvantaged in terms of academic and occupational advancement.

As we show concern for the social groups who are being left behind the opportunity and achievement race, it is time to attend to the Mixed population. They should no longer remain as orphans in the analyses on educational opportunity and equity – or even in political debate. As Catholic Archbishop Finbar Ryan said of the Catholics, the Douglas too have a powerful electorate franchise.

## HUMANITARIANISM

When a child is born as a human being, he or she is assumed to be equal to all other children, and entitled to the same privileges and rights that all other children enjoy. It is from here, basically, that the human right philosophy 'all men are born equal' emerges. But the research evidence from this and other studies in education demonstrates that, as life comes on, as the child grows up, this is not so.

Equality of opportunity and equity become sharply dependent on what social class-type of parents this child has, his or her colour, race or religion, what type of school he or she attends and even where this child lives. The education system is supposed to be the major legitimate vehicle for escape. However, some children grow into comfort and prosperity, others into distress and poverty. Education is not a neutral process.

For this latter group of children, the humanitarian violation is that, firstly, all these restraining factors are no fault of the child at all. But the society, the existing hierarchy of power, privilege and status imposes itself so harshly upon this growing child that he or she has to struggle, much more than others, to move up so as to enjoy the same privileges that the 'better-born' child gets.

These youthful 'strugglers,' however, are the politically voiceless, not yet franchised. They are expected to reach the same finishing line at the same time, though they started far behind.

Even so, and accepting that the society is vertically based on ability, effort, merit and scarce resources, our fundamental argument is that, in this post-colonial society, greater policy efforts must be made to improve the psychological and academic status of the racial, social class and gender groups who find themselves consistently left out or behind in the secondary school placement and examinations, and university entry levels. The required remedies will fall within a humanitarian philosophy.

## COMPETITION BY MERIT: ANOTHER VIEW

There is a view different from our own, mostly a merit-driven conservative one, which could claim to be more realistic. That is, with limited places in the preferred secondary schools, there is equal opportunity to write the same entrance examination, and places are awarded on the basis of the marks gained. Those who score high marks deserve to get their preferred places.

Those who didn't score high are responsible for not getting their preferred places – they did not make the effort required. This is the doctrine of individual responsibility which fits well into capitalist thinking, part of which is 'work hard and sacrifice to achieve.' This perspective sees 'limited places' as a static condition, not as the artificial one that it is – a variable.

It also does not consider the cut-off entrance mark as another artificial variable. Both conditions, limited spaces and the cut-off mark, arise mainly because of institutional deficiencies and public policy. The conservatives, however, would fear that moving down the cut-off point may well water down standards.

They see the education system as necessarily competitive, serving the social and economic order, and where many are called but few necessarily chosen. These 'left-overs' deserve to go into technical/ vocational programmes or eventually fall into welfare programmes. Given the persistent qualitative differences between the denominational and government secondary schools, this seems to be the pervasive view in this country. The conservatives will tend to preserve the system. Our arguments, however, are designed to defrost the system and inspire a change.

## FIX THE SCHOOLS AND THE CONCORDAT

As educator Lennox Bernard indicated, the longer it takes to 'fix' the governments schools – primary and secondary – the worse the situation will become for the social groups now systematically left out or far behind. We agree. Of course, the role of parents or guardians is important, but it is for the government to take leadership especially since it has several relevant ministries and social agencies.[14]

As discussed earlier, the Concordat, the 1960 school-control compromise between government and the church, presents a special case. Repeated calls have been made to review or change the Concordat.[15] Change is very difficult because as the evidence has shown, the Concordat church schools are generally the high-performing schools and highly attractive to parents, not necessarily with regard to religious affiliation. The Concordat allows secondary school placement for 80% by ministry placement and 20% discretion by Principals.

The court has ruled – with outstanding questions - that the Concordat is currently embraced by the Constitution and settled practice.[16] The Concordat is also protected with an ethnic solidarity and political clout for which the government shows great appreciation. One government after another has kept its safe distance. In other words, it depends on which government is prepared to take the political risk in this multi-religious society with several marginal constituencies. The Concordat is about education but it is also about the politics of education.

## INEQUALITIES BY DISTRICT AND ZONING

The evidence also revealed significant and consistent inequalities between one educational district and another. Assuming the Concordat is shut down, would there still be a secondary school entrance examination? Even if students are zoned or selected randomly for secondary schools, there will still be some schools that are strongly preferred and others not, the latter category being mostly governments schools.

Places at high-performing schools will still be limited. There is strong public opposition to zoning. One view is that 'zoning will only handcuff bright children in failing communities and reward those who have the money to move to wealthy neighborhoods.'[17] Until the government takes serious, sustained action to make the government schools more attractive to parents and students, changing or removing the Concordat will make little or no difference.

# THE 1993-2003 EDUCATION PLAN

In 1993, the Government National Task Force on Education itself recognised these deficits when it complained that the ministry was 'strong on philosophy and weak on empirical research' for policy action.[18] In fact, that Education Plan should have been adopted, with few changes, by succeeding governments. That 1993–2003 Plan was detailed enough, with enough forward and backward linkages to move into implementation towards the equality and equity challenges. This Education Plan 1993-2003 had already laid a foundation, even though that, too, while recognising the challenges, did not spell out a specific programme for healing the wounds of inequality and inequity. With the 2011 to 2015 Strategic Plan, there is also no evidence that the gaps of inequality and inequity have been closed or will be empirically tackled in any significant way.

What the country has been annually having are media-driven celebrations of the 'first 100 or 200 top places' in the SEA and scholarships, with the Prime Minister and Education Minister shaking hands with the 'winners,' and seeming oblivious to the significant racial and social class inequities left behind each year.

# A STRATEGIC FAILURE: THE 2011-2015 PLAN

The evidence we have examined not only confirms the conclusion from that 1993-2003 Education Plan but points to the unfortunate fact that in spite of such early and repeated warnings over the challenges of inequality and inequity in education, the required action is yet to be seriously taken. Policies and promises of 'quality education' keep being repeated year after year.

In the Ministry's Strategic Plan 2011-2015, little or nothing was said about how the ministry plans to deal with the inequalities found so consistently within ethnicity, social class, residence and family background. No clear strategic direction given, except for superficial attempts to reinvent the wheel and even so, quite incompletely. The other question to be answered is this: How is the society expected to enjoy racial harmony when ethnic inequalities and inequities persistently exist in its education system? When its main engine of socio-economic mobility and equity is defective?

In this respect, the government's 2011-2015 Strategic Plan, approved by cabinet and full of still-born promises, has failed to deal effectively with the No. 1 challenge in the education system, that is, equality of educational opportunity and equity, and setting a precise pathway for improving under-performing government schools.

The Strategic Plan lacks an appropriately configured and derived operational plan directed towards the outstanding challenge of equality of educational opportunity and equity. But then in the Strategic Plan, there is no situational analysis to know where exactly to go, and from where exactly.[19] Educator and Lecturer, David Subran, described the 2010-2015 Strategic Plan as 'a glaring failure' because of the way it was prepared.

## REMOVING THE MASK

Considering that all the relationships identified so far are statistically significant, when they are combined with other evidence, it appears that the public education system has failed terribly in achieving any reasonable amount of equal opportunity and equity among the different races, social class, family types, place of residence and even gender. As the Secondary School Placement Study remarked, proportionality and historical disadvantages are to be taken into account.

Even so, some further inquiry should soon be undertaken to answer the usually controversial question: What contributes today to the significant differences between these two historically deprived groups, Africans and East Indians, in secondary school achievement, university attendance and academic and occupational status, even after leaving secondary school? There is a mask that needs to be removed.

## THE MOBILITY MATRIX

In order to put some of our data into a socio-economic mobility perspective, five categories are created. We use university as the criterion.[20] These pertain to persons three years after they left Form Five.

1. *The Retainers:* Those middle and upper social class persons who held on to their original class position three years after leaving Form Five (77%).

2. *The Skidders:* Those middle and upper class persons who skidded down from their original position (35%).

3. *The Gate-Crashers:* Those low social class persons who moved up from their original class position to a higher class position (47%).

4. *The Drifters*: Those persons from all social classes who neither studied nor worked. The idlers. (7%).[21]

5. *The Stagnants*: Those low social class persons who remained in their original low class position (14%).

## The Drop-Outs

Students who reach Form Five in secondary school are of the 'O' level type or, if going on to 'A' levels, that would be within three years after Form Five. The point is our sample did not drop out of school at Form Three, Four or before, but, presumably filled with some measure of academic ambition and occupational aspirations, were determined to go on to Form Five. Yet, their social class and ethnicity made a difference. It means therefore that the students who dropped out before Form Five would likely be worse off, academically and occupationally, than those who reached and graduated from Form Five. It is likely, also, that the vast majority of such 'drop out' students would have come from the Government Schools. The academic and occupational deficits (by proportion) found for the government school Form Five graduates would therefore be multiplied if a systematic analysis were to be done with such 'drop-out' students.

# UNIVERSITY THE DOMINANT VALUE

The policy thrust towards technical and vocational education as a means of responding to multiple intelligence or varying aptitudes does have a place in the educational system. But, as explained earlier, such a policy and practice clash severely and worryingly with the over-riding and widely-celebrated preference for a university education and the occupational and professional benefits which flow from such education (e.g., elite positions, public respect, professional independence, policy influence, etc.).

At Form One, as earlier indicated, almost 80% of the secondary school students sampled (denominational and government), held university aspirations. As these same students went to Form Three, 75% of them chose university and at Form Five 70% of these same students held on to university aspirations. Less than 5% chose technical/vocational training as their post-secondary option.[22] But having aspirations does not necessarily mean they will be fulfilled, especially when faced with social class and ethnic mediators.

The university ethos, enjoying strong elite validation, is strongly tied to entry into prestige schools. In her 2013 International Youth Day message, the country's former prime minister, lamenting the dangers of youth gangs, again upheld the dominant value of the education system this way: '*We must watch our young men grow. We must be proud of them when they graduate to be doctors, lawyers, teachers, engineers.*'[23]

The SEA and scholarship winners are, with public acclamation, grammar-types with ambitions for the professions. The value domination of grammar type education and the professions persist, a domination which the 1959 Maurice Committee Report and the 1993à2004 National Education Plan frowned upon, and which continues to occupy the society's stratification system most prominently. The early gateway is the prestige school with all the racial, social class, gender and family-background implications.

## PRESTIGE SCHOOLS

As unpalatable as it may sound, the term 'prestige school' remains justifiable – until there is no need to make such discernment. Of course, the labelling consequences especially for the 'non-prestige' schools remain troublesome. But the fact that some schools clearly and consistently show higher academic performance for well-known reasons, cannot be hidden in an open society.

Whatever description we use – whether 'high-performing' schools, 'schools of excellence,' etc., the differentiation and parental preferences will persist. The public will still provide a name. Work must be done to improve the performance standards of the under-performing government secondary schools, making them attractive for enrolment. It is unfair to blame prestige schools for their high performance. Either fix the placement system or fix the under-performing government schools for equitable competition, and with remedies or 'opportunity pluralism' for those who may be left behind.

After all, many of today's prestige schools, driven by the management advantages of the 1960 Concordat, were not all that prestigious at their beginnings. But it is more than this.

It is well known that students with high marks, over 80% of the standardized 100%, get shunted into schools they did not choose, depending on residence, gender, etc. But what makes the students in prestige schools relatively successful? Is it only because of their SEA marks, parents?

University Lecturer and President of a denominational board,[24] Nasser Mustapha, provided a clue:

> At the 'prestige schools' themselves, a culture of high achievement develops through peer and sometimes teacher influence. Through its system of rewards and punishments, there is pressure to achieve, to compete and to conform. There is an established culture which students must internalise. The public preference for these schools at all costs leads to competition and rivalry.'

## COMPETITION

Now, many will say a lot in life is about competition, especially in our highly education conscious society. Accepted, but efforts should still be made to prepare all our children to be able to compete later in life, win or lose. Our view here is that these children are still too young to experience and be traumatized by such inequality and consequent inequity in the education system. Such early trauma, and it is intense trauma from what is annually seen from the SEA results, does prematurely hold many of them back from their full potential as they move into later life. It is an emotional scar, too early and unfairly in life.

This is the reason for the extended discussion on egalitarianism, liberalism, opportunity pluralism, etc. in our earlier chapters. It is for this reason, too, that we discussed the differences and implications between merit, equality of opportunity and equity, to help energise the movement towards helping our socially disadvantaged groups in this post-colonial era.

## TECHNICAL/VOCATIONAL DILEMMA

As desirable as it is, technical/vocational programmes in secondary schools have not met with the success expected. As pointed out, the failure rates are quite high – 76% in one year failing to get a full certificate. Additionally, as also pointed out, less than five percent of Form One and Form Three secondary school students saw technical/vocational training as their desired option.

As pointed out earlier, the government National Task Force of Education, like the IDB study on Education Access and Opportunity, advised the government to provide such programmes *after* secondary school. The major reason being the obvious need to enable students to get a basic education before entering the technical/vocational programmes. All this, though, faces the holy grail barrier – the cultural preference for university.

# THE MASQUERADE OF NUMBERS

It must be noted that the discovery of inequality becomes meaningful only when one thing, person or group is compared with another within some defined criterion. These concepts are based on sociological relativity. That is why the group by group or school by school differences within the examination passes cited earlier are important. It isn't only how many, in total, are brighter than last year's group. Disaggregated data, when published by the ministry, will be usually given for age, regional and sex differences, but usually none for ethnicity, social class or family background differences. How then would we know how large the gaps are, or how much more effort needs to be made to achieve or come close to equality of educational opportunity? Furthermore, the system of education in this country is dual – state and church schools. After all, the public already has a general sense how the social class and ethnic distributions exist. Publication of the distributions may well help inspire the already socially advantaged to help, and also compel even those at the weaker end to tighten up their efforts towards equality of educational opportunity. In this overall context, three policy-related issues arise:

6.  Numbers are important when equality of educational opportunity or equity is considered. But aggregate numbers by themselves tend to mask inequalities. For example, when the minister proudly announced that 'students did better this year than last year' in the SEA or CAPE, or that 'those getting five or more passes increased from 2010 to 2015', this tells nothing about equality or inequality – except possibly, that one group of students are brighter than another group. The sociology of education remains masked. After all, the ministry cannot tell us, as they have told us, that there will be equality of educational opportunity regardless of ethnic, religious, family or gender background and not produce the proportions to establish how far that policy pledge has reached in outcomes.

7.  There is the related issue of biblical repute, that is, to those who have plenty, more will be given, and to those with little, less will be given. The evidence from several sources showed that,

proportionally, more advantage was gained by the smaller group of already advantaged students (middle and upper class), while less advantage was gained by the larger group of already disadvantaged students (lower class). More precisely, as the evidence showed, the student population contained a much larger proportion of low class students than middle and especially upper class students. Yet, lower proportions of these lower class students, compared to middle and upper class students, gained access to prestige schools, to university and into full-time studies. In terms of the sociology of educational inequality and its relation to the social order, the general point here is that the education system, with all its promises, does not seem able to improve the social stratification system to any significant extent. The essential point is the continuity of the inequitable social reinforced by the education system.

8.  The third issue is how the education system treats the socially disadvantaged and academically marginalized. Providing remedial education is of course part of helping to restore educational equity. What happens, unwittingly, is that boasts are made of the large numbers of students so 'remedied' with programme expansion and increases from year to year, and as a demonstration of a 'caring' ministry. However, there should be some evidence that the numbers so 'remedied' are being decreased from year to year and their performance improved. Given the previously cited criticisms of compensatory education, the challenge is how to prevent the proportion of disadvantaged students from growing.

## IDEOLOGIES AND EQUALITY NOT EXACT SCIENCE

There are those who argue that the current education system, even in developed countries, remains captured by an exploitative capitalist economy and stagnant social stratification order. These argue that, for all practical purposes, the merit-driven education system is inextricably and reciprocally tied to the economic structure of the society and as such, schooling largely becomes a matter of training people to serve the competitive economy, even a capitalist one as Trinidad and Tobago's. There are others who emphasise that the deficiencies in the education system - for example inequality of opportunity or social disadvantages - can be healed by compensatory programmes – to restore equity.

Within each ideological position, the debates swirl around three pivotal concepts – equality of educational opportunity, merit and educational equity. This country's educational policies largely operate on the merit premise, that is through examinations, with a set of back-up remedial education programmes.

As the evidence has shown, this merit-based system, while it can claim equality of opportunity in the sense that everyone legitimate can write a common examination, there remain significant imbalances by student ethnicity, social class, family background, gender and place of residence. As our research and the Study of Secondary School Placement[25] indicated, for example, the annual recurrence of such imbalances makes it appear that the students so adversely and consistently affected are inherently intellectually challenged, a situation which has possibilities of unwittingly creating a marginal racial underclass of young people.

That such educational imbalances seem to systematically and disproportionally affect certain specific social groups entering and emerging from the government secondary schools particularly, make it imperative for the government itself to recognize the seriousness and injustice of this inequitable situation, and implement remedies. In other words, the merit principle – between primary and secondary school - leaves behind an unfortunate wastage of human resources. It leaves behind a visible amount of inequalities and social injustice among certain groups of young people.

## TEACHER EXPECTATIONS

As has been indicated earlier, the compounding problem for the working class student in our government schools is the prevailing public stereotype that many government schools, as evidenced by their persistently low academic achievement output, will not lead to high academic achievement. The added danger for students is that the teachers themselves may possess the stereotype such that the desired extra effort required to help working class students overcome their social disadvantages may not be made.

As Carl Braun explained from available research, '*the self-fulfilling prophesy has been coined to imply the tendency for the teacher to create a reality commensurate with his perceptions. Furthermore, the learner, while creating his own reality, shadows the reality forming in the teacher's mind.'*[26] The role of teacher as a 'significant other' in the school does have tremendous influence over the student. In fact, the teacher may well be the only real 'significant other' the working class student has during his school life.

Perhaps, worse yet, parental support for the students in these government schools, as reported by the teachers themselves, is much, much less than required.[27]

## FURTHER ISSUES

Many of the issues within the early debates over equality of educational opportunity in Europe, Britain and the United States still have relevance to the attempts to transform the education system of this country.

Bowles, for example, said:

> The burden of achieving equality of educational opportunity should not, and cannot, be borne by the educational system alone. The achievement of some degree of equality of opportunity depends to a very large degree upon what we do elsewhere in the economy, in the polity, and in the society as a whole.[28]

Agreed. However, given the complex policy challenges facing such conditionalities, if any improvements in equality of educational opportunity and equity are to be undertaken, they will have to be of the more pragmatic and practical kind in this country. Here, it will take too long, if ever at all, to make significant changes in the economy, in the polity and in the society as a whole.

Take the issue of poverty, for example. By demanding that government secondary schools, with their under-performing students, improve their academic performance in a stipulated benchmarked manner, the poverty and family disadvantages of their students will also have to be attended to.

In such circumstances, the first major step required here is to sensitise the population over the extent to which educational inequality and inequity exist in their society. And for them to be energized enough to press for the policy reforms required. The masks have to be removed.

## THE POLITICAL LANDSCAPE

In its 2015 two-page supplement headlined 'Achievements in Education,' the Ministry of Education stated: *'Education is the most effective means by which people can improve themselves, the cycle of poverty can be broken and a nation can achieve the ideal of sustainable development.'*

And once again, the Ministry spoke extensively, among other things, about its successes in school construction, in testing, curriculum reform, teacher training, school feeding, etc., all commendable, but nothing about identifying and closing the existing gaps of educational inequalities in the system. There are identifiable barriers.

Enough researchers, professional institutions and civic commentators - even calypsonians – have pointed out some of these inequalities. The quest for equality of opportunity and especially equity is based not merely on 'having opportunities for all' but from a serious consideration of the extent to which social and economic disadvantages persistently keep back certain groups from effectively participating in these opportunities. To achieve this, some things require a long journey, others a shorter one.

We believe that fixing the under-performing government schools so as to make them more attractive for enrolment is short-term project. A few have already started to improve. More are required if only to ease the current tensions around the Concordat and the relentless chase after prestige schools. The other structural and psychological disadvantages affecting many students should also be tackled as long term projects. In a broad sense, all this is also for the good of the entire community since as has been earlier indicated, the marginalised and demoralized youth go on to damage themselves and the community. They become criminogenic.

## STEPS TO EQUITY

The Organisation for Economic Co-Operation and Development (OECD), noting the extent to which enrolment expansion adversely affects quality and equality in education, explained the various ways in which inequity in education could arise. The OECD stated: '*A fair and inclusive system that make the advantages of education available to all is the most powerful levers to make society more equitable.*'[29]

They then proposed ten steps to improve equity. Among these are: limit early testing and streaming students, provide attractive alternatives in secondary education, identify and provide systematic help to those who fall behind, respond to diversity, direct resources to students with greatest needs, set concrete targets for more equity.[30] While we have already proposed these interventions, the OECD confirmation should help stimulate the action required by the policy makers here.

During the 2015 general elections, education had a place in the manifestos of the two major political parties, People's Partnership (PP) and the PNM. The governing PP manifesto said '*education is available for all who would have it and the quality of education is improving.*'[31] At the tertiary level, there are further promises for skills' training, curriculum diversification and, generally, for school by school improvement.[32]

The PNM manifesto promised, among other things, teacher training, widened access to education, improving tertiary education, developments in the arts, technology, curriculum, sports, research and educational administration.[33] The PNM manifesto added: '*To emphasise the richness of our cultural diversity and eliminate any dissonance that may arise from ethnic. cultural, religious and class differences.*'

These political pledges are quite relevant to the general purpose of this book. In fact, while celebrating the country's ethnic diversity as all such public officials have done, they should also be reminded of the pledge in several government education reports, one of which pledged: '*That every child has an inherent right to an education which will enhance the development of maximum capability regardless of gender, ethnic, economic, social or religious background.*'[34]

This is an equality of educational opportunity and equity pledge. Having seen the data produced so far, to what extent has the country achieved this pledge? Given what the politicians have promised, it seems we have much more work to do.

# ATTACKING INEQUITY: TOWARDS POLICY-MAKING

As explained in Chapters One and Two, given this country's colonial, plantation-type society, education quickly became the treasured passage after political independence in 1962 for restoring dignity and achieving socio-economic mobility among its citizens. As the education system rapidly expanded, there were great expectations. Therefore, in the competition for social status and mobility within the society's ethnic diversity, any evidence of persistent educational inequality or inequity naturally leads to broken expectations, dissatisfaction and even public controversy. These consequences and their causes were presented as the book moved from Chapter Three to Sixteen.

The denominational boards of education and the Concordat attract ethnic controversy especially since, as Chapters Nine to Fourteen show, these denominational schools consistently produce higher academic performance than the government-managed  schools. Students from a working (low) social class background, more precisely, experience persistent inequities in the educational system. Social class gets compounded by race and school type: students of African descent of low social class background from government secondary schools persistently suffer a relatively high degree of educational inequities.

These inequities make the educational system appear as a racially segregated system. As pointed out in Chapter Fifteen, these latter inequities have very serious consequences for the society as a whole, consequences such as youth alienation, delinquency and youth crime. Therefore, this makes it necessary for a quickened policy response to the under-performing government schools. We now take a look at some of the puzzles in educational policy-making here.

The right of the child to education is widely recognised as a moral and more precisely a legal right at least up to primary school. The Declaration of the Rights of the Child states that the child:

> shall be given an education which will...enable him on a basis of equal opportunity to develop his abilities, his individual judgement, and his sense of moral and social responsibility, and to become a member of society. [35]

## Ten Conundrums of Educational Equity

Resting on the U.N Declaration, part of this country's educational philosophy states:

> Every child has an inherent right to an education which will enhance the development of maximum capability regardless of gender, ethnic, economic, social or religious background.[36]

When the ministry's educational philosophy is combined with the U.N. provisions for equal opportunity, eleven fundamental issues arise in the policy pursuit of educational equity. Based on the data and analyses in the preceding Chapters, these can be called *The Ten Conundrums of Educational Equity*:

I.   What does it mean to provide equal educational opportunity for every child regardless of gender, ethnic, economic, social or religious background? To what extent does 'equal educational opportunity' lead to 'inequality of educational achievement' among the different social groups in the society? The literal meaning to this is that no racial, social, economic or gender barrier should stand in the way of a child's getting an education. This is the general position of human rights. But how should we deal with children in a society that is gripped by a hierarchy of social status, privilege and power and where educational opportunities are related to students' race, religion, social class, gender, school type and even place of residence? Consequently, the educational opportunities are present, but not equal, especially in their outcome. The reason for this inequity has empirical foundation. This therefore essentially means that while universally every child should get an education, the provision of equal opportunity for 'every child' offers some leverage to pay special attention to children who persistently suffer from relative disadvantages. Let us select two sociological facts in this ethnically diverse, formerly colonial society: (1) Children from rich, white, upper class families already enjoy educational opportunities. They too have the right to get an education, but they don't really need the protection of this human rights provision. (2) On the other hand, children from poor, black families do not enjoy the same educational opportunities. These need the protection. The gap is significant.

One of the major objectives of the education system in this post-colonial society is to use education for both socio-economic mobility and also a means to close the significant gaps between the rich and the poor. There is a public policy to give free university (tuition) education to all students. Given the objective of the education system and the existing rich-poor gap in the society, should all university students, regardless of socio-economic background, get free tuition? Should those who can afford to pay tuition for higher education be treated the same way as those who cannot afford to pay? Should unequals be treated equally? If so, will inequality be perpetuated? How then will the social stratification system get adjusted? How will the poor get an opportunity to close the status gap if the rich get the same benefits as the poor – benefits which are in addition to the resources they already have?

In terms of providing equal educational opportunity, there are serious qualifications required for public policy action. Consider this: It is said that 'everyone is equal in the eyes of the law.' But it is not an absolute condition in practice. All are not equal before the court. Certain adjustments are made in the name of social justice. For example, legal aid. So too, remedial adjustments have to be made in order for socially disadvantaged students to help them achieve educational equity.

There is a related issue; in the first place, while it sounds fair and legally upright, equal educational opportunity, like its first cousin, meritocracy, could lead to protracted inequality since in a society afflicted by social class, racial and school type inequities, all students will not be starting from the same point of advantage. Unequals will be treated equally from the start so that academic achievement, the finish line, will very likely be one of inequality, leaving the initially disadvantaged, as a group, still relatively disadvantaged. In this competition, without social adjustments, equal educational opportunity and merit may lead to perpetuate inequality among the various ethnic and social class individuals or groups. In the competition, some 'disadvantaged' individuals escape, but others fall in after to fill the space. Social stratification remains unmoved. It therefore depends on how far we wish to insert remedial or compensatory interventions, as a welfare policy, to enable socially disadvantaged students to compete in a 'level playing field' and without being unfair to the already advantaged students. Unless, of course, we accept that in this capitalist-driven system, educational opportunity and promotion by individual merit is a fair method to serve social stratification. And the most effective policy is to improve the under-performing government schools.

2.  When the provision of equal educational opportunity results in significant and persistent inequalities within students' race, social class, gender, school type and religious background, how should public policy respond in a 'free-choice' society? More precisely, how should the government treat with these disadvantaged groups? Before remedial or compensatory interventions are considered, the specific nature of the disadvantages should be examined to see what is possible and desirable through structural adjustment and what is possible through individual or group effort. Merit by examination in an education system has its limitations which can be countered by policy adjustment.

3.  How will redress or compensatory policies for the disadvantaged affect the rights of the already advantaged individuals who share equal opportunity with the disadvantaged? For example, in writing an examination that is common to all. As students move up the educational ladder, opportunities and places become more and more limited, competition increases. In this sense, as the initially disadvantaged gain in competitive advantage, more of the limited places at the top will move from the already advantaged to the new entrants, the formerly disadvantaged. In this way, no rights are violated. However, the already advantaged persist in holding on to their top position and, with apprehensions, stand to lose ground the more the socially disadvantaged rise up.

4.  In comparing one social group to another, when does 'educational inequality' become 'educational inequity' in academic achievement? In the examination-driven education system inequalities are bound to arise. Some will get high marks, others low marks. The ideal condition is when such inequality is randomly distributed among the various social and economic groups from one period to another. Such random distribution will help ensure that consequent opportunities for advancement also have a fair distribution. Inequity

arises when year after year, the same racial, social class or gender groups persistently suffer significant failures and opportunity disadvantages in comparison to other racial, social class or gender groups. When such persistent inequities are consistently ignored by the education system, a charge of discrimination could possibly arise.

5.  How will equality of educational opportunity by merit be reconciled with evidence of educational inequity (educational outcomes) among the different ethnic, economic, or gender groups? The social and psychological assets of the already academically-advantaged do not arise only from the educational system but from a range of other enhancing factors, for example, parental support, personal effort, role models, protective environment, etc. The socially disadvantaged, especially through their low social class status or cultural differences, generally lack these assets. To a significant extent then, such differentiating conditions help make the education system in this multi-racial, post-colonial society an object, a captive, of the values and social structure of the wider society rather than an agent for social change. The widespread practice of occupational selection and promotion by political patronage and 'social contact' also contributes to distortions in the relationship between the education system and socio-economic mobility for all groups in the society.

6.  What are the defined and quantitative criteria used to determine educational inequality and especially educational inequity? In other words, could there be specific benchmarks so as to guide public policy on when educational equality or more critically, educational equity is attained in the educational system? Yes, there should be quantitative criteria especially since such terms are often used so self-servingly and controversially. If, for example, there is a consistent difference of around 25% between one school type and another in the SEA, CAPE or national scholarships, this will be enough to claim educational inequality and provoke policy action. A 5% difference will not matter much,

    Benchmarks on a sliding scale, year to year, should be used to improve school accountability and help reduce the inequities now so widely present in the education system. Such quantitative criteria should be used to assess inequity between students' academic achievement and their race, social class, gender and place of residence. Such criteria should be an integral part of the Ministry's Strategic Plan. In this way, too, the difference between ethnic perceptions and the reality of deprivation will be uncovered, thus soothing some of the controversies over relative deprivation.

7. Given the fact that within each disadvantaged racial, gender, economic, social or religious group, there are individuals who achieve excellence, to what extent will the policy response consider personal effort (e.g., academic diligence) alongside structural constraints (e.g., school type). Personal effort and motivation are critical drivers. The educational reforms required to achieve educational equity and social justice also require individual and family effort and support. This implies that inter-agency collaboration is a key element in such reforms.

8. In such assessment, to what extent will historical deprivations and disadvantages be combined, if at all, with contemporary deprivations and disadvantages? This is a public policy issue which can be unduly clouded depending on whose hands the public policy rests, or more precisely, which ethnic group is in political power. In this society with recognisable ethnic diversity, any attempt to mix historical with contemporary educational deprivations will not only be controversial but very difficult to measure and implement. Not all ethnic groups in the society suffered similar historical deprivations. It is already difficult to apply public policy to present deprivations in the education system.

9. To what extent will the policy response to such educational deprivations and disadvantages emphasise individual rights or group rights, especially when the pursuit of rights for one individual from a particular ethnic or economic group may well ignore the rights of other individuals from that same group? The country's constitution provides rights against discrimination and unequal treatment to *individuals*. (Section 4) A group response by public policy will depend on the number of individuals who suffer persistent discrimination or unequal treatment. Of course, the inequity suffered by one individual student could be used to draw wider attention to other deprived students in his or her same racial, social class or gender group.

10. To what extent will an ameliorative policy for *group rights* (e.g., race, social class, gender) include many from that group who are already well-advantaged? If an edited group response is taken, that is *omitting* the relatively few individuals already advantaged in the disadvantaged group, this few may well charge discrimination, unequal treatment. (Issues of affirmative action or quota system for educational placement or promotion are inferred here but not discussed)

The other half of the country's educational philosophy states:

> *That the educational system of Trinidad and Tobago must endeavour to develop a spiritually, morally, physically, intellectually and emotionally sound individual, that ensures that cultural, ethnic, class and gender needs are appropriately addressed.*

This pledge does bring further power to the concerns over educational inequities cited above. In other words, the pledge to 'develop a spiritually, morally...sound individual' is sharply related, either directly and reciprocally, to the extent to which students enjoy a good measure of educational equity and success. Conversely as earlier explained, the extent to which these spiritual, social, and psychological virtues are not achieved by students, to that extent they will likely drift into deviance and youth crime.

Further, the government's assurance that 'cultural, ethnic, class and gender needs' will be 'appropriately addressed,' is one which speaks directly to the help needed by students who suffer from racial, social class and gender disadvantages in the education system. In other words, the pledge is there. However, based on the evidence uncovered, and now that the mask has been removed, the required policies to help reduce the educational inequities are yet to be effectively implemented. Reforming the examination system, school placement policies and the government schools are top priorities. For these reasons, a selected list of actionable recommendations are made.

## Selected Recommendations

1. Government should immediately establish a twelve-member Task Force to consider the significant quality differences in academic achievement between the government assisted denominational schools (prestige) and the many government under-performing secondary schools, and make actionable recommendations. The

need to make the government secondary schools more attractive to parents and teachers is now a matter of utmost urgency. Through a recent court judgement (2012), the Concordat has now taken on the controversial status of law, as 'settled pratice.'

2.   As a 'work in progress' measure, consider expanding by 100% the number of Form One places in the Secondary Schools now known as high-performing schools.

3.   Given the educational and occupational challenges affecting youth, especially along the East West corridor, the government should, as a matter of urgency, form a partnership between the private sector, labour, Trinidad and Tobago Unified Teachers Association (TTUTA), National Parents Teachers Association and the universities to establish 50 Career Empowerment Centres along the East West Corridor in the first instance. This is the recommendation made in the 2006 Public Services Asociation (PSA)-commissioned study entitled 'African Youths in Danger along the East West Corridor.' In this regard, and driven by the evidence, a special emphasis should be given to the black, urban youth.

4.   Do a baseline study every seven years of secondary school student placement and achievement to assess the pursuit of equality of educational opportunity and attainment in terms of their socio-economic, ethnic, social class and gender background. Repeat the 1994 Secondary School Placement Study, with modifications, to help kickstart the process and the reforms required.

5.   Use the current 'school watch' assessment system in the primary schools to insert the required resources and guidance in order to stimulate significant year by year improvements. The benchmraks should inlude academic performance, student discipline and extra-curriculr activities. This 'school  watch' system should also be applied to the secondary schools. In both cases, this system should be part of an accounting matrix for each school, with continuous improvement objetives. Each school should be assessed within its own criteria and results – annually.

6.   To help specify what is exactly needed and what could be improved in the under-performing government secondary schools, a pilot project of ten (10) such schools can be selected, and staffed with a

select group of appropriately trained teachers. Enrol as a start only Form One students who did not get into their preferred school, and see, with appropriate teaching techniques, etc, the extent to which these students eventually matched up with the success rate (e.g., CSEC, CAPE) of the students who got into their chosen (prestige) schools.

7. The Education Act (No.of 1966) needs urgent revisions especially in the areas of accountability and performance. This should be done in collaboration with a review of the Teaching Service Regulations.

8. The role and functions of the multi-sectoral National Advisory Committee on Education (Education Act, Section 8) should be activated and strengthened.

9. Finalise the Ministry's 20-school pilot project on having single-sex secondary schools and develop all government secondary schools into single-sex schools, comparable with the single-sex schools of the denominational boards.

10. Review the Ministry's examination system and secondary school placement policies. The primary schools especially have become exceedingly examination-congested and besieged by the tyranny of a testocracy.

11. Like the challenges of crime reduction and prevention, such educational reforms are better served with well thought-out, medium and long-term programmes. Overnight solutions become counter-productive.

12. The responsibility of parents and guardians should be further defined and clarified either through the Education Act or by a 'Parent-School Contract.' There have been too many evidence-backed complaints from teachers about the need for improved attention and support by parents in treating with their children's welfare in school.

13. Decentralise the Ministry of Education in relation to the existing seven educational districts in Trinidad while treating the Tobago Division as a special case. This decentralisation will improve accountability and administrative services to teachers. Decentralisation will also achieve more effective  coordination with the relevant agencies in the districts, such as the police, regional corporation, hospitals,

etc. Depoliticise the Ministry's prgramme development and implementation for fuller and more effective success.

14. In view of the growing challenges facing the education system, there is a critical need for the Ministry of Education to establish a skills-appropriate Research and Public Policy Centre (RPPC) to gather and provide reliable and readily available information and policy-directed reports to the Minister, senior ministry staff, other ministers and where practical, to the general public. The present research unit in the Ministry would serve reciprocally as a guide and feeder system to this centre. There is an obvious and growing need for sound, evidence-based policy making.

## NOTES

1. The concepts of equality of educational opportunity, merit and educational equity have been discussed in some detail in Chapters 4, 8 and especially Chapter 9.
2. We used occupation to measure parental status. See Method and Measures in Appendix M.
3. A high correlation was found between 'studying only' and 'entering university.'
4. UWI=University of the West Indies, UTT= University of Trinidad and Tobago, USC= University of the Southern Caribbean.
5. Full-time studies included university. Note: One can also 'work and study' and still attend university as the data indicate.
6. Even so, it is likely that the upper class students will get 'better' jobs that lower class students.The proportion that went into early employment, low class jobs, was quite even across the three racial groups – Africans, Indians and Mixed.
7. See multiple regression statistical test in Chapter 14.
8. ith regard to technical/vocational training, Figure 10 shows that while 57% of Africans went into such training, 37% East Indians did so.
9. Study on the Secondary School Population (Summary Report): Placement Patterns and Practices. UWI: Centre for Ethnic Studies. 1994. p. 28.
10. Cabinet-appointed Committee to examine 'youth at risk,' especially the young black male in certain areas. (2013). The authors emphasized the urgent attention now required for these youths and also for their female counterparts. This, too, is the concern of our study.
11. Ethnic Studies Centre Summary Report on Study of Secondary School Placement. St Augustine: University of the West Indies. 1994. p. 28.

12. Data drawn from tables in Chapter 14, as well as from study entitled 'Project Safeguard: Tracing Youths 2001-2010, Post-Secondary Experiences', Report submitted to Ministry of Education. July 2010.pp. 38, 84.
13. Address on Revolution and Dignity. March 23, 1970.
14. For example, the Ministry of the People and Social Development, Ministry of Youth, Gender, etc. All this apart from the Ministry of Education's outreach programmes and the schools' Parent-Teachers Associations.
15. Among such calls have been the Trinidad and Tobago Unified Teachers Association (TTUTA), many educational commentators and letters to the editor. These and more have also called to stop the SEA.
16. Jagessar vs Teaching Service Commission.
17. Evron Legall, *Newsday*. July 16, p. 19.
18. National Task Force on Education. Education Policy Paper 1993-2003. p. 29.
19. *Express*. February 17, 2015. p. 15.
20. University, as the highest educational factor, holds the potential for middle and upper class status. Of course, others could get into family business, etc. Both middle and upper class are combined for this analysis.
21. This is the average for the three groups. Low social class alone, however, had 14%, the other two had 3% and 5% respectively.
22. 'Tracing Youths 2001–2010: Project Safeguard', Ministry of Education. No. 2. 2010.
23. Mrs. Kamla Persad-Bissessar, S.C., *Guardian*. August 13, 2013. p. A8.
24. Trinidad Muslim League.
25. Ethnic Centre Report on Secondary School Placement. 1994.
26. C. Braun, 'Teacher Expectation: Sociopsychological Dynamics', *Review of Educational Research*. Spring, 1976.46, (2).pp. 185–213
27. From interviews and surveys with 1100 teachers from 20 'high risk' Secondary Schools. R. Deosaran, 'Voices of the Teachers', 2005. Study commissioned by Ministry of Education. 2005. Two reports submitted to Ministry. Over 90% expressed great dissatisfaction over parental interest and support regarding their children's academic work and discipline.
28. S. Bowles, 'Towards Equality of Educational Opportunity', in *Harvard Educational Review*: Special Issue on Equal Educational Opportunity. 1968. 38 (1). p. 95.
29. OECD Policy Brief. January 2008.
30. Ibid. pp. 5-7.
31. Manifesto. 2015. pp. 35–37.

32. PP manifesto. 2015. pp.47–52.
33. PNM manifesto. 2015. p. 14.
34. National Task Force, Education Policy Paper 1993–2003. p.xvii.
35. United Nations/UNICEF Declaration of the Rights of the Child, Principle Seven. This provision is further founded in the UN Declaration of Human Rights, e.g. Article 26: (1) Everyone has the right to education... Elementary education shall be compulsory. Technical and professional education shall be generally available and higher education shall be equally accessible to all on the basis of merit. (2) Education shall be directed to the full development of the human personality and to the strengthening of respect for human rights and fundamental freedoms. (3) Parents have a prior right to choose the kind of education that shall be given to their children. For a useful  discussion on the role and effects on human rights in developing  countries, see, e.g. Z. Arat, *Democracy and human rights in developing countries*, London: Lynne Rienner Publishers, 1991
36. Ministry of Education National Task Force on Education 1993–2003.

# Appendices

## Appendix A

### The Concordat, 1960

The Concordat of 1960

**THE CONCORDAT OF 1960**
**Assurances for the Preservation and Character of Denominational Schools**

*As approved by Cabinet*

The Minister of Education and Culture wishes to clarify for general information some of the proposals on Education with reference to the re-organization of Education so far as those proposals affect the Denominational Boards of Management, the Governing Bodies and Principals of Assisted Secondary Schools.

1. In relation to property, the ownership and right of direct control and management of all denominational primary and secondary schools will be assured to the denominations in whatever modifications of the existing system that may subsequently be introduced in the New Education Ordinance, and all existing rights, so far as property is concerned, will be respected.

2. In denominational schools, no books or apparatus to which the denominational authority formally objects, will be introduced or imposed.

3. In denominational schools (unless the Denomination concerned otherwise gives its consent) the religion of the particular denomination which owns the school will be taught exclusively and by teachers professing to belong to that Denomination. In Government Schools all recognized religious denominations will have access through their accredited representatives during the times specified in the time-table for the teaching of Religion to the pupils belonging to their faith. Pupils attending the schools of a denomination not of their own faith will not be compelled to take part in the religious exercises or lessons of that denomination.

4. The right of appointment, retention, promotion, transfer and dismissal of teachers in Primary Schools will rest with the Public Service Commission. A teacher shall not be appointed to a school if the denominational board objects to such an appointment on moral or religious grounds. Similarly, if a teacher be found unsatisfactory on these very grounds, moral or religious, the denominational authority shall have the right to request his removal to another school after due investigation. For these reasons it is proposed (provided the legal and constitutional arrangements allow) "that vacancies as they occur in all schools should be advertised and applications submitted in the first instance to the respective Board of management which will examine them and forward them all, with their recommendations, to the Public Service Commission for final action."

**SECONDARY SCHOOLS**
5. The existing relationship between Government and the Governing Bodies and teachers in Assisted Secondary Schools will remain subject however, to negotiated changes inevitable with the introduction of Free Secondary Education and to a system of inspection of these schools by

persons authorized to do so by the Ministry of Education and Culture. The Governing Bodies of these schools will continue to be responsible for the administration of these schools and for their maintenance, repair and furnishing. Those schools will continue to qualify for Government Aid. The Principals of Assisted Secondary Schools will make available a minimum of 80 per centum of the First Form entry places to those who, by passing the test, qualify on the results of the Common Entrance Examination for free secondary education. The Principals will be represented on the panel of examiners to be set up to administer the test. The Principals will be free to allocate up to 20 per centum, the remaining places as they see fit provided normally that the pass list of the Common Entrance Examination serves to provide the pupils. Entry above the First Form will be under the control of the Ministry of Education and Culture and will require the approval of the Minister.

6. Where the need arises for disciplinary reasons or unsatisfactory progress to remove a pupil from the school, the right to request such removal will remain with the Principal who may for the same reasons suspend a pupil pending investigation. Authority to expel a pupil is vested solely in the Cabinet. For disciplinary reasons the same principle will apply to Primary Schools.

7. All new Central Schools may be established only by Government for the simple reason that these schools are to be fed from the Primary Schools of all Denominations, as well as Government Schools, which may be in the area served by the Central School. Where, however, the need arises for converting an existing denominational school into a secondary school, the denominational character of that school will be allowed to remain.

8. The selection of teachers for training at the teachers' college is to remain solely with the Ministry of Education and Culture. Selection of teachers for training in the existing denominational training colleges may be made by the Denominational Boards, but such selection must be approved by the Ministry of Education and Culture.

9. It is the desire of the Government that all teachers be trained at the teachers' college under Government supervision and administration. Government will however respect the rights of the existing training colleges conducted by the denominations; but no expansion of those facilities will be allowed without the expressed permission of Government.

**Signed by Hon. J.S. Donaldson,**
**Minister of Education & Culture,**
**on behalf of Cabinet on 22 December 1960,**
**and published on 25 December, 1960**

# Appendix B

SENATE OF THE REPUBLIC OF TRINIDAD AND TOBAGO
NOTICE OF MOTIONS PAPER 1988 SESSION

The undermentioned Motion which has been accepted by the President and entered in the Order Book is hereby forwarded for the attention of the Minister concerned and for the general information of all Members

| No. Of Motion | Date Received | Date Released | Person giving Notice of Motion | Subject | Date Motio Qualifies fc Order Pap |
|---|---|---|---|---|---|
| 2 | 26.2.88 | 29.2.88 | Senator Dr. Ramesh Deosaran | Whereas a major goal of our educational system is equality of educational opportunity as a means towards effective political independence.<br><br>Whereas there has so far been no published comprehensive study of the extent to which such goal has been attained within the context of our scare financial resources.<br><br>Whereas there is now a need to develop basic measures of equality of educational opportunity so as to assist effective educational and manpower planning.<br><br>Whereas the educational system has undergone extensive physical expansion since 1975 but without any systematic evaluation of the quality of education.<br><br>And whereas there is now a specific need to examine the degree to which our educational system has helped close the gap between the economically disadvantaged and the economically advantaged.<br><br>Be it resolved that the Government undertake a nationwide study of all schools in 1988, in the first instance, of<br><br>1. Common entrance passes and the consequent allocation of places among the different secondary schools.<br>2. The results of the respective national examinations in secondary schools.<br>3. The student intake (Year One) at the University of the West Indies, St. Augustine,<br><br>using as its major student background variables<br><br>2/... | 10.3.88 |

# Appendix B (continued)

-2-

| No. Of Motion | Date Received | Date Released | Person giving Notice of Motion | Subject | Date Moti Qualifies Order Pa |
|---|---|---|---|---|---|
| 2 (cont'd) | | | | a. Social class status (e.g. as obtained from parental or guardian occupation. | |
| | | | | b. Family type, for example, | |
| | | | | 1. Living with mother and father | |
| | | | | 2. Living with only mother | |
| | | | | 3. Living with only father | |
| | | | | 4. Living with neither mother nor father | |
| | | | | 5. Living with guardian | |
| | | | | c. Sex | |
| | | | | d. Student resident (district) and | |
| | | | | e. Religion | |
| | | | | With a view to taking early and systematic steps to help ensure the effective attainment of equal educational opportunity. | |

29th February, 1988.

N. Cox
Ag. Clerk of the Senate

# Appendix C

EXPRESS
PG. 39
19·11·11

## SERVICE COMMISSIONS DEPARTMENT
Cipriani Plaza
52-58 Woodford Street, Newtown, P.O.S.
Tel: 623-2991-6 / Fax 623-5972

# PRESS RELEASE

The Teaching Service Commission wishes to issue the following statement on the impasse at the Tunapuna Hindu Primary School.

The TSC is the independent body with the power to appoint, transfer and discipline members of the Teaching Service. To date, no allegations of misconduct have been made against the Principal of the Tunapuna Hindu School by the Ministry of Education which will require the suspension from duties of the Principal.

At its meeting of 13th July, 2011, the Commission noted the contents of a letter dated 17th June, 2011 from the Principal of the School, copied to the School Supervisor, wherein she informed of problems being experienced by her at the School and requested a transfer to a Government Primary School.

The Commission acknowledged that the issue was not properly before it, having not come via the Permanent Secretary, Ministry of Education, but in an effort to avert a potentially volatile situation when the School re-opened, it took the initiative to facilitate an informal intervention while referring the matter to the Permanent Secretary for investigation.

In this regard, the Commission held separate discussions with the School Supervisors, the Principal and Mr Satnarayan Maharaj, Secretary, SDMS Education Board of Management.

Subsequently, the Commission received correspondence from Mr. Satnarayan Maharaj requesting that the Principal be transferred to a Government Primary School. The Commission in keeping with Regulation 137, asked Mr. Maharaj to give specific reasons for the request for a transfer in respect of the Principal. The Commission submitted all correspondence on the issue to the Permanent Secretary, Ministry of Education for investigation into the matter. The Commission further directed that while the investigation was ongoing, that the Principal should carry out her duties at the School.

On November 18th, 2011, the Teaching Service Commission received an unsigned report from the Permanent Secretary, Ministry of Education, which indicated that investigations were inconclusive and ongoing. The Commission therefore again directed the Ministry of Education to take steps to ensure that the Principal discharge her duties at the School.

**Teaching Service Commission**
November 18th, 2011

# Appendix D

Performance of SEA Students scoring in the 90% and Above, 60% and Above and 50% and Above Bands by School

| Denomination | Number who wrote | Above 90% | | Above 60% | | Above 50% | |
|---|---|---|---|---|---|---|---|
| | | No. | % | No. | % | No. | % |
| Private School | 1320 | 157 | 11.9 | 1058 | 80.2 | 1140 | 86 |
| Private Candidate | 152 | 4 | 2.6 | 81 | 53.3 | 95 | 63 |
| ASJA | 334 | 13 | 3.9 | 254 | 76.0 | 285 | 85 |
| Vedic | 342 | 27 | 7.9 | 257 | 75.1 | 287 | 84 |
| Baptist | 122 | | .0 | 49 | 40.2 | 73 | 60 |
| Anglican | 1697 | 22 | 1.3 | 724 | 42.7 | 987 | 58 |
| Government | 4741 | 139 | 2.9 | 2164 | 45.6 | 2888 | 61 |
| KPA | 67 | 5 | 7.5 | 35 | 52.2 | 44 | 66 |
| Methodist | 231 | | .0 | 92 | 39.8 | 146 | 63 |
| Moravian | 33 | | .0 | 10 | 30.3 | 20 | 61 |
| Presbyterian | 2421 | 180 | 7.4 | 1658 | 68.5 | 1965 | 81 |
| Roman Catholic | 3866 | 98 | 2.5 | 2078 | 53.8 | 2677 | 69 |
| SDMS (Hindu ) | 1470 | 102 | 6.9 | 1049 | 71.4 | 1236 | 84 |
| SDA | 182 | 2 | 1.1 | 92 | 50.5 | 121 | 66 |
| TIA | 117 | 3 | 2.6 | 77 | 65.8 | 90 | 77 |
| TML | 166 | 34 | 20.5 | 138 | 83.1 | 148 | 89 |
| AME | 19 | | .0 | 10 | 52.6 | 14 | 74 |
| Total | 17280 | 786 | 4.5 | 9826 | 56.9 | 12216 | 70.69 |

*Ministry of Education, SEA Report 2011.*

# Appendix E

Mean SEA Scores x School Type (2011)

| Denomination | Mean/Standard Dev./ No. | Mathematics (100) | Language Arts (100) | Creative Writing (20) |
|---|---|---|---|---|
| | N | 33 | 33 | 33 |
| Presbyterian | Mean | 74.1 | 62.9 | 11.4 |
| | Std. Deviation | 23.4 | 19.5 | 4.0 |
| | N | 2421 | 2421 | 2421 |
| Private Candidates | Mean | 59.4 | 56.9 | 9.5 |
| | Std. Deviation | 29.9 | 23.7 | 3.9 |
| | N | 152 | 152 | 152 |
| Private School | Mean | 79.6 | 70.7 | 12.6 |
| | Std. Deviation | 21.8 | 17.4 | 3.9 |
| | N | 1320 | 1320 | 1320 |
| Roman Catholic | Mean | 65.0 | 57.0 | 10.4 |
| | Std. Deviation | 25.3 | 20.0 | 3.8 |
| | N | 3866 | 3866 | 3866 |
| SDA | Mean | 61.1 | 55.0 | 10.0 |
| | Std. Deviation | 26.5 | 21.2 | 3.5 |
| | N | 182 | 182 | 182 |
| SDMS | Mean | 77.2 | 62.9 | 117 |
| | Std. Deviation | 21.2 | 18.5 | 3.9 |
| | N | 1470 | 1470 | 1470 |
| TIA | Mean | 71.3 | 58.8 | 11.3 |
| | Std. Deviation | 24.8 | 20.1 | 3.4 |
| | N | 117 | 117 | 117 |
| TML | Mean | 83.1 | 73.0 | 13.8 |
| | Std. Deviation | 22.3 | 17.4 | 3.9 |
| | N | 166 | 166 | 166 |
| National | Mean | 67.1 | 58.1 | 10.5 |
| | Std. Deviation | 25.9 | 20.7 | 4.0 |
| | N | 17280 | 17280 | 17280 |

# Appendix F

Distribution of SEA Students Placed by School Type in Secondary Schools for the Period 2008–2014 (Ministry of Education, SEA Report, 2014)

| Type of Institution | 2014 | 2013 | 2012 | 2011 | 2010 | 2009 | 2008 |
|---|---|---|---|---|---|---|---|
| Seven & Five – year (Gov't and Gov't Assisted) | 17059 (93.5%) | 16797 (93.2%) | 16684 (95.8%) | 16042 (92.8%) | 15964 (94.6%) | 16109 (95.0%) | 16035 (89.8%) |
| Private | 598 (3.3%) | 548 (3%) | 476 (2.7%) | 483 (2.85%) | 506 (3.0%) | 364 (2.1%) | 580 (3.2%) |
| Pre-vocational (Servol centres) | 415 (2.2%) | 262 (1.5%) | 332 (1.9%) | 347 (2.0%) | 399 (2.4%) | 491 (2.8%) | 109 (0.6%) |
| Total Placed | 18072 (99.1%) | 17607 (97.7%) | 17492 (97.9%) | 16872 (97.6%) | 16867 (97.7%) | 16964 (96.3%) | 16964 (93.6%) |
| Primary School (Students repeating SEA) | 167 (0.9%) | 417 (2.3%) | 371 (2.1%) | 408 (2.4%) | 401 (2.3%) | 651 (3.7%) | 891 (6.4%) |
| TOTAL | 18239 | 18014 | 17863 | 17280 | 17270 | 17615 | 17855 |

# Appendix G

| Score | 2014 | 2013 | 2012 | 2011 | 2010 | 2009 |
|---|---|---|---|---|---|---|
| Above 90% | 8.9% (1620) | 3.6% (645) | 4.8% (860) | 4.5% (786) | 5.9% (1027) | 6.3% (1111) |
| Above 60% | 65.2% (11898) | 56.3% (10125) | 57.1% (10195) | 56.9% (9826) | 54.0% (9319) | 54.4% (9587) |
| Above 50% | 78.7% (14360) | 71.7% (12793) | 71.2% (12723) | 70.7% (12216) | 67.5% (11661) | 68.0% (11972) |
| 30% or below | 4.4% (795) | 8.9% (1602) | 9.1% (1630) | 9.9% (1718) | 11.6% (2001) | 11.2% (1973) |

# Appendix H:

Distribution of Number and Percentage of Students scoring Above the Mean during the period 2008 to 2014

| Subject | % and No. of Students Scoring Above the Mean | | | | | | |
|---|---|---|---|---|---|---|---|
| | 2014 | 2013 | 2012 | 2011 | 2010 | 2009 | 2008 |
| CAC- (Drama, Science, CCE) | 59.5% (10851) | | | | | | |
| CAC- Creative Writing | 52.9% (9643) | 50.3% (9068) | | | | | |
| Creative Writing | | | 53.9% (9628) | 48.2% (8332) | 50.7% (8749) | 53.6% (9434) | 51.3% (8733) |
| Language Arts | 57.8% (10543) | 55.6% (10021) | 54.5% (9729) | 54.7% (9462) | 56.2% (9710) | 57.3% (9930) | 53.1% (9040) |
| Mathematics | 54.6% (9963) | 56.1% (10116) | 56.2% (10055) | 57.8% (9996) | 55.3% (9554) | 55.7% (9628) | 54.7% (9312) |

Ministry of Education, SEA Report, 2014.

# Appendix I:

Percentage of Male and Female Students Scoring in the 30% and Below Band

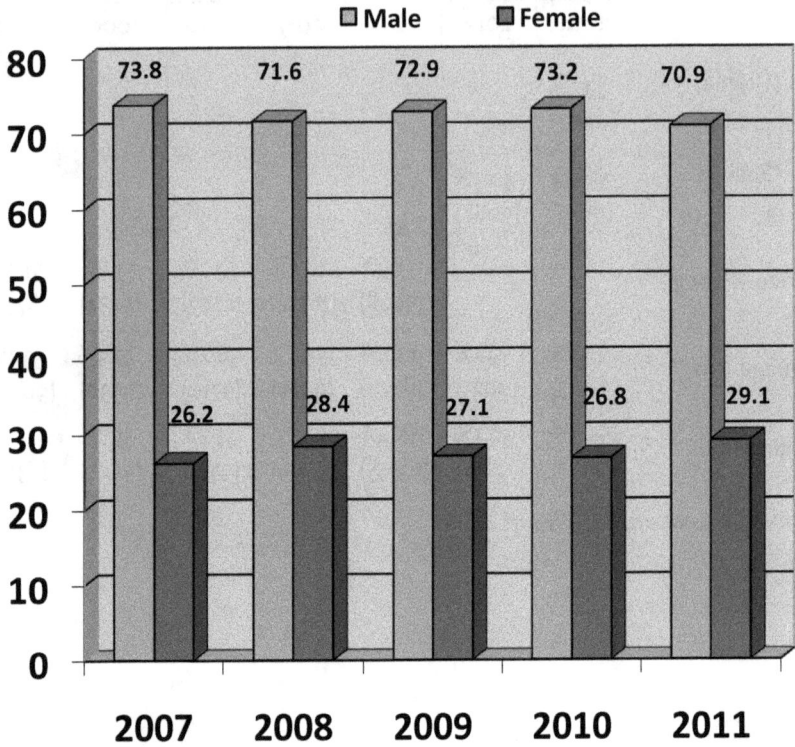

# Appendix J

This Table shows the number and percentage of students getting between 0 and 8 passes by school type. Sixty-seven percent, 67% (10,278) of the students registered for the NCSE Examination were in Government Secondary Schools. Twenty-six percent, 26% (2644) of the students in Government Secondary Schools obtained five or more passes as compared to 60% (2,762) in Denominational and 19% in Private Schools. The percentage of students in Government Schools (32%) and private Schools (38%) who were unsuccessful in any subject was higher in the Denominational Schools (9%). The percentage and number of students passing between 0 and eight subjects by school type is shown below.

**Number and Percentage of NCSE Students passing 0–8 subjects by School Type for 2011**

| School Type | Entered | 0 Passes | 1 Pass | 2 Passes | 3 Passes | 4 Passes | 5 Passes | 6 Passes | 7 Passes | 8 Passes |
|---|---|---|---|---|---|---|---|---|---|---|
| Government | 10278 | 3263 | 1563 | 1100 | 915 | 793 | 749 | 725 | 825 | 345 |
| | | 32% | 15% | 11% | 9% | 7% | 8% | 7% | 8% | 3% |
| Denominational | 4575 | 429 | 276 | 277 | 352 | 479 | 920 | 748 | 983 | 111 |
| | | 9% | 6% | 6% | 8% | 11% | 20% | 16% | 22% | 2% |
| Private | 422 | 160 | 62 | 39 | 40 | 42 | 31 | 28 | 20 | 0 |
| | | 38% | 15% | 9% | 9% | 10% | 8% | 6% | 5% | 0% |
| All Schools | 15275 | 3852 | 1901 | 1416 | 1307 | 1314 | 1700 | 1501 | 1828 | 456 |
| | | 25% | 13% | 9% | 8% | 9% | 11% | 10% | 12% | 3% |

*Ministry of Education NCSE Report, 2011. (Administrative Report 2010-2011)*

# Appendix K:

Summary of Secondary Schools (Govt X Denominational)

| Denominational Boards | Caroni | North Eastern | Port of Spain | South Eastern | St. George East | St. Patrick | Victoria | Total |
|---|---|---|---|---|---|---|---|---|
| Anglican | | | 2 | 1 | | 1 | | 4 |
| ASJA | 2 | | | 1 | 1 | | 2 | 6 |
| Baptist | | | | | | | | 1 |
| Pentecostal | 1 | | | | | | | 1 |
| Presbyterian | | | | | 2 | 1 | 2 | 5 |
| Roman Catholic | 2 | 2 | 6 | | 1 | 2 | 3 | 16 |
| SDMA | 2 | | | | 1 | 1 | 1 | 5 |
| SWAHA | | 1 | | | | | | 1 |
| | | | | | | | | |
| Government | 13 | 12 | 16 | 13 | 12 | 9 | 11 | 86 |
| | | | | | | | | |
| Total | 20 | 15 | 24 | 16 | 17 | 14 | 19 | 125 |

# Appendix L

## Summary of Private, Denominational and Government Primary Schools

| Denominational Boards | Caroni | North Eastern | Port of Spain | South Eastern | St. George East | St. Patrick | Victoria | Total |
|---|---|---|---|---|---|---|---|---|
| African Methodist Episcopal | | | 1 | | | | | 1 |
| Anglican | 2 | 3 | 11 | 8 | 6 | 7 | 10 | 47 |
| Baptist Fundamental | | | 1 | | | | | 1 |
| Baptist Union | | | | 3 | | | | 3 |
| Baptist Shouter | | | | | 1 | | | 1 |
| Hindu APS | 2 | | | 1 | 2 | 2 | 2 | 9 |
| Hindu KPA | 1 | | | | | 1 | | 2 |
| Hindu SDMS | 12 | 2 | | 2 | 10 | 8 | 9 | 43 |
| Methodist | | | 1 | 1 | | | 1 | 3 |
| Moravian | | 1 | 1 | | | | | 2 |
| Muslim ASJA | 2 | | | 2 | | 1 | 2 | 7 |
| Muslim TIA | 1 | | | | 3 | | 1 | 5 |
| Muslim TML | | | | 1 | 1 | | 1 | 3 |
| Presbyterian | 16 | 9 | 1 | 12 | 7 | 8 | 19 | 72 |
| Roman Catholic | 12 | 13 | 29 | 12 | 28 | 12 | 9 | 115 |
| Seventh Day Adventist | | 2 | | | 2 | | 1 | 5 |
| Roman Catholic/ Government | | 1 | | | | | | 1 |
| Government | 19 | 11 | 24 | 7 | 29 | 17 | 17 | 124 |
| Special Schools | *1 | | 4 | | 2 | 1 | 3 | 11 |
| Private Schools | 4 | 1 | 25 | 2 | 24 | 4 | 7 | 67 |
| Total | 72 | 43 | 98 | 51 | 115 | 61 | 82 | 522 |

*The Interdisciplinary Child Development Centre at Caroni Education District is Government Special School. It is included as one of the Government Special Primary Schools although the pupils who attend are between the ages of three (3) and five (5) years.

# APPENDIX M

## Method and Measures

This 'post-secondary destination' study of 1293 Form Five students in 2010 was derived from a ten-year tracer study which began in 2001 with 2760 Form One students from 20 secondary schools.[1] The tracer study aimed to examine the changes in a range of students' social, psychological and behavioural characteristics (academic aspirations, civic attitudes, locus of control, violence and delinquency, etc) as these same students moved from Form One through Form Three up to Form Five. The Form Ones were randomly chosen in each school.[2] The detailed results on these measures as students moved from Form One, through Form Three up to Form Five are published in the text, Crime, Delinquency and Justice.[3]

The sample of Form Five students used for this preliminary 'post-secondary destination' study was substantially representative of the original tracer study sample in terms of social class background, race and gender. This implies that attrition (via migration, transfer, drop-outs etc) within each factor was largely random, thus making the Form Five sample viable.[4]

**Students' social class** background was measured in terms of their household head occupation.[5] **Parental structure** was measured in terms of students living with both-parents, mother/father only, guardian, step-mother/father, aunt/uncle, others.[6]

These 'post-secondary' students left Form Five in 2005. Data was collected three years after. The summary tracer study report was written up in 2009, with eighteen separate reports subsequently written up in 2010- and submitted to the Ministry of Education. Given the lack of tracer study data in this country or the region for that matter, and the challenges of attrition, this study is exploratory, setting a data-base for further work.

Given the research findings and widespread public concerns over the differences in student performance and behaviour between the various types of secondary schools in the country, it was necessary to get schools, at that time, from the six secondary **school types** to participate in this study. Since this study began, the Government changed the category-names of many of its secondary schools.

Hence, in order to retain relevance of the data, the 20 secondary schools were condensed into three types: Government Denominational Assisted – 7, Government College/Secondary- 4 and 'Govt. Schools' – 9 (i.e.

Composite, Comprehensive, etc.) These schools, spread across the country, were randomly selected from their respective types in co-operation with the Ministry of Education.[7] Ranking: 1. Denominational; 2. Govt College/ Secondary; 3. Govt. Schools.

Each student was given an ID which was also listed on their questionnaires. No names or addresses were written on their questionnaires. The questionnaire itself contained a list of social and demographic data. (e.g. gender, parental occupational, school type, race, religion) The interviewers then verbally got students' names, phone numbers and addresses and stored them in a separate list of IDs for subsequent tracing. The students' completed questionnaires were subsequently matched with the IDs from the tracer study on file. The procedure was applied to the students by ten trained interviewers across the 20 schools. Given attrition for various reasons (e.g. migration, school transfer, drop-out, etc) the study got 1,293 students in Form Five from the original 2760 measured in Form One.[8] The representative nature of the tracer sample compared to the original sample is noted.

Calling their homes three years after they graduated from Form Five provided some difficulty in applying the post-secondary interview (by telephone), for example, families relocated, graduates migrated, etc. Through such attrition, we obtained a final number of 812 completed interviews, that is, three years after the students left Form Five - 63% of the 1293 Form Five sample. Social and demographic background were then obtained.

For these post-secondary interviews – three years after secondary school - persons were contacted and asked about their employment and educational status, that is, where they were working (part or full-time), what type of job they were doing, where they were studying, what type of studies (part or full-time) they were undertaking. Their answers were matched with their social, demographic and school type data on the files..

The data were analysed in two major ways. The frequency percentages were obtained for each measured group (e.g. social class, sex, race, school type, parental type) and then cross-tabulated with their educational or occupational status. This was done in order to provide a quick overview of the trends regarding what students did three years after leaving Form Five, and how this post-secondary action was related to their social and demographic background. The data were also analysed with Pearson's correlation, the Chi-Square and Multiple Regression tests for significance. ($p < .05$) In all cases, the statistical tests were significant at $p < .05$, some at $p < .01$.

## Limitations

1.  Tracer (longtitudinal) studies are usually affected by attrition. That is, persons migrating, moving residence etc, thus reducing the initial sample as the study moves forward. The study was so affected - the difficulty in finding all students who left Form Five three years before. However, the fact that the initial sample of 2760 *(drawn from randomly selected Form Ones)* and the later Form Five tracer sample of 1293 shared similar proportions in their respective social and demographic distributions helped make the tracer sample reasonably representative. In any case, while a larger sample may be desirable and random sampling be done at the post-secondary stage, we believe that the results will be similar or more significant compared to the trends discovered in our study.

2.  This tracer study did not measure students' actual academic ability but rested on the reasonable assumption that generally those who gained very high marks at the secondary school entrance examination would have entered the Government Assisted Denominational Schools (prestige) and the others with relatively lower scores would have gone to the Government Secondary and other Government schools. Furthermore, those students who dropped out before reaching Form Five would have likely ended up with relatively lower academic and occupational status than those who reached up to Form Five in our sample. (This does not include those who transferred or migrated to another Secondary school, etc.

3.  While we made a qualitative distinction between grammar-type and university education compared to technical/vocational training, the following must be noted: Slight improvements were noticed with very few Government Schools, for example, by gaining very few additional academic-type scholarships. Scholarships for professional studies gain wide officially-driven media attention. Such attention is not given as much to graduates of technical and vocational education. Of course, while having a degree makes a

difference, the line between technical and vocational education and university education can be blurred. For example, draughting, surveying,etc.

4. It is also important to note that in counting the persons three years after leaving Form Five, some of them might still have been writing the A levels for university entry. This possibility did not disturb the trends cited in the Figures earlier presented.

## NOTES

1.  For reasons of unavailability, four (Govt) of the original 24 schools were omitted.Denominational Schools = 41% of sample. Govt Secondary/ College = 18%, Government Composite, Comprehensive, etc = 38%. The three private schools (3%) used for the original Tracer Study were omitted.This 'post-secondary study' is part of a larger longtitudinal study (2001-2009) which traced students from Form One through Form Three to Form Five and three years after. The Tracer Study Report submitted to Ministry of Education. R. Deosaran. Project Safeguard: Tracing Youths 2001-2010, Post-Secondary School Experiences. Ministry of Education, Trinidad and Tobago, July 2010.

    As is usual with such tracer studies, it took great effort to reach students three years after they have left their Form Five. School records, addresses etc, were used to reach them.

2.  The Form One to Form Three to Form Five results have been written up in 18separate reports and submitted to the Ministry of Education. This derived tracer study was written up in 2010.

3.  Published by Ian Randle Publishers, Kingston, 2008.

4.  ***Original Sample (Form One)***: <u>social class</u>: (1)low=49%, (2)middle=34%, (3)upper=7%, other=10%. <u>Sex:</u> (1)male 54%, (2)female=46%. <u>Race:</u> (1) African descent=38%, (2)East Indian descent=33%, (3)Mixed=25%, Others=4%.<u>Parental:</u> (1)Both Parents: 67%, (2)Mother Only = 16%, (3) Others = 17 (i.e. father only, guardian, aunt/uncle, relative, stepfather etc

    ***Tracer Study Sample: Form Five*** : <u>social class</u>: (1)low=47%, (2) middle=37%, (3)upper=7%, (4)Others=9%. <u>Sex:</u> (1)male=48%, (2)female=52%. <u>Race:</u> (1)African=34%, (2)East Indian=40%, (3) Mixed=24%, Others -White, Syrian, Chinese, etc = 2%.<u>Parental:</u> (1)Both Parents = 63%, (2)Mother Only = 17%, (3)Others = 20%.

5.  (e.g. Upper class (1) = senior engineer, senior lawyer, university professor, CEO of large company, etc. Middle class (2) = teacher, public servant, librarian, pilot, IT specialist, etc. Low class (3) = vendor, chauffeur, shoe-maker, store-clerk, etc. Others = pensioner, retired, unemployed, etc.

6.  Given the distributions obtained, it became convenient to use only three categories: (1) Both Parents, (2) Mother Only, Others.

7.  As advised, the names of the schools are not published but submitted to the Ministry of Education.

8.  This was a 47% retention rate from Form One. The representative nature of this post-secondary sample, as compared to the original sample, remains a viable group for the study.

# References

## Selected Books, Journals and Research Reports.

Agnew, R. Foundation for a General Strain Theory of Crime and Delinquency. Criminology, 30, pp 47–87

Agnew, R. A Revised Strain Theory of Delinquency. Social Forces, 1985, 64, pp. 151–167.

Anderson, C. The Political Economy of Social Class. New York: Prentice Hall, 1974.

Arat, Z. Democracy and Human Rights in Developing Countries. London: Lynne Rienner Publishers, 1991.

Aron, R. Social Class, Political Class, Ruling Class. European Journal of Sociology, 1960, 1, pp. 260–281.


Bacchus, M. Education, Social Change and Cultural Pluralism. Sociology of Education. 1969, 42, 4 (Fall) pp. 368–385.

Baksh, I. Caribbean Sociology: Introductory Readings. Jamaica: Ian Randle Publishers, 1984.

Beckford, G. Persistent Poverty. New York: Oxford University Press, 1972.

Bendix, R. and M. Lipset (ed.) Class, Status and Power (2nd ed.) New York: Macmillan, 1966.

Bernstein, B. Education Cannot Compensate for Society, New Society, February 26, 1970, pp 344–7.

Bennett, R. and J. Lynch. Towards a Caribbean Criminology: Problems and Prospects. Caribbean Journal of Criminology and Social Psychology. Jan 1996, vol. 1 (1), pp. 8–36.

Bernstein, B. Social Class, Codes and Control, vol. 1, New York: Routledge and Kegan and Paul, 1971, pp 170–89.

Bierlein, L. Charter Schools: Initial Findings. Denver, Colorado: Education Commission of the States, 1996.

Binder, A., Geis, G. and Bruce Jnr, D. Juvenile Delinquency. Cincinnati, Ohio: Anderson Publishing Co., 1997.

Boudon, R. Education, Opportunity and Social Inequality. New York: John Wiley, 1974.

Bourdieu, P. and J. Passeron. Reproduction in Education, Society and Culture, London: Sage, 1977.

Bowles, S. and H. Gintis. Schooling in Capitalist America, London: Routledge and Kegan Paul, 1976.

Bowles, S. Towards Equality of Educational Opportunity. Harvard Educational Review: Special Issue, 1968, 38 (1), p. 95.

Bowles, S. Unequal Education and the Reproduction of the Social Division of Labour, Review of Radical Political Economics, 1971, 3.

Braithwaite, L. Social Stratification in Trinidad: A Preliminary Analysis. Social and Economic Studies, 2 (2, 3), 1953, pp 38–61.

Braun, C. Teacher Expectations: Sociopsychological Dynamics. Review of Educational Research, Spring, 1976, 46 (2), pp. 185–213.

Brereton, B. A History of Modern Trinidad 1783–1962. Kingston, Jamaica: Heinemann, 1981.

Brereton, B. The Experience of Indentureship 1845–1917. In J. La Guerre (ed.) Calcutta to Caroni. Trinidad: University of the West Indies School of Continuing Studies, 1985, pp. 27–30.

Brown vs. Board of Education of Topika, 1, 347 US 483, (1954).

Brown, M. (ed.) Still Not Equal: Expanding Educational Opportunities in Society. New York: Peter Lang, 2007.

Brown, S., Esbensen, F. and Geis, G. Criminology: Explaining Crime and Its Context. Cincinnati, Ohio: Anderson Publishing Co., 1998.

Bryden, D. West Indian Slavery and British Abolition. Cambridge: Cambridge University Press, 2010.

Campbell, C. A Social History of Education in Trinidad and Tobago 1834–1939. Jamaica, Mona: The Press University of the West Indies, 1996. p.11.

Campbell, C. The Young Colonials: A Social History of Education in Trinidad and Tobago, 1834–1939. Mona, Jamaica: The Press, University of the West Indies, 1996, pp. 11–117.

Carmona, A. Speech on Indian Arrival Day celebrations, Newsday, May 30, 2015, p. 7.

Carnoy, M. Education as Cultural Imperialism. New York: David McKay and Co, 1974.

Calvo-Armengol, A. and Zenou, Y. Social Networks and Crime Decisions: The Role of Social Structure in Facilitating Delinquent Behaviour. International Economic Review, 2004, 45, pp. 439–458.

Centre for Ethnic Studies, A Study of Secondary School Population in Trinidad and Tobago: Placement Patterns and Practices, UWI, 1994, p 440.

Clarke, E. My Mother Who Fathered Me. Jamaica, Kingston: The Press University of the West Indies, 1999.

Cloward, R. Illegitimate Means, Anomie and Deviant Behaviour. American Sociological Review, 1959, Vol. 24 (2), pp. 164–176.

Coleman, J. The Concept of Equality of Opportunity, Harvard Educational Review, Winter, 1968, 38, (1), pp 7–22.

Coleman, J. Equality of Educational Opportunity. Washington, D.C.: U.S. Government Printing Office, 1996, p. 325.

Collins, R. Functional and Conflict Theories of Educational Stratification, American Sociological Review, 36, 1971.

Collins, R. Some Comparative Principles of Educational Stratification, Harvard Educational Review, 1977, 47 (1).

Cooley, C. Social Organisation. New York: Schocken Books, 1972.

Corning, P. The Fair Society. Chicago: University of Chicago Press, 2012.

Coward, R. and L. Ohlin. Delinquency and Opportunity. New York: Free Press. 1960.

Cross, M. and A. Schwartzbaum. Social Mobility and Secondary School Placement in Trinidad and Tobago. Social and Economic Studies, 18, 2, 1969.

Curtis, S. and M. Boultwood. A Short History of Educational Ideas. Surrey, Great Britain: University Press, 1977.


Davis, K. and W. Moore. Some Principles of Stratification, American Sociological Review, 10, (2),1945, pp. 242–240.

Davis, K. and Moore, W. Principles of Stratification. American Sociological Review, 10, 1945, pp 242–49.

De Lisle, J. Secondary School Entrance Examination in the Caribbean, Caribbean Curriculum, 19, 2012, pp 109–143

Deosaran R. (ed.) Crime, Delinquency and Justice: A Caribbean Reader. Ian Randle: Jamaica, 2007, pp 89–148.

Deosaran, R. African Youths in Danger. (Research Report partly funded by Public Services Association.) Trinidad: University of the West Indies, Psychological Research Centre, 2006.

Deosaran, R. Benchmarking Violence and Delinquency in Secondary Schools: Towards a Culture of Peace and Civility. Trinidad: Ministry Education, 2003 (Phase One), 2006 (Phase Two)

Deosaran, R. Demographics and Six Categories of Deviance. Report No. 12, Project Safeguard: Tracing Youths 2001–2010. Report commissioned and submitted to Ministry of Education, April, 2010.

Deosaran, R. Juvenile Homes: in1997, An Analytic Basis for Reform, Intervention and Rehabilitation. Submitted to Ministry of Social Development, October 1997. CIDA/UWI grant.

Deosaran, R. Project Safeguard: Tracing Youths 2001–2010. Post-secondary School Experiences (educational and employment status) Three Years after Form Five. Report commissioned by and submitted to Ministry of Education, July 2010. (18 separate reports also submitted).

Deosaran, R. Psychonomics and Poverty: Towards Governance and Civil Society. Kingston: University of the West Indies Press, 2000.

Deosaran, R. School Type and Students' Fear of Being Bullied and Classroom Disorder. Report No. 18, Project Safeguard: Tracing Youths 2001–2010. Report commissioned and submitted to Ministry of Education, April, 2010.

Deosaran, R. School Type and Students' Level of Comfort and Self–Esteem. Report No 17, Project Safeguard: Tracing Youths 2001–2010. Report commissioned and submitted to Ministry of Education, April, 2010.

Deosaran, R. School Type x Demographic and Civic Attitudes. Report No. 16, Project Safeguard: Tracing Youths 2001– 2010. Report commissioned and submitted to Ministry of Education, April, 2010.

Deosaran, R. School Violence and Delinquency: The Dynamics of Race, Gender, Class, Age and Parenting in the Caribbean. In R. Deosaran, (ed.) Crime, Delinquency and Justice: A Caribbean Reader, Ian Randle: Kingston, 2007.

Deosaran, R. The Agony and Ecstasy of the SEA, Newsday, July 3, 2010, p.10; The Quest for a Good School, Newsday, June 26, 2010, p. 10; Youth and Broken Expectations, Newsday Sept 25, 2010, p. 10. The Prestige School Dilemma, Newsday, July 21, 2013, p. 10).

Deosaran, R. Tracing Youths 2001–2010: Project Safeguard, Ministry of Education (Report No. 2), 2010.

Dewey, J. Democracy and Education, New York, Macmillan, 1953

Dewey, J. Moral Education. New York: Free Press, Glencoe, 1961

Douglas, J. The Home and the School, London: MacGibbon and Kee, l964

Durkheim, E. Suicide: A Study in Sociology. New York: The Free Press, 1951.

Durkheim, E. The Division of Labour in Society, New York: Free Press, 1947

Dyer, P. The Effect of the Home on the School. Trinidad: UWI, Social and Economic Studies, 1968, 17, 4.

East Indians in the Caribbean: A Symposium. Trinidad; University of the West Indies, Faculty of Arts, 1979.

Fanon, F. Black Skins, White Masks. Great Britain: MacGibbon and Kee Ltd, 1968.

Fanon, F. The Wretched of the Earth. New York: Grove Press, 1968.

Figueroa, P. and G. Persaud (eds.), Sociology of Education: A Caribbean Reader. Oxford: Oxford University Press 1976

Fishkin, J. Bottlenecks. New York: Oxford University Press, 2014.

Flicker, B. (ed.) Justice and School Systems: The Role of the County in Education Litigation. Philadelphia: Temple University Press, 1990.

Ford, J. Social Class and the Comprehensive School. London: Routledge and Kegan Paul, 1969

Freire, P. Education: The Practice of Freedom. London: Writers and Publishing Cooperative, 1974.

Freire, P. Pedagogy of the Oppressed. New York: Seabury Press, 1974.

Giddens, A. Capitalism and Modern Social Theory. London: Cambridge University Press, 1971.

Goffman, E. Stigma. New Jersey: Prentice Hall, 1963

Gordon, S. A Century of West Indian Education. London: Longman Group, 1963.

Gorski, P., Zenkov, K., Osei-Kofi N. and Sapp, J. (eds.) Cultivating Social Justice Teachers. Virginia: Stylus Publishing, 2013.

Gottfredson, M. and Hirschi, T. A General Theory of Crime. Stanford: Stanford University Press, 2000.

Guinier, L. The Tyranny of the Meritocracy. Boston: Beacon Press, 2015.

Gurley, J. Challenges to Capitalism. California: San Francisco Book Company, 1976.

Hagan, F. Introduction to Criminology. California: Nelson Hall Publishing, 1994.

Hagan, J. The Poverty of a Classless Criminology. Criminology, 31 (1), p. 2.

Halsey, A., A. Heath and J.M Ridge, Origins and Destinations. Oxford: Clarendon Press, 1980.

Halsey, A., J. Floud, C.A. Anderson (Eds.) Education, Economy and Society. New York: Free Press, 1965.

Haraksingh, K. Aspects of the Indian Experience in the Caribbean. In J. La Guerre (ed.) Calcutta to Caroni. Trinidad: University of the West Indies Extra Mural Studies Unit, 1985.

Haralambos, M. and M. Holborn. Sociology. London: Collins International, 1995.

Harrison, L. Underdevelopment is a State of Mind: The Latin American Case. Boston: Center for International Affairs and Harvard University Press, 1985.

Horowitz, D. The Courts and Public Policy. Washington: Brookings Institute, 1977.

Howe, K. Understanding Equal Education Opportunity: Social Justice, Democracy and Schooling. New York: Teachers' College Press, Columbia University, 1997.

Hutmacher, W., Cochran, D. and Bottani, N. (eds.) In Pursuit of Equity in Education. New York: Springer Publications, 2001.

Hyman, H. The Value System of Different Classes: A Social Psychological Contribution to the Analysis of Stratification. In Bendix, R. and Martin

Lipset, S. (eds.) Class, Status and Power (2nd ed.) New York: The Free press, 1966.

Illich, I. Deschooling Society. New York: Penguin, 1973.

Inter-American Development Bank Report. Access, Equity and Academic performance. Washington: IDB Bookstore, 2002, pp. 24–30.

James, CLR. The Black Jacobins. New York: Random House, (2nd ed.) 1963.

Jencks, C. Inequality: A Reassessment of the Effects of Family and Schooling in America. London: Penguin, 1975.

Jensen, G. and Rojek, R. Delinquency and Youth Crime.(2nd ed.) Illinois: Waveland Press, 1992.

Karabel, J. and A. Halsey, P. (Eds.) Power and Ideology in Education. London: Oxford University Press, l977.

Keenan, P. Report Upon the State of Education in the Island of Trinidad. Dublin: Alexander Thom for Her Majesty's Stationary Office, 1869.

Kennedy, R. For Discrimination: Race, Affirmative Action and the Law. New York: Vintage Books, 2013.

Kipple, K. The Caribbean Slave Trade: A Biological History. Cambridge: Cambridge University Press, 1984.

Klass, M. East Indians in Trinidad: A Study of Cultural Persistence. Illinois: Waveland Press, 1961.

Kozol, J. The Shame of the Nation: The Restoration of Apartheid Schooling in America. New Jersey: Crown Publishing, 2005.

La Guerre, J. (ed.), Calcutta to Caroni (2nd ed.) Trinidad: University of the West Indies, School of Continuing Studies, 1985.

Lemert, E. Human Deviance, Social Problems and Social Control. New York: Prentice Hall, 1967.

Lowenthal, D. and L. Comitas (eds.) The Aftermath of Sovereignty: West Indian Perspectives. New York: Doubleday Anchor, 1973.

Lowenthal, D. West Indian Societies. London: Oxford University Press, 1972.

Louis, H. (ed.) Classic Slave Narratives. New York: Penguin Books, 2002, esp. pp. 231–297.

Mahabir, C. Crime and Nation-Building in the Caribbean. Cambridge, Mass: Schenkman Publishing Co., 1985

Marshall, G. and A. Swift. Social Class and Social Justice, British Journal of Sociology, June 1999.

Matza, D. Delinquency and Drift. New York: Wiley, 1964.

McCaghy, C., Capron, T. and Jamieson, J. Deviant Behaviour: Crime, Conflict and Interest Groups. (5ᵗʰ Ed.) London: Allyn and Bacon, 2000.

McClelland, D. The Achieving Society. New York: Feffer and Simons Inc., 1961.

Mead, G. Mind, Self and Society. Chicago: University of Chicago Press, 1934.

Memmi, A. The Colonizer and the Colonized. Boston: Beacon Press, 1967.

Merton, R. Social Theory and Social Structure. New York: The Free Press, 1968.

Morrish, I. The Sociology of Education. London: George Allen, 1976

Mustapha, N. and N. Ali-Mustapha, Socioeconomic Status, Self-Esteem and Common Entrance Exam Results, Educational Practice and Theory, 1997, 19, (2),

Mustapha, N. and R. Brunton (eds.), Issues in Education in Trinidad and Tobago, School of Continuing Studies, University of the West Indies, 2002.

Mustapha, N. Denominational Boards and the Education Act. In R. Deosaran (ed.) Cultural Diversity. Trinidad : University of the West Indies, Ansa McAL Psychological Research Centre, 1995.

Mustapha, N. Education and Stratification in Trinidad and Tobago, in N. Mustapha and R. Brunton (eds.), Issues in Education in Trinidad and Tobago, School of Continuing Studies, University of the West Indies, 2002, pp 143–162.

OECD Study, 2009. Programme for International Assessment (PISA). Cited In Ministry of Education Annual Administrative Report, 2010–1, pp. 23–25

Osuji, R. The Effect of Socio-Economic Status on the Educational Achievement of Form Five Students, Institute of Social and Economic Research, 1987, p. 128.

Parkin, F. Class, Inequality and the Political Order. London: MacGibbon and Kee Ltd., 1971.

Parsons, T. Structure and Process in Modern Society, Chicago: Free Press, 1960.

Persad-Bissessar K. Speech to formally open the new Maloney Police Station, May 27, 2015

People's National Movement Manifesto, 2015, pp. 35–37.

People's Partnership Manifesto, 2015, pp.14, 47–52.

Quinney, R. The Social Reality of Crime. Boston: Little, Brown and Co., 1970.

Rafter, N. and Heidensohn, F. International Feminist Perspectives in Criminology. Buckingham: Open University Press, 1995.

Rawls, J. A Theory of Distributive Justice. Cambridge, Mass: Harvard University Press, 1977.

Rebell, M. Courts and Kids: Pursuing Educational Equity Through the State Courts. Chicago: University of Chicago Press, 2009.

Reid, D. The Constitutional Politics of Educational Opportunity. Princeton: Princeton University Press, 2000.

Reid, L. School and Environmental Factors in Jamaica, In P. Figueroa and G. Persaud, Sociology of Education. Oxford: Oxford University Press, 1976.

Rowe, K. Understanding Equal Educational Opportunity. New York: Columbia University Press, 1997.

Rubenstein, D. and C. Stoneman. Education for Democracy. Middlesex: Penguin Books, 1972.

Rubin, V. and M. Zavalloni. We Wished to be Looked Upon. New York: Teachers College Press, l969.

Russell, B. Education and the Social Order. London: Unwin, 1977

Ryan, S. and J. La Guerre. Ethnic Centre Report on Secondary School Placement. St Augustine, University of the West Indies, 1994.

Ryan, S. Race and Nationalism in Trinidad and Tobago. Toronto: University of Toronto Press, 1972.

Ryan, S., Thorpe, M., Bernard, L., Mohammed, P., Rampersad, I. No Time to Quit, Engaging Youth At Risk, Report submitted to Cabinet of Trinidad and Tobago, 2013.

Samaroo, B. The Presbyterian Church as an Agent of integration in Trinidad and Tobago during the 19th and 20th Centuries. Caribbean Studies, XIV, 4, Jan. 1975.

Schur, E. Labelling Deviant Behaviour: Its Sociological Implications. New York: Harper and Row, 1971.

Sheal, B. Schooling and Its Antecedents: Substantive and Methodological Issues in the Status Attainment Process, Review of Educational Research, 1976, 46 (4), pp. 463–526

Simon, B. and W. Taylor. Education in the Eighties: The Central Issues. London: Batsford Academic and Educational Ltd, 1981

Skrla, L. and Scheuriel, J. (eds.). Educational Equity and Accountability. London: Routledge, 2004.

Smith, M.G. The Plural Society in the British West Indies. Jamaica: Sangster's Book Store, 1974.

Sorokin, P. Social and Cultural Mobility. New York: The Free Press. 1964. p. 502.

Stark, R. Deviant Places: A Theory of the Ecology of Crime. Criminology, 1987, 25, pp 893–909.

Swann, L. Education for All: A Brief Guide (HMSO), London, 1985 U.S. Office of Education, Equality of Educational Opportunity and Supplemental Appendix, 1966, 1966.

Taylor, I., Walton, P. and Young, J. The New Criminology. London: Routledge and Kegan Paul, 1977.

Thornberry, T., Moore, M. and Christenson, R. The Effect of Dropping Out of High School on Subsequent Criminal Behaviour. Criminology, 23, 1985, p. 3.

Trotman, D. Crime in Trinidad, Conflict and Control in a Plantation Society, 1838–900. Knoxville: University of Tennessee Press, 1986.

Tumin, M. Some Principles of Stratification: A Critical Analysis. American Sociological Review, 1953, 1(2), pp 387–393.

U.S. Brown vs. Board of Education of Topeka, Kansas, 347 U.S. 483 (1954).

U.S. Civil Rights Act, 1964.

UNESCO. Addressing Male Underperformance in the Education System: Intervention Strategies. Final Report of Regional Conference Nov 26–28, 1997.

United Nations/UNICEF. Declaration of the Right of the Child. (Article 26).

Weber, M. The Protestant Ethic and the Spirit of Capitalism (trans). New York: Charles Scribner's Sons, 1958.

Vidich, A. (ed.) The New Middle Classes. New York: New York University Press, 1959.

Weiner, M.(ed.) Modernisation, The Dynamics of Growth. New York: Basic Books, 1966.

Weiss, J., Crutchfield, R. and Bridges, G. Juvenile Delinquency (2nd ed.) London: Sage Publications, 2001.

Williams, E. Education in the British West Indies. New York University Place Bookshop, 1968.

Williams, E. Inward Hunger, London: Andre Deutsch, 1971.

Williams, E. Public Lecture on Secondary Schools, Woodford Square, October 26, 1965.

Williams, E. Selected Speeches. Trinidad, Port of Spain: Longman Caribbean, 1981, pp. 242–3.

Williams, E. Speech to House of Representative, December 8, 1965.

Wilson, J. Capitalism and Morality. The Public Interest, 1995, 12 (1) Fall, pp. 42–60.

Wood, D. Trinidad in Transition. London: Oxford University Press, 1968.

Young, C. The Politics of Cultural Pluralism. London: University of
    Wisconsin Press, 1979.
Young, M. The Rise of the Meritocracy. Middlesex: Penguin Books, 1976

# Index

www.ingramcontent.com/pod-product-compliance
Lightning Source LLC
Chambersburg PA
CBHW060132280326
41932CB00012B/1495